Intimate NIGHTS

Intimate NIGHTS

The Golden Age of New York Cabaret

James Gavin

LIMELIGHT EDITIONS

New York

First Limelight Edition October 1992

 Published in the United States by Proscenium Publishers Inc., New York, and simultaneously in Canada by Fitzhenry & Whiteside, Limited, Toronto.

LIBRARY OF CONGRESS CATALOGING-IN-PUBLICATION DATA

Gavin, James, 1964–
Intimate nights : the golden age of New York cabaret / James Gavin.—1st Limelight ed.
p. cm.
Originally published : New York : Grove Weidenfeld, 1991.
Includes discography (p.) and index.
ISBN 0-87910-161-X
1. Music-halls (Variety theaters, cabarets, etc.)—New York (N.Y.)—History. I. Title.
[PN1969.C3G3 1992]
792.7'09747'1—dc20 92-22558
CIP

For my parents, Viola and Jack,
who have never set foot in a nightclub
in their lives

ACKNOWLEDGMENTS

First, to all those who submitted graciously to my questioning, my deepest thanks.

To the following, who supplied me with recordings, photographs, and other materials that collectively made this book possible, a fond thank you for your generosity: Bret Adams, Sylvia Albert, Peter Allen, Steve Allen, Jeff Austin, Jean Bach, Marshall Barer, Mae Barnes, Judy Bell, Richard Rodney Bennett, Joanne Beretta, Richard Blair, Gene Bland, Michael and Joy Brown, Nathan Bupp, Ann Hampton Callaway, Otis Clements, Charlie Cochran, Steve Cole, Betty Comden, Eric Comstock, Robert Conaway, Barry Conley, Jane and Gordon Connell, Frances Coslow, Lesley Davison, Dolly Dawn, Charles DeForest, Fred Ebb, Ross Firestone, June Ericson Gardner, Mary Genovese, Alice Ghostley, Scott Gleason, Murray Grand, Tammy Grimes, Marsha Harkness, Herb Hartig, Jane Harvey, Alex Hassan, Harry Haun, Goldie Hawkins, William B. Hay, Skip Heinecke, Daphne Hellman, Jack Holmes, Marshall Izen, Laura Kenyon, Sandra King, Jackie and Roy Kral, Joel Kudler, Cam Walter LaGianussa, Paula Laurence, Arthur Laurents, Kevin Lawler, Maryann Lopinto, Christine Lyon, Loonis McGlohon, Rod McKuen, Gerry Matthews, Mark Murphy, Allen Murray, Portia Nelson, Bibi Osterwald, Audrey and Richard Pohlers, Lovelady Powell, Michael Pritchett, Rex Reed, Rex Robbins, Fred Rogers, William Roy, Denny Santos, Bob Schulenberg, Bobby Scott, Daryl Sherman, Arthur Siegel, Joel E. Siegel, David

Smith, James Spada, Roger Sturtevant, John Wallowitch, Ronny Whyte, Lucy Chase Williams, Mary Louise Wilson, and Miller Wright.

Special thanks to Gary Allabach, Larry Carr, Michael Chertok, Greg Dawson, Barry Dennen, Will Friedwald, Steve Grant, Steve Gruber, Lee Hale, Bart Howard, John Paul Hudson, Irving Joseph, David Litofsky, Harry Locke, Richard Norton, Ted Ono, Guy Riddick, Steve Ross, Joe Savage, Larry Sharpe, Bob Shaver, and Tom Toth, whose generosity exceeds my ability to thank them sufficiently.

Then there are those who are responsible for some of my most treasured evenings out over the last five years, which have in turn given this book much of its life: Mario Buatta, Harry Locke, David Lotz, Rhoda Minowitz, Jim Randolph, William Roy, Roy Sander, and Sara Widness.

For their warm encouragement and advice at various stages of this project, thanks to Edward Albee, Marie Brenner, Michael Brown, Eric Comstock, Buster Davis, Anita Ellis, James Kirkwood, Jr., Bruce Laffey, Barbara Lea, Leo Lerman, Susannah McCorkle, Helen Merrill, Charles Michel, Terry Miller, Bobby Scott, Daryl Sherman, Joel E. Siegel, Treva Silverman, Donald Smith, Michael Sommers, Richard Sudhalter, Marlene VerPlanck, Stuart Wilk, and Julie Wilson.

Thanks to ace copy editor Joel Honig for making me look so good; to Jed Mattes, agent for this project; to Anne Sikora, assistant to my fortunate editor; and to Grove Weidenfeld's director of publicity, Ken Siman, one of the few who really cares—probably because he is an author himself. My gratitude also to Ken's tireless colleagues Katherine Beitner and Susan Nover, and to the entire staff of Grove, who went miles beyond the call of duty.

I reserve my greatest thanks for a group of people who have gone to heartwarming lengths to convince me of this project's (and my own) value. I hope all of you have at least a clue of how much your support has meant to me: Ben Bagley, my editor Walt Bode, Kim Hartstein, Stephen Holden, Bart Howard, Verlyn Klinkenborg, Steve Ross, and Pat Sheinwold.

Intimate
NIGHTS

INTRODUCTION

Friday, November 28, 1958, was a day marked by early preparations for the holiday season. A CBS-TV news feature showed workmen hanging wooden stars on the great tree in Rockefeller Center, as a pair of Salvation Army Santas down below tolled small handbells. Nighttime shows were already interrupted by Christmas commercials. In a magazine article on yuletide shopping, a department store buyer revealed new concepts for visual merchandising. "Everything must move," he said.

Everything did move, and Christmas may not have been entirely to blame. As Dick Gregory, a controversial young black comic, kept repeating in his act, "Oh, I'm telling you, so much is happening all over the world." That week the government announced plans for eight space probes in 1959, including Mars and Venus, and eight to twelve each year thereafter. In California the nation's third major rocket base, costing $1 billion, would begin testing next month. Defense spending had reached $40.8 million. Nuclear arms no longer seemed like a reassuring safeguard.

Those were the topics of the day, but as the dinner dishes dried and the six o'clock news ended, they became quite distant. This weekend's possibilities seemed a lot more exciting, even for those who could not afford to spend much. Late '50s salaries sound low today (clerk-typists earned about $50 a week; skilled professionals such as engineers, especially in the burgeoning aerospace field, started at around $300), but entertainment prices as well as living expenses were comparatively much cheaper. Broadway tickets cost between $2.30 and $9.90, and tonight's shows included *West Side Story*, Judy Holliday in *Bells Are Ringing, Jamaica* with Lena Horne and Ricardo Montalban, *The Music Man*, and Rodgers and Hammerstein's *Flower Drum Song*, then in previews. The wealthier could afford Metropolitan Opera tickets, which topped out at $9.35. Most movie theatres charged a dollar, and a burger and fries at P. J. Clarke's could be had for ninety cents, five courses at the Plaza Hotel for $9.75.

For those who liked the intimacy of a small, nonjazz nightclub—where singers made Broadway ballads sound as personal as a talk between lovers, and where comics addressed day-to-day worries as if they were chatting in their living rooms—choices were widest of all. Near Third Avenue on 55th Street stood the Blue Angel, a lavishly upholstered room famous nationwide as a launching pad for Pearl Bailey, Harry Belafonte, Phyllis Diller, Eartha Kitt, Johnny Mathis, Shelley Berman, and later Woody Allen and Barbra Streisand. The Angel wrapped you in a cloak of sophistication as soon as you walked into its gleaming black-and-white cocktail lounge, where you could rub elbows with Lena Horne, Beatrice Lillie, Truman Capote, Tallulah Bankhead, and other regulars. A year before, beneath the tiny plaster angel that hung above the stage, the unknown Carol Burnett had introduced a comic tribute to the secretary of state called "I Made a Fool of Myself Over John Foster Dulles"; soon after she sang it on the Jack Paar Show, and the rest was history. Tonight's acts included an improvisational comedy team from Chicago, Mike Nichols and Elaine May, who had come to New York on borrowed carfare.

A fifteen-cent subway ride to Greenwich Village brought you to the Bon Soir, a Mafia-owned cellar club best remembered for giving Barbra Streisand her first important showcase. At other times, anybody from Dick Cavett to Ethel Waters might show up on its little stage. The raucous young crowd shouted and stamped its approval of acts it liked, especially at a gay bar inside the room that existed through police payoffs. The club's all-black company of regulars included Mae Barnes, a five-by-five singer with dark saucer eyes, a grainy powerhouse voice, and the sassiest good-time spirit ever to haunt a nightclub stage. She loved to poke fun at ballads that

Blue Angel acts sang in dead seriousness, such as Harold Arlen's "One for My Baby (and One More for the Road)":

It's quarter to three
There's no one in the place except you and me
So stick 'em up, Joe . . .

When the laughs died down she might tear into "On the Sunny Side of the Street" with the blast of a DC-10 at takeoff, keeping time by beating her arm against the piano and even bursting into a spontaneous tap dance.

The headliner was comedienne-singer Kaye Ballard, known later as Eve Arden's costar in the television sitcom *The Mothers-in-Law.* Ballard's act consisted of original material by such fledgling writers as Fred Ebb (who would go on to write the lyrics for *Cabaret* and *Zorba*, among other shows) and Charles Strouse (*Bye Bye Birdie*, *Annie*), plus shtick of her own creation. A lot of it would have gotten Sophie Tucker the hook, but Ballard's audiences adored almost everything she did. "I saw two ladies go by who obviously hadn't seen each other in a long time. One said to the other, 'My God, what did you do to your hair? It looks like a wig!' And the other one said, 'It *is* a wig.' She said, 'Well, you'd never know it!' "

Uptown on West 56th Street, the former John Wanamaker mansion housed the Upstairs at the Downstairs and the Downstairs at the Upstairs, two clubs run by a tall, dandyish North Carolinian named Julius Monk. He presented a series of revues that dissected Gristede's gourmet shop, the *New York Times Book Review*, Kabuki theatre, and other subjects of East Side interest. Some thought his shows the essence of chic, while others found them merely pretentious, but somehow the revues captured the sense of priggish sophistication that many New Yorkers felt in the '50s. Tonight at the Downstairs, a smaller room designed for comics and singers, a scratchy-voiced singing actress named Tammy Grimes was making her nightclub debut. Among those to discover her there was Noel Coward, who would cast her in two Broadway productions.

On Madison Avenue and 37th Street, in the basement of the Duane Hotel, the Den in the Duane provided a scruffy setting for such singers as Thelma Carpenter, an ex–Count Basie, Teddy Wilson, and

Broadway songbird; and Felicia Sanders, who welcomed you with a passionate invitation by Kurt Weill ("We'll go away together, just we two, just you and I . . .") then gave fiery interpretations of songs associated with her beloved Edith Piaf as well as obscure ballads that few singers attempted thereafter. In two months Lenny Bruce would make his New York debut there, blowing sky-high the surface values espoused by Monk's shows and by most of the country. People who found public discussion of vibrators, hypocritical priests, and Filipino sex habits offensive could opt for the gentler humor of Milt Kamen at the Den tonight, or, elsewhere that month, Phyllis Diller and Tom Lehrer.

No conversation in a bar or lounge seemed complete without a pianist playing showtunes and standards in the background. At Peacock Alley in the Waldorf-Astoria, pianist-arranger Norman Paris (the lover and later husband of comedienne-singer Dorothy Loudon) tickled the keys of Cole Porter's own Steinway. And at the Weylin Hotel's Weylin Room, the revered Cy Walter provided an eminently melodic backdrop for chatter, drink, and seduction. Listeners who wanted to hear the lyrics as well had their pick of about twenty singer-pianists, among them a boyish thirty-four-year-old Bobby Short at the Living Room on 49th Street and Second Avenue, a cozy club with sofas and a working fireplace.

Many fans and performers made their last stop the RSVP, a hatbox-size room opposite the Blue Angel where the beloved Mabel Mercer sang from eleven until four in the morning. A refined black Englishwoman in her late fifties, Mercer possessed an almost magical ability to lighten the weary heart and to elevate the lovestruck spirit. Frank Sinatra, Peggy Lee, Tony Bennett, and Leontyne Price were among the singers who revered her. Around 3:00 A.M., when the crowd had dwindled to six or seven, she rose from her chair on the tiny stage and sang requests at your table. Club performing could not become more intimate.

If you still didn't want to go home, you could head over to Bickford's at 51st and Lexington for breakfast—a restaurant visible in the Marilyn Monroe film *The Seven Year Itch* just before a gust of wind from a sidewalk grating blows Monroe's skirt up. While opening the front door of your apartment building you learned what "doing the town" meant, as the sun rose behind your shoulder.

New Yorkers stayed up later in those days, largely because they had more to stay up late for. In three or four years most of the country would choose to spend their nights at home watching TV, safe from the mounting dangers of the night. But the city's great era of nightclub entertainment still flourished, and nearly everyone, regardless of budget, could take part in it in some way. Cover charges were rare, so you could clubhop all night for the price of your drinks.

Today, when only a few intimate clubs remain, and when the cost can exceed $60 a person, it becomes fitting to remember the time when Manhattan played host to dozens of them. From approximately 1945 to 1963 it seemed as if every other block had one. They seated anywhere from thirty to two hundred, and often had suitably homey names—the Little Club, the Red Carpet, the Tender Trap. Writers compared them to living rooms, for the best performers could make them seem like an after-dinner gathering of friends. Some were decorated smartly and with genuine elegance; others were as stylish as an Iowa roadhouse. All were crammed with as many tables and chairs as the fire laws allowed, and often more.

But comfort did not seem to matter when one had a chance to discover such talents as the ones encountered on that not-untypical November evening. Despite their frequent shabbiness, the most durable clubs had an electricity that outshone almost any act: a subtle romantic or sexual aura, an air of sophistication that made you feel like a member of the elite, or some similar magnetism that left you grateful you lived in New York—or sorry you didn't. As Spivy, a foghorn-voiced female singer-pianist who owned a room called Spivy's Roof, told the *New York Star* in 1948, "In a club all is atmosphere. Without it you are a couple of chairs and tables in a bare room. You've got to make the trade feel they are in something more than a cheap bar. They've got to feel like guests in a parlor of gaiety. Got to feel the bar tinkle."

The field's earliest significant roots are in Paris. As Lisa Appignanesi notes in *The Cabaret*, the first cabaret opened there in 1881 in the slumlike, underdeveloped district of Montmartre. Newly rebuilt, Paris boasted an apparent economic and political stability, yet its streets were full of prostitutes, poverty, and degenerate street life—which the "respectable" newspapers of the day exploited. A subversive poet-painter named Rodolphe Salis recognized this hypocrisy and in turn founded the Chat Noir (Black Cat) for outspoken poets, composers, and artists to share their work. Its very nature as a "club" attracted curious outsiders to see what they were missing, and when Salis started to serve drinks a true nightclub was born. It developed into a nightly celebration of young talent (notably composer Erik Satie, the pianist there) and of contempt for the political and social prevarications of the day, and its regulars included Debussy, Maupassant, and the prince of Wales.

By 1900 the reputation of the Chat Noir and of clubs like it had spread to Germany, where young artists and intellectuals were gaining the courage to satirize the political, religious, and artistic repression they had known all their lives. They created the scathing style of club performance portrayed in the Berlin stories of Christopher Isherwood, which would inspire the musical *Cabaret.*

A distinctly American influence came from speakeasies, an industry unto themselves. At first Prohibition had a deadly effect upon New York nightlife, wiping out Bustanoby's, Delmonico's, Maxim's, and other famous cafés and restaurants. But within six months their chefs relocated to speakeasies, making them the best places to drink *and* dine. To circumvent the law these establishments called themselves "nightclubs" and issued membership cards. If you didn't have one, all you had to do was "knock three times and ask for Joe." Performers were often hired in an attempt to make these clubs appear legitimate, as well as to encourage booze sales. One singer who managed, quite literally, to rise above her surroundings and make these rooms her own was Helen Morgan, the prototypical '20s torch singer and one of the first to win recognition as a genuine artist.

Morgan's life sounds like a series of pulp magazine clichés. Born in Danville, Illinois, in 1900, she was partly blinded as a child when a companion hurled a can of paint in her face. She began singing in Chicago speakeasies in 1922, before winning a Montreal beauty contest. With her $1,500 prize she moved to New York, where she got a job singing at Billy Rose's Backstage Club. Five days later Broadway producer George White heard her there and hired her for his *Scandals of 1925*; thereafter she went on to stardom in *Show Boat* and in saloons across the nation as well as to a life scarred by alcoholism, divorce, and illness. She died of a kidney ailment in 1941.

Morgan distilled the pain of these misfortunes into a singing style that remains moving today on her many recordings and in such films as *Show Boat* and *Applause*. It was at the Backstage Club that author Ring Lardner lifted her to the top of the piano, allegedly because she was too drunk to stand up. Thereafter it became her trademark perch in about forty speakeasies and saloons. Four were even named for her: Helen Morgan's 54th Street Club, Chez Morgan, the House of Morgan, and Helen Morgan's Summer Home. The last of these was raided by federal agents in 1928, and Morgan was arrested and charged as an accessory to the illegal sale of liquor.

Even after she became a star, her speakeasy past made her feel like something less than a respectable artist. Morgan knew that a saloon singer's professional function was to sell booze—the reason why clubs didn't have to charge covers. *New York Post* columnist James Cannon recalled sitting at the bar of Frankie and Johnny's on West 45th Street one night in the '30s when Morgan came in alone (May 17, 1957):

"When it came time for the second round, Miss Morgan whispered to me to take my money off the bar. 'I'll sing them a couple of songs,' she explained. 'They'll start buying.'

"There was no piano in that place, but the tiny voice didn't need one. I can't tell you how many songs she whispered in that private concert, but the guys there bought a lot of booze. 'What did I tell you,' Miss Morgan said, as if I doubted the persuasion of her talent. 'A kid like you shouldn't be throwing his money away in saloons.' "

The art was further refined in Paris in the '20s and '30s, when that city became a refuge for such expatriate American artists as Cole Porter, Gertrude Stein, Ernest Hemingway, F. Scott Fitzgerald, and John Steinbeck. Most of them gravitated to a club on the rue Pigalle run by Bricktop, a stylish hostess and singer with short-cropped red hair. Bricktop sang briefly at intervals and presented a cosmopolitan lineup of acts that included Mabel Mercer. "The moment you entered her club," recalled Julius Monk, "she'd exclaim to Mabel a good twenty yards away, 'Mabel, just look who's here!' One would immediately feel ten feet tall and order a bucket of wine."

Prior to 1945, the six or seven such clubs that opened in New York were overshadowed by the splashier rooms of the day. The famous Latin Quarter offered twenty-seven chorus girls, two dance orchestras, and from five to a dozen acts; the Copacabana's regular headliners included Joe E. Lewis, Jimmy Durante, and Sophie Tucker. The sweet-and-swing band era was almost over, but there were still over thirty ballrooms in town for fox-trotting the night away, often under ceilings of simulated starlight. Many hotels had their own supper clubs for dining, dancing, and performances by celebrity acts; notable among them were the Cotillion Room of the Hotel Pierre, the Plaza's Persian Room, and the Wedgwood Room of the Waldorf-Astoria. At the Stork Club and El Morocco, the wealthy went to eat, dance, vie for the best tables, and have their pictures snapped by a flurry of photographers.

Not until World War II ended did the craving for escape give way to a longing for quieter, more personal sentiments. As small clubs began to multiply, the demand for acts grew, and New York was in a unique position to meet that demand. The greatest lure was live television, centered in town and growing rapidly. Record companies were signing an unprecedented number of young singers, who had replaced big bands in the country's heart. The McGuire Sisters, three of the most popular hit-makers of the '50s, recalled their fairy-tale introduction to both media in 1989 at Rainbow and Stars, a club on the sixty-fifth floor of 30 Rockefeller Plaza. Their experience, though not typical, illustrates the sort of breaks that made '50s Manhattan seem like the land of opportunity. "We decided we were gonna leave Ohio," explained Phyllis McGuire, "and come to New York to try for the big time. We checked in at the Barbizon for Women and came over to the RCA Building. We didn't know a soul, and we didn't have an agent. We said, 'We would like to audition for RCA Records.' The next thing we knew we were down in a studio singing our little arrangement for Mannie Sacks, the big cheese then. In walked Ted Collins, Kate Smith's partner, and we were hired for twelve weeks on *The Kate Smith Show*. So after that ended, we thought, 'Wow, we got lucky over there! Let's go to CBS and see if we can get on the *Arthur Godfrey Talent Scouts* show. And you know something? We did!" A contract with Coral Records followed almost immediately.

Just as important was musical comedy, which required the efforts of hundreds for every show. Most tantalizing to young hopefuls were revues: compilations of songs and sketches by a variety of writers, performed by sizable casts and often elaborately staged. Today most of them, even the hits, are forgotten—*Angel in the Wings*, *Touch and Go*, *Lend an Ear*, *Three to Make Ready*, *Tickets, Please!*—but one that is a permanent part of theatrical lore is Leonard Sillman's *New*

Faces of 1952, the biggest smash in a series that had featured Imogene Coca, Henry Fonda, and many other future stars. The cast included Eartha Kitt, Alice Ghostley, and Paul Lynde, all of whom Sillman plucked from small clubs and gave the kind of break that youngsters dreamed of. Syndicated columnists such as Dorothy Kilgallen and Walter Winchell wrote about these success stories every week, inspiring young people around the country to race to the nearest Manhattan-bound bus or train. For a lot of them, intimate clubs were the first stop.

Under the guidance of Julius Monk, the Blue Angel's Herbert Jacoby, and others, performers learned that nightclubs were more challenging than theatre or TV. Every flick of an eyelash, every intake of breath could be noticed—especially with singers. Most devotees remember the club era best for its music, which wrapped itself around the most personal aspects of their lives. The '50s are usually regarded as the most forgettable decade in pop music, characterized by *Sing Along with Mitch*, "How Much Is That Doggie in the Window?" and primitive rock and roll. Within small clubs, however, popular singing became an art form of unexpected subtlety and depth. Unlike such belters of the day as Georgia Gibbs, Frankie Laine, and Kay Starr, club singers had a refreshing way of singing to you rather than at you, almost as if they were confiding. As the gifted Sylvia Syms told *Down Beat* magazine, "Maybe there's a boy and girl in love sitting there . . . well, when I sing to them, I'd like to become part of their love affair. I'd like to make them fall more in love with each other."

Intermingling so closely with the public had its ups and downs, though, as actress-comedienne Pat Carroll remembers. "The things you were fighting had nothing to do with performing, they were negations of performing: liquor, sex, and conversation. Saturdays were the worst, because everyone seemed to have had their champagne cocktails before they came. Sometimes you wanted to say, 'Doesn't anyone inhale?' because the pall of cigarette smoke was so thick, and the smell of booze. Often the level of conversation was so high that no one could hear the performer, and the sexual activity could be unbelievable. My jaw dropped many a night. But you continued no matter what. You were being paid. If they didn't want to listen to you, too bad."

Not all performers reacted so philosophically. Actor Lee Goodman, half of a popular nightclub comedy team with author-playwright James Kirkwood (*A Chorus Line*), told of comedienne Connie Sawyer's emotional response to a drunken customer at Le Ruban Bleu, an East 56th Street boîte presided over by Monk.

"One night all of us learned we were being reviewed by *Variety*, which was very important for a nightclub act in those days. Jimmy and I finished our act, and Connie followed us. There was a drunk sitting up front who didn't like the liquor, didn't like the service, and didn't like Connie. He droned on and on through her act. She was doing a number with a cowboy hat, and finally her eyes welled up with tears. 'You son of a bitch!' she sobbed. And she took off her hat and started beating him over the head with it. 'You lousy creep! You're screwing up my goddamned act!' Tears were pouring out of her eyes."

Drunks and lechers aside, audiences were usually of above-average intelligence and sophistication, and performers designed their shows accordingly. Singers searched for unjustly neglected showtunes; special material writers satirized film, TV, books, and plays at a level that often escaped the typical viewer. Many comics reveled in a more intellectual brand of humor: Irwin Corey, for example, whose blustery, incoherent college professor tore pedantry to shreds, and Pat Carroll, with a witty satire of Dame Edith Sitwell's *Facade*. To take this material outside the major cities was to risk disaster, as Kirkwood and Goodman found. Their act, which included a takeoff on an Uncle Tom folk song called "Downy Little Brownie Man" and a choreographed lampoon of Khachaturian's "Sabre Dance," did not impress viewers at the Royal Palace in Duluth, Minnesota, circa 1950. "Before the show we looked out from behind the curtain," says Goodman, "and the audience was full of chubby little balding men in black suits with steel-rimmed glasses and women in black lace dresses. Nobody under fifty-five. The headliner, a tenor named Carl Ravazza, was making his entrance from the back of the room with a follow spot, singing 'I Kiss Your Hand, Madame' as he kissed the hands of all the ladies and handed them long-stemmed red roses. Jimmy said, 'Holy shit, I think we're in trouble.' There was a full orchestra, but we didn't get to sing with it, because we were the cheapie act. They gave us an electric organ, a saxophone, and drums. In the middle of our first number we saw everyone's heads go down, and for the rest of the act we stared into a bunch of bald spots. We walked off, and some guy came over and said, 'Hey, the boss wants to see you.' He took us down under the stage into a basement office, and there was a guy in shirt sleeves with his feet up on the desk and his hat tipped back. He said, 'Where the fuck did you guys fall from?' Jimmy said, 'It just takes time to warm up a new audience. They'll love us next time, you'll see.'

" 'OUT!'

" 'Well, what about our money?'

" 'Forget it!' He said to the thug, 'Get someone from the local radio station to fill in.'

" 'But we've got a contract!' Jimmy said. With that the guy took off his jacket, and there was a gun holster underneath.

" 'Now, how was that about a contract?' "

New York's big commercial rooms were often only a cut above Duluth. Record and revue producer Ben Bagley and songwriter Bud McCreery were hired to write the Latin Quarter act of Marie ("The Body") McDonald, a movie sex goddess best remembered for a phony kidnapping stunt intended to boost her fading career. "Her manager said it was supposed to be a class act," says Bagley. "But the woman had no taste whatsoever and wouldn't listen to anything. All her clothes looked like they were made of paper. She had a pale blue evening gown covered with what looked like crepe-paper pink ruffles. She was no longer 'The Body.' Her waist was pinched in very tightly with a corselet, with a big pot belly underneath. But we gave her some really nice things to sing, including a beautiful medley of spring songs, because she was opening on the first day of spring. She could barely sing them, but I directed her to talk a lot of things. She didn't like anything we suggested, but her manager kept saying, 'We're gonna do a class act, Marie, the critics'll eat it up!'

"She went along with it until the first dress rehearsal with the orchestra, exactly two hours before the show. She stopped in the middle of Rodgers and Hart's 'Spring Is Here' and said, 'You know, I'm so tired of all this Ben Bagley chic shit. I'm gonna throw it all in the trash can and sing 'When the Saints Go Marching In,' and I'm gonna close with 'Rock-a-bye Your Baby with a Dixie Melody.' The musicians said, 'But Miss McDonald, we don't have any charts on those songs.' She turned to them and stamped her foot, and said, 'Wing it!' That night she went through most of our clever, chic, tasteful act, and it was moderately received. But when she launched into 'When the Saints Go Marching In,' tapping her high-heeled foot to keep time while the orchestra deliberately played sour notes to louse her up, the crowd went wild with appreciation. That tone-deaf, half-drunk Latin Quarter audience stood up and cheered.

"Backstage, after she walked off in triumph, she turned to her manager and said, 'Don't give them their final check.' We were so embarrassed that we didn't even ask for it."

The recherché feeling that bored the Latin Quarter crowd made smaller clubs feel all the more exclusive. Their customers, in fact, considered this an essential part of New York's charm. The city's cultural life, its manic pace, its self-imposed superiority—all these are qualities that New Yorkers crave, just as they crave the company of people who feel likewise. And yet no other city keeps its dwellers involved in such an exasperating love-hate relationship. "New York is a vile place to live," declared writer Richard Gehman, ex-husband of actress Estelle Parsons, in a 1953 issue of *Cue*. "It's a noisy, dirty, stinking, stinkingly expensive, crowded, traffic-throttled, complex-inducing embalmer's parlor for the living. I am leaving it for good, and I wouldn't come back for the Aga Khan's weight in plutonium." Off he went to live in his hometown of Lancaster, Pennsylvania. Six months later he moved back.

The things New Yorkers complain about today have changed little in two centuries. Bumper-to-bumper traffic? Careless driving? In the mid-eighteenth century horse-drawn carriages jammed the streets, causing so many accidents that the mayor ordered bridges built across several streets to protect pedestrians. Speeding was a problem three centuries ago; the first speed limits date from 1652, when New York was still New Amsterdam.

The decline of Broadway? In 1954 *Cue* decried the plight of theatregoers "who either can't afford or refuse to pay Broadway's high prices, or who aren't satisfied with the fare there." (The fare included *The Caine Mutiny Court-Martial* with Henry Fonda, Cole Porter's *Can-Can,* T. S. Eliot's *The Confidential Clerk* starring Claude Rains and Ina Claire, *The King and I, Kismet, Teahouse of the August Moon,* and *Wonderful Town.*)

The high cost of city living? In 1947 Kaye Ballard drew gales of laughter at the Blue Angel with a parody of "My Man":

It cost me a lot
But there's one thing that I've got
My apartment . . .

Even the nightclub era was mourned long before its passing, when Rogers Whitaker of the *New Yorker* alluded to "a time when there are hardly any reasons for staying up late." The "time" was 1956.

Every generation of New Yorkers is regaled with stories about the downfall of a great city, but certain indisputable advantages of the 1940s and '50s are lost forever. As dirty and gray as much of the town looked, there were fewer skyscrapers to block out the sun, making the streets much brighter by day. "Fifth Avenue and Park Avenue were pristine," recalls Pat Carroll, "and some of the most beautiful people walked there. The men dressed in suits and overcoats and homburgs, the women in furs and hats and gloves. I used to walk along Fifth Avenue to go to Brentano's and other bookshops, and I loved to just look at the people."

Others tell how there was seldom a line at the bank or post office, how clerks and cashiers smiled and said thank you. A unanimous memory is that you could ride the subways or walk the streets at any hour—even cross Central Park at 2 A.M.—and not feel a qualm.

Yes, it was a less complicated time, a safer, more romantic time, a more innocent time—and intimate clubs reflected this. Rarely did comics try to enlighten you politically or sociologically; their goal was to entertain. Phyllis Diller bemoaned her inadequacies as a cook: "I was making a pudding and I knew something was wrong. I couldn't get the spoon out. The Food and Drug people tried to stir it and the whole room went around." Mike Nichols and Elaine May depicted a pretentious couple talking in bed after their first meeting in a bar: "Too many people think of Adler as a man who made mice neurotic. He was more. *Much* more." This was the stuff of '50s life, interpreted with a sophistication that few comics before them had shown.

The glamour of these clubs was something of an illusion, however. They were hard work, offering less money and exposure than television, theatre, or recordings. Most performers stuck it out in hopeful anticipation of the big break that would take them out of there. During her run in the 1961 Broadway musical *Carnival!* Kaye Ballard told *Theatre* magazine, "I hope *Carnival!* blasts me out of nightclubs once and for all! Clubs are the most heartbreaking field for a performer. You've got to be made of steel to combat all those warring elements: booze, food, chatter, clamorous china, smoke billowing down your throat as you open your mouth to sing! It's not only a battle for attention, it's a struggle for survival!" Even Helen Morgan, a year before her death, told the *New York World-Telegram* (March 9, 1940), "I want to finish with nightclubs. I hate the smoky tiny places. There's no excitement in it anymore."

Afternoon shed new light on these rooms. "You would never have wanted to see them in the daytime," says singer-comedienne Dorothy Loudon. "They all looked like men's rooms and ladies' rooms." Suddenly you saw smoke-stained walls, faded banquettes, and decor that looked cheap and tacky. They came to life only at night, when darkness and an eager clientele transformed them into something magical. No theatre or television studio could have engendered such artistry, for it contained one precious element: intimate human contact, rare in a city known for impersonality. As *Horizon* magazine lamented in 1962, "New York has only one gift to bestow on the newcomer: a majestic indifference, the absolute privacy which may or may not mean loneliness, the precious right to go and come without being welcomed or missed."

And yet this was the time when Manhattan often regarded the efforts of its talented youngsters with fatherly pride; when it was somewhat kinder to newcomers with a childlike trust in the city's ability to help their dreams come true. Many of them found the key to that success inside the tiny quarters of intimate nightclubs, where, in the eyes of several generations of elegant New Yorkers, less was assuredly more.

Much *of New York's* café entertainment, often referred to as tasteful, had its roots in a tasteless style of performance. From the 1920s through the mid-'40s Manhattan was filled with singer-pianists who specialized in the risqué song. This dubious art form flourished in Prohibition speakeasies and brothels, where pianists who were hired to supply background music found they could draw a few glances over to the upright in the corner by singing lewd numbers.

In the '30s, lounge and hotel players made the same discovery. It was still easy to shock or titillate with mildly racy material, and an evening of "sophisticated songs," as they were called, became a rite of passage into Manhattan adulthood. Seventy-eight RPM recordings of such titles as "Little Richard's Getting Bigger" or "Every Girl I've Ever Known Has Had One," filed in the party or novelty sections of record stores around the country, gave notice of the forbidden pleasures available in New York, the most permissive of cities. These were the days when the Motion Picture Production Code forbade the use of such words as "tart," "pregnant," "lousy," and "nerts" and cautioned that "seduction and rape should never be more than suggested. They are never the proper subject for comedy."

Not everyone was amused by this prurient musical pastime. As Irving Drutman reflected in *Cue* magazine (May 15, 1937):

> Why it is mandatory for nightclub entertainment to be on the dirty, or boys' boarding-school side, will remain one of the deeper

mysteries. . . . Come eleven P.M., all the barriers fall and "sophistication" reigns supreme . . . the arias turn out to be those stories that Stinkie Watson used to whisper to you behind Miss Horton's back, in the sixth grade.

One of the earliest masters of this sport was Nan Blakstone, an older woman with silver-gray curls and the air of a spinster aunt who couldn't wait for Mother to leave the room so she could read the kids some dirty stories. She wrote most of her lyrics and recited them while pounding out a rudimentary accompaniment. One number, "Life on a Donkey Island," told of a land near England where donkeys were the main source of transportation:

The mayor has an ass that no one looks at
But with his wife, it's a different affair
For between you and me, she has one of the most terrific asses
Ever seen on that island there!
Why, when she goes to market they all form in line
Just for one glimpse of that ass so divine!

Blakstone began her career in New York speakeasies, notably the Club Abbey on West 54th Street, a hangout for some of the more volatile gangsters of the day. Late at night, after an evening of bathtub gin, customers tended to get hot under the collar. It was Blakstone's job to keep them smiling as they approached the boiling point.

Few entertainers did so better than she, but one night a lethal combination of booze and clientele put an end to the Abbey and very nearly to Blakstone. At about 2 A.M. on a January morning in 1933, the revelers included Arthur Flegenheimer, also known as Dutch Schultz, a prominent beer mobster; racketeer Charles Sherman; "Marty the Wolf," a local thug; and Detective John J. Walsh, who like many of "New York's Finest" offered his silence in return for all the free food and booze he could consume.

Wolf was dancing with a girl while Sherman sat alone, drunk and jealous. After glowering at the couple for a few minutes he rose, pulled Wolf away, and planted a fist in his left eye. Suddenly the room went black. Tables and chairs crashed, shots cascaded into the walls and ceiling, and a chilling silence fell over the room. The crowd outside watched as Mavis King, the Abbey's cigarette girl and resident gun moll, dragged Sherman's body out onto the sidewalk. He had been stabbed ten times and shot at least three. Blakstone emerged unharmed; at the sound of the first gunshot she had ducked behind the battered upright.

Performing in speakeasies posed other hazards. Old-timers claimed that Blakstone started her career with a pleasing high voice, but that in the '20s she drank a glass of gin containing wood alcohol, a cheap and deadly substance that occasionally found its way into moonshine. Many unsuspecting customers who drank it died within minutes. Luckily for Blakstone, a friend rushed her to the hospital, but all that remained of her voice was the hoarse whisper preserved on dozens of recordings.

After the repeal of Prohibition Blakstone performed regularly in New York for about fifteen years, pausing in 1937 to recover from an automobile crash that necessitated two months of hospitalization and extensive facial surgery. This left the already unattractive entertainer even uglier, and privately she cringed every time she looked in a mirror. But like many homely comediennes she kidded her appearance onstage. "I hope you're aware that I am known as the Helen of Troy of the East Side," she told her audience. "My skin is so bad that Cary Grant has named me 'The Face That Launched a Thousand Pits.' "

Standards were more restrictive outside New York, making it difficult for these songsters to go on tour. In Boston, controversy over Blakstone's act ended a hit booking three weeks early. As the *Boston Post* reported on December 8, 1944:

> Testimony that Nan Blakstone, well known night club performer, entertained patrons in the swanky Satire Room of the Hotel Fensgate with obscene, suggestive and smutty songs and made profane comments in the course of her act, was given by police and a representative of the Watch and Ward Society yesterday afternoon.
>
> Special Officer Blake briefly recounted one suggestive song about Princess Pocahontas. He got as far as stating that Princess Pocahontas, according to the song, was married to Chief Sitting Bull and that the chief was not romantically inclined.
>
> Under cross-examination Blake testified that the patrons laughed at the obscene and suggestive points in Miss Blakstone's songs and at her smutty jokes.
>
> "Because they thought they were funny?" asked Councillor Muchnick. "I suppose so," answered the officer.

"Did you laugh?"
"No."
"Not at all?"
"Oh, I guess I did some."
"At what lines did you laugh?"
Chairman Mary E. Driscoll broke in to halt that line of inquiry.

Then there was Charley Drew, whose "songs teacher never taught" raised besotted eyebrows in the Tap Room of New York's Hotel Taft from the '30s through the '60s. Located in the heart of the theatre district at 50th Street and Seventh Avenue, the Taft garnered much of its trade from tourists, senior citizens, and occasionally prostitutes who used the Tap Room for pickups. The backdrop for this activity was provided by a round-faced, grinning fellow who played and recited original stories in verse that seldom lived up to their titles ("She Got Them Caught in the Wringer," "You Can't Fool the Boys Behind the Desk," "It's Better Than Taking in Washing"). When Drew came to a lewd phrase his face glowed with the naughty smile of a schoolboy looking at a girlie magazine during history class:

Gladys lived upon a farm far away from any harm
Until a city slicker came along one day
It didn't take him very long to teach this lady right from wrong
The trouble is, he taught her wrong before he taught her right . . .

She sighed and cried and tried to hide
For days and days she pouted
But just like all of us, she found out she was nuts about it!
She left the village in disgrace
Now she lives on Sutton Place
Gladys isn't gratis anymore!

One of the oldest sites in New York for naughty fun is the Monkey Bar of the Hotel Elysée on East 54th Street, a room once described as "a place where old jokes go to die." A lot of old jokes have died there, for it opened in 1933 and continues to this day. A dozen or so tables crowd the small room, opposite a prominent baby grand. Monkey figures decorate the walls. Its first pianist, a Southerner named Johnny Payne, set its tone as a place not designed to impress your date. The *New York Times* scoffed (April 30, 1939):

> Mr. Payne is a phenomenon, though not a very pleasant one as far as we're concerned. His songs are for the most part screeching obscenities without even a trace of wit, and his main talent seems to lie in drinking an endless series of double Scotches straight. [He averaged ten to fifteen per set.] The glasses are tossed over the piano to crash on the floor. Now and then he obligingly removes ash trays from adjacent tables to dump their contents behind the piano amid the broken glass . . . Throughout this spectacle the faithful sit in little huddles following the master's antics with a fervor that is almost religious. As for us, we were grateful for the fresh air afterward. The Elysee's Monkey Bar is well-inhabited.

Even so, it was a favorite nightspot of celebrities who loved its outrageous atmosphere: Dorothy and Lillian Gish, Helen Hayes, Joe DiMaggio, Vladimir Horowitz, and Johnny Weissmuller, to name a few. In the suites upstairs, the preponderance of call girls, divorced women eager to change their status, and "torch-bearing bachelors" (to use novelist Robert Ruark's term) won the Elysée in those days the nickname of the Hotel Easy Lay. Foreign correspondent Walter Duranty enjoyed terrorizing the chambermaids by chasing them around with his spare wooden leg. A society lady, in love with a golfer, used to place golf balls on the windowsill and practice hitting them out the window. Musical comedy star Gertrude Niesen's English bulldog even committed suicide by jumping off the roof.

The Elysée's most famous resident was Tallulah Bankhead, who at various times shared her suite with a monkey and a lovebird. Her monkey was named official mascot of the Monkey Bar, and she occasionally uncaged the bird to soar and dip through the room before it perched on the rim of the piano, listening intently to the songs of Johnny Andrews or former Ziegfeld girl Consuelo Flowerton, mother of the distinguished stage actress Nina Foch.

One pianist went further than any other in exposing the lubricious interests of his listeners: Dwight Fiske, whom *Variety* christened "King Leer." Fiske recited original tales that pried into the sex habits of everyone from "Ida the Wayward Sturgeon" to Lucrezia Borgia, emblazoning every nonsubtlety with winks, grins, shrieks, and mock-dramatic silent movie–styled accompaniment. Born in 1892 in Providence, Rhode Island, Fiske had studied at the Paris Conservatory of Music but liked to amuse guests at parties with salacious songs. Bankhead heard him and recommended him for a two-week tryout at the Café Anglais in New York, and after thirty-four weeks there Fiske abandoned all plans for a concert career.

During the '30s his headquarters was at the Café Lounge of New York's Savoy-Plaza Hotel, but his recordings for the Liberty Music Shop and Gala labels made him a household word far beyond Manhattan, as his friend Michael Pritchett recalls. "In that era, a young lady had not experienced living if she had not seen Dwight Fiske. At every party you went to, you had to hear one of his records. Socially, he saw all the top people. Dwight was invited everywhere."

Fiske's stories told of such characters as Pomona the Deer, a charming doe out to make an honest buck; Queen Isabella, whose frustration grew unbearable during Columbus's long absence ("She didn't give a damn whether the earth was flat or round!"); and Salome, so driven with desire for John the Baptist that she performed the dance of her life in order to seduce him. "Which only goes to prove," declared Fiske, "that if you want something *long* enough . . . and you want something *hard* enough . . . you're always bound to get it in the *end!*"

SOPHOMORIC as all this may sound, it helped establish New York's intimate clubs as places where entertainers could indulge some of their most shameless whims. The business took its first step toward true sophistication in 1934, when the Village Vanguard began to showcase more serious local talents. Max Gordon, who ran it until his death in 1989, was the first of a new breed of club owners with the taste to spot potential in young performers and an eagerness to help it blossom. More than nearly any other club manager he won admiration as the most honest, level-headed boss an act could have.

A short, owlish-looking man with glasses, teakettle ears, and a brow knit with worry, Gordon was born in Lithuania in 1903 and raised in Portland, Oregon. He moved to Greenwich Village in 1926 to become a writer but drifted into the club business to support himself. A relatively cheap and not yet fashionable place to live, the Village played host to a community of poets, painters, writers, and musicians who were broke but could flourish artistically among sympathetic comrades. Because most of the local club owners were nearly as poor, their rooms were usually tiny, sparsely furnished dumps that took whatever charm they had from the clientele. The neighborhood "joints," as Gordon called them, bore such names as the Black Cat, the Alimony Jail, and the Gypsy Tavern. He decided to open a more respectable room, undeterred by the fact that he had no money. In 1932 he borrowed some to open the Village Fair in a Sullivan Street basement, and invited such neighborhood poets as John Rose Gildea, Joe Gould, and Maxwell Bodenheim—as well as Clifford Odets—to give fervent readings of their work. One woman danced to records; another strolled through the room singing Hungarian folk songs. Customers brought their own booze (a requirement in Prohibition days) and observed a seventy-five-cent food, coffee, or tea minimum. The waitresses dressed in pajamas and served free Sunday breakfast to customers who could get up before noon.

The Village Fair was shuttered after about a year by a Prohibition agent who discovered employees selling liquor under the table. Undaunted, Gordon opened the first Village Vanguard in February 1934 on nearby Charles Street. He lit the rat-infested basement by tapping into the hall lights of the tenement upstairs and installed an exhaust fan through a sidewalk grating. Because he could not afford chairs, his first customers sat on old barrels. But despite the seediness, Gordon managed to create the atmosphere that he described in his 1981 memoir *Live at the Village Vanguard*: "You dropped in, met your friends, heard the news of the day, read the daily papers provided by the house. When it got crowded at night, as I hoped it would, and the conversation soared and bristled with wit and good feelings, perhaps a resident poet would rise and declaim some verses he had composed for the entertainment and edification of the guests." Humble intentions—but enough to fill the room nightly with a bohemian crowd of WPA employees, jazz musicians, prostitutes, and neighborhood characters.

Success enabled Gordon to move to a larger, more modern location a bit north, on Seventh Avenue South (where the club still resides), and to reopen on December 5, 1934. Money was still tight, so Gordon covered the walls with magazine pages and sheet music and tacked cartoons on the chipping ceiling. The local avant-garde poets and personalities didn't mind a bit and again made it their home. The entertainment took a dramatic turn upward in 1938 when he hired a song-and-comedy quintet called the Revuers: Judith Tuvim (later to become actress Judy Holliday), Betty Comden, Adolph Green, Alvin Hammer, and John Frank. The group wrote and performed musical sketches that tackled show business, New York City life, and human foibles from a razor-sharp urban perspective. They spoofed the sensationalistic murder coverage in the daily rags, denounced plans to dismantle the Sixth Avenue el and sell it as scrap metal to the Japanese, lampooned Gilbert and Sullivan, and even recorded an original "minimusical" about a search for the girl who left two left footprints in the cement outside "Plowman's Japanese Theatre." A parody of the hatchet-job literary condensations in the *Reader's Digest* announced:

In these days of hurly-burly everyone must hurry
There's no time for reading books, but you don't
  have to worry
You may not have the time, but perhaps you'll
Learn to take your culture in a capsule
For though the field of literature's immense
There's a magazine that knows how to condense
Don't sweat for weeks and weeks over just one book
The *Reader's Digest* gives it to you in one look

Les Misérables:
Jean Valjean, no evildoer
Stole some bread 'cause he was poo-er
A detective chased him through a sewer
THE END!

Gone with the Wind:
Scarlett O'Hara's a spoiled pet
She wants everything that she can get
The one thing she can't get is Rhett
THE END!

War and Peace:
Napoleon did not beware
He attacked the Russian bear
He came home on his derriere
THE END!

Young and inexperienced though they were, the Revuers took nightclub comedy to the most ambitious level of the day. They found a perfect home at the Vanguard, where audiences admired risks. "We weren't an act," Holliday later said. "We were a Vanguard act. We made mistakes. The Vanguard forgave us our mistakes." Comden later claimed that their style was born of necessity. "We usually did scenes of people on a subway platform or out on the street reading. This was so we could wear our hats and coats and mufflers, because it was very cold at the Village Vanguard."

Conditions proved even chillier elsewhere. Within six months the group had received an offer from the Rainbow Room, a ballroom and supper club atop New York's RCA Building where they faced audiences more interested in their dinner than in material they had to pay attention to. Later tours taught them that their act was too recherché, too "inside New York," to appeal to out-of-towners. "No place ever seemed to want us back," said Holliday. Nearly all the footage they shot for their first film, 20th Century-Fox's *Greenwich Village* (1944), fell to the cutting room floor, although the studio signed Holliday to a seven-year contract. As the group discovered, to take satire out of the realm of the obvious and then bring it into settings where people were drunk, distracted, and interested only in a little mindless diversion had its commercial limitations.

After the Revuers in 1944, the Vanguard moved into a phase of folk and blues singing with such artists as Leadbelly, Burl Ives, Josh White, and Richard Dyer-Bennet. From the late '40s until 1957, when Gordon adopted an all-jazz policy, his club became a forum for everyone from singers, comics, and jazzmen to poets and harpists. The acts in those years included Pearl Bailey, Eartha Kitt, Wally Cox, Pat Carroll, and Charlotte Rae, all of whom moved uptown to the more prestigious Ruban Bleu or to the Blue Angel.

Unlike some of them, Judy Holliday never forgot her roots, and she dropped into the Vanguard for periodic visits, especially in the mid-'60s when her lover, saxophonist Gerry Mulligan, was appearing. Holliday would always associate her days as a Revuer with butterflies in the stomach. Just before her death she told Gordon, "Nightclubs used to scare me. They still do. Playing a role on the stage is a cinch compared to playing in a nightclub. You're projected on the stage. You're not there playing yourself, where they can get at you."

AROUND THE TIME the Revuers were making their debut, a dour Frenchman named Herbert Jacoby was giving the café business a Parisian flavor of elegance. On December 28, 1937, he opened Le

Ruban Bleu (The Blue Ribbon) on East 56th Street, a room that celebrated the flair of a group of performers known mainly to Europeans.

Jacoby himself shared little of their charm. Six foot two, fond of black suits, with a ruddy complexion and accusing brown eyes, his appearance alone intimidated most people; as Max Gordon said, "Jacoby is the only man I ever met who looked like a nightclub owner." "He was a *thing*, this dark, caustic, introverted man," says singer Anita Ellis. "He looked like a Hitchcock character. He appeared to stoop, but he didn't—he was just so tall. His voice sounded like water rolling out of broken pipes." He was also a cold, shrewd businessman who always balanced his superb taste with his financial sense.

Born in Paris in 1900 to a French-Swiss-Jewish mother and a British father, Jacoby spent his early years at a Manchester boarding school and saw little of his parents. His father was an alcoholic and behaved coldly toward his son, causing the already quiet child to withdraw into himself. He never quite emerged for the rest of his life. In his twenties he would struggle with his own alcohol and drug problem, shaking both before he moved to America. Almost friendless in his youth, he compensated by becoming a brilliant student. At a Paris college he majored in economics and diplomacy, then traveled all over Europe as a diplomatic courier for the French war department. A few years later Léon Blum, head of the Popular Front in France, hired Jacoby as his secretary and as editor of his newspaper *Le Populaire*.

When Blum's government fell in June 1937, Jacoby took the first job offered him, as press agent for the Parisian nightclub Le Boeuf sur le Toit (The Steer on the Roof), named after a theatrical spectacle by Jean Cocteau that incorporated dance, mime, acrobatics, orchestra, monologue, and drama. The club offered a similar mix that had made it a favorite meeting place for the French cognoscenti of the '20s. Lisa Appignanesi describes the clientele in *The Cabaret*:

> Jean Wiener [a student of French composer Darius Milhaud] played with his partner, Clement Doucet; black musicians dropped in or stayed; Artur Rubinstein, or indeed anyone giving a formal concert, would come in after hours to entertain and improvise. The sound of Gershwin, Cole Porter, jazz and more traditional airs, would emerge from the Boeuf amidst incessant chatter. Picabia's painting of an enormous eye, "L'Oeil Cacodylate," looked on over everything.

Jacoby tried to make the club even more diverse by creating a showroom upstairs and calling it Le Ruban Bleu, for it opened on the day the French liner *Normandie* set a new transatlantic speed record. He presented three or four acts per show, among them Hildegarde, Bricktop, and Mabel Mercer.

Gershwin, Porter, and other Americans urged him to create a replica of the Ruban back home. Almost by necessity, he did. Seeing the thunderheads rolling toward Paris, he knew he had to flee the country or probably lose his life. "He arrived in New York penniless," says Michael Pritchett. For the rest of his life he seldom discussed his political past, except for an occasional terse statement. "I am not a martyr," he told *Cue* (September 4, 1943). "I don't want to die and I have no politics."

In the fall of 1937 Jacoby walked into Theodore's, a fine Italian restaurant at 56th Street and Fifth Avenue. Its owners were Theodore Tietze, a wealthy restaurateur, and Anthony Mele, a wine steward and chef from Naples who had come to Manhattan on a cruise ship to seek his fortune. Jacoby offered Mele his services as press agent, maître d', or anything available. When he learned that Mele and Tietze owned a vacant room upstairs, he argued that he could convert it into the most sophisticated nightclub in New York. Knowing little about his past, they agreed to give him the chance. Thus was born New York's Ruban Bleu.

A staircase inside Theodore's brought you up to a landing with men's and ladies' rooms, a banquette, and a doorway leading into the club. The room itself, a square, low-ceilinged box, seated about 125 at banquettes and tiny tables. The stage was positioned at an angle in the front left-hand corner, and Jacoby arranged the seating so that all eyes were directed toward it. On that small platform he placed two grand pianos, topping them with fresh flowers and candelabra.

Despite these elegant touches, little was spent on decor and Jacoby never tried to make the room comfortable. "The only audience participation at Le Ruban Bleu," wrote a *New Yorker* columnist (November 18, 1939), "is the kind that results from the patrons' being practically within handshaking distance of the entertainers. Claustrophobes and people who hate the adjective 'intimate' complain about the Ruban's size, or lack of it, but that really is the point of the place." It was just as cramped onstage, but performers then were so used to primitive conditions that little unnerved them. They simply planted their feet onstage and performed. The Ruban lacked a sound system, and its lighting consisted of a couple of spotlights with gels and no expert to run them. "Nobody had heard of that in those days," says actress Paula Laurence, whose comedy act opened there in 1940. "All these jobs have been invented as they've invented machines to go with them, and they're totally unnecessary, most of them. The more machinery you have, the more chance there is of it breaking down. A mike? Good heavens, who needed a microphone in such a small room?"

From the beginning the Ruban had the air of a private club, perhaps an illicit one—the essence of any memorable boîte before or after. Recalls Julius Monk, who took over its management in 1942, "In the foyer there was an enormous papier-mâché hand that Cocteau asked Jacoby to bring over here, perhaps to sell, and the police would come in nightly to ask about the pornographic implications of the hand. It was so suspect, you know, the candelabra, the hand, the performer Marie Eve, a Swiss mimic who sang something called 'Je suis Cléopâtre' in what would now be known as a body stocking."

For five years Jacoby brought together a truly cosmopolitan group of performers and audiences, the likes of which existed no place else in Manhattan. With World War II fast becoming a reality, many Europeans sought refuge in the United States. The war discouraged wealthier globe-trotters from traveling, so they settled down and made New York City their home. When they arrived they flocked to Jacoby, delighted to find that he had created a club that felt so much like Paris. Jacoby was just as pleased, for most of them were artists or friends of artists and made an ideal audience. But as Laurence points out, "There was no reason to go to the Ruban except to see the artists perform. It was too crowded for comfort, and the food was minimal. But Jacoby attracted a very chic crowd. There was a whole floating populace of pleasure-seekers in New York at that time. You always saw a good number of champagne coolers next to the tables. It was not unusual to see men in tails. It was all very elegant, and it was the last gasp of that kind of life."

The familiar faces in the first year included Cole Porter, Moss Hart, Robert Benchley, Cocteau, Noel Coward, Tallulah Bankhead, Clifton Webb, Marlene Dietrich, and Dorothy Parker, who from 1934 to 1937 reviewed nightclubs for the *New Yorker* under the nom de plume Lipstick. Wrote the *New York Times* (December 3, 1939):

"Usually the tiny tables disappear under a huddle of such naive sophisticates as once bore the label 'expatriate' and indulged in bitter reflections on life while sipping pernods on the Left Bank."

Jacoby's first lineup consisted of Elsie Houston, a fabled Brazilian soprano; Marie Eve; Jimmie Daniels, a debonair black singer who later hosted several Manhattan clubs, notably the Bon Soir; and twin pianists Cy Walter and Gil Bowers. Jacoby was the imperious emcee, stepping onstage at eleven to introduce the first act in funereal tones. There was no cover or minimum.

Elsie Houston drew the most attention. Born in Rio de Janeiro, Houston sang with concert orchestras and as a soloist between 1926 and 1937. Then she moved to America with an arresting nightclub act of Brazilian folk melodies, songs by her friend Heitor Villa-Lobos, and some chilling voodoo songs for which she put the candelabra on the floor. It was unlike anything club audiences had seen.

Middle-aged by this time, Houston dressed elegantly but austerely, making it a shock when she began to wail like a woman possessed. Her beautiful but metallic soprano ranged all the way from birdlike highs to fierce, animallike sounds. She was an erratic performer, however. "When she really had the spirit moving in her it would make your hair stand on end," says Laurence. "But there were nights when she wasn't interested, or she was depressed, or people were smoking too much. She would come out and wave away all the smoke and glare." Her occasional bursts of temperament betrayed a melancholy spirit, and after a long period of depression Houston committed suicide on February 20, 1943, leaving behind a son barely in his teens. Allegedly a romance had gone sour.

On April 7, 1938, Lotte Lenya came to the Ruban for her first American appearance, with songs by her husband Kurt Weill and by American composer Marc Blitzstein. Wrote *Variety* in a passing mention (April 17, 1938): "Miss Lenya is an engaging young lady and she does full justice to her husband's efforts, concerned to some extent with the lesser souls on this earth." Nevertheless she was only moderately successful and closed in four weeks. "There was such a convention in America and particularly in Europe of women having to be pretty in a certain way," Laurence recalls. "There was another woman at the Ruban named Marianne Oswald, who was quite remarkable. She was very homely. She had Mercurochrome-red dyed hair and a voice that sounded as if she'd gotten hoarse from shouting on top of the barricades. She had been a great friend of many of the avant-garde and surrealist writers, who all loved her and gave her material. She was not successful there, and Jacoby began to learn he needed prettier singers."

Along these lines he presented Vera Sanoff, whose smoldering French and English torch songs were made even more dramatic by her all-white wardrobe and by the white streak dyed in her hair. He also booked Mabel Mercer in 1938, years before the rigors of club performing had robbed her of her sweet mezzo-soprano and given her in its place extraordinary powers of interpretation. That year Jacoby brought to America the beloved Austrian diseuse Greta Keller, whose performances of German and American standards, full of the charm of old Vienna, were evidently quite affecting in person. On recordings this appeal is a mystery; years later a detractor said she sounded "like Madeline Kahn doing Marlene Dietrich." Dietrich, however, named Keller as one of her own influences.

Also popular was Caspar Reardon, a small, studious-looking young harpist from Little Falls, New York. He had performed as a classical soloist under Leopold Stokowski and other prominent conductors before entering nightclubs full time. His act combined pop songs such as "Honeysuckle Rose" and "Summertime" with blues and classical selections, all played with unusual technical virtuosity and an enveloping, sensual sound that transported listeners far beyond their cramped confines.

Reardon's promising career was cut short on March 9, 1941, when he died of uremic poisoning. "I was devastated," says Laurence. "It seemed so senseless to me. He led a very regimented life. He would never even eat the food at the Ruban and brought sandwiches from home on bread that he baked himself, with sprouts and all kinds of things no one had heard of in those days. I was appearing at the Brevoort supper club, and his friend came to tell me, and it was raining, and the two of us were standing there crying. I couldn't believe it, it happened so quickly."

Not all the entertainment was dramatic or serious. Nan Blakstone and her fellow risqué songstress Hope Emerson brought the sometimes high-flown proceedings down to earth with their lusty playing and singing. Billie Haywood and Cliff Allen, a lively black vocal-piano duo, did the same. Haywood had appeared in *New Faces of 1934*, and her light, sweet voice bounced along infectiously as Allen's fingers flew over the keys. He couldn't read music but always put a sheet of music in front of him, sometimes upside down. "They were a marvelous opening act," says Paula Laurence, "because they were ebullient and created a lovely atmosphere. Most acts I had seen seemed to be giving more than they had. But Billie always had something back in the dressing room that she wasn't showing at the moment, and if you hung around, she might. She had a charming, relaxed style, and I realized that that's what club entertainment was about—setting an atmosphere that made people think they were in some wonderful living room."

It didn't take long for Laurence to master that skill. The tall, dark-haired actress-comedienne, who once called herself one of the ugliest babies born in Brooklyn, nevertheless went on to build an enviable career. In 1937, at age twenty-one, she played Helen of Troy at New York's Federal Theatre in *Dr. Faustus* opposite Orson Welles. Subsequently she joined his famed Mercury Theatre company, then co-starred on Broadway with Ethel Merman in Cole Porter's *Something for the Boys* and with Mary Martin in the Kurt Weill–Ogden Nash musical *One Touch of Venus*. Between stage appearances she headlined frequently at the Ruban and other clubs with an act that had no loftier intention than to entertain. She specialized in parodies of silly popular songs, and her show was a celebration of high camp. With flowers and fruit on her head and a box full of props, she massacred such silly pop favorites as "Amapola (Pretty Little Poppy)" and "Jungle Drums" ("Those jungle drums are calling to me . . . PAULA-PAULA-PAULA-PAULA . . .")

As the 1930s ended, intimate clubs were still few and posed no threat to the grander rooms of the day. Most were so unpublicized that they were hardly noticed, except by local regulars who appreciated having their own hideaways for late-night cocktails, conversation, and romance. The cozy Penthouse Club, atop 30 Central Park South, featured a working fireplace, a panoramic view of the park from candlelit tables, and the talents of such singers as Maxine Sullivan, the jazz vocalist best known for her swing version of "Loch Lomond."

Another favorite hangout was Tony's West Side, a bar-restaurant popular among theatre and newspaper folk. Located on 52nd Street and Sixth Avenue amid the jazz clubs that lined "Swing Street," Tony's is best remembered for Mabel Mercer, who sang there throughout the '40s and influenced a legion of singers, composers, and cafégoers. The proprietor, an Italian named Tony Soma, had come to New York in 1922 and worked as a waiter while studying opera. Although highly regarded by Enrico Caruso, one of his customers at the Knickerbocker Hotel, he abandoned his musical ambitions in 1928 to open Tony's. He created a relaxed, breezy atmosphere where you could "take off your coat, put your feet on the chair and unwind for hours," as the *New York Herald Tribune* wrote (August 2, 1939). In the peppermint-striped rear dining room Tony seated customers and chatted with such regulars as Beatrice Lillie, Charles Laughton, Robert Benchley, Dashiell Hammett, and George S. Kaufman, all of whom became subjects for caricatures that lined the walls. Another frequent guest was film director John Huston. There Huston met Tony's daughter Enrica, a beautiful young ballerina who appeared on the cover of *Life* in 1947. They married in 1949 and were the parents of future actress Angelica Huston.

Still a frustrated singer, Tony combined those yearnings with his mastery of yoga by standing on his head in the corner during business hours and singing arias for up to twenty-three minutes. "At first I was pretty terrible," he told a reporter, "but I'm getting better all the time."

One Fifth Avenue, a bar on the ground level of a Greenwich Village hotel, has offered casual entertainment since 1934. Although ill designed for that purpose, with a large mirrored pillar in the center that blocked sight lines, it had an undeniable living room charm. Number One cost less than the uptown clubs, making it a favorite place for college boys from nearby New York University to take their dates. Its attractions included twin pianos, a palm reader who worked for tips, old silent movies, a talent contest on Monday nights, and mostly second- or third-rate acts, one of whom, a torch-singing Dorothy Lamour, played a brief and barely noticed engagement in 1935, a year before her screen debut in *Jungle Princess*.

That year the room gained the services of Julius Monk, who had had a colorful twenty-three years since his birth in Salisbury, North Carolina. Monk's physician father provided well for the family, but life amid Southern plantations held no appeal for the young man. In his early teens he tried to sneak away from home disguised in his mother's clothes; deterred, he had to wait until age sixteen, when he left to enter Manhattan College. An aspiring pianist, Monk dreamed of a career in New York. He enrolled at the Cincinnati Conservatory of Music but quit in his third year to play on cruise ships. When he finally settled in Manhattan he was hired by Victor Gilbert, the owner of Number One, to play during cocktails for $13 a week.

There Monk met Herbert Jacoby, in town as interpreter for Louis Moyses, the owner of Le Boeuf sur le Toit. He also met Elizabeth Allen, a wealthy sculptress with impressive social connections in Europe and America. Despite being homosexual he married her in 1935, and off they sailed to Paris for their honeymoon. The union failed, but it brought Monk into European high society. He began a series of piano jobs in Cannes, St. Tropez, and Paris, where he worked at the Dingo Bar, incorporated by Ernest Hemingway into *The Sun Also Rises*, and at Le Boeuf sur le Toit. Monk's sphere of acquaintance grew even more prestigious when he allegedly became the lover of the duke of Kent, who introduced him to many English peers. When Monk returned to New York, Jacoby hired him to play the piano at the Ruban and at his new club in the basement of the Brevoort Hotel on lower Fifth Avenue, but his days as a cocktail entertainer were numbered.

THE SNOBBERY that played a harmless role in the popularity of many of these clubs had far uglier manifestations elsewhere in town. Stork Club owner Sherman Billingsley made no secret of the fact that he barred blacks and noncelebrity Jews; for many years blacks were even discouraged from walking on Fifth Avenue. A former shoe store partner from Trenton, New Jersey, named Barney Josephson took a significant step against discrimination in 1938 when he opened Café Society Downtown, where Billie Holiday, Lena Horne, Sarah Vaughan, Mildred Bailey, Teddy Wilson, Imogene Coca, Zero Mostel, Jack Gilford, Art Tatum, and others performed for the first truly integrated nightclub audience in America.

Josephson had gotten his first taste of racism when he befriended a black classmate in junior high school and was subsequently beaten up by white students. When he moved to New York in the 1920s he noticed that whites received priority seating at Harlem's Cotton Club to hear Duke Ellington or Ethel Waters, while blacks sat in the rear. "I thought, 'Look what they're doing to these people,' " said Josephson. "The only unique thing we possessed culturally in this country was the music that black people gave us. Everything else was brought over from Europe."

When his family's shoe business went bankrupt during the depression, Josephson took the $7.60 in his pocket, added $6,000 borrowed from friends, and opened Café Society on December 18, 1938, in a basement at 1 Sheridan Square in Greenwich Village. The name was suggested by Clare Boothe Luce as a parody of the Stork Club, El Morocco, and other racist uptown rooms. Josephson hired WPA artists to paint scathing murals on the walls, one of which showed a rich East Side "fat cat" with a walrus mustache, wearing red underwear and dancing with a fan. He paid $200 a month rent, with no deposit or security. The club was large enough for a small dance floor and six-piece band, whose members worked by union regulations: six nights a week from 7 P.M. to 4 A.M., for dancing and three shows, plus afternoon rehearsals. The musicians earned $40 a week, the leader $60. Customers paid a $1.00 table minimum during the week and $1.50 on weekends.

Josephson sent out press releases to black papers around the country, inviting readers to visit. Jazz critic and promoter John Hammond helped him book acts. The first bill included Billie Holiday; boogie-woogie pianists Meade Lux Lewis and Albert Ammons; and Jack Gilford, a white comic later known for his Broadway appearances in *A Funny Thing Happened on the Way to the Forum* and *Cabaret.*

Despite the potentially explosive mix of customers, Josephson created an atmosphere of tolerance; white customers who complained—"What have you got here, a nigger joint?"—received a check and were asked to leave. "One night," recalled Josephson, "I was sitting at the bar when my featured singer at the time, Hazel Scott, arrived for her early show, radiant in a new gown and a new hairstyle, and obviously in an 'up' mood. I gave her a nice compliment and a fatherly good-luck kiss on the cheek as she left to do the show. A well-dressed woman farther down the bar left her stool, glared at me, and spat out, 'Nigger lover! Only a Jew could kiss a nigger!'

"I ignored her and turned to the bartender, telling him to give her a check and get her out. The bartender made me promise to hide the incident from Hazel, but some employee must have leaked the news, because as she left the club later she very dramatically planted a kiss on me and at the door turned and said, 'Only a nigger would kiss a Jew!' "

Josephson sent promising singers to a vocal coach, worked with them on material, and even took them to Bergdorf Goodman. "I'd like to see this young lady gowned," he would say to the horrified saleswoman. Lena Horne was his first project. "John Hammond urged me to go see her with Charlie Barnet's band at the Paramount in 1940. She sat up there in a chair the way all band singers did, every now and then getting up to sing a chorus. The Paramount was a big theatre, and you couldn't tell if she was black. I was impressed not so much by her singing but by her looks, the way she carried herself. I went to the dressing room, introduced myself, and said, 'Lena, people who come here don't know who the devil you are. You're a singer with Charlie Barnet—where are you gonna get with that? How would you like to come into Café Society? You'll have no less than Teddy Wilson playing for you.'

"She left Charlie and came in, and I worked with her on material. All her movements and routines were done in Latin rhythms, which were very big then. I asked her if she was a Negro, and she bristled and said yes. 'I don't dig you,' she said.

" 'Lena,' I answered, 'there are dozens of nice Jewish girls from Brooklyn doing the Latin rhythms. Let me present you as a Negro talent.' I got her to sing blues and things like 'Summertime,' but she didn't have any contact with the audience because she wasn't putting feeling and meaning into what she sang. She closed her eyes when she sang or looked at the ceiling. I asked her if she was afraid to look white people in the eye. Finally she got to the point where people would stand up and shout whenever she sang the blues."

Josephson made one of his few missteps in 1947. "I auditioned a young white lady, a singer with a comedy sense. I listened to all her material and told her there was one piece I didn't want, an imitation of Ethel Waters singing 'Cabin in the Sky.' Now, Ethel Waters was to me and to many black people an Uncle Tom. I explained that Café Society was integrated, and if she did this number she would probably get booed.

"She came in and started doing her shows, and at every performance she bombed out. Her feeling was, the reason she's not doing well is that I've taken away her best material. One night she turned to Teddy Wilson and said 'Cabin in the Sky,' and they went into it. Sure enough, the audience became restless and irritated, and couldn't wait for it to end.

"When she walked off I said, 'I told you not to do that, and you will take your two weeks' notice.' "

"A year later she's appearing in a Broadway revue called *Lend an Ear,* and then she's in *Gentlemen Prefer Blondes.* Did I miss? No. The Broadway casting directors saw something in Carol Channing that wasn't there in a nightclub. But I still don't like her—in shows or anywhere."

Josephson opened a second club, Café Society Uptown, on October 8, 1940, on 58th Street between Park and Lexington avenues. Both the entertainment and the admission policy were the same as Downtown's. By now Josephson had won national recognition for his work in promoting racial equality. "It's the only thing I'm proud of," he said shortly before his death.

THE LAST INTERESTING new café to open before World War II held neither the Continental chic of the Ruban nor the social purpose or musical thrills of Café Society, but it was there that the sophisticated song finally became sophisticated. Spivy's Roof occupied the penthouse of an office building at 139 East 57th Street. In the slow, creaky elevator ride to the ninth floor patrons might rub elbows with Clifton Webb, inhale the perfume that Gertrude Lawrence dabbed behind her ears, or crush the gold slipper of decorator Elsie de Wolfe. By midnight most eyes were glued to the corner piano, where a stout, fortyish woman played the piano with gusto, talking and singing in a Tallulah Bankhead register. One of her numbers, "The Last of the Fleur de Levys" by Broadway composer John Latouche, told of a society doyenne who had long passed her prime:

Two men were standing in a swanky hotel bar one day
Their chatter grew more frivolous with each new Dubonnet
A woman who came trickling in incited one to mirth
He giggled and he tittered and he pointed, "What on earth?"
But the other held his arm and said, "Hold on, you'd better not!
Though she's frowsy and she's blowsy and undoubtedly a sot,
Though her eyes are dead and rimmed with red and her nose is bright blue,
She once was the empress of 103rd and West End Avenue!"

This was Spivy. Her black hair was combed and lacquered into a pointed pompadour with a white streak running through it, and she often wore a black dress with shoulder pads and large sequined lapels shaped like those on a double-breasted dinner jacket. "Spivy was *squat*," says one of her pianists, "and she looked like a bulldog. We used to call her the Bulldog Bulldike."

Spivy first came to attention at Tony's, where composers such as Latouche admired her dexterity with a tongue-twisting triple rhyme and her flair at projecting the character of a comically world-weary, overpartied, underslept New Yorker always ready to rise in time for the next soiree. They wrote songs for her filled with half-mocking references to Elsa Maxwell, Benzedrine, plastic surgery, Salvador Dali, and other components in the lives of upper-crust New Yorkers. Audiences laughed empathetically when she sang of her efforts to banish a hangover after an all-night drinking spree ("I searched for rubbing alcohol to rub away the ache / But I couldn't find the stuff at all, I'd drunk it by mistake!") and nodded at her response "to a man who tried to induce me to live on a farm":

I want to live in town
Where you hunt in Jaeckl's when you want a foxhide
And you see fair hair of purest peroxide
And you breathe fresh air of carbon monoxide
I love town!

"She was magic!" said Buster Davis, one of her pianists and later the vocal arranger for forty Broadway shows. "There was such glee when she sang those saucy lyrics, and her energy was boundless."

Details about her background are scarce. Spivy mixed nightly with the wealthy, the socially prominent, and the insufferably snobbish, altering her humble life story accordingly. She called herself Spivy Le Voe, pretending to be a cultured, intellectual legend in her own time, Russian by birth, who had worked her way up from playing the organ in Catholic churches to speakeasies to East Side house parties (where she claimed to have entertained guests with Chopin waltzes) to New York notoriety. She was actually born in Brooklyn in 1906 to an impoverished Russian Jewish family and quit high school to help support them by playing the piano in speakeasies and gin mills.

According to Marsha Harkness, the sole backer of Spivy's Roof, "Her real name was Bertha. I got hysterical when I heard it. She had a sister who couldn't say 'sister' so she said 'Spivy.' "

Try as she did, she couldn't conceal her coarseness. Bart Howard, composer of "Fly Me to the Moon" and her pianist in 1946, recalls that "Spivy always talked about what a great cook she was and how much she liked gourmet food. One night she asked Kurt, the headwaiter, for something to eat. 'I'll just have my usual,' she said, 'and tell them to put a piece of salami in with the bologna!' "

But a smash nightclub is not created without some kind of talent, and Spivy's was for penny-pinching. At Tony's she met wealthy young socialite Harkness, persuaded her to loan her $5,000 to start her own club, leased the penthouse for $200 a month, opened in January 1940, and characteristically never returned a penny of Harkness's money. "Spivy was famous for not paying anybody unless you put a gun to her head," Harkness says. "There were long periods when the money was rolling in, but if you didn't put her over the barrel you wouldn't see any of it."

Spivy persuaded Vernon MacFarlane, known for his zebra-striped designs for El Morocco, to decorate her club for practically nothing. With so little funding, MacFarlane hardly rose to his stylish standard. "The place was glittery, with a lot of mirrors and chrome, and tiny cheap tables anywhere they could jam them in," says Buster Davis. An almost perfect square, the room possessed an attractive L-shaped terrace overlooking Lexington Avenue and 57th Street. Spivy placed two baby grands in the front right corner of the club, hers facing the bar and tables diagonally. Peppermint-striped banquettes lined the blue walls, which held paper sculptures of Katharine Cornell, Gypsy Rose Lee, and others.

For ten years Spivy ran the club on a shoestring, avoiding bills whenever possible and treating her underpaid staff like servants. Pianists came and went constantly, with the exception of Davis, who stayed two years. "I started to go to Spivy's Roof with other Princetonians and their dates. It was *the* place in those days, especially for men. Spivy was the patron saint of the fags. They loved her. It wasn't certifiably gay, but there were a lot of young men at the bar, and since it was so dark a little fumbling around went on. Spivy didn't care for that, but she let her girlfriends sit there, so fair is fair. When she was in a rotten mood she'd walk into the room, which was always packed in those days, take one look around, and announce, 'GET ALL THESE FAIRIES OUT OF HERE!'

"To the left of the elevator was one of the smallest ladies' rooms in New York and a tiny office. In it sat this poor woman who was madly in love with Spivy. Her name was Dora. She had white hair, and she looked like a sophisticated version of Andy Hardy's mother—really sweet and nice, but Spivy growled at her all the time. Occasionally Spivy would come out of the office screaming and slam the door behind her.

"God, she cheated us on the bills. But we were all dizzy Princetonians and would never have quibbled about a dollar or two. They'd throw the bill at you, and there was very little light, and they'd say, 'Please, sir, I'm needed at the next table!' You'd see the amount and say, 'Isn't that too much? Oh, never mind. Isn't she marvelous?' Finally I met her, after I'd come there often enough. She was very gracious. I was Princeton to her, so I meant money.

"I had promised my family I would get a respectable job for one year, so I went to work for Texaco. I hated it. I didn't know what else to do except play the piano, and a waiter there told me that Spivy's pianist had been drafted and she needed someone in a hurry. She probably thought I'd bring in a lot of people from Princeton, so she hired me. Soon I realized I was her slave. I'd never worked in a nightclub before, so I didn't know the union entitled you to ten minutes off an hour to pee, or whatever. I'd be playing and playing, and every once in a while I had to pee. Then she'd come strolling through, and I could feel her presence. I didn't dare get up from that piano."

Spivy reserved two tables in the back for buddies such as Tallulah Bankhead or singer-comedienne Patsy Kelly. She was supposed to do two shows a night and three on Fridays and Saturdays, but she never paid attention to the time. Every evening she sat in the back and gabbed for hours, so that customers who came for the ten o'clock show were still waiting at 11:30. Some shouted "Spivy! Spivy!" and banged their glasses on the tables. Finally a waiter would approach her.

"Spivy, they're waiting."

"Oh, fuck 'em! I'll be there in five minutes!"

She would go to the terrace from a doorway near her table, walking to the front along a pathway obscured by hanging flowers and ferns. A waiter signaled the pianist to begin her fanfare, the lights dimmed, and over to the piano she charged. Pounding out an introduction, she tore into her opening number, often "The Madame's Lament":

> *They all go upstairs—but me!*
> *Me with my fine silk dress, and furs, too*
> *I wouldn't feel so low*
> *If they'd look and* then *say no*
> *But there's not one guy it actually occurs to.*
>
> *Every night I get the drinks exactly right*
> *The lemons squeezed, the rind pinched*
> *I get the ice cubes every night*
> *But I don't get my behind pinched . . .*

Her repertoire amounted to about fifteen numbers. It took her so long to learn new lyrics and to master a new accompaniment that she gave up trying to learn anything else. "People used to ask, 'Why doesn't she learn some new songs?' " said Buster Davis. "But her fans didn't *want* her to learn any."

She closed with a medley of piano duets. "Her accompanist was expected to play every key on that keyboard and make her sound marvelous," said Davis. "She would suddenly go into 'Wildflower' by Vincent Youmans. I would play fancy-fancy, then she'd suddenly switch to 'Wait Till You See Her' or God knows what. You couldn't avoid fumbling a bit. One night she walked over to the audience and said, 'Why doesn't he know this? We rehearsed for twelve hours. Sometimes I think he masturbates up there!'

"At the end she'd take a big bow, like Horowitz after performing a Scriabin etude. The other pianist sat in the dark, and she never even acknowledged him."

Though always the star entertainer, Spivy featured a series of opening acts that included Mabel Mercer, Thelma Carpenter, and impressionist Sheila Barrett, whom Dorothy Kilgallen dubbed "the nightclub Bernhardt." Barrett performed at Spivy's on the heels of a glamorous heyday marked by frequent appearances on radio and at the Palace Theatre, the Paramount, the Waldorf-Astoria, and the Rainbow Room. During the '30s she received up to $2,300 a week and enjoyed an equally auspicious personal life as the mistress of

Cissy Patterson, proprietor of the *Washington Times-Herald,* and Evalyn Walsh McLean, who owned the Hope Diamond.

Unlike most of her competitors, Barrett avoided the predictable imitations of Tallulah Bankhead, Bette Davis, or Hildegarde. Her routines included a scene from *Hamlet* enacted by Bert Lahr and Lynn Fontanne, Mae West as Juliet, and Fanny Brice as Scarlett O'Hara opposite W. C. Fields as Rhett Butler. She also created several original characterizations, many of them downtrodden women to whom she brought an unexpected dignity. In one monologue, "Victoria Station," she became an English prostitute fighting back tears as she bids goodbye to an American soldier to whom she'd grown too close in their one night together. "Speakeasy Girl" depicted an alcoholic who spends every night in a gin mill hoping someone will talk to her, but finally summons enough self-respect to decide she is better off alone.

Tragedy had dogged the impressionist since 1940, when an auto accident nearly disfigured her permanently. It took four operations to save her right hand and restore her features, leaving her with badly blemished skin but allowing her to resume her career within a few months.

She spent the rest of the '40s mostly out of town, accepting any brief bookings offered her. After returning to Spivy's in 1948 she performed at La Commedia on West 52nd Street where Thelma Carpenter, Sylvia Syms, and other talented singers appeared. She had been booked there by Milton ("Doc") Bender, an agent who not only handled performers but also supplied male prostitutes for the likes of Cole Porter and Lorenz Hart. "He had a whole stable of gentlemen, including a lot of weightlifters," says composer Murray Grand, who accompanied Barrett. "But he would only book acts who were unknown or who had peaked and were now near the bottom of the ladder. Sheila was hopelessly alcoholic by the time I met her. While I could see that she was probably pretty good when she had her wits about her, by this time she'd be so drunk that I didn't know if we'd get through a show. Fortunately she designed her act so that a lot of the characters were drunks, and when she got up you thought she was faking it. She would enter as a drunken woman who interrupts the emcee—'Now, wait a minute, mister!'—but she really *was* drunk."

Still unknown in 1941, when Spivy booked him, was a young pianist known as Walter Liberace. He wore white tie and tails, and a toothy smile shone beneath his wide, cowlike eyes and dark curly hair. Hired to warm up the audience with standards and an occasional vocal, Liberace had an obvious thirst for showmanship. Each night he cranked up a Victrola behind the piano and set down the needle on a Gershwin orchestral record. Then he played the piano part to the scratchy accompaniment of the NBC Symphony Orchestra or the Boston Pops.

Neither that engagement nor a second in 1943 lasted long; he proved too sensitive to tolerate Spivy. "One night," says Davis, "he was up there playing and Spivy's fans were getting restless for her to go on. Dora came over and said, 'Spivy, are you ready?' She answered in that booming voice, 'Oh, tell the fairy to keep playing! I'll be right there!' Liberace heard her, as did half the room, and not long after that he quit."

During her prime in the early '40s replacement pianists were always available, as well as celebrity friends such as actress-singer Anne Francine or Martha Raye, who often performed. "Martha and Spivy would vie with each other as to who could be the filthiest," says Marshall Barer, lyricist of the Broadway musical *Once Upon a Mattress* and a frequent patron. "They would try to break each other up. When Martha went onstage Spivy would hide on the balcony, where only Martha could see her, and take out this enormous tit and flash it at her. Then Spivy would go on, and Martha would step on the balcony and stick a finger up her nose, pull it out, stare at it, then make a flicking motion over the rail."

Another of Spivy's regulars was a man who had lost an eye in a fishing accident. He had three artificial eyes: one brown, one blue, and one with an American flag in the iris. Often he stood at the bar and waited for a sedate-looking couple or young square to glance over. Then he would remove his eye, take the other two out of his pocket, and ponder them for long moments before popping one in, shouting 'Whoops!' and replacing it with the third. Whenever Spivy heard a glass crash to the floor she knew the cause.

No one wanted the nights to end, but during wartime the midnight curfew put an end to the fun just as it was getting started. To cheer people up, Spivy placed a tiny white spinet in the elevator and played for them on their way out, sometimes bringing along her featured girl singer to place her arm around the shoulders of visiting GIs and coo "Goodnight, My Love" in their ears.

In view of such efforts as Spivy's and Josephson's, it was inevitable that European bons vivants and the wealthy and artistic elite would no longer dominate the town's nightlife. The war itself had much to do with deflating that late 1930s frivolity, as Paula Laurence noticed.

"In May 1940 I went to Canada with Hume Cronyn, Keenan Wynn, and Tamara [a singer-actress who introduced "Smoke Gets in Your Eyes" in Jerome Kern's *Roberta*]. The British War Relief and the American Theatre Wing had joined forces, and we were going to entertain at the various installations in the Royal Canadian Air Force in Toronto. It was the first experience I had of looking out at an audience, fifty percent of them eighteen-year-olds off the farms and far reaches of Canada, and knowing that half of them would never come back. Horrifying. These well-born women with houses full of servants, scrubbing floors and washing dishes and cooking and cleaning, who'd never done it before in their lives. It was a great equalizer, I can tell you."

Like others who had reveled in the ultrasophistication of the Ruban's early years, Laurence regretted its passing. "It was not perceptible at first, but after a few months you suddenly looked up at Bergdorf's, and a woman who had clearly never been there before was buying a pocketbook for two hundred and fifty dollars, which she'd earned in a defense plant. There were very marked strata of society in New York, and they all began to melt. Many people suddenly had money, along with all the trappings. But when they went to places of entertainment, they really weren't that interested in Elsie Houston, say, or even Lotte Lenya. Things had to be popular in order to succeed. Jacoby was very sharp in keeping up with trends. He had Mildred Bailey at the Ruban for a whole season in 1941, and it was like a jazz club. She was remarkable, but he would never have hired her when I started there."

Whatever exclusivity the room lost, its shift in clientele allowed it to embrace a greater variety of acts and to place more emphasis on American talent. Jacoby also realized, of course, how much money and publicity this could bring him.

But he would take this knowledge elsewhere. By now Julius Monk had become quite familiar at the Ruban, as pianist and substitute emcee. Jacoby spent many evenings at the Brevoort, thereby giving Monk a chance to gain the upper hand. Unlike Jacoby, who cast a dark shadow over the proceedings, the flamboyant Monk was charm itself, and he ingratiated himself with the entire Ruban staff. His colorful introductions of acts drew a lot of attention, and customers gradually began to associate the club with him.

Jacoby grew angrier as he realized Monk's intentions, and the tension finally mounted into an angry confrontation. It ended when Jacoby announced that he was through with the Ruban and that Monk could have it. Jacoby seldom gave up easily; in this case, he didn't mention that he had decided to buy his own club. But that didn't interest Monk. Now he was in charge.

When Jacoby opened the Blue Angel in 1943 a lifelong rivalry started between the two men. Monk turned up his nose, calling the Angel a "commercial" room, while Jacoby scarcely acknowledged the Ruban or his successor there. Sometimes he referred to Monk as Jules Monkey. "He really does look like a monkey," he would say.

Though both men would dedicate their careers to the discovery of talented unknowns, Spivy persisted in showcasing herself above anyone else on the bill. By the end of the war her fans had grown bored, while younger clubgoers overlooked her in favor of the more exciting goings-on in other rooms.

She did have an eye for talent but treated performers so badly that few stayed for long. By the late '40s business had so dropped that two of her opening acts, Charlotte Rae and Carol Channing, were hardly noticed and left quickly. Marshall Izen, a classically trained pianist who used handcrafted puppets to enact an endearing set of opera satires, might have given the club a boost when he appeared in 1950, but true to form Spivy sabotaged it. As ever, she hired him for a bargain fee. "Union scale was seventy-five dollars a week in those days," says Izen. "Spivy said, 'Now, darling, business is very very slow, as you can see. The arrangement is that I will pay you scale, but you have to give me back seventy-five dollars under the table.' " While there Izen won a spot on the *Arthur Godfrey Talent Scouts* television amateur contest. Contestants were limited to three minutes, and Spivy advised him to perform highlights from all his routines. "I said, 'Spivy, if I do that it will just be a hodgepodge and nothing will hold together.' She said, 'Darling, you must listen to your mother and do as I say!' "

"Well, I didn't. I auditioned with a satire on *Die Walküre* and won, and Spivy was so pissed that she fired me that week. I said, 'Spivy, if I get on the show and win I can mention that I'm working here.' She said, 'Darling, you don't think anyone who watches Arthur Godfrey would come up here!' "

"I appeared on a Wednesday night, and Godfrey mentioned the club. That weekend the place was packed, but I wasn't there anymore. Godfrey invited me to appear on his television series, and I was recognized everywhere I went. Spivy wanted to kick herself in the ass. She had hired some young comic in my place, and he wasn't doing too well. Later in the week I got a phone call. 'Darling, this is Spivy. Irv has had an appendicitis attack. Could you stand in for him for a few days?' "

By now she had eliminated her ten o'clock show, and on some nights she didn't perform at all. She cut her staff to the minimum and raised drink prices, still refusing to face the truth. "She owed everybody," says Murray Grand. "The place was falling apart."

Few were around in 1951, her last season, to applaud comic Paul Lynde in one of his first nightclub appearances, prior to his Broadway debut in *New Faces of 1952*. "Spivy was too broke to pay him, so she told him he had no talent," says Grand. "Instead of being honest she made him feel so awful that he quit. She wouldn't pay me either, so I quit too. She would sit with guests saying awfully witty things—she thought—and people bought it for quite a while. Then the world turned against her all at once, because they finally caught on that she was just a tacky lady from Brooklyn." Spivy's Roof finally closed in the summer of 1951. "They dispossessed her," says Anne Francine. "Friends of mine went by and said, 'What the hell's happening here?' Everything was out on the street."

Spivy filed for bankruptcy to avoid her debts but faced such hostility that she decided to skip town and fly to Paris, where older clubgoers remembered her fondly from her appearances in the '30s. Early in 1952 she opened the first of several Paris clubs bearing her name, financed by unsuspecting French investors. All failed, even with such a talent as Bobby Short performing at one of them. Once more Spivy endeared herself to few. Thelma Carpenter, singing throughout Europe, stopped in Paris in 1953 and decided to look her up. "I had a hard time finding her. Nobody would tell me where she was—that's how she was disliked. And she was a slave driver. The French wouldn't stand for it."

Later she appeared at London's lavish Café de Paris, an ideal setting for the talents of Marlene Dietrich and Noel Coward but not for

Spivy's more intimate style. Ventures in Rome and other parts of Europe were also flops. She returned to New York in 1957 when Herbert Jacoby hired her at the Blue Angel for old time's sake. By now she seemed like a relic of nightclubs past, and young audiences found her songs all but meaningless. Spivy never again worked a New York club.

Thereafter she began a brief career as a character actress, playing small roles in such films as *Requiem for a Heavyweight*, *The Fugitive Kind*, *The Manchurian Candidate*, and *A Walk on the Wild Side* and making a memorable appearance in 1959 on television's *Alfred Hitchcock Presents* as the hostess of an exclusive restaurant where the house specialty is human flesh. In the late '60s she moved to an inexpensive apartment in Hollywood, where she spent most of her time with friends. "We'd go to Patsy Kelly's house a lot," says Thelma Carpenter. "She and her pals would all be drunk and they'd always fight with each other. But they could never get the better of Spivy. She was a bitch but an intelligent one. She lived by her wits."

In 1969 cancer forced her into a series of hospitals and nursing homes. She was only sixty-two and full of bitterness at having to rely on nurses after a lifetime of self-sufficiency. "Spivy was such a bad patient," says Anne Francine, "that they'd kick her out. She'd scream and yell, and if they didn't take care of her she'd throw her plate against the wall." Finally, Patsy Kelly arranged for her to move to the Motion Picture County Home and Hospital in Woodland Hills, California, where she died on January 8, 1971. The only mementos of her offbeat talents are a few rare 78s, her Hitchcock episode, and a handful of film cameos that give no indication of the illustrious nightclub career that preceded them.

Chapter TWO

To most of 1940s America, nightlife in New York City was synonymous with grandeur, audience participation, and—most of all—money. As a *Life* reporter wrote in 1943, "The nightclub boom is fed by a national surplus of cash which cannot be spent on consumer goods and thus flows into entertainment . . . It reflects the wartime need for escape."

The formula for success: make it big, loud, lavish and, if possible, Latin. Dozens of rooms brought all four qualities splashily to life, among them Havana-Madrid, La Martinique, Casa Mañana, Club Gaucho, Riobamba, La Conga, El Chico, El Borracho, Don Julio—and, of course, the Latin Quarter. Their glorification of South American life, a ubiquitous '40s craze, was partly an offshoot of President Roosevelt's efforts to keep Latin America as an ally. But other foreign lands held an escapist fascination in those stormy years, hence the Persian Room, the Hawaiian Room of the Hotel Lexington, Casino Russe, Féfé's Monte Carlo, Bal Tabarin, Zimmerman's Hungaria, and a host of similar clubs.

All were places to eat and drink heartily, dance, and forget your wartime troubles by watching floor shows that often rivaled Busby Berkeley. For the finale of the extravaganza staged at the enormous International Casino a bit north of Times Square, girls atop miniature airplanes descended from the ceiling, a train charged onstage as planes rolled out onto runways alongside the wings, and two staircases dropped from the roof bearing tap-dancing chorines in one-piece costumes that might have gotten them thrown off the beach. Viewers preferring a more modest display could go to the Casino Russe on West 56th Street, where a man did a fire dance with half a dozen flaming torches in his mouth.

Many dance-crazy Americans were just as happy to create the excitement themselves, crushing their partners' toes as they whirled around packed dance floors to the strains of Ray Noble, Jimmy Dorsey, or Harry James at any of Manhattan's forty or so ballrooms. Wherever one spent the evening, color overwhelmed the eyes. Féfé's Monte Carlo swam in tropical shades of yellow and green; red stars twinkled in the electric blue sky above El Morocco; and at the St. Regis Roof's Viennese Room a man named Pinky did the conga in a pink elephant suit, followed by a dancing couple who pranced out of a red-and-white striped tent to the fanfare of an orchestra dressed in bright crimson uniforms decorated with gold braid and pompons.

Few people looked for escape in a small, quieter room, where alcohol, the midnight hour, and some gentle, persuasive music could multiply wartime sorrows tenfold. To a typical clubgoer "intimate" might have meant the sprawling Café Lounge of the Savoy-Plaza Hotel on 58th Street and Fifth Avenue, home of such entertainers as Dwight Fiske and The Incomparable Hildegarde, a Milwaukee-born singer-pianist who represented a compromise between big-scale glamour and the more personal style that was emerging in New York. For her highly elaborate performances Hildegarde chose many fine new showtunes by Coward, Kern, Rodgers and Hart, and Vernon Duke, gilding her pallid renditions lavishly enough to give wisecracking critics—and nearly every impressionist in town—a field day. In a typical show she floated out into a sea of complex lighting by her manager Anna Sosenko, composer of her signature song "Darling, Je Vous Aime Beaucoup," wearing a gown by the celebrated Hollywood couturier Adrian and a pair of elbow-length white gloves. Then she sat down at a grand piano adorned with a bouquet of American beauty roses. Staring at the keys, she played in the careful manner of a second-year music student giving her first recital, and sang in a pleasant but unremarkable voice. A spotlight on the edge of the keyboard cast mammoth shadows of her head on the wall.

After every few songs she walked to ringside to chat with the audience. "Tell me, the lady with the red dress, are you in love?" "Is this your first, second, or third marriage, Colonel?" "May I see your dental work, sir?" Finally she distributed her roses to the ladies and invited their mates to sniff her perfumed handkerchief.

Amusingly dotty as it was, Hildegarde's act hardly resembled the sort of intimacy that Herbert Jacoby and Julius Monk were trying to create. In many ways their clubs were a reaction against such excess. They were decorated in dark blue and gray and black so as not to detract attention from the performers. A singer, a pianist, a lone comic, and a vocal quartet continued to be the order of the night. It was not surprising that *Life* looked elsewhere for its photo spreads or that movie stars and society couples found the glare of the Stork Club a better place to have their pictures snapped.

But truly intimate rooms were growing in esteem among listeners who preferred more intelligent fare. In 1941 the *New Yorker*, in a passing mention of Le Ruban Bleu, allowed merely that it was "upstairs and rather dark," but by 1944 reviewer Rogers ("Popsy") Whitaker wrote in the same pages:

> Someday, years after most of us nightowls have gone to our reward, a committee of antiquarians will place a commemorative plaque beside the entrance of No. 4 East Fifty-sixth Street. This plaque will say something about the Ruban Bleu and a few of its alumni—people like Paula Laurence, Caspar Reardon, Richard Dyer-Bennet and Maxine Sullivan, to name names. There will not, of course, be room to deal with everyone, because it has evidently been the theory of the management that all the acts on a given bill, and not just the headline act, might as well be as good as possible.

Like Jacoby, Monk began there with a vast following of royalty, literati, film stars, and others who trusted his taste. He oversaw every detail of what his acts sang or spoke, how they delivered it, and what they wore. For a performer new in town, with little confidence or showbiz savvy, this personal attention meant a lot. Monk sometimes spotted qualities in them that few perceived, and fought for them to stay on, even against the wishes of owner Anthony Mele. Says Pat Carroll, "Oh, my dear, I found him wonderful to work for. He had a great sense of humor, so whenever he gave you notes about why your material might not be working he was so amusing that your feelings were never hurt. He made me feel I was wonderful, and he was the most elegant gentleman I'd ever seen. He always dressed in such a dapper fashion, and the way he carried himself was exquisite. I thought he was right out of a Noel Coward script."

In keeping with the nationalistic wartime mood the Ruban downplayed European entertainers in favor of American singers, jazz pianists, vocal quartets, and comics, many of them black. The club was redecorated in 1943 with similar intent. The black patent leather walls, which seemed too frivolous for wartime, were stripped and recovered in deep blue Celanese, and blue carpeting was laid. When the ball sconces on the walls dimmed, only the performers were visible—just as Monk wanted. The only Continental touch came from Monk himself, who emceed in a Southern twang with incongruous English overtones, a result of his elbow-rubbing with nobility and high society.

The standout acts in the mid-'40s included petite, honey-voiced jazz singer Maxine Sullivan; boogie-woogie pianist Maurice Rocco; Liberace, who played there for a few weeks in 1943, during which he borrowed the idea of placing candelabra on his piano; and Imogene Coca, six years before millions of viewers welcomed her into their living rooms as costar of *Your Show of Shows*.

Even in 1944, when she first appeared at the Ruban, Coca was no stranger to clubs. Born in Philadelphia in 1909 as Imogene Fernandez y Coca, daughter of a Spanish bandleader and a retired vaudeville dancer, she worked her way up in showbusiness as a chorine in vaudeville and speakeasies. One of them, the Silver Slipper, became known for its "imported champagne," a corrosive mixture of ginger ale and medicinal alcohol that sold for $55 a bottle. Emcee Danny Healy dubbed the room "the upholstered sewer," a moniker that lives on as the description of any basement club.

Coca's career as a comedienne began in *New Faces of 1934*, and for the next fifteen years she alternated between nightclubs and theatre. Her act consisted of original parodies of opera stars, torch singers, ballerinas, and a female trombonist in Phil Spitalny's all-girl orchestra, for which she played a few licks on the slide trombone. She also satirized fads in female sex appeal, from Clara Bow and other silent film sirens to the movie goddesses of the '40s, whose glamour was judged, Coca said, by "how far they stick out in front and behind." She showed how far removed from reality they were—quite the opposite of Coca herself who, though no beauty, radiated a warmth and believability that audiences identified with. Coca would grumble in an often-quoted moment of candor, "I'm spending three-fourths of my life out of work, and the rest of it among people so chic you can hardly understand them."

Coca helped pave the way for a legion of singer-comediennes whose stock-in-trade was pointed satire, not the knock-'em-dead brashness and vivacity of a Martha Raye or a Betty Hutton. But the shy, insecure entertainer would prefer TV, where audience reaction was not so close and immediate. Customers at the Ruban may have been a little more refined, but the booze there was just as strong. "In nightclubs," she told the *New York Post* (October 10, 1954), "people often bring their emotional problems and with the help of a few drinks take them out on the first person they see. Usually, it seemed to be me."

Even the rowdiest audiences couldn't intimidate Thelma Carpenter, a picture-pretty young black singer with, to date, over five decades of nightclub and musical comedy experience. Carpenter sang standards in a sweet, melodic voice with a trace of vinegar around the edges, revealing some of the gritty street savvy of her Harlem upbringing. She sang on radio as a child and belted out songs on 42nd Street for tips. In 1937, at age fifteen, she won a week's engagement at the Apollo Theatre by singing "Stormy Weather" in one of their famous amateur contests. Thereafter she performed at several forgotten black clubs from Greenwich Village to Harlem and sang with the bands of Teddy Wilson, Coleman Hawkins, and Count Basie. Finally she broke through to the white club circuit when she debuted at the Ruban in 1944. "Julius took me out and bought me clothes from a shop on Madison Avenue, and he introduced me as the Downbeat Diva. He really took great pains with me—like a mother. He supervised what I wore, and he was right. I met all the right people through him."

It helped that Carpenter had enormous natural poise and authority, as well as the sort of repertoire that Monk encouraged for girl singers: "The Man I Love," "September Song," "Happiness Is a Thing Called Joe," "Porgy" by Dorothy Fields and Jimmy McHugh (from *Lew Leslie's Blackbirds of 1928*), and other great ballads.

Her Harlem roots kept her down-to-earth, no matter how grand the setting. As one club owner said: "Don't mess with that chick, man. She's tough." Carpenter could comfortably work such mob-run rooms as the Valentine Club on West 48th Street, which was just the sort of place that helped inspire the snobbery common at the Ruban and similar rooms. "That place could have been really nice," she says, "but a lot of these new clubs wanted to be chic and didn't know how. One night I came to work and there were all these whores sitting there. Now I knew these men's wives, and I was the kind of singer where men wouldn't dare bring another woman in, 'cause I've got a big mouth. I'd stand there and say, 'That ain't your wife! *I'm* the only broad in the room!' And I'd sing.

"In those days even when the gangsters were sitting up front I used to take chances. I'd say to their girls, 'OUT! This is my room. Out! No woman's in here but me!' The big boss would come over to start trouble, and I'd say, 'Uh-uh!' You had to learn to roll with the punches and make sure you were superior to them, because you were on the stage. And when you're on that stage, you are immortal. I could come offstage and love you to death, but onstage? Up your ass, kid. You wanna play rough? Let's play rough."

The Valentine Club struck a familiar chord in its treatment of homosexual customers, especially flamboyant ones. Clubs like the Ruban, which were managed by homosexuals and catered to a generally tasteful clientele, were tolerant; but heterosexual rooms, especially black- or Mafia-run, were not. "They didn't want any gays in there," says Carpenter. "Some gay people would come in and sit at the bar, and the bartender would get kind of smart with them. One guy I knew was a hairdresser, as gay as he could be, but he was a tough guy. The bartender made fun of him, and I said, 'Don't say that. These are my friends.' He made some other comment, and the boy reached behind the bar and beat the shit out of him. And he said, 'Now, how does that feel, being whipped by a sissy?' One of the mob guys came over to me and said, 'What kind of people you got coming in here?'

"I said, 'Listen, they spend a lot of money. You can't insult anybody. They're better gentlemen than the people you got coming here. You see them bothering anybody? They come in, they keep quiet, they pay their bills.'

" 'But it looks like you've got nothing but men in here all the time.'

" 'So what?' "

But homosexual entertainers did not dare speak the truth. The few acknowledged gays tended to be sequestered in safe, remote categories such as drag performing. Perhaps the most notorious in that area was Ray (Rae) Bourbon, a flamboyant female impersonator of the '30s, '40s, and '50s whose campy songs and monologues were shocking enough in their day to land him in jail repeatedly. Bourbon was the sort of figure who helped perpetuate the stereotype of gays as freaks and transvestites. Born in 1893 near the Mexico–United States border and raised in Texas, Bourbon began appearing in drag in the grueling English music hall and American vaudeville circuits. In the '20s he worked extensively as an extra in silent films, including four with Rudolph Valentino; thereafter he played in nightclubs throughout America and Europe. While homosexually oriented, most of them were not bona fide gay gathering places but virtual sideshows, where a few men in makeup and permanent waves paraded around as straights pointed their fingers and laughed. The repression of those years destroyed the pride of many homosexuals, leading them to caricature themselves. Such was the case with Bourbon, who plied his trade in a legion of dives whose names speak for themselves: the Glory Hole in Central City, Colorado; the Coon Chicken Inn in Reno, Nevada; Dante's Inferno in Kansas City.

Naturally he never won the acclaim of such stylish and dignified female impersonators as Julian Eltinge, Francis Renault, and Bert Savoy, who appeared on Broadway and in more prestigious clubs. But he behaved as grandly as if he were a combination of Mae West and Katharine Cornell—an irony in view of his material, which he wrote himself and which stretched the single entendre to its limits:

> Emmy, Peter, darlings! Mother's gonna read you a bedtime story. Come and sit over here . . . Peter, will you stop picking your nose? All right, but don't wipe it on me. Wipe it on your father. Now sit down. Mother's gonna tell you all about Cleopatra and her famous asp. ASP! It was a snake . . . Now, Cleopatra was a very lovely Egyptian queen. *Queen*, dear. Yes, they had 'em in those days, too. A little different, but they had 'em . . .

His songs were similar. "Mr. Wong" told of a Mandarin who "controls a bandit band . . . And in Chinaland they call a band a tong":

> *When he puts the spot on a rival guy*
> *The guy says, OOOH! What a way to die!*
> *Mr. Wong has got the biggest tong in China . . .*

Bourbon's primary aim was to shock, and in those innocent years his mastery of this was rewarded by one of the longest record of imprisonments ever held by an entertainer; he was even arrested in a California club for simulating the use of toilet paper. But as a rebellious figure who gloried in camp, he enjoyed several illustrious years. Top designers dressed him, and stars such as Johnny Weissmuller, Lupe Velez, and Bing Crosby were amused by his work and saw him often. In 1944 Mae West hired him to play a French hairdresser in the Broadway production of her comedy *Catherine Was Great* and featured him four years later in *Diamond Lil.* He even appeared before Generalissimo Franco in Spain as part of Josephine Baker's *Paris Revue* and occasionally performed in respectable rooms such as the renowned San Francisco drag club Finocchio's, La Vie Parisienne, and the Blue Angel. Though he tried to tone down his material for the Angel, audiences were sufficiently appalled for Jacoby to cancel the booking, leaving Bourbon heartbroken.

Such experiences left him bitter, bitchy, and self-aggrandizing. Robert Wright, who with his partner George Forrest played duo piano for Bourbon in the '30s before writing the lyrics for *Kismet*, *Song of Norway*, and other musicals, recalls that "Ray told so many lies about so many things that no one could say anything certain about him unless it happened while you were present."

Bourbon was capable of kindness, as when he helped get Wright and Forrest their first film job at MGM, where they wrote for such productions as *Maytime*, *Sweethearts*, and *The New Moon*. But he also exaggerated his generosity, telling friends that he discovered Rudolph Valentino at the Vernon Country Club in Hollywood, where the future movie idol worked as a tango dancer for $35 a week. Thereafter, claimed Bourbon, he became Valentino's lover and helped arrange for his first screen test. But as soon as he was signed, Valentino "deserted him," later "throwing him a bone" by getting him tiny parts in several films.

Bourbon often developed crushes on young men he worked with, but few ever took him seriously, providing another cause for his insecurity. Recalls Bart Howard, who played for Bourbon in 1935 at the Rendezvous in Hollywood, "Ray was very kind to me, and I even lived with him awhile because we were working together so closely. But he didn't want me to have any other friends. Whenever anyone came over he put sugar in their gas tanks or punctured their tires. He tried to treat me like his possession." Howard left to accompany impressionist Elizabeth Talbott-Martin at the Rainbow Room, his first New York job and an auspicious one. Shortly afterward the management received a letter from Bourbon stating that the two were degenerates and not to be trusted.

Bourbon worked steadily throughout the '40s, but by 1950 or so his act seemed so passé that jobs became scarce. He devised a ploy to get publicity. Wrote the *New York Journal-American* (May 28, 1956):

> Female impersonator Ray Bourbon, who wore dresses when he performed with Mae West on the Broadway stage, has undergone sex transformation surgery and today can wear dresses all the time.
>
> "Yes, it's true," said Ray—oops, it's been changed to Rae—"I am now a woman."
>
> According to Rae . . . the operation was performed last September by a Hungarian refugee doctor in Juarez, Mexico . . . The doctor also gave Rae a certificate that reads in part, "Bourbon is now more woman than man."
>
> "And there's no doubt about it," Rae asserted. "My hair is thicker, my voice is higher, and my shape is like a woman's—a big woman's. I measure 44-36-40. That beats Mae West, doesn't it?"

It was all a hoax, of course, but it brought him little attention. Now sixty-four and penniless, Bourbon accepted any job, often driving hundreds of miles to small towns. He was humbler now and desperately lonely, but since most of his old friends no longer saw him he turned to his dogs for affection. He eventually acquired fifteen, which he loved so obsessively that he purchased a rickety trailer and took them with him around the country.

In 1965 he was driving through Texas on a 105-degree day. His old jalopy suddenly burst into flames, and the trailer caught fire. Luckily a nearby farmer came to his assistance and doused the vehicles with crop spray. Bourbon and his pets were unharmed, but the car and trailer were destroyed, along with most of his gowns. He was forced to leave the animals in the care of the owner of a local pet shop.

Over the next three years his fortunes went from bad to worse. Whenever possible, he sent money for the care of his "kids," but by 1968 there was so little work that he couldn't spare a penny. The next time he called the store he learned that his dogs had been sold.

A few weeks later the pet shop owner was found murdered. Bourbon, then appearing at the Jewel Box in Kansas City, was arrested and charged with masterminding the murder. He pleaded innocent, claiming that he would never have killed the one man who could help him reclaim his dogs, but the State of Texas gave him ninety-nine years. His lawyer filed for an appeal, but Bourbon's prison record made this hopeless. On June 3, 1970, *Variety* published the following letter:

> Editor, *Variety*:
>
> This is the town where they pulled "Midnight Cowboy" for being obscene. I am sure it must be obvious to you now what chance I had here for getting a fair trial.
>
> I'm hoping you will mention this as I seem to have been completely forgotten by everyone, especially ones I have done favors for.
>
> I'll be grateful for anything you can say to attract any kind of aid. I am now on an appeal. But I need help.
>
> The address of the jail where I'm in is 212 N. Broadway, Brownwood, Texas 76801.
>
> Ray Bourbon

Nothing came of the appeal or of his plea for help. On Christmas Day, 1970, a friend called him in prison, where Bourbon had entered the final stages of a three-year bout with leukemia. "All I want is to die on the outside," he said. But a heart attack claimed him on July 19, 1971, and he died in the state hospital under confinement. Bourbon outlived by at least twenty years the shock value of his act, making it rather pathetic that so few noticed his genuinely sad demise.

BOTH HERBERT JACOBY and Julius Monk liked to experiment with acts that East Siders would never have ventured into Harlem or Greenwich Village to see, but listeners were not always with them. In 1944 Monk hired Billie Holiday with disappointing results. Efforts at that time to make the great jazz singer more commercial, including a series of string-backed recordings for Decca Records, had little success; white audiences were slow in catching on to her magic. Le Ruban Bleu was the first and last such club she sang in. She found Monk's crowd uptight and snobbish, while they were indifferent to the jazz delivery fashioned so devastatingly around her soul-baring interpretations. As a result she displayed even more bitter mistrust than usual of the whites around her, even scoffing at having to share a dressing room with golden-haired harpist Daphne Hellman. "I'm not gonna dress in there with that society bitch," she complained. The irony was that most club owners would have made her enter through the kitchen.

Most of the time the Ruban's warm, inviting atmosphere put everybody at ease, whereas the Blue Angel's formality almost challenged guests to rise to their surroundings. Consequently, it gained a great deal more prestige. From 1943 to 1964 dozens of performers began their careers at its red-carpeted entrance, including Barbra Streisand, Mike Nichols and Elaine May, Carol Burnett, Johnny Mathis, Tom Lehrer, Phyllis Diller, Shelley Berman, Pearl Bailey, Harry Belafonte, and Woody Allen. This list illustrates Jacoby's unequaled eye for fine talent with commercial appeal. But the club itself had an electricity that attracted people regardless of who was appearing. "You've *got* to go to the Blue Angel before you leave," said many a New Yorker to visiting friends.

The all-black decor was considered the height of '40s and '50s New York chic, and the cocktail lounge looked like an extension of the night itself. The bar was black, as were the booths and banquettes on the right. The walls were upholstered in black patent leather with white trim, and nearly everyone wore dark evening clothes.

Around nine o'clock the maître d' escorted patrons through a pair of white swinging doors in the back of the lounge into an oblong room crowded with dozens of tiny black round tables that afforded no room for stretching your legs. In contrast with the austere bar, the back room contained a bright red carpet, padded gray velour walls pegged with pink rosettes, and pink leather banquettes along the right and left. At the far end was a stage just large enough for the trio, a stand-up microphone, and (comfortably) one performer, who could not stray far. Even if there had been more room, the single pinspot and bodylight didn't move. "It was like trying to do an act on top of a cocktail napkin," says comedienne-singer Dorothy Loudon, who performed there between 1955 and 1962.

Some found the decor morbid. "I never liked that room," says Bobby Short, who played and sang in the lounge during the early '60s. "It was long and somewhat narrow—and madly upholstered. It was decorated within an inch of its life. I used to call it the Coffin Room." Ben Bagley, hired in the late '50s to select material for comics and singers, agrees. "In the dim light the piano onstage looked like a casket, and when you saw the vase of gladiolas on top you felt as if you were in a funeral parlor. Then Herbert walked in and you *knew* you were in a funeral parlor."

But that stately interior made it clear that the Blue Angel was a serious listening room and that Jacoby's acts were the crème de la crème. "Just walking in the door every night made me feel like a man of the world," said late pianist Jimmy Lyon, whose trio accompanied the main room acts between 1950 and 1963. "I think it had that effect on almost everybody. When people went there they held their chins up high and moved with a little more grace. They knew they were in the chicest place in town, and they wanted to rise to the occasion."

Jacoby chose its name because he loved the Marlene Dietrich film of the same title and considered blue his lucky color, having triumphed (artistically if not financially) with Le Ruban Bleu. But he never relied on good fortune. He was a cold, clever businessman with an uncanny skill for getting what he wanted. Early in 1942 he and playwright William Saroyan had made plans to open a club called The Time of Your Life, named after Saroyan's play. "Right on Third Avenue," Jacoby explained. "People will love to go slumming right around the corner from El Morocco."

When Saroyan went off to war, they reluctantly abandoned the project. A few weeks later Jacoby learned that Café Life, a supper club at 152 East 55th Street, had closed. At least two other rooms, the East End Club and the Kit-Kat Club, had foundered there, but that did not discourage his decision to lease the property. Nor was he deterred by the $10,000 needed to open a new club. Falling about $9,500 short, he persuaded a wealthy friend to invest half the money and prevailed upon Max Gordon to furnish the balance and become his equal partner.

The Vanguard was less lucrative than Jacoby believed. Usually Gordon just met expenses, and he had no extra money either. But after nine years in a Village cellar he found the prospect of an East Side club tempting. He postponed a month of liquor payments, scraped together $5,000, and began a twenty-year partnership with Jacoby.

Because the Vanguard occupied so much of his time, Gordon left the decoration, booking, and supervision almost entirely to Jacoby. During some periods in the '50s Gordon spent nearly every night uptown, but no one close to the Angel in those years questioned who really took charge. "Herbert always knew what he wanted," says singer Portia Nelson, a mainstay in the '50s. "It was his taste that made the Blue Angel."

Jacoby towered almost a foot above Gordon and pointed his nose even higher. Few ever got close to him, and he was certainly not a man to take advantage of. "He was deadly serious about his business," says Michael Pritchett, "and there was no freeloading. He was there every single minute." What private life he had he kept private indeed. His homosexuality was well known, but he seldom discussed it, even with friends. Sexual partners laughed about Jacoby's foot fetish, particularly his fixation with toenails, but when James Kirkwood made the mistake of mentioning it to him at the club, Jacoby was mortified and did not speak to him for the rest of his engagement. Max Gordon recalled that despite the Angel's high quota of homosexual customers, Jacoby was determined to keep that element under control, even warning the bartenders not to serve men who seemed to be on the make.

Such edicts helped give him his deserved reputation as a snob, and Gordon unfortunately bore the brunt of his partner's attitude. Privately, Jacoby called the Village Vanguard a sewer, sneering that Gordon had as much taste as a Vanguard hamburger. He considered the humble, businesslike man a necessary evil—a $5,000 ticket into a club he could not afford to buy alone. "They fought over everything," says Otis Clements, a Blue Angel pianist and emcee for eight years. "I don't think their tastes were at all alike. Herbert was running a different sort of room than the Vanguard. Max's taste in acts would have never worked."

And yet Gordon contributed more to the room than most people acknowledged. Pearl Bailey, Harry Belafonte, and Eartha Kitt were only a few of the Vanguard performers who came uptown at Gordon's urging. A sharp talent scout in his own right, he spotted dozens of Angel candidates that Jacoby might have overlooked. And everyone at the club found him more approachable and personable than his partner, whom many loathed.

Deservedly, however, Jacoby took most of the credit for the room's success. He may have discovered very few of his biggest acts—usually he waited until they had proved themselves elsewhere—but his good judgment was usually indisputable. He exuded an authority that comes only to those who are sure that their decisions are impeccable, when most of them are, and when everyone around is too frightened to question them.

THE BLUE ANGEL'S prices carried an implicit welcome for only the most fashionable crowd. For the main room Jacoby set a minimum of two dollars during the week and three on weekends—more expensive than El Morocco, the Stork Club, the Casbah, and the Waldorf's Starlight Roof. Even so, the club took about six months to hit its stride; in his efforts to create a serious atmosphere, Jacoby threatened at first to put audiences to sleep. Appearing on April 21, 1943, when he opened, were Mme. Claude Alphand, an austere Frenchwoman who sang Parisian ballads to her own guitar accompaniment; classical harpsichordist Sylvia Marlowe; Hector Montverde, a Venezuelan tenor; and British revue comedienne Brenda Forbes. Of Alphand, Noel Coward, there for opening night, said, "Good God, don't you know how dangerous that woman is? That's France's Secret Boring Weapon." Wrote *Variety*'s Abel Green, "Jacoby needs something boffier to put his new spot on the map. The lush interior merits something fancier."

By 1944 he had begun to find acts that were both tasteful and fun: Mildred Bailey; the Revuers; Yul Brynner, who sat on the piano and sang Russian folk songs while playing the guitar; Irene Bordoni, New York's favorite French musical comedy star in the '20s and '30s and now a nightclub sensation; comic-impressionist Eddie Mayehoff, who offered whimsical portraits of New York's ham poets, cab drivers, concession stand dealers, and other local characters; and George and Gene Bernard, two brothers who did pantomime impressions, some in drag, to recordings by the Andrews Sisters, Mary Martin, and Bing Crosby.

Appearing in 1945 was the twenty-year-old Bobby Short, a lanky, boyish dynamo in white tie and tails who already bore his familiar veneer of Harlem highbrow. Born in Danville, Illinois, to a coal miner and a maid Short began playing and singing in roadhouses at the age of nine to help support his family during the depression. In 1937 he came to New York. Short had champagne tastes at an age when most children were still drinking chocolate milk; audiences were amused by his attempts to copy the sophistication of Ethel Waters, Duke

Ellington, Ivie Anderson (Ellington's vocalist in the '30s), and his other idols. That year he appeared at the Frolics, a club above the Winter Garden Theatre on 51st Street and Broadway. *Variety* complained about the thirteen-year-old "little colored kid's" choice of adult love songs such as "Gone with the Wind" and "It's a Sin to Tell a Lie." "He's too much on the torch side. Being a sweet little pickaninny type, different song material might suit him better."

After returning to Danville to finish high school, Short played in Chicago, Omaha, Milwaukee, and once more in New York, this time at the Blue Angel. With him were Irene Bordoni, Mildred Bailey, and Eddie Mayehoff, in whose company he finally felt he had arrived. At that time he met Mabel Mercer, who helped inspire in him a prophetic yearning. "I longed to belong to Mabel's intimate circle," he later told Whitney Balliett of the *New Yorker*, "and I knew I had to come back to New York one day on a more permanent basis."

One of Jacoby's proudest finds of the '40s was Florence Desmond, probably the finest impressionist of her generation. Born in England in 1905, Desmond came to prominence in the '30s as a star of British nightclubs and musical comedy. Wrote William Hawkins in the *New York World-Telegram* (April 3, 1946): "[Her] name is as much a household word in England as Gracie Fields' or Beatrice Lillie's." Desmond had seldom worked in America, but after only three days at the Angel, Jacoby doubled her engagement. Blonde and sexy, she sashayed around in tight, strapless gowns as she portrayed all the guests at a Hollywood party attended by Gracie Fields, Tallulah Bankhead, Katharine Hepburn, Marlene Dietrich, and Bette Davis; re-created a scene from Noel Coward's *Private Lives* as performed by Coward and Gertrude Lawrence; and added seven or eight more rapid-fire impressions. As she moved from character to character she pulled glasses, handkerchiefs, and other props out of her cleavage, dropping them to the floor as she finished.

Unlike other impressionists, Desmond knew that the most effective parody was the least exaggerated. With a slight change in tone and the addition of a scarf or gloves she seemed to become her subjects, mimicking them so precisely that when she later appeared on Tallulah Bankhead's radio series *The Big Show* listeners could not tell them apart.

Her most celebrated impression was of Hildegarde. Desmond entered with an armful of dying zinnias, which she dumped on the piano as she took her place on the bench. Lowering her head with a perplexed look, she found enough correct keys to approximate a Rachmaninoff prelude. Then, scooping up some crumbling flowers, she stepped to ringside and smiled at an elderly man seated with his wife. "Tell me, the man in the gray flannel suit, are you *in love*?"

In 1946 another beloved performer made her nightclub debut at the Blue Angel, singer-comedienne Alice Pearce, whom critic Douglas Watt in the *New Yorker* called "probably the funniest woman to come along since Beatrice Lillie." (February 21, 1953). A Leonard Sillman alumna (*New Faces of 1943*), Pearce later played in about fifteen other Broadway musicals and appeared in films. Television audiences remember her on *Bewitched* as Gladys Kravitz, the gossipy neighbor of the Stevens's whose head always hung out the window in search of scandal.

In nightclubs Pearce gave a harebrained portrait of "a complete moron with a high, high squeak and a recurrent giggle," as the *New Yorker* wrote (October 4, 1947). With her buck teeth, large ears, and receding chin, Pearce looked a lot like Bugs Bunny, and her rubber-face expressions made even the most innocent asides sound hilarious. She wore thrift store gowns, a moth-eaten fur stole, and a series of trampled, wide-brim hats, one an upside-down handbag. With a wave of her leopard-skin hankie she took listeners on a nightmare tour through the hoariest annals of popular song, lip-synching "Shortnin' Bread" to a scratchy recording by Nelson Eddy, intoning a traditional folk song for which she accompanied herself on a "five-string Scottish fluke," and producing two cigarettes and smoking them both herself for "Two Cigarettes in the Dark."

Pearce's gift for transforming any number into a comic gem endeared her to writers of special material, especially John Latouche, who created the role of spinster schoolmarm Miss Minerva Oliver for her in his 1954 musical *The Golden Apple*. (Pearce was not available, so it went to Portia Nelson. When she saw the show and heard its complicated score, Pearce remarked that she came out "whistling the scenery.")

Her very presence on the Blue Angel stage could turn that restrained audience into a 2 A.M. crowd at the Roxy. One evening two women sat ringside with their red-nosed companion, then on his fourth or fifth cocktail. He turned to one of the women and said, "I have to pee!"

"Shhhhh! After the show!"

"I have to pee!" he repeated angrily.

"Will you be quiet?" both women whispered. "People are staring!"

"I SAID I HAVE TO PEE!" With that he stood up, unzipped his fly, and peed on the carpet directly in front of Pearce, literally stopping the show. "What an uproar!" recalled Max Gordon. "Jacoby was sitting in the back with Noel Coward, who was in New York for a couple of days. The next thing you know, Coward jumps out of his chair with a big wet stain on the front of his trousers. Jacoby was so horrified that he knocked his drink right into Coward's lap. 'This never happened with Claude Alphand!' he growled."

WHAT ABOUT those who were looking for an elegant place to drink and relax with only a soothing lull of showtunes in the background to add a lilt to the conversation, perhaps to orchestrate anything from a business deal to a seduction? Or those who belonged to New York's theatrical and artistic community, whose egos did not necessarily bloom under the glare of flashing cameras or gelled spotlights?

Until the early '40s there were few hangouts where they could enjoy the company of their own kind in relative privacy, so they decided to create some themselves. One of the first was 1-2-3, a plush, dimly lit restaurant-lounge at 123 East 54th Street that Cole Porter had originally conceived. The club showcased pianist Roger Stearns, a friend and former lover of Porter's from about 1920, when Stearns studied architecture at Porter's alma mater Yale. An aspiring actor, he appeared with Rudy Vallee and Monty Woolley in *Out to Lunch*, a Yale varsity show that included a few Porter songs, and in *New Faces of 1934* and the Arthur Schwartz–Dorothy Fields musical *Stars in Your Eyes* (1939), but his lack of marketable charisma led him toward a career in lounge piano. His fortunes crested when he met Leonard Hanna, a millionaire coal magnate and friend of Porter's. The composer had long suggested that Stearns preside over a room where he and his friends could escape from the limelight, and Hanna finally bought him one with the help of Porter, producer Dwight Wiman, and a few other rich friends. For the January 1942 opening Porter and Hanna assembled a stellar guest list: Ethel Barrymore, Walter Pidgeon, Eddie Cantor, Ethel Merman, Vincent Price, Burgess Meredith, William Powell, Mary and Vincent Astor, Gertrude Lawrence,

Clifton Webb, Danny Kaye, and others. Once they told *their* friends about 1-2-3, its success was assured.

Never had they had such a sumptuous hideaway. Spacious and high-ceilinged, it was decorated in taupe with paneled mirrors, thick, luxurious carpeting, love seats, and armchairs. In the far corner sat Stearns at a baby grand, playing showtunes in a drooping fashion that nevertheless adhered carefully to the written note, a demand of Porter's for performances of his own music. Between tunes Stearns hopped from table to table greeting customers, most of whom he knew, before returning to the keyboard, a Scotch and soda beside him, for another set of "Love for Sale" and "You're the Top" and "I Got Rhythm."

Besides Stearns, the only divertissements were Myra Kingsley, a "hand analyst" (palm readers were a fixture in most '40s nightclubs), and gin rummy tournaments. Dinners started at $2.50 (top dollar in those days), and "midnight breakfasts" were served from eleven until three. The general public took little notice of the room—just as Stearns wanted. He even barred photographers from the premises, which irritated many publications. As the *New Yorker* sniped (June 13, 1942), "The 1-2-3 Club is one of those places where friends gather to play gin rummy, preferring a room that looks like the lounge of a movie theatre to the loathsome privacy of their own homes." But during the war years those "friends" stood in line to get in. "Wendell Wilkie, we've been told, couldn't get a table on one occasion. Lillian Gish, and Tallulah Bankhead's party, including Ruth Gordon, parked themselves on beer cases, so packed was the room." (December 26, 1942)

The success of 1-2-3 proved the potential of such clubs in those peak theatre years, when performers, investors, and audiences had no desire to head home after the final curtain. Similar rooms opened, notably the Barberry Room of the Hotel Berkshire on 52nd Street and Madison Avenue, a favorite of the staff members of CBS around the corner. Another was Tony's Trouville, a posh restaurant–piano bar two blocks east. The *New Yorker* listed its assets as "French food, smart decorations and clientele." Buster Davis, who played there after leaving Spivy's Roof in 1943, remembers an example. "Each afternoon at five, in came my biggest fan—a very, very pretty boy whom you've seen on the dust jacket of one of his most famous books. He'd trot in, arms swinging by his sides, and shout in a voice that could cut through glass, 'HELLOOOOOO, BUSTER, HERE WE ARE!' It was Truman Capote, who was then working as an office boy at the *New Yorker*. 'Now play me "Alone Together," and sing!' With him were Gloria Vanderbilt and all these society girls. As soon as Tony saw Truman he'd start to growl. He had a very voluptuous wife, Rose, who looked like Rita Hayworth. She'd say, 'Now, darling, shut up. He pays the bill.'

" 'And now do me, mmm . . . "Wait Till You See Her." ' And that voice would carry, because the room was empty at that hour. Rose would come up to the table and ask how they all were. 'Oh, we're all FIIIIINE, thank you very much! BUSTERRRRR! Now play me . . .' The girls would sit there and giggle."

The usual terms for that piano style—cocktail piano, lounge piano, drawing room piano—are unfortunate descriptions of what is, at its best, a sublime art of playing that incorporates jazz elements but is essentially a loving examination of some of the best pop melodies. These pianists used all the harmonic and technical resourcefulness at their command to underscore those melodies, to bring them to life as vividly as a vocalist would animate lyrics. They phrased a lot like singers did, playing the words as much as the notes. As Rogers Whitaker noted in his essay for the 1959 album "Julius Monk Simply Plays! (and/or vice versa)," "After you and your loved one had settled down in a nice dim recess in a nightclub for a long talk about life and love and happiness and each other, someone now and then sat down at a piano and played what we still call mood music or background music . . . We people who like to go out at night and think we want to be alone together can't bear it if there isn't a pianist ten feet away."

The dean of café pianists was Cy (Cyril) Walter, a superbly imaginative player whose slicked-back graying-blond hair, tortoiseshell glasses, jowly cheeks, and conservative suits made him look like a Harvard history professor. Born in Minneapolis in 1915, Walter studied the piano with his mother and supplemented his lessons by studying the recordings of Art Tatum and other great jazzmen. But he preferred showtunes and adapted his jazz-influenced technique to a repertoire so tasty and offbeat that he wanted to keep its melodies intact.

While still a teenager, Walter came to New York and played for four years with bandleader Eddie Lane, then teamed with pianist Gil Bowers at Le Ruban Bleu and at the Algonquin. Thereafter Walter played solo in at least a dozen rooms, notably the Drake Room of the Hotel Drake, from its opening on December 21, 1945, through 1951 and then from 1959 until his death in 1968. In that brown-and-green lounge-restaurant, dominated by a glittering ceramic magnolia tree forever in need of dusting, Walter sat at a Steinway baby grand and polished off song after song until the wee hours. Customers ranged from the familiar diners and talkers to the sing-along crowd (whom he discouraged by changing keys several times per song) to those who, like Whitaker, liked to sit beneath the tree after a long evening, sipping a daiquiri and serenaded by tunes sure to rekindle memories of tuneful shows and lost romances. "A minor art, but one of the more important ones," he wrote. Walter influenced nearly every pianist of his kind, not only in person but through a coveted series of 78s on the Liberty Music Shop label and a long-running radio show entitled *Piano Playhouse*, which he shared with Stan Freeman, a brilliant technician and entertainer in the Victor Borge–Oscar Levant tradition. Composers were his fans as well, even those as finicky about the treatment of their work as Alec Wilder and Richard Rodgers. Wilder wrote in his liner notes for Walter's Atlantic album of Rodgers songs, "Anyone who has heard his own songs played by Cy immediately has a greater respect for his own work." Rodgers himself, who tolerated nothing less than note-perfect renditions of his songs, even agreed to pose with Walter on the cover.

Walter was also identified with Tony's West Side, where he played in the early '40s. Tony's always retained the status of a "local secret," beloved by newspapermen and by well-heeled homosexuals in the arts who appreciated the talents of a Spivy or a Cy Walter. When Walter left in 1943 to join the army, he recommended a replacement who made the room her own for the next seven years. Lee Goodman stumbled upon her in 1945 by accident, as one often did.

"I was in New York on furlough, walking around in uniform and not knowing what to do with myself. I passed a brownstone on West 52nd Street. On the ground floor was a little window behind an iron grille, and because it was a warm summer night the louvers were open. I saw a piano player and the back of a woman seated on a stool with a spotlight on her. People were sitting on striped banquettes, rapt. Something just drew me in. I went down a long hallway, and there was an older, rather glamorous, light-skinned black woman, with all these beautiful people around her. She was singing a Hoagy Car-michael song, 'How Little We Know,' about the uncertainty lovers feel when they start a relationship, and between phrases everyone tapped a spoon against their wine or champagne glasses. She sang all these other wonderful love songs. Couples were holding hands. I thought, 'I've found it!' "

From the 1940s until her death in 1984 Mabel Mercer was regarded by everyone from Frank Sinatra to Leontyne Price as the definitive café singer, an artist who struck a deep personal chord in nearly everybody who came to hear her, while elevating the often seedy rooms she sang in to grandeur. She used the sparest means. Seated in a chair, hands folded or held at elbow length before her, her voice seldom raised above conversational level, she could draw listeners into a mood so tranquil and reflective that time seemed to stand still. "Whenever you were in love, you always took the person to see Mabel," said Goodman. In the late '40s Tony's became a magnet for composers and singers who listened in wonderment, trying to figure out how she did it.

No one ever explained how, although the externals are obvious. Despite a voice that grew frail with the years, Mercer had flawless diction, the phrasing of a great actress, and a repertoire filled with treasurable obscurities that many singers borrowed. Underneath it all lay a natural, unpretentious regality that led critics to call her a "queen" or "doyenne," although Mercer was much happier weeding her country garden in a pair of overalls than holding forth in a gold lamé evening gown.

Her greatest gift, however, was simply the ability to communicate, a talent as rare as it is difficult to fathom. Some of it came from her eagerness to subordinate herself completely to the great lyrics she sang, acting as their purest and most selfless instrument. But the "spiritual grace" with which Buddy Barnes, her finest accompanist, credits her is also a key. "She was a devout Catholic, but she was spiritual in many other ways, like about nature. You'd go out walking in the woods with Mabel, and she made you feel like you'd gone into a cathedral in Rome. People wanted to be where she was. They wanted to touch her. They felt blessed by her presence." Regrettably, recordings and films never captured this quality.

For all this adulation Mercer showed a remarkable lack of ego, maybe because she had to work for a living all her life. She was born Mabel Alice Wadham on February 3, 1900, at Burton-on-Trent in

Staffordshire, England. Her father, a black American jazz musician, died before her birth, and her Welsh-English vaudevillian mother deserted her in early childhood, leaving her with relatives. The pain of growing up a virtual orphan haunted her for years; not until 1938 did she see her mother again.

Mercer spent her early years in a Manchester convent school, where the nuns coached her in elocution and taught her impeccable manners. Penniless, she left at age fourteen to join a touring vaudeville troupe, one of the few showbusiness options for a mulatto—even one with a precise mezzo-soprano voice. Mercer spent sixteen years of hand-to-mouth life on the road; despite the fun she could never shake the feeling of homelessness or the grief of having only brief friendships. Around 1930 she settled in Paris, where she began a solo singing job at a club called Chez Florence. The next year she went to work for Bricktop, whose famous club on the rue Pigalle was at its peak. Bricktop knew that Mercer would help maintain a classy atmosphere amid so much drunken revelry. "I didn't want her for her singing," she said in her 1983 memoir. "I wanted her because she was very shy and reserved, a lady. Beautifully friendly, but never familiar. I knew I could sit her down at a table and she wouldn't use any bad language or tell any dirty jokes, and that she'd laugh at the right times."

Mercer's singing, indeed, excited no one. "I'd go over to the tables and say, 'Well, what did you think?' and the clients would say, 'Wellllll, Bricky . . .' And I'd say, 'But she's an awfully nice girl!' " Within a year she had gained more confidence and began to develop her intimate approach, particularly when she sat at tables to sing in the early morning hours. "It's very tricky to sing for a small group or even a small room full of people," she told *Stereo Review*'s William Livingstone in 1975. "You have to learn to sing *for* them and somehow sing *at* them, but not sing *to* them in a way that makes them uncomfortable. So I tried singing *at* them, but ignoring them, and they'd suddenly relax and become interested not in me, but in what I was singing and how they could apply it to themselves." She also learned a lesson that she would pass on to countless singers: less is more. "To do anything very dramatic, you have to underplay to get it over. It does no good to shout a meaning in someone's ear. But when you are quiet, people will listen to the words."

Mercer grew to love that unconventlike setting. As she told Livingstone, "Bricktop's closed about five or six in the morning, and a place called the Breakfast Club would still be open, so everybody would troop over there. I remember one morning Louis Armstrong with his trumpet and Django Reinhardt with his guitar were playing for each other. I went home and to bed. I got up around noon for some milk or something, and they were *still* there playing duets."

In the south of France she became a friend of Joe (Marion Barbara) Carstairs, a socialite who raced speedboats for fun and profit. The philanthropic Carstairs paid for Mercer to travel to New York in October 1938 for her first Manhattan engagement, at Le Ruban Bleu. A few months later she left to sing in the Bahamas, where she became trapped by the outbreak of World War II, unable to return to England or to the United States. Finally she met Kelsey Pharr of the jazz vocal quartet the Delta Rhythm Boys, who offered her a paper marriage in order to get her to the States. Once back in New York, Mercer was understandably reluctant to leave and traveled as little as possible for the rest of her life.

In 1941 she went to work at the Onyx Club on West 52nd Street, a jazz room where the noise level allowed for little intimacy. Nevertheless she stayed for several months and attracted such fans as Thelma Carpenter, then singing nearby at Kelly's Stable. "I'd go every night and listen to her. Mabel had a high voice then, but people still had to get used to it. But what made me enthusiastic about her was, with that soprano voice she was singing all these good songs, and she could swing." In 1942 Mercer moved to the Three Deuces on the same block and the next year replaced Cy Walter at Tony's. Her arrival was well timed. She began in a period when big bands were on the decline, and when their former vocalists—Frank Sinatra, Peggy Lee, Kay Starr, and others—were seeking their own direction, as were a slew of singers interested in the burgeoning café field.

In 1943 popular singing was still a relatively primitive art, seldom aspiring beyond the secure intonation and rhythmic acuity required of band vocalists or the bravura style of Broadway performers. Few singers sensed the impact that they could have through a close examination of the words, maybe because such subtlety would be lost on noisy 78s, across the static-laden airwaves, or in enormous auditoriums such as the Paramount. A few exceptions—Bing Crosby, Sinatra, Mildred Bailey, Billie Holiday—recognized the potential of a more personal approach to lyrics; even their early recordings find them lingering over key words, holding back before a measured climax, telling a story. Not until intimate clubs began to crest, however, did singers find the ideal setting for extracting all the nuances of a fine lyric. These rooms were small enough so that they did not have to worry about the slightest gesture going unnoticed. They were free to paint their lyrical pictures with as much detail as they could muster. Mercer was the first singer to put this knowledge to full use—and undoubtedly the most influential.

Her impact was not immediate, however. Knowing of her reputation, many singers made their way to Tony's expecting to be dazzled; instead they found her understated, untheatrical readings and ladylike voice a letdown. "A lot of times," says Carpenter, "I brought people there and they didn't take to her right away. If they say they did, they're liars. Billie Holiday hated her in the beginning. I said, 'But you've *got* to go back!' At first Lena didn't dig her. '*Listen* to the woman,' I told her. Margaret Whiting says she loved her right from the start. Bullshit! But after two or three visits you'd see them sitting there with pencils and paper, hanging on her every word."

Among the obscure showtunes that Mercer introduced to other singers and helped make standards were Rodgers and Hart's "Little Girl Blue" and "Wait Till You See Him" and Jerome Kern and Dorothy Fields's "Remind Me." Mercer began to receive new numbers from younger writers who hoped for the same, notably Alec Wilder, composer of such ballads as "Trouble Is a Man" and "While We're Young," and Bart Howard, her accompanist from 1946 through 1949 and the composer of "Fly Me to the Moon" and dozens of other songs that café singers took to their hearts.

Tony's remained her headquarters until 1949, when the building was torn down to make way for a parking lot. Thereafter she began a series of long engagements in other local rooms. The handful of out-of-towners who knew of her through her albums for Atlantic Records thought of her as café elegance personified. But Mercer never thought about such things, grateful just to make a living doing what she loved. Her refined presence gave New York's nightlife much of its character, while the city itself provided her with the long-term employment and security that she could find nowhere else. As she told Richard Dyer of the *Boston Globe Magazine* in 1974, "The value comes in not travelling, because this is how you establish friendships that last for years. This is something I find important."

The *intimate*-nightclub business truly took off at the end of World War II, when thousands of men returned home to build new lives from scratch. Crushing military demands, giant goals, a national team effort that might fail—all these had led to triumph. In June 1945 America possessed $140 billion in liquid assets, and New York itself had become the world's wealthiest and most powerful city. Jan Morris, chronicling the postwar months in her book *Manhattan '45*, quotes a Bankers Trust publicity booklet from that year that boasts the city's plans for "huge new housing projects, the largest bus terminal in the world, an airport eight times as big as the one they had already, huge new hotels, skyscraper offices, department stores, dozens of new schools, marvelous new hospitals, telephone systems, TV transmitters."

After the initial six months of celebration a calm fell over the country. The trumpet voices of newsreel announcers had faded; people yearned to plant new roots, to reestablish a sense of permanence. Couples wanted to get involved in each other and in their plans. As Pat Carroll recalls, "Everyone sat down and said, 'I don't want to hear big things anymore. I went through big. It stinks.' I think the fellows who came back wanted to get on the GI Bill, get into their professions, get a house in the suburbs with a barbecue on the weekend, raise their families. They'd kicked up their heels in Paris and Berlin and Tokyo. They'd been places they'd never seen before. That was enough world-saving."

Grand clubs would thrive for a few more years, but solo acts started to outnumber extravaganza floor shows. The headliners in 1946 included Charles Trenet at the Embassy and Jean Sablon, Morton Downey, and Frank Sinatra at the Wedgwood Room of the Waldorf, all of whom tried to make listeners feel they were singing just for them. Customers had limited attention spans, though, based on what a *New Yorker* columnist wrote of Sinatra: "He sang from twelve-fifteen to one twenty-five, and while he's every bit as good as he's supposed to be, I don't think even Cicero could hold an audience that long."

In 1947, ex-vaudevillian and Broadway hoofer Billy Reed opened his aptly named Little Club, a tiny nightclub-restaurant at 70 East 55th Street. The *New Yorker* described it as "one of those places so narrow that two people can't sit face to face but have to squeeze in alongside each other on banquettes against the wall." Jane Harvey, who sang there for up to five months at a time, remembers it as "quite a place for successful men-about-town and their girls. It was a high-class pickup place. Everybody was dressed to the nines—the guys wore star sapphire pinkie rings, and the ladies were in full makeup with spiked heels and jewels. It was very chic. At the end of this long, narrow room was a set of glass doors that led to another tiny little room, the Champagne Room, and that was where I sang. It was carpeted and upholstered in red velvet, with crystal chandeliers and mirrors. When the show was about to begin, the doors closed, the chandeliers and sconces went out, and I sat on a stool next to the piano and sang with no microphone. Nobody uttered a word during the show." Soon after it opened the *New Yorker* called it "an unpretentious East Side hall, cheerfully decorated and offering peace and quiet during dinner and casual dancing to a trio later in the evening. There's also a singer."

The singer was Doris Day, the club's first solo act, just prior to her film debut in *Romance on the High Seas*. Day had recently finished a long stint as vocalist with bandleader Les Brown, a collaboration that yielded such hits as "Sentimental Journey" and "My Dreams Are Getting Better All the Time." For now she was a happy newlywed, living with her second husband, Brown saxophonist George Weidler, in a trailer. Needing the money, she accepted Reed's offer of a one-month engagement at the Little Club for $100 a week and all the food she could eat.

Day chose a program of songs she liked, among them "How Are Things in Glocca Morra?" "How About You?" and "Too-Ra-Loo-Ra-Loo-Ral." The only challenge was to stay awake. As she wrote in her 1976 memoir *Doris Day: Her Own Story*, "I enjoyed the dinner show, but every night the late show was a struggle. My nature is to fold early. I should have been a bird or a flower. I had had to struggle through the late hours when I sang with the bands, and now I had to struggle to keep myself from falling asleep before the late show—not only before, but during."

Day was such a hit that Reed tried to keep her for an additional four weeks. That month she received a letter from her out-of-town husband telling her he wanted to end their marriage. She was on the brink of stardom, he felt, and he would never be more than a sideman in a band; for him to become Mr. Doris Day would destroy their relationship, so they had better end it now. Day was devastated and every night learned the hazardous effects of singing about love and loss in a room with dozens of sympathetic faces looking up at her. They in turn got an unflinchingly honest look at the singer in one of the lowest periods of her life. "My engagement at the Little Club was a battle with tragedy. I was crying all the time. Poor Billy, such a dear man, tried to console me, but there was no way to stop my interminable flood of tears. I even cried when I was out on the floor singing. 'Little Girl Blue' was one of my numbers, and I cried all the way through it. Every night I had to struggle to finish 'Glad To Be Unhappy' before my tears overcame me. I'm sure the audience never heard a performer so touched by her songs." Day ran into the same problem when she auditioned halfheartedly for Michael Curtiz, casting director at Warner Brothers. Attempting "Embraceable You," she broke down repeatedly. Curtiz, however, recognizing her deep sensitivity, cast her in the first of her thirty-seven films.

The Little Club remained a favorite until the early '60s, featuring such acts as pianists Arthur Ferrante and Lou Teicher, who went on to considerable fame of their own; and Jane Harvey, whose breathy, catch-in-the-throat vocal style and stunning good looks invited every man to set down his drink and move a little closer.

Throughout the '40s and '50s, One Fifth Avenue continued to offer some casual fun on a tour through Greenwich Village. Still cheaper than many uptown clubs (for several years there was no cover or minimum), it presented performers who ranged mostly from fair to ghastly. But audiences weren't hostile; if they didn't like a show they simply talked through it or left. The better acts used it as a workshop. "Number One was like working in my living room," says Pat Carroll. "On late evenings when there were not that many people I was able to try out material there, because it was so relaxed. I even said to them, 'Look, I'm trying this out. Tell me what you think.' "

It was hardly well constructed for performers, however. "There were two square mirrored pillars in front of and behind the grand piano. You literally stood beside the piano, so most of the time you were playing to yourself. On weekends, though, they opened up a second room, with a lot of medallions in it, to accommodate the overflow crowd. Those people always seemed angry that they weren't in the other room with the big kids, so you kind of disliked going in there. I used to say there were medallions for all the acts that had died in there."

The backbone of Number One consisted of its three resident pianists: Hazel Webster, an earthy middle-aged brunette who played during interludes; Harold Fonville, a short, neurotic little man who reminded some of Peter Lorre, ever staring up from his cigar through shifty eyes; and Bob Downey, who ran the room and formed a piano team with Fonville. Downey selected candidates for the club's weekly Monday night amateur contests, voted on by the room's established acts. Most winners were never heard from again after their honorary engagements, but there were exceptions: Paul Lynde, who auditioned with a monologue that he later performed in *New Faces of 1952* about a man who goes on a safari with his wife and barely lives to tell about it; and actor Jack Cassidy in a brief stint as a standup singer.

A more familiar face there was comedienne-singer Nancy Andrews, who went on to perform on Broadway in *Touch and Go*, *Plain and Fancy*, and *Little Me* and then appeared in hundreds of television commercials until her death in 1989. The Minneapolis-born entertainer grew up in California, where she studied acting and musical composition. Occasionally she played the piano and sang, a skill that launched her career in 1944. "One day a boyfriend took me to a nightclub Bud Abbott owned in the Valley. It was a slow night. We were talking about a certain song, and he asked me to play and sing it at the piano. I did a couple of songs, and I started getting requests. So Bud Abbott came over. He was a gross man—pitiful. He said, 'How'd ya like to work here?' I said, 'What do you mean, work here?'

I thought he meant as a waitress or something. He said, 'You know, doin' what you're doin' now. I'll give ya seventy-five dollars a week.' Well, I was making twenty-five a week working from eight-thirty to five-thirty in an advertising agency in Hollywood, so I thought, fine."

Andrews went from one California gangster dive to another, singing mostly "sophisticated songs" that she wrote herself such as "I Was Investigated by Congress for Having Too Many Foreign Affairs," tunes rescued by her deft timing and hearty comic flair. Not surprisingly, she became almost as tough as the gangsters she worked for. One mob joint was run by a thug named Benny, who carried a pearl-handled revolver. "One night he said, 'We want you to do a third show—a special show. Tonight.' I went onstage, and there was just one table of hoods. One of them stood up and said, 'Hey you, I want you to sing "Happy Birthday" to Willy Sutton.' Willy Sutton had just gotten out of the can."

For much of 1948 Andrews shared the bill with the young comedy team of James Kirkwood and Lee Goodman, who had won the talent contest that April. Kirkwood, probably best known as the librettist of *A Chorus Line*, was the son of stage and film actor James Kirkwood and silent film star Lila Lee. His parents divorced when he was a child, and through their shared custody agreement he traveled from Hollywood to Ohio to New York and anywhere else they happened to be working. After graduating from high school he settled in New York and got a job as an usher. By day he studied acting and took singing lessons with Harold Fonville, where he met his partner. Already an experienced actor from age nine, Goodman was studying through the American Theatre Wing and taking singing lessons with him as well.

"I finished my lesson one day," recalled Goodman, "and Harold said, 'You have got to stay and hear this boy who comes to me every week. He can't sing on key, but he's got more enthusiasm. You're gonna scream with laughter.'

"Jimmy arrived. He complained when he saw me there, but Harold told him not to worry. He started to sing, and he couldn't hit one note on. I was shaking my head. He said, 'What's the matter?'

" 'Well, God, you're way off key!'

"I started to sing something with him, and it helped him to stay in tune. Harold said, 'There is something about the two of you together that is so funny.' " Goodman had a long, funereal face, slightly protruding ears, and a put-upon expression, whereas Kirkwood was a bundle of manic energy that burst forth in every direction. "When I met him," said Goodman, "he was literally starving. He was a bright, cute kid, and he could always get somebody to take him to dinner. He was very ambitious and desperate to accomplish something." Recognizing Goodman's solidity, Kirkwood persuaded him to become his partner—"over my dead body," as Goodman said. "In fact, that's almost what happened."

The two became lovers for a brief period, sharing a cold-water flat for $28 a month in Hell's Kitchen. "There was no heat," said Kirkwood. "We froze our asses off. The bathtub was in the kitchen, and we shared a hallway bathroom with an Irish dockworker and his family. And it was a tough area. We'd walk home and they'd throw buckets of paint and hot water on us."

Since they had no money for special material they borrowed numbers wherever they could find them. "I wrote a parody of 'Tea for Two' in hipster lingo," said Goodman, "and brought in some funny props. Jimmy found some terrible old art songs. One of them, 'Downy Little Brownie Man,' was unbelievably racist. It was introduced by Dame Clara Butt." Most of the laughs came from the chemistry between them, like a stern young English professor babysitting for his adorable but bratty kid brother. Fonville arranged for them to enter a Number One talent contest. They won easily and began their engagement a few weeks later on the bill with Andrews.

"All of us dressed in a tiny little room," recalled Goodman. "Jimmy and I were only in our early twenties. Suddenly there we were with this tough lady who took off her bra, and every other word was 'fuck.' Jimmy was pacing back and forth. Nancy said, 'Here, kid, have a drink,' and handed him a tin can of Johnny Walker Black. No glass."

Nevertheless they were a hit. As *Variety* wrote, "Lads are both cleancut but possess the elastic mugs necessary for good comedy delivery." They expanded their repertoire, staging Khachaturian's "Sabre Dance" as a duel with swords and soup strainers and spoofing the titles of *Reader's Digest* articles ("I Did Not Live Through Menopause," "America's Number One Killer—Zippers," "We Bought Dad an Electric Chair for Christmas"), emphasizing targets ignored by big-time nightclub comics. "Martin and Lewis came to see us once, and Jerry wanted to buy the 'Sabre Dance.' We said, 'That's our biggest number!' He said, 'Well, you gotta come and hear Dean and me at the Copa.' He booked us a ringside table, and we hated the show, because they were a symbol of the broad humor we were fighting against. Television was just beginning, and they were all going back to seltzer-squirting and pie-in-the-face. So all our efforts to be sophisticated were against the time."

But they were never too sophisticated for the rumpus room atmosphere of Number One. After Andrews left, they shared the bill with Hope Emerson, another risqué singer-pianist. "She was about six feet one," said Goodman, "with an ass that covered the whole piano seat and a voice that could shatter glass. People had to stand back." The *New Yorker* called her "as vigorous and commanding as a camp director, although her songs aren't exactly suitable for the youngest group. 'I'm going to sing a song!' she'll shout at the patrons, and darned if they don't quiet down just as docilely as if they were in a recreation hall." In "Did I Do Wrong?" she asked an advice columnist if she had compromised her virtue:

> *It was in a little bar at a table*
> *I was waiting for Great Aunt Mabel*
> *When I saw a man who made me want to* shriek!
> *His hair was sealskin sleek*
> *His smile had a new technique*
> *And his profile can best be described as "chic Greek"*
>
> *Oh, I dropped my eyes so modestly, he couldn't help but see*
> *And then I dropped my handkerchief, he picked it up with glee*
> *And then I dropped all pretenses and he picked up me!*
> Did I do wrong?

That bill was even more popular than the last, and Kirkwood and Goodman began to receive radio offers. For several months they hosted *Teenagers Unlimited*, a variety show that gave Kirkwood another chance to exasperate his partner. "The show had something called the Junior Achievement Awards," Kirkwood recalled, "which we presented to kids who had achieved something in the community by raising funds for a hospital, or opening up a day care center for kittens, or whatever. We did a routine, we played records, the kids all yelled and screamed, then we presented the awards. Before one show the producers said, 'There's a boy and a girl today. Lee, you take the little girl, and Jimmy, you take the boy.' Lee interviewed the girl, and then it was my turn. He was a little Chinese boy who had helped raise two hundred thousand dollars for some hospital wing. I said, 'What's your name?'

"He said, 'Harry Dong.'

"Harry Dong?"

"Yes."

"I started to laugh, and I just couldn't stop. There were a couple of hundred kids there, and the producers were standing a few feet away. I got up and walked into the hall, and I stood there and shrieked. Lee had to interview Harry Dong. They wanted to kill me."

More often it was Kirkwood who wanted to kill his partner. An angry young man, especially when drunk, he later attributed his behavior to a transient childhood spent with an alcoholic mother and an inattentive father. But it also stemmed from insecurity about his slender singing and dancing abilities and his inadequate comic timing. Goodman had these talents in abundance and ended up bearing the brunt of Kirkwood's violent resentment. "Lee was by far the more talented comedically. He had an ease about him. I wanted to rehearse every day, all day, all night, but Lee didn't like to rehearse, which became a big problem for us. In all our numbers I played the fuckup, but I was the one who got the new material, got the agents, did the hard work. Everyone thought Lee was doing it, which used to burn my ass. They really thought I *was* the fuckup. I had a terrible, terrible temper. I used to beat the shit out of him."

One incident in 1949 foretold their rocky collaboration. "We were riding home after finishing at Number One. Somebody had invited Jimmy over for a few drinks, and he was not a good drunk. He suddenly picked a fight with me in the cab about a sketch we had done. 'You know when you're supposed to say such-and-such and I'm supposed to say so-and-so? You did it too fast! Why did you do it that way?' I said, 'Because I felt like it!' The next thing I knew the door was open, and I was rolling down Broadway from a moving cab."

"I screamed at the cab driver, 'DON'T STOP THIS CAB!' " Kirkwood said. "But the guy knew he had a nut, and we picked Lee up. The next night we had to announce that he'd been in a car accident, because he was covered with scratches."

DECADES AFTER ITS CLOSING in 1957, the more polite Ruban Bleu remains irreplaceable to those who worked there. "I think it came closest to the swank supper clubs I'd seen in the movies," says Dorothy Loudon. "The waiters were all Italian, and dressed in bow ties and tails. If they really liked an act it was hard to get them to wait on tables, because they'd stand in the back and applaud and yell 'Brava! Brava!' It was like a big family."

In the late '40s the room's atmosphere outshone most of its acts, which were novel and accomplished but not too exciting. According to Monk, girl singers were hired as much for their abilities in the greenroom as for their singing; niceness was often the main qualification.

One performer with both qualities in abundance was singer-composer-pianist Michael Brown, a brown-haired, winsome Texan with an ingenuous smile and about as much sophistication as a college freshman working behind the desk of the campus library. Brown debuted at the Ruban in a typical manner. In 1943, after graduating from the University of Virginia, he came to New York and said, "Mr. Monk, I think I would like to be a performer." Monk said, "Stay here tonight and watch the entire show. When everybody's gone, play something for me." Afterward Monk said, "I think you should come back when you've had a little experience."

In 1949, after a stint in the air force, the young man returned. "Well, Mr. Monk, I've had a little experience." He played and sang another number.

"Can you possibly come in and begin tonight?" Monk asked. "I must be truthful with you. There's a magician on the bill who is so dreadful that I'll take almost anybody."

"Sure, I'll be there!"

Brown loved to research historical events, and from his findings fashioned some wonderfully evocative songs, among them "Lizzie Borden," a showstopper in *New Faces of 1952* and, later in the decade, a hit single for the Kingston Trio; and "Ruth Snyder," a rundown of the sensationalistic 1920s scheme of a Queens woman and her lover to murder her husband.

In 1947 came pianist Norman Paris, whose trio supplied sparkling interlude music and accompaniment there for nine years. Born Norman Pawlak in Philadelphia, he made a prodigious debut at age six with the Philadelphia Orchestra. As a teenager he decided that greater rewards lay in popular music, and became a nonpareil accompanist and arranger. He formed a trio with bassist Justin Arndt and Frank Cerchia, whose amplified electric guitar gave the group a resonant, ethereal sound.

Paris's influence on the singers there equaled Monk's. Intuitively he found material that suited them, arranging it and rehearsing for free—a blessing for many struggling young vocalists. His painstaking care earned him a reputation as one of the kindest and most generous men in the business, one of the few about whom no one could say a bad word.

Paris's trio held special rewards for Bibi Osterwald, a brassy blonde singer-comedienne who first came to attention in *Sing Out, Sweet Land*, a 1944 Broadway musical that she stopped nightly when she belted out "Casey Jones." In 1948 Monk heard her at New York's Knickerbocker Music Hall and asked her to sing at the Ruban. "I went to David Craig, the vocal coach who's married to Nancy Walker, and we got a very sophisticated act. *Wrong!* We did all these sophisticated songs like 'It Never Entered My Mind' and 'Bewitched, Bothered, and Bewildered'—bullcrap! I can do them, but forget it. I flopped the first show, it was terrible. Julius said, 'Where are all those wonderful numbers you used to sing like 'The Oceana Roll' and 'Casey Jones' and 'Mention My Name in Sheboygen'? I said, 'Oh, I've got those.' He said, 'Can you do them for the second show?' We had a quick rehearsal with Norman Paris, and we did them. I was booked for two weeks and stayed for five years. Married the bass player and got the hell out of there."

After that night Osterwald had a surer sense of direction. "I went to the library and read the reviews. I didn't take the ballads or the hit numbers like 'Bewitched, Bothered, and Bewildered.' I took numbers that stopped the show. And those were the comedy numbers. They used to have comedy numbers in shows. They don't have those anymore. Then I put my act together. It cost twenty-two dollars and fifty cents."

And it worked. "Bibi had one of the best nightclub acts in the business," says Ben Bagley. "She was tough, she was hard, she was a red hot mama, and nobody looked the other way when she was on." Wrote columnist Lee Mortimer in 1950, "Bibi Osterwald is a big buxom lass who makes with ditties that evoke a special response from elderly wolves. She has a large following of this class." Some of those ditties were familiar, such as "Ballin' the Jack," "Hard Hearted Hannah," and "The Begat" from *Finian's Rainbow*; others were written especially for her, such as Earl Brent's "One Stinkin' Magnolia," the saucy complaint of a girl who didn't receive the expensive gifts she required.

But she preferred the theatre. In 1954 John Latouche created the role of Lovey Mars, the baking champion of Mount Olympus, for Osterwald in *The Golden Apple*. She sang one song, "Goona Goona," while performing a hula. One evening Ben Bagley went backstage to say hello. "God, Bibi, you look wonderful. Have you lost weight?"

"Yeah, honey, they told me I'd have to shake my ass a lot, so I figured I'd better look good."

THE ADVENTUROUS PROGRAMS at the Blue Angel in the late '40s made an evening there a lot more offbeat. Max Gordon brought a number of folk acts uptown from the Vanguard, among them Burl Ives, Josh White, the Weavers, and even future actor Alan Arkin, then a teenage folk singer–guitarist; but by 1948 the club had spawned its own company of regulars who often appeared for weeks at a time. As long as the phones rang with inquiries about whether so-and-so was still there, Jacoby asked that act to stay another week. The familiar faces in that period included singer-actress Josephine Premice, star of such musicals as *Jamaica* and *Bubbling Brown Sugar*, who wore West Indian garb and gave fiery, emotive performances of Creole and calypso songs; Evelyn Knight, a pretty blonde with a mere wisp of voice who sang English, Scottish, and Irish tunes with "hot" Dixieland accompaniment; and John Buckmaster, a suave blond Englishman who delivered droll comic monologues on Shakespeare, Oscar Wilde, the British nobility, and other topics not often covered in nightclubs.

Sometimes there were stars in their formative years, before they had developed much finesse. "Then there's a fellow named Andy Williams," wrote Douglas Watt in a December 1949 *New Yorker* review, "who used to be a part of Kay Thompson's highly stylized act and is now a highly stylized solo performer. There is no body to his tones but he is remarkably persuasive as he bawls and coos his way through fresh-sounding arrangements of some aptly chosen solo numbers."

In 1946 Jacoby launched the most enduring club career in the business when he introduced Kaye Ballard to an instantly smitten audience. The auburn-haired singer-comedienne has never been out of work since. A national audience remembers her best as one of television's *Mothers-in-Law* (the other was Eve Arden), but that two-year series has been a small part of a career that now spans almost fifty years of Broadway and off-Broadway, recordings, nightclubs, and television. Of all '40s and '50s café stars Ballard stayed loyal to that field the longest, deciding only in 1989 that she was through competing with booze.

She had just turned twenty when Jacoby hired her. Much of her intense desire to succeed grew from childhood insecurities. Ballard was born Catherine Gloria Balotta in Cleveland to a staunchly traditional Italian family. Her mother did her best to quell the youngster's acting ambitions. "Are you crazy? The way you look? Movie stars are pretty. They're tramps, but they're pretty." When a high school drama teacher refused to admit her for the same reason, Ballard turned to comedy, discovering that making people laugh gave her ego a powerful boost. One didn't need beauty to be funny; it may have even gotten in the way. Many women in her profession adopted a self-deprecating comedy style, finding it easier to make fun of themselves before others did. Once Ballard approached forty she seldom missed a chance to spoof her weight, looks, and age, but with such good humor that it only added to her appeal.

After graduation she began two years of vaudeville appearances, finally winning a job with the Spike Jones orchestra as a singer, comic, flutist, and tuba player. *Variety* singled her out on July 19, 1946, when the band played at New York's Strand Theatre:

> High spot on the bill, for laughs and boffo entertainment, is new member of the unit, Kaye Ballad [sic], who justly garners top returns of the show. Opening slowly with "You Gotta Have a Beat," comicanary croons the Jones version of "My Heart Sings," worded like a masochist's moan. Housing shortage is given clever treatment in "My Apartment," with music of "My Man." Has to beg off.

Theatre producer John Murray Anderson brought Jacoby to hear her, and Jacoby offered her a job. "I started at the top and worked my way down," she says. "I didn't realize what a thrill it was to work at the Blue Angel." In the vaudeville tradition, her overriding goal was to give everybody a good time, whether they came from Park Avenue or Nebraska. "Kaye's act was class," says Ben Bagley, "but it wasn't chic, so it appealed to everyone." Her formula was simple: she sang a few funny songs, told some jokes and stories, clowned with the audience, and once in a while played an accomplished flute chorus. Anyone could appreciate her satirical targets: a narcissistic movie star who sings a love song to herself in a hand mirror, a torch singer with hiccups struggling to make it to the end of Rodgers and Hart's "Where or When," and a decrepit Sophie Tucker's annual "final farewell appearance" in a monologue by Charles Strouse and Lee Adams (*Bye Bye Birdie*, *Golden Boy*, *Applause*): "I'll *nevah* forget my first show. It was at the old Hippodrome Theatre. I don't mean the old *new* Hippodrome Theatre—I mean the old, old, *old* Hippodrome Theatre. The show was called *Bim-Bam Baby*. There were six great songs in that show, ladies and gentlemen, and *yours truly* sang them all!"

Ballard had a clear, tuneful singing voice, but except for "Love Is a Simple Thing," the hit ballad from *New Faces of 1952* by her accompanist Arthur Siegel, she stuck to comedy. "I was too self-conscious to sing, except for comedy singing, because I thought I was so ugly. In the theatre, I'd sing a straight song and stop the show. But Herbert would say, 'I don't want you to sing, I want you to do comedy. We have Charles Trenet to sing.' " Yet Ballard went on to introduce "Lazy Afternoon" in *The Golden Apple* and to make the first recording of "Fly Me to the Moon."

Still, the Angel was an exciting place for a starstruck girl in her twenties. "That's where I got to meet Josephine Baker, Cole Porter, and Mistinguett. I'd sit in the first booth with Herbert, and he'd introduce them to me. You could count on seeing a celebrity almost every night."

The Angel practiced a staunch policy of racial tolerance, hiring dozens of black performers and never barring a black customer. "I was from the Village," reflected Max Gordon, "and Jacoby was from Paris, and we didn't have any prejudices, even though this was a smart East Side club. Most of the guys running the uptown places were afraid that if they put in black performers they would attract black clientele, and they didn't want that. We didn't have any serious problems with white audiences because of it. We had some people come and bawl the hell out of us afterward—'What sort of a place are you running?'—but most people were tolerant. It was the kind of place where you just didn't make a fuss." And so it became one of the foremost midtown showcases for black talent, presenting, among others, Pearl Bailey, Josephine Premice, Barbara McNair, Diahann Carroll, Johnny Mathis, Dick Gregory, and Godfrey Cambridge.

Billie Holiday never sang there but came occasionally as a customer. Holiday fought to retain her dignity as an artist and human being in the face of nearly every humiliating obstacle a black performer of her generation could meet, and seldom would she tolerate condescension. Ben Bagley recalls an evening at the Angel with Holiday and her agent Joe Glaser. "Billie was chicer than almost any white woman who went there and really glamorous with a black dress, and pearls, and an orchid in her hair. Two snotty women from out of town came over to the table. 'Oh, Miss Holiday,' they said, 'we want you to know that if you ever come to Cleveland you're welcome to stay in our homes.' It was obvious they would ordinarily never allow a black person to stay with them, but in this case they would make an exception. Billie looked at them and their ghastly plastic handbags and plastic shoes and awful hairdos, and said, 'If your homes look anything like your clothes, I wouldn't set foot in your kitchen.' They walked away in embarrassment."

It was ironic—and tragic—that the career of the man who helped create a more racially tolerant atmosphere was nearly destroyed in 1948. The House Un-American Activities Committee, under the direction of Senator Joseph McCarthy, had begun its witch-hunt of actors, writers, and intellectuals whom it suspected of Communist involvement. That year it subpoenaed Barney Josephson's brother Leon, an avowed member of the German Communist underground who had participated in a plot to assassinate Hitler in 1934. Leon refused to respond to their questioning on the grounds that it was a violation of the Fifth Amendment and was cited for contempt, tried, found guilty, and sentenced to ten months in prison. Leon was one of the committee's first victims, and the vast publicity made a lot of the fact that his brother was Barney Josephson. The Hearst newspaper chain's syndicated columnists, among them Dorothy Kilgallen, Lee Mortimer, Westbrook Pegler, and Walter Winchell, began a campaign of innuendo and guilt-by-association that sabotaged Café Society. As Josephson told Whitney Balliett in the *New Yorker* (October 9, 1971), "Pegler devoted a column to Leon implying that he was a drug addict, and the last line was 'And there is much to be said about his brother Barney.' Just that, no more. So I was the brother of a Communist drug addict, I allowed Negros in my clubs, I had introduced inflammatory songs like 'Strange Fruit' and 'The House I Live In,' and on and on."

Critics would no longer review his acts; when a reporter from the *New York Herald-Tribune* wrote a favorable notice, his editor squelched it before publication. Josephson tried to bring in stars who would not need reviews, but they were afraid to work for him. Within three weeks Uptown business dropped 45 percent. He kept both clubs running for almost a year, but after losing $90,000 he was forced to sell them in 1950.

Uptown didn't remain vacant for long. With $75,000 of their profits from the Blue Angel, Jacoby and Gordon bought the club and created an opulent new room with a dance floor and acts too elaborate for the Angel. They named it Le Directoire, junked all the old furnishings, and spent a fortune redesigning it as a showcase for Kay Thompson and the Williams Brothers, then the hottest act in show-business and one that Walter Winchell proclaimed the greatest in nightclub history. A renowned MGM vocal arranger, Thompson created a song, dance, and patter presentation that was choreographed to the hilt. It featured her own complex arrangements, executed with the assistance of Andy Williams and his three brothers, four wholesome boys with crewcuts and Pepsodent smiles.

In 1948 the *New Yorker* described this whirlwind of energy:

> The Williams Brothers bounce onto the floor shouting some kind of welcoming song and flinging themselves about with such faultless unanimity of movement that they appear to be one person reflected in a set of mirrors. Kay Thompson, dressed in pink satin slacks, follows them, waving her hands and singing her hellos while the band churns up an enormous fanfare. Then, suddenly, you are in the midst of something about a jubilee down south, with the angular Miss Thompson hurrying about the stage, leaping into the air every now and then with the odd grace peculiar to the very long-legged, while the Williams Brothers follow her about, grouping themselves into various formations around her as she sings and stamps.

Jacoby's decorator Bill Pahlmann created one of the city's most elegant designs, complete with plush taupe carpeting and walls covered in woven threads of pink, silver, and gold. To accommodate Thompson he built a hinged stage that was lowered onto the dance floor at showtime, as well as a glass-enclosed bar for latecomers. On the afternoon of the opening, while setting up the chairs and tables, Jacoby and Gordon discovered that they had inadvertently reduced the seating capacity from 300 to 212—a disaster when the room overflowed every night of the ten-week engagement with customers who had, in many cases, bribed the maître d' for seats. (The next year he opened his own club with the tips.) The patrons were outnumbered by those alienated at being turned away.

After Thompson left, the partners booked Abe Burrows, Pearl Bailey, and others, but no one could fill that space as Thompson did. "Every act we tried felt anticlimactic," wrote Gordon. "A cab would drive up, the doorman'd open the door, a face'd lean out. 'Is that woman, Kay what's-her-name, and her brothers on tonight?' When given a negative reply, the cab door would bang shut and off they'd drive." After losing thousands of dollars, Jacoby and Gordon reluctantly closed, gave the club back to Josephson, and auctioned off as many of the furnishings as they could. Pahlmann's enormous stage brought them $100.

Back at the Blue Angel, rewards and headaches came in equal measure in the person of Pearl Bailey, whom Gordon brought uptown from the Village Vanguard in 1944, where she had an avid following. Bailey had spent most of her time performing in clubs; her Broadway debut in the Harold Arlen–Johnny Mercer musical *St. Louis Woman* would not take place until March 30, 1946. Both at the Angel and the Vanguard she sang the wry ballads and tongue-in-cheek comedy songs that she made famous, including "Tired," "Legalize My Name," and "It's a Woman's Prerogative," but this was a subtler Bailey than the hearty Pearlie Mae of later years. Sleek, sexy, and still in her twenties, she held much of her humor in reserve, allowing it to sizzle beneath the surface of a teasing half-smile. An impudent flash of her eyes or wave of her hand drew laughs at a suggestive reference in a song heard a hundred times.

Audiences never seemed to tire of her, but by 1951, her last year there, Bailey had grown more than a little tired of the Blue Angel. One of Jacoby's shrewder policies was to sign acts at a three-time option, allowing him to rebook them twice if he wished—in many cases after they had hit it big and did not care to return. With Bailey it backfired. Songwriter-pianist Bud McCreery, who with singer Paula Drake shared Bailey's last bill, recalls that time. "Pearl was contract-bound to fulfill a return commitment, so she was not overjoyed about that. She was appearing simultaneously at the Angel and in a revue called *Bless You All*, which required more energy than Boulder Dam could supply. She would sometimes be so late that it was second-show time before she arrived. People who'd made reservations for the first show kept getting embalmed on the house Scotch, while the second-show reservations waited out front at the bar and even in the street, making all sorts of threatening noises. So Herbert, a nervous wreck by this time, kept turning up the heat and turning off the ventilators to drive out first-show patrons, until we all came down with galloping pneumonia.

"I think Pearlie Mae must have been getting 'a little help from her friends' to keep the adrenalin pumping, because her shows were full of surprises. At one jubilant moment she asked if anyone remembered when the girls used to take the money off the tables. An' when some joker gave you a hot quarter . . . *Hon-eeee!*' I didn't recall any such amusement from my sheltered childhood, but when I saw *Lady Sings the Blues* I realized Pearlie Mae wasn't putting us on. At one performance she lifted her petticoats to demonstrate, and *that* was a night to remember. Herbert almost turned flesh-color!"

ANOTHER FABLED CAFÉ opened on September 6, 1949, in a basement at 40 West 8th Street in Greenwich Village. Much of the Bon Soir's appeal came from its out-of-the-way, almost illicit feeling. A walk down thirty-one steps led to a square black room owned and run by the Mafia, where blacks and whites, gays and straights mingled without a trace of tension. On one side of the room was a gay bar. Those seeking a highbrow atmosphere had to look elsewhere. But that did not detract from the club's impressive list of graduates, topped by Barbra Streisand. Most of the others—Phyllis Diller, Kaye Ballard, Alice Ghostley, Jimmie Komack, Larry Storch, Joey Carter—offered comedy, which suited the room's plaster walls and raucous audience.

The Bon Soir was the culmination of a line of clubs that featured, in various combinations, the same all-black company of regulars: singer-emcee Jimmie Daniels, a stylish Texan adored by New York and Paris society; Mae Barnes; the instrumental-comedy trio the Three Flames; pianist Garland Wilson; and pianist-singer Norene Tate.

A native of Laredo, Texas, Daniels sang in clubs throughout Europe in the '30s, acquiring an air of elegance that never seemed as pretentious as Monk's often did. He was a private, childlike man who seldom said a bad thing about anyone—including the many second- and third-rate acts he had to introduce. That ingenuous quality, combined with his boulevardier manner, proved irresistible to many wealthy society women, although his actual involvement with any of them is questionable. In 1939 he opened a club called Jimmie Daniels' at 114 West 116th Street in Harlem and ran it until entering the army in 1942. Modeled after the genteel French boîtes where he had worked, it was hardly noticed outside his circle. "By Harlem standards, this is a model of dignity and respectability," wrote the *New Yorker* (May 4, 1940). "It's a Negro version of a supper club: no dancing, just a few singers and piano-players, most of them good and none of them too loud."

A closer foreshadowing of the Bon Soir came at Cerutti, a supper club at 59th Street and Madison Avenue, half a block from the Copacabana. The featured act was Mae Barnes, who sang to the twin piano accompaniment of Garland Wilson and his partner Eddie Steele. There Barnes came to the attention of the white audiences who would love her for the rest of her career. Born Edith May Stith in 1907 in the Village to a dockworker and his wife, she revealed an enormous natural talent even before kindergarten. One afternoon her mother took her to the 14th Street Theatre, a vaudeville and movie house. "A guy came out on the stage to sing, the band was playing, and I was sitting on my mother's lap. I knew the song he was singing, and I got up and went into the aisle to sing with him. He stopped and had the spotlight turned on me. I was singing my heart out, and the house was applauding, the band was applauding. That's when I knew I had to go into show business."

For her eighth birthday her father bought her a secondhand upright. "I could never understand the notes, but I'd watch the teacher's fingers, and whatever she'd do I'd do. After about two weeks she came in to give me my lesson. She called my mother and said, 'I want you to listen to this.' I was playing like mad, and the piano books were on the floor. She told my mother, 'You are wasting your money!' "

After school Barnes hung around the Village and tap-danced for tips. She left school at twelve, telling the administration she was moving to Cleveland. Falsifying her age, she got a job as a chorus girl at the Plantation Club in Harlem. Then she joined the touring black vaudeville circuit in the South booked by TOBA (Theatre Owners' Booking Association but dubbed "Tough on Black Asses" by performers). In 1924 she made her Broadway debut in *Runnin' Wild*, in which she is credited with introducing the Charleston on Broadway. Her dancing in the national tour of *Shuffle Along* and *Rang Tang* led Bill ("Bojangles") Robinson to call her the greatest living female tap dancer, but in 1938 an auto accident fractured her pelvis and impaired her precision tapping. "So I took the rhythm from my dancing and put it in my songs," she says. She worked in gin mills, singing and playing dirty songs, table singing, hip shaking, "giving the customers plenty of leg," even grabbing dimes off the tables with her crotch. Gradually she drifted toward the standards she preferred, "On the Sunny Side of the Street," "I'm Gonna Sit Right Down and Write Myself a Letter," and "Sweet Georgia Brown." A Cerutti regular was Peggy Hopkins Joyce, an oft-married showgirl of the '20s and '30s and a charter member of café society. "Peggy came in one night with a soldier," remembers Barnes. "The place was packed. I was singing at tables, and the guy was so interested in the funny things I was doing that he was ignoring her. I got to the table next to them, and he was applauding and laughing and carrying on. She said to him, 'It seems as though you're more interested in that nigger than you are in me!' I finished my song, then I went over to her table and I said, 'You say that word again and I'll kick you square in your ass!' She started to scream, 'MR. CERUTTI! MR. CERUTTI!' He came right over, a little fat guy, and asked me what happened. I told him just what she said. And he told Peggy Joyce to pay her check and leave."

In February 1946 the Little Casino, a tiny cellar club at 245 Sullivan Street in Greenwich Village, brought together Daniels, Barnes, Garland Wilson, and Norene Tate. Owned by Phil Pagano and Ernie Sgroi, a pair of slick Mafiosi, the dim little black room reminded some of a hallway, with ceiling lights and wall mirrors trying to make it seem a little less claustrophobic. But lack of space did not squelch its party atmosphere, from the bustle at a gay bar near the entrance to the tables that crowded the room all the way up to the stage. Seated with customers, Barnes would often sing along with Daniels at the end of his set, before joining him alongside the twin spinets onstage with the other performers for a rousing finale.

At its opening the Little Casino featured a trio led by trumpeter Frankie Newton as well as Stella Brooks, a white girl with a pageboy hairdo and a reputation as one of the saltiest, most eccentric singers in blues and jazz. Brooks infuriated Billie Holiday by commenting that "Billie sings like her shoes are too tight" but revealed no doubts about her own abilities when she called her 1948 Town Hall concert "Exit Singing: 99 Minutes of What's Left of Jazz." After Brooks left, Sylvia Syms, Rae Bourbon, and other entertainers took over.

The Little Casino closed in 1949, reportedly due to a suicide on the premises. Don Julio, a Mexican nightclub-restaurant on West 8th Street, had just closed, and Sgroi and Pagano took it over, renaming it the Bon Soir. They brought in Wilson, Tate, and Jimmie Daniels, who functioned as host, singer, and sometime artistic advisor. Because Barnes would not be available for a few months, they hired Mildred Bailey for one of her last engagements before she died in 1951. Bailey's enormous girth allowed her little freedom on the tiny stage; she stood between a pair of grand pianos and bounced back and forth.

The Bon Soir did not take off until Barnes came aboard after a year. "They say she had been one of the best tap dancers alive," recalls Thelma Carpenter. "Those big eyes and that Kewpie doll face—you had to see it to believe it. I can't even describe the energy that came from her. She could throw away a line and you'd be laughing for five minutes." Wrote Douglas Watt in the *New Yorker* (November 14, 1953), "She may begin a song softly and sweetly, but after no more than a few bars she is rocking like a houseboat in the rapids. Singing 'Ol' Man Mose' with a murderous beat, or delivering 'Summertime' in an indescribably racy manner, she is tremendous."

Most of the performers recall their shady employers as perfect gentlemen—Pagano and Sgroi even fed them pots of Italian food after closing—but at least two acts remembered otherwise. Nancy Andrews doubled at the club during her run in the musical *Plain and Fancy*. "One night I came to work and they said, 'We're closed. The roof fell in. We'll call you when you can come back.' So, OK. We came back, and that week we were docked for the days we were out. Well, we were under Local 802 contract because I played the piano, and boy, you don't fool around with the musician's union. All the others you can, but not that one. I got everybody together and said, 'Listen, they can't do that. They have to pay us.' They were all afraid to call the union, so I did. The next night I got my money, but some swarthy, spooky guy pulled me in the back room, really threatening me. He said, 'You ain't never gonna work for us again.' And I didn't."

Kirkwood and Goodman once arrived ten minutes late for their show after having gotten caught in a traffic jam. Cornering them as they pushed their way through the crowds along the front staircase, Pagano smacked Kirkwood across the face. Immediately he turned contrite. "Christ, you made me hit you, do you know what that means? Goddammit, don't you ever do that again! What do you drink?"

"Scotch."

Pagano yelled to an assistant, "Hey, get this kid a case of scotch!" Then he moaned, "I'm so ashamed! This place is my home, this is class! That's why we run this place, for class. Then you make me do something like that. You're never gonna do that again, are you?" Then he chucked Kirkwood on the chin and said, "Go to church!"

The room took its true class from Daniels and from Norene Tate, a beautiful, light-skinned woman in her forties with a streak of gray in her hair and a dignified, stately presence. Tate sang and played such standards as "But Not for Me" and "I Cover the Waterfront" during intervals, her prim voice and ladylike piano style establishing her more as a lovely ornament than as someone to pay close attention to. She especially liked "Tenderly," singing it in a rendition that seemed to make it about twice as long. As soon as she started to intone its long opening phrase about the evening *breeeeeeeze* caressing the *tree-eeeees*, someone was sure to groan, "Oh, my God! She's singing 'Tenderly' again!"

Chapter FOUR

By 1950 intimate clubs had fully come into their own. No longer would they remain local secrets hidden away in cellars or down side streets and given only passing mentions by the press. The greatest reason? Television—the very medium that would, ironically, help tear them down about ten years later. TV had existed experimentally since the '30s but only after World War II would it become affordable for a mass audience. In 1946 about 7,000 sets were in use. Four years later that number had grown to 4.4 million and would escalate at a rate of 20,000 per day until 1956. (By then Americans spent a higher average of weekly hours before the set than on the job.) In 1960 the total number of units surpassed 60 million.

As TV developed it required a growing number of performers and writers to fill airtime, especially for its wealth of variety shows. Ed Sullivan featured about eight guests every Sunday at eight; the *Tonight Show* had 105 minutes to program each weeknight. Dave Garroway, Steve Allen, and other hosts looked to clubs for many of their guests, caring not if they were unknown but only if they were good. And since these shows, like most of television, originated in New York, they didn't have to look far.

All this exposure alerted the nation to the existence of the Blue Angel, Le Ruban Bleu, the Bon Soir, and other intimate clubs. It also inspired thousands of aspiring performers to pack their bags and head for Broadway. Revues were especially popular, and Leonard Sillman's *New Faces of 1952* in particular drew much attention to the fact that several of its stars, among them Eartha Kitt, Alice Ghostley, Robert Clary, Paul Lynde, and Ronny Graham, had come from nightclubs. "[Bistros are] doing the job in Broadway today which was once so magnificently accomplished by a gimmick called vaudeville," wrote Emory Lewis in *Cue* (1954). These "discoveries" sparked the daily syndicated columns of Walter Winchell, Dorothy Kilgallen, and Lee Mortimer, helping make many an unknown nationally famous, seemingly overnight.

But most of these big breaks resulted from years of hard work. Such was the case with Alice Ghostley, the lovably dithery singing comedienne whose showstopper in *New Faces*, Sheldon Harnick's "Boston Beguine," depicted a haughty "bachelor stenographer's" near-seduction in the Boston Common.

Raised in Henryetta, Oklahoma, Ghostley could hardly have landed in a stranger setting when she debuted at the Bon Soir in 1951. Jimmie Daniels, Mae Barnes, Norene Tate, and Garland Wilson had just been joined by the Three Flames, who combined expert piano, bass, and guitar playing with the salty streetcorner comedy that had made their 1947 recording of "Open the Door, Richard!" a hit. They kicked off the evening at ten o'clock with a half-hour set. "Serious" numbers quickly ran amok, as the trio spouted wisecracks to one another and to the audience ("Oh, you're all so sick, *sick*, SICK!"). The misty-eyed romance of the East Side rooms was reduced to a pile of tattered handkerchiefs:

I'm in love with you
But you're in love with Jim
Jim's in love with Joan
But Joan is gone on Slim
Slim just worships Faye
But Faye idolizes Fred
Fred dreams of the day
That he and Kaye will wed . . .
They're all so much in love
That they're about to flip their lids
And I'm convinced that they're a lot
of crazy, mixed-up kids . . .

"LET 'EM SUFFER!" yelled a Flame.

But they were also full of solemn romantic advice, as in "Stay on the Road of Love": "When the one you love begins to lie and cheat on you / Ain't no sense in cryin' / You start cheatin' too!"

Daniels and Tate followed, then came the headliner, who didn't go on until about eleven, even during the week. All the pot smoked backstage didn't slow the frenzied pace, and the atmosphere out front sometimes got out of control, as James Kirkwood remembered. "Usually the room was well patroled by the bartender and Jimmie Daniels, but one Saturday night was like fucking mayhem. The bar was seven deep, and the noise was unbelievable. During our act this midget was sitting at the front table with two tall ladies. He got very drunk and was trying to play with one of the broad's tits, and he fell off his chair. The two amazons picked him up and sat him back down. And we're supposed to do our act. Well, I was outraged.

"About twelve men were having steak dinners in the greenroom hosted by Phil Pagano, all very dignified and well dressed. We finished our act, and when you came off you went through the kitchen and past the greenroom. I said, 'Phil, who the fuck is running this? It's like a zoo out there! There's a little drunk midget trying to crawl down some broad's tits, and the bar is completely out of hand—they're all groping each other. What's going on? I'm not gonna do the second show unless somebody takes care of it. This place has turned into a toilet!'

"All the men looked up at me. Phil said, 'Jimmy, just wait a minute. I'll come out and talk to you.' Well, it turned out that they were the police and inspectors Phil paid off to keep the place legit, and they were all in there having their annual dinner."

Into this chaos came Ghostley. Until then she had held a number of jobs as a meat market checker, a typist at *Life* magazine, and an usherette. She had even worked for a detective agency, sitting at bars to check that bartenders weren't pocketing money or giving out free drinks.

She and her partner, pianist-composer G. Wood (his first name was George, which he hated), had just closed at the Fireside Inn on West 24th Street, where their admirers included Tennessee Williams and José Quintero. Ghostley, with her oversized poodle haircut and "one suspicious eye" (as Kaye Ballard called it), looked more like a loan officer in a New Hampshire bank than a club entertainer, and her appearance gave an outlandish dimension to her characters: a straitlaced society matron, for example, who gets lost on the Boston train system for hours and amuses herself by trying to seduce a parade of attractive commuters; or Mona Lisa, shown as a prostitute disappointed at da Vinci's intentions ("That long song and dance about ants in your pants to have me on canvas / Well, I never heard that one before in all my years as a poor senora / Working from street to street trying to make ends meet!"). "The material was so far out for the time," says Murray Grand. "Alice had studied opera, so G. wrote arrangements to use that big range of hers, like a very dramatic version of 'When Johnny Comes Marching Home.' She would start off sounding like a mezzo, then she'd be way up in the clouds. And since G. was from the South, some of the material was folk-oriented, like 'Red River Valley' and 'There's a Hole in My Bucket.' "

At that time Charlotte Rae had done months of backers' auditions for the upcoming *New Faces of 1952* and was slated to appear in it until comic Abe Burrows, director of the new musical *Three Wishes for Jamie*, hired her away and appointed Grand, composer of several *New Faces* numbers, as rehearsal pianist. "We weren't making any money with Leonard," says Grand. "He never paid anybody a penny. He called me, screaming 'YOU TRAITOR! HOW DARE YOU! And what am I going to do about Charlotte?'

" 'What are you screaming about? There's a perfectly good girl to do Charlotte's part. Her name is Alice Ghostley and she's down at the Bon Soir."

" 'I saw her. She's terrible.'

" 'She's not terrible, she's wonderful.'

" 'Well, I didn't like what she was singing.'

" 'I'll get her to sing something else.'

" 'Well, you better get her here fast!'

"And here it was, ten o'clock at night. 'Tonight?'

" 'TONIGHT!'

"I called Alice and said, 'Listen, would you like to audition for Leonard Sillman?' She was up to her elbows in hot water doing dishes in this terrible apartment on Third Avenue where she lived. She said, 'What am I going to sing?' I said, 'Guess Who I Saw Today.' " That song, a sophisticated tale of adultery from *New Faces*, is sung by a city housewife who coolly exposes her husband's infidelity as they sip martinis. Ghostley portrayed the spurned mate so touchingly that Sillman hired her at once.

"We all thought Charlotte was *the* singing comedienne until Alice arrived and just mopped up the town," says Grand. "She replaced Charlotte with everybody. Anybody who had any taste was mad for Alice."

Sillman plucked French singer-actor Robert Clary, later known as Le Beau on TV's *Hogan's Heroes*, from La Vie en Rose, an East 54th Street club owned by Monte Proser, proprietor of the Copacabana. That same room marked the New York debut of Eartha Kitt, for whom *New Faces* opened the door to national stardom. It also gave her her first signature song, "Monotonous," a blasé rundown of an existence so jaded that even a gift of the Black Sea as a swimming pool didn't excite her. Kitt was just the sort of original that Herbert Jacoby dreamed of finding, even if she proved to be anything but a dream offstage. The feline comparison was unavoidable: her widely set eyes burned forth from a light-skinned face, and her remarkably lithe body moved with the tension of a cat about to pounce. Her voice, a thin, nasal hum, had a tight vibrato and undercurrent of ferocity, even when it pretended to caress. Both her figure and vocal style would remain almost unchanged forty years after *New Faces*—as would her reputation as a tigress and no mere kitten.

Kitt blamed much of this on her childhood. Born on a South Carolina cotton plantation around 1926 (she claims to have no birth certificate), she spent her early years in poverty, picking cotton at a penny a pound. "When people come backstage and announce themselves as relatives of mine, they get the brushoff treatment," she told *Cue* (November 27, 1954). "I'll never forget how my own people treated me and my mother. I had reddish hair and I was too light. Everyone called me 'that yellow girl,' and nobody wanted me, Negro or white."

At about seven she moved to Harlem with an aunt and as a teenager joined dancer Katherine Dunham's dance troupe, touring London, Paris, Switzerland, and Scandinavia. In 1950 she performed her first nightclub act at a Paris room called Carroll's for eleven months. Fairly well known as a lesbian nightclub, Carroll's was run by "Frede," allegedly an ex-lover of Marlene Dietrich's. The waitresses, who wore double-breasted suits, and the rest of the staff adored Kitt. Returning home, however, she received an unexpected critical lashing at La Vie en Rose. *Variety* (December 19, 1951) injected a typical racist undertone:

> Miss Kitt seems to have plenty of confidence, but she lacks pace and needs to be sharply routined. Her voice is good enough, without being socko . . . She could conceivably build a rep along novelty lines, as a colored songstress who bases her catalog on French tunes . . . One number, "C'est Si Bon," indicates that she has a light touch and can work up a French chantoosey idea . . . Miss Kitt has a habit of dropping her voice during the introductions, and she shifts from the overhanging mike at inopportune moments to leave her inaudible.

"I was a horrible flop," she admitted in the *New York World-Telegram and Sun* (August 22, 1959): "I was so embarrassed, I didn't want to see anybody." Max Gordon recognized her potential, however, and booked her at the Vanguard in February 1952. Here, with a more balanced program, she was a smash. The *New York Herald Tribune*, like most of the press, admired her as a novelty but felt that "a vibrant Negress" should not attempt Cole Porter (February 21, 1952):

> Once she's gotten past Porter's "Just One of Those Things," she's dramatically appealing in the old English lament, "When I Lay Me Down to Die, Do-Die, Bury Me Where He Passes By." The sophisticated "Since I Fell for You" and "Live the Life" suit this Village cellar, and "I'm Gonna Live to Find Something to Sing About in My Soul" has the power to pull Vanguard customers to the edge of their chairs.

Gordon and Jacoby wasted no time in bringing her to the Angel. By now she had polished her act to a blinding gleam, calculating each purr and stretch so that no effect was left to chance. Her sex appeal was totally manufactured, yet both white and black men found it beguiling. Her unusual repertoire, combining sex-kitten special material, French, Spanish, and African songs, and American standards, yielded a dozen or so numbers that became her trademarks, among them "I Wanna Be Evil," "Santa Baby," "Uska Dara," and "C'est Si Bon."

Jacoby begrudgingly admired her onstage charisma, even while considering her style an affectation and privately mocking her French pronunciation and cultivated airs. He cared even less for her temperament, particularly her habit of snubbing VIPs who asked him to introduce them to her. Finally he began to make excuses rather than embarrass himself and his guests. "I believe she's changing her gown," he would say. "But have you met Anita Ellis?"

Others would not tolerate it. Mae Barnes had known Kitt since her Katherine Dunham days, but when Kitt snootily pretended to Alice Ghostley never to have heard of her, Barnes was outraged. "You tell Eartha Kitt that she's a goddamned liar," shouted Barnes, "and if you can't say it to her I'll write it down on a piece of paper and you give it to her!"

"A few nights later," says Barnes, "I was standing at the bar of the Bon Soir having a ball with the boys, when Eartha Kitt came over and said, 'Hi.' I said, 'Hi my ass!'

" 'I didn't know you were the one Alice was talking about.'

" 'How many Mae Barneses do you know?' "

But Kitt protested her icy reputation. "I'm not cold, just a little numb sometimes, courtesy of my childhood," she told *Cue*. A few years later she stated in the *New York World-Telegram and Sun*, "I'd be a liar if I said I wasn't somewhat temperamental, but there's always a reason. I expect my friends to understand that and when I do something evil, to be able to forgive me." Jacoby did not have to suffer her behavior for long. After *New Faces* her price rose so high that he could never have afforded her, try though he did.

Harry Belafonte was another black performer who captivated white audiences at the Angel. Matinee-idol handsome at a time when there were no black matinee idols (besides himself, for a short period, and Sidney Poitier), he appeared in tight black pants and a half-buttoned shirt, and applied his soft, husky voice to folk songs, work chants, calypso tunes, and spirituals with a controlled fervor and a beat accentuated by his hands and body. Few folk singers, white or black, had such sensual appeal.

Born in the slums of New York to a Jamaican domestic and a seaman from Martinique, Belafonte grew up with an explosive resentment of his disadvantages in life, including his color; he was regularly beaten up by white neighborhood thugs. His performance in school suffered and he became angry and disaffected. "My mother's greatest victory was that she kept my brother and me out of jail," he told Irwin Ross in *Coronet* (May 1957). After two years of high school he joined the navy and decided to pursue acting after he was discharged.

Months of lessons and rounds produced nothing, and he wound up pushing a hand truck in New York's garment district.

His career as a singer began by accident when he sat in one night at the jazz club the Royal Roost and won a two-week engagement as a popular singer for $70 a week. He finished twenty-two weeks later at $225. But the pop song mainstream did not interest him much; he was lazy about learning new tunes and after about a year and a half called it quits. An effort to run a Village hamburger joint ended in bankruptcy, once more leaving Belafonte penniless. But when he teamed with Jack Rollins, one of the city's most sought-after agents and a major factor in the success of Nichols and May, Woody Allen, and other performers, he switched to his real love, folk and calypso music. Under Rollins's aegis he opened at the Village Vanguard in November 1951 and played for fourteen smash weeks. Then he moved up to the Angel, where he drove the elegant white women mad for four months.

The image of a sexy but unintellectual native boy seemed to bother him, however. In interviews he tried to mask his lack of education by using big words, often incorrectly. To Irwin Ross he reflected on his career longevity, postulating that he "would probably have lasted only five years—on a maximum mobilization basis." Criticized for a tendency to "hoke up" his nightclub material and to clown too much with the audience, he agreed that "there's been a delineation in the act that hasn't been good."

Well-delineated or not, by the mid-'50s Belafonte was earning almost $500,000 a year, racking up such hit records as "Matilda, Matilda" and "The Banana Boat Song." He seemed a natural for films and appeared in *Carmen Jones*, *Bright Road*, *Island in the Sun*, and others, but America was not ready for a black movie star. His TV spots were also relatively few; blacks didn't fit in with the laundered, antiseptic image that TV wished to present. In 1950s television, racism, sexism, and poverty were seldom portrayed as national crises, for most of America still did not view them as such. Blacks were rarely seen except as servants (Jack Benny's Rochester) or as stereotypes (Amos 'n' Andy). A 1956–1957 variety show hosted by Nat King Cole ended for lack of a sponsor; none would touch a series starring a black singer. So Belafonte, like Cole and Kitt, carved out his success through recordings and live appearances. His popularity at the Angel and the Vanguard was another reminder that whatever their snobberies, such rooms were above all a celebration of talent, black or white, and a haven for performers whom *Variety* and much of the country were content to pigeonhole as "novelties."

In 1950 the *New York Herald Tribune* named Herbert Jacoby "King of the Intimaries," placing him above even Monk as a talent spotter. He spent much of his time at other clubs scouting out potential Angel acts, but most of them came to him first.

Everyone seemed to know everyone else in his exclusive community, and each week somebody was sure to throw a party or brunch. Blue Angel acts were invited to all of them. The best host in this circle was John Latouche, who joined not only club and theatre people but sculptors, poets, architects, and painters for some of the most stimulating parties in New York.

Often these affairs were just what they seemed: a group of artists with similar ambitions enjoying one another's company. Latouche held a party game in which guests took turns describing, in ascending order, their five best sexual experiences. Tennessee Williams detailed bondage scenes, and Carol Channing's eyes widened as she expressed her love for "*biiiiig* men, with big torsos and biceps—football players." Kaye Ballard and Eudora Welty could be seen tiptoeing toward the door before their turns came.

At other times vitriol was hurled in many an undeserving face. Bagley recalls a Sunday brunch given by a top nightclub pianist-composer. "He was sitting at the piano entertaining some friends. He said to them, 'Now wait till you hear this piece of shit.' He reached over and took out a folio of songs from *The Golden Apple*, which was about to open at the Phoenix Theatre. He started to play 'Lazy Afternoon,' one of the most beautiful songs I'd ever heard and probably the best song John Latouche, who happened to be gay, had written. But this man was making fun of it. 'Who does *she* think *she* is?' he kept asking."

Writers were even more rivalrous. Considering the number of revues produced in the '50s and all the club acts in need of material, it might seem as if there were plenty of work to go around; but the supply far exceeded the demand. A revue producer might receive up to 150 submissions, and most club performers could not afford to spend much on material. Therefore even the best writers had to play for rehearsals, work as cocktail pianists, or find some other way to support themselves until steady TV or theatre work came along. According to Michael Stewart, whose superb nightclub comedy material led him toward a career as librettist for *Carnival*, *Hello, Dolly*, and *42nd Street*, "Material of all sorts was sold for about one hundred dollars apiece or one hundred-fifty on a good day, often paid in installments. I always had a sale before going to Europe, and numbers went for a great deal less, sometimes as little as fifteen dollars. Even at that price one had to go down to the clubs, usually at four in the morning, to talk to the performers and change lines that were not working. How I ever found the money to visit those clubs I will never know, but a beer was less than a dollar in those days, and one usually stayed at the bar."

The larger supper clubs were enjoying their own heyday in the early '50s as venues for established stars, who took sumptuous advantage of their big stages and orchestras. At the Plaza's Persian Room were Jean Sablon, Jane Froman, Celeste Holm, and Lisa Kirk; the Cotillion Room of the Hotel Pierre presented Nelson Eddy, June Havoc, Yma Sumac, Gisele MacKenzie, Mimi Benzell, and Hildegarde. The Versailles became famous as the headquarters of Edith Piaf and Kay Thompson, as did the Copacabana for Jimmy Durante, Joe E. Lewis, Danny Thomas, Billy Daniels, and ex-Met opera star Helen Traubel. And at the Empire Room (formerly the Wedgwood Room) of the Waldorf-Astoria, Maurice Chevalier, Peter Lind Hayes and Mary Healy, Patachou, Dolores Gray, and Gloria DeHaven held forth. DeHaven's 1952 engagement unearthed a discovery of its own. Wrote Douglas Watt in the *New Yorker* (February 9, 1952):

> Maybe I had better mention that before Miss De Haven comes on, a skinny dancer named Bob Fosse, with wild eyes and unruly blond hair, taps and runs and leaps his way around the floor with astonishing energy. He is still young enough to be in an imitative frame of mind, and in the course of his exhibition he imitates Chaplin's walk and, hatless but with cane, Fred Astaire's "Top Hat" dance. The night I saw him, he even read, in an immature voice, a scene, originally done by Gene Kelly, from William Saroyan's "The Time of Your Life." He really shouldn't talk at all, but dancers in supper clubs have been growing remarkably garrulous lately (maybe it's because dancers don't have a chance to get listened to anyplace else) and I suppose Fosse is just going along with the tide.

But a young singer or comic who needed less floor space usually longed for the Blue Angel. Jacoby was inundated with auditions and could therefore be as selective as he wished. Auditioning for him was no pleasure. Whereas Julius Monk laughed at and applauded even mediocre acts, Jacoby glowered at the best as welcomingly as Count Dracula. Recalls Dorothy Loudon, who auditioned for him in 1950 and 1951, "I remember Herbert getting up in the middle of one of my songs and saying, 'This is supposed to be funny?' "

What he wanted was star quality. Not for him the homogeneously pretty singers of the day, who sat on stools and sang ballads in a dreamy but lackluster fashion. Instead he sought out such vocalists as Felicia Sanders, later known for her intense, emotive style, similar to her idol Edith Piaf's. Sanders spent her whole career in nightclubs. She dreamed of a serious singing role on Broadway and in 1964 almost got her wish when producer Claire Nichtern announced plans to star her in *Sparrow*, a musical based on Piaf's life. It never materialized. In the '70s she tried to assemble a Piaf show herself but died of cancer before completing it.

Sanders sang with big bands and on radio in the '40s but abandoned this to become a Hollywood housewife and mother. The life of a homemaker bored her, and in 1950 she got a job dubbing film vocals. This led to an engagement at the Bandbox, a club on the Sunset Strip where Bobby Short was performing, and to a contract to record a brief vocal chorus on "The Song from Moulin Rouge (Where Is Your Heart?)," arranged and conducted by Percy Faith. Sanders finished in about a half hour and left.

Within weeks the record had sold a million copies. Although it did not earn her much money (her contract called for scale, with no royalties) or make her a star, it launched a twenty-year career in nightclubs. Jacoby booked her in 1953, admiring the fact that here was a *woman* singer, not a girl singer (she was then thirty-two), with natural poise and showbiz savvy. More important, Sanders had the power to touch audiences and to excite them. She and husband Irving Joseph, her gifted accompanist and arranger, tried to bring a Piafian approach to such ballads as "When the World Was Young," "Come Rain or Come Shine," and "It Might As Well Be Spring." Sanders even modeled her appearance after Piaf's by dressing in plain, high-necked black dresses and wearing her hair in a poodle cut. Her penchant for drama occasionally went too far—detractors laughed at the tear that rolled down her cheek night after night during the same phrase of "This Nearly Was Mine" or "Music, Maestro, Please!"—but her combination of vulnerability and bravado kept most listeners on the edge of their seats. Hecklers were no match for her. One night a drunk started to sing along with her at the top of his lungs. Instead of starting to cry (as most girl singers would) she stopped the music, turned to him, and said, "Oh, do you like to sing? Good. Why don't you come up on stage with me? We'll do a duet." He sat in silence for the rest of the show.

In the spring of 1952 Anita Ellis, another superb singer, debuted at the Angel. For much of the '40s Ellis had provided the "ghost voice" for Rita Hayworth and other nonsinging film stars. A naturally dynamic performer with sex appeal and star quality of her own, Ellis unfortunately had none of Sanders's dauntless confidence; chronic stage fright limited her appearances and led to an early retirement in 1960.

In 1973 she returned with a seven-week booking at Michael's Pub, an East Side club, and won greater publicity and attention than ever before. She cut two albums, became the subject of a television documentary, made some infrequent but highly touted appearances, and even found herself dubbed a "legend" by the press.* By now she had grown into a more subdued singer who gave her material an art song quality, but at the Angel she was theatrical, uninhibited, and sexy, with a velvety voice and control that enabled her to sing high *piano* tones with ease and to take four bars of a ballad in one breath.

The sister of Broadway's Larry Kert, Ellis was petite and buxom, with shoulder-length brown hair, big blue eyes, and a Marilyn Monroe sort of sexiness—not always subtle but hair-raisingly effective. During "I Loves You, Porgy" from *Porgy and Bess* she choreographed the phrase "when he take hol' of me with his hot han' " by rubbing her right hand across the thigh of her skintight electric blue sequined gown. Eartha Kitt's purrs and slinky movements were familiar at the conservative Blue Angel, but to find such sex appeal in a singer of Ellis's musicality and taste was a surprise.

* Her 1978 concert at Lincoln Center's Alice Tully Hall could have sold out five times, but Ellis was too petrified to think of repeating it. "That afternoon Miss Tully called me and said, 'Can you do two tonight?' I said, 'Two? I can't even do one!' "

Her repertoire included such standards as Cole Porter's "You Do Something to Me" and "What Is This Thing Called Love?" and Rodgers and Hart's "Wait Till You See Him," plus many offbeat numbers almost nobody sang: "The World Is in My Arms," a Burton Lane–Yip Harburg song from the Al Jolson musical *Hold on to Your Hats;* "Roller Coaster Blues" by Marshall Barer and Dean Fuller (a none too oblique song about oral sex); the Gershwins' "I Ain't Got No Shame"; and others identified with her to this day.

Ellis was one of the few nightclub singers with legitimate musical training. Born in Montreal in 1920, she graduated from the Cincinnati College of Music, majored in music and psychology at UCLA, and studied voice extensively, including opera. At sixteen she became a radio singer in Hollywood and in the mid-'40s began to dub the singing voices of Hayworth, Vera-Ellen, and Jeanne Crain in such films as *Gilda* (in which she introduced "Put the Blame on Mame"), *Belle of New York*, *Three Little Words*, and *The Lady from Shanghai.* She cherished the privacy and anonymity of the studio and could match the vocal inflections of these actresses so closely that few noticed the difference—including, in one case, the actress herself. Bud McCreery, who worked as an MGM group singer in the '40s, remembers an example. "Vera-Ellen, as all the world knows, was a dancing fool but certainly not a singing fool. However, Vera wanted to do her own singing on a number entitled 'Come On, Papa.' Now, there is a crack in the human voice between chest tones and head tones. Every note Vera hit was in that crack. I don't know how she did it. The musical director did several takes with her and several with Anita while we backup boys ooh'd and aah'd, and then played them back to prove to Vera how wrong she was. With a bright, victorious smile, she said, 'See? You can't tell the difference!' MGM could tell the difference, so the voice you hear is Anita's—not Vera's crack."

Screen musicals, like radio, began to fade in the early '50s, and Ellis flew to New York to find a new direction. "I didn't come here to sing in clubs. Radio was over, and I came to appear on *Your Show of Shows*. When I got out on that stage, in a big enormous theatre with millions of people watching, I couldn't do it. But I stayed in town. Luther Henderson, who had played piano in the first trio at the Angel, suggested I try a nightclub. We walked around town and found one on East 54th Street. He said, 'How do you like this little place, La Vie en

Rose'—all red plush. I said, 'Terrific.' We went inside and met Monte Proser, and Luther told him he wanted to present me. Monte knew of my radio work and said, 'OK, let me hear you sing. Not on the radio. Now.' I sang something and he said, 'You start in two weeks.' "

Ellis opened on January 6, 1952. Jacoby heard her and instantly booked her at the Angel. She stayed ten weeks, discovering just how torturous it was to perform live, even before warm audiences. "I could never get up on that stage. They'd have to pull me, push me—it was horrendous. Every once in a while I'd realize I was up there, and I'd have to stop. But the trio—Mundell Lowe, the guitarist, was there the first few weeks, and that was thrilling. And to listen to Jimmy Lyon play the piano and to Milt Hinton, the bassist, was one of the joys of being there. I'd bring songs no one had ever heard of. They were given to me by Frank Loesser and Ira Gershwin and Burton Lane and the Kern people.

"But nightclubs were not my home. Radio was my home. The privacy—oh, I just worshiped it. I went into analysis to try and find out what caused this awful stage fright. And I haven't found out."

Ellis learned that one way to control her nerves was to have a few drinks beforehand. Jacoby forbade the bartenders and waiters to serve her before a show, as he did whenever he thought a performer might become drunk. He had never forgotten the case of a female singer-pianist who had performed regularly in the '40s at the Monkey Bar and other lounges until her drinking problem got out of control. Around 1952 Jacoby heard that she was on the wagon and booked her cautiously. Recalls Bart Howard, by that time the Angel's emcee and intermission pianist, "She came out of her dressing room and stood at the foot of the stairs waiting to go on. I asked her if everything was all right, and she said yes. I went onstage to introduce her, and as she stepped up and sat at the piano I walked off. Then I heard a big commotion. I looked back, and there she was lying under the piano."

Jacoby was determined that this would never happen again. One evening just before showtime he stopped Ben Bagley on his way up to Ellis's dressing room.

"Where are you going with that rock and rye?"

Bagley, then a somewhat naive twenty-two-year-old, answered, "Miss Ellis needs it for her head cold."

"You turn right around and bring that back to the bar!"

"Herbert was worried that she'd go on drunk," says Bagley. "She never did. The booze relaxed her enough to give a great performance, but Herbert never understood that."

Her appearances grew fewer and fewer, an important component in the making of this particular legend. Composers regretted this even more than audiences. Friends warned her that "I Loves You, Porgy" would never work in a club, but she insisted on trying it. Wrote Douglas Watt in the *New Yorker*, "Her steamy version of 'I Loves You, Porgy' is a minor masterpiece of singing and acting." Ira Gershwin called it the best version of his song he'd ever heard, and Richard Rodgers told Jacoby he had never heard it performed so well.

Ellis's Blue Angel repertoire is preserved on her 1956 Epic album "I Wonder What Became of Me." Regrettably the producer commissioned Davis Grubb, author of the novel *The Night of the Hunter*, to string the songs together with a melodramatic, B movie–style narrative ("When your heart dies . . . why doesn't the rest of you die too?"). Skipping the monologues makes it clear why so many authorities placed Ellis at the top of a formidable list of café singers.

Even when Jacoby chose a singer closer to the image of the pretty young canary, he did so with an eye for the unusual. Barbara Cook had neither Sanders's fearlessness nor Ellis's anxieties but a midwesterner's sense of wide-eyed wonderment at getting to sing in such a swank place. After two brief engagements the apple-cheeked blonde became one of the most popular musical comedy ingenues of her generation, lifting her warm soprano voice in *Candide*, *The Music Man*, *She Loves Me*, and other productions. Not until 1974 did Cook become a full-time nightclub and concert performer, still sounding, as Douglas Watt had written in 1951, like a "little lamb."

Another youngster who came to Manhattan to seek her fortune in the theatre, Cook arrived from Atlanta in 1948 at age twenty-one. "I came with my mother for a two-week visit, and I packed everything I owned. She said, 'Why are you taking so much?' I said, 'Because I'm really gonna stay and see what I can do in New York!' She was very upset when she saw that I meant it. I *loved* New York. I couldn't believe I was here. After my mother went home I stayed with her friends, who lived near Columbia University, and that area was glorious. It was very neighborhoody. People used to say, 'If you think this is nice you should have been here twenty-five years ago,' but that's always been going on, I'm sure. I didn't go out much at night because I was so poor, but still I thought I was in heaven."

Composer Vernon Duke did his best to open doors for her, and recommended she sing at Camp Tamiment, a summer resort in the Poconos where a remarkable welter of talent performed every year. In 1950 Max Gordon heard her there and invited her to call Jacoby when she returned. After her audition Jacoby asked, "Can you start in three days?" She said, "You bet!"

Cook not only sang but looked like a little lamb in those days, with her childlike smile and blonde hair tied back with a ribbon. Beneath her renditions of "Little Girl Blue" and "The Boy Next Door" lay an uncluttered, heartrending quality that sounded like a sensitive youngster's first expression of love and heartache. According to Jimmy Lyon, "She didn't have an act. All she did was stand there and sing ballads in that gorgeous voice, but everybody adored her. Herbert said, 'I think this one might go on to something,' which is as effusive as he ever got."

Cook seemed not at all intimidated by her surroundings. "Ignorance is bliss, I guess. Just the fact that I was singing anywhere in New York and that Walter Winchell was putting me in his column—that was high cotton, as we say."

IN ALL, it was a storybook time for café singers. The Broadway musical still gave them volumes of material, as did a multitude of aspiring Broadway composers who were eager to have their songs performed. New York teemed with pianists and accompanists who had a rich knowledge of popular songs—a boon for singers in search of repertoire.

One of these musicians was Bart Howard, who hosted and played at the Angel from 1951 to 1959. A blonde, impeccably dressed man who spoke and carried himself with supreme elegance, Howard, like most of his colleagues, came from an unsophisticated background—in his case, Burlington, Iowa. Howard began to study the piano as a child, and dreams of big-city life so preoccupied him that he left home at sixteen to play with dance bands and in roadhouses. At twenty-two he came to New York, accompanying Ray Bourbon and playing solo at 1-2-3 and other lounges. "My dinner jacket got to be my uniform. Everybody went out at night, all the time. If you liked a show, you saw it two or three times. You'd say, 'What should we do tonight? Oh, let's go see *One for the Money* again.' And you could do it, for three or four dollars a seat."

Mabel Mercer was the first to sing one of his songs, "If You Leave Paris," and after stints at Spivy's Roof and other clubs Howard became her accompanist at Tony's in 1946, remaining with her until the room was torn down in 1949. Mercer introduced dozens of his songs to the singers and fans there, and by the time he reached the Angel he had developed a sizable following. Jacoby hired him for $193 a week and never offered him a raise in eight years. Howard never asked for one; it was enough to have access to the best café singers in town, most of whom were eager for his sort of material, and to other top figures in show business. "I kept meeting wonderful people every night. One didn't go to the table unless asked, but in the lounge I'd always get to meet them."

He also needed the money. Special material writers sold numbers at a flat fee, but composers such as Howard simply wrote songs and hoped to get them sung and eventually recorded. "Steady jobs were hard to come by for musicians in Bart's category," says singer Portia Nelson. "You either worked on a show or played piano for cocktails and rehearsals." In 1951 Rosemary Clooney cut a single of his song "On the First Warm Day" that earned him $7,500. Most other singers asked for "In Other Words," which Mercer, Nelson, and Sylvia Syms had claimed for their own after Felicia Sanders introduced it at the Angel and Kaye Ballard on record in 1953. He wrote it in response to his publisher's plea for a simpler song: why did he always bring such convoluted lyrics? It began with a lovely verse that most singers dropped:

Poets often use many words to say a simple thing,
It takes thought and time and rhyme to make a poem sing,
With music and words I've been playing,
For you I have written a song,
To be sure that you'll know what I'm saying
I'll translate as I go along . . .

That song would become a hit only when Peggy Lee sang it on the *Ed Sullivan Show* in 1961 and recorded it under what most listeners believed was the actual title, "Fly Me to the Moon."

"I used to keep copies at the Blue Angel. I just kept throwing them out to people. In those days all the young singers were given record contracts to see if any of them surfaced, and they all did my song. They thought it was so chic."

Until then Howard had to settle for modest success as a composer of ballads that seldom left New York. His colleagues admired him as a writer and as a distinguished, elegant man who stood for all the good taste and refinement that the Blue Angel symbolized. Says singer-pianist-composer Charles DeForest, who played at the lounge in 1954, "Bart is so erudite and classy, he just looked wonderful and sounded wonderful and epitomized what you hoped the Blue Angel would be."

Besides working as pianist and emcee he operated the lights; functioned as taskmaster when things ran behind schedule; sometimes advised Jacoby, who respected his opinion; and in general went far beyond the call of duty. "I was the backstage psychiatrist, too. They all had problems. Kaye Ballard used to say before she went on, 'Oh, tell me I'm good!' " And he helped the severely myopic Anita Ellis down the stairs from her dressing room. "I'd practice a lot of Bart's songs," says Ellis, "then I'd be afraid to sing them, because he was there. 'In Other Words' was my favorite. They were always about something so sensual, and they reminded me of art songs. Steve Sondheim's are more or less there too. But I like Bart's songs better than Steve's, although I love Steve. I shouldn't say better—they're different. Steve's songs are much harder. Bart's can become part of you. He leaves room for that to happen. Not so with Steve."

Few composers in his field glorified romance or mourned its failure as passionately as Howard. Most of his songs spoke of commitment, of one great love that lasts forever, or of the crushing pain when it ends. They were perfect cameos of a time when relationships and stability meant a great deal, and when the thought of spending a lifetime with someone seemed so appealing:

Let my love be the love you remember
Let my heart be the heart you keep
Let my face be the face you dream of
Every time you smile in your sleep . . .

["Year After Year"]

His love songs had a fragile quality: a sense of losing yourself in the first flush of romance or of reaching the defenseless moment when it crumbles. One lover begs another not to leave Paris, for the stars will fade and the sun won't rise; another remembers a fourth-floor walk-up as "a hop, skip and jump to the stars" when shared with the right person.

But not all his songs were dramatic. He wrote about romping on a hillside on the first warm day in May, gave teasing invitations in "Sell Me" and "Let Me Love You," and said loving goodbyes in "Thank You for the Lovely Summer" and "Take Care of Yourself." Because his songs seemed intended for spaces as intimate as a bedroom or a candlelit dinner table, small clubs were their ideal setting. Often these rooms were just as intimate, especially after midnight.

ANOTHER BLUE ANGEL FIXTURE was the husband-and-wife piano team of Eadie and Rack. Between 1949 and 1953 they became as much a trademark as the angel that hung above the stage; their sound lifted patrons' spirits from the moment they walked in. They specialized in showtunes and could improvise duets on request from their encyclopedic repertoire. As their friend Bruce Laffey says, "They sat facing each other at twin uprights on either side of the swinging doors in back of the lounge, and Eadie never took her eyes off Rack as they played. He would change keys, he would change songs, and they never faltered."

Eadie was Eadie Griffith, a tall redhead who had spent most of the '30s touring with Babe Eagen and Her Hollywood Redheads, an all-girl orchestra. In 1942 she got a job playing and singing at the Café Gala, a club on the Sunset Strip in Hollywood with a distinct New York feeling, making it popular among displaced Manhattanites. Its emcee and host was John Walsh, an extremely handsome silver-haired man who sang obscure show music of the Mabel Mercer variety. In 1945 Eadie formed a piano team there with Rack, the former rehearsal pianist for *Panama Hattie*, *Louisiana Purchase*, and other Broadway shows. Rack was reportedly born in Texas as H. Godwin, with no actual first name until producer John Murray Anderson nicknamed him Rack, after Rachmaninoff. He and Eadie married, and in 1949 Jacoby brought them to New York for an unlimited engagement at the Blue Angel.

Between them Eadie and Rack knew almost every prominent theatrical and café figure on either coast, especially Beatrice Lillie, whom they accompanied in her one-woman show *An Evening with Beatrice Lillie*. They were so in demand socially and professionally that they had to devise a scheme to save at least one day a week for themselves. On Saturday night after work they checked into the Algonquin Hotel, where they spent Sunday in bed, watching TV and ordering room service. Everyone thought they were in the country.

Casual acquaintances marveled at their offstage harmony, but their relationship had a stormy underside. Rack was a homosexual and suffered from a drinking problem that placed a great strain on their marriage. "Eadie was like Gibraltar, very warm and very real," says Bruce Laffey, "but Rack was like a spoiled kid. He fell apart easily, and Eadie had to mother him like mad. It was very rough on her. He'd go out and get drunk and not come home, and suddenly my doorbell would ring at four in the morning. Finally Eadie said to me, 'Just call and let me know if he's there. I don't care where he is, so long as you call.' At one point she hired me to come over and keep him company all night. We'd play records and talk, and in the morning Eadie would get up and cook breakfast for us.

"Rack relied on her totally. She managed their careers all by herself—she arranged the jobs and got the PR, worked out their contracts, did everything. The only thing that kept them together was the fact that they loved each other very much."

Their marriage ended tragically in Detroit in 1957. "Eadie woke up in their hotel room in the middle of the night complaining of indigestion. Rack said, 'Well, stop eating doughnuts before you go to bed.' A couple of hours later he heard a very odd sound, and she was gone. She'd had a heart attack and died immediately."

Rack was on the phone for two hours, hysterical and almost incoherent. One of those he called was Lillie, then performing in *The Ziegfeld Follies* on Broadway. A young lady in the cast knew Rack, and Lillie sent her off to Detroit, paying all expenses. But there was no comforting him. He never quite recovered from the shock of Eadie's death and from the feeling that he might have prevented it, although through financial necessity he continued to play. Even though he had become unreliable, Herbert Jacoby invited him to work in the Blue Angel lounge. He quit after one night. Says Buster Davis, "He told Jacoby that every time he looked up he saw Eadie's face staring back at him."

UNTIL THE '70s, stand-up comedy remained primarily a man's field; with sex roles so arbitrarily defined, it was simply considered too uncouth for a woman. Ginger Rogers, guesting on *The Steve Allen Show* in 1960, pointed this out in a sketch that examined how the public might envision a female comic. Sashaying around her boudoir in a negligee and gazing into a hand mirror as she brushed her long blonde hair, Rogers tilted her head back and murmured through half-closed lips, "Good evening, ladies and germs."

But singing comediennes were common from the earliest days of vaudeville and musical comedy, which required both vocal and comedic skills. That rich tradition, which included Beatrice Lillie, Fanny Brice, Martha Raye, and Cass Daley, continued in cafés with Imogene Coca, Carol Burnett, Pat Carroll, Charlotte Rae, Bibi Osterwald, and Dorothy Loudon, among many others. Most of them were not too pretty, a little overweight, short on sex appeal, and determined to use these failings to their advantage. They were a tough breed of women, struggling to succeed in a field where men did the hiring and made the business decisions. They fretted constantly over whose act was the best, who received the longest bookings for the highest fees, and who made the most frequent TV and theatre appearances. More than other entertainers they felt constant pressure to stay "on" and to keep everyone amused. Many longed for dramatic roles but were seldom taken seriously as straight actresses, even though several had that capacity.

One of these was Charlotte Rae, widely considered the best singer-comedienne of the '50s. A short, plump woman with close-cut brown hair, tousled bangs, and the doting look of a Jewish mother, Rae is best known as star of the long-running TV comedy series *The Facts of Life*. But her club act, a montage of satirical songs, monologues, and parodies of female personalities, revealed the full range of her abilities. She could handle a wider variety of material than any other comedienne, much of it targeted at ladies who left themselves open for laughs—Kathryn Grayson, for example, whose bout at the Hollywood Bowl with a buzzing fly as she tried to sing Victor Herbert's "Italian Street Song" received a merciless ribbing. She also portrayed a thinly disguised Zsa Zsa Gabor lecturing on life, love, and the secret of glamour ("Many many times when I am little girl Mama take me on her knee and say, 'Lala—whenever you get divorced, let your husband keep the children, but always keep the house!' ").

Rae's warm, flexible voice enabled her to sing ballads charmingly, but she used it mostly for comedy. One of her few straight numbers was Rodgers and Hart's "Why Can't I?" a wistful plea for romance from their 1929 show *Spring Is Here*. That song, like much of her material, poked fun at the comically lovelorn, a group Rae was visually well equipped to portray. But no one could deny her professionalism. "Charlotte was very consistent and very reliable, which is what made her so valuable in nightclubs," says Ben Bagley. "If there were six people in the audience and three were sleeping, she'd come out and give an opening night performance."

Besides the short-lived *Three Wishes for Jamie*, Rae appeared in the classic 1954 Theatre de Lys production of *The Threepenny Opera* (as Mrs. Peachum) and in Ben Bagley's *The Littlest Revue*, which closed after a limited run, despite her exceptional notices. Nevertheless that was a happier experience than *Li'l Abner*, Johnny Mercer and Gene de Paul's Broadway adaptation of the perennial comic strip. Rae was signed to play Mammy Yokum, but shortly afterward Mercer and producer Norman Panama decided the ideal actress for the part was Billie Hayes, a pint-sized blonde who had just closed in *New Faces of 1956*.

"They did everything they could to get Charlotte to leave," says Bagley. "Johnny Mercer decided he absolutely loathed her and her performance. They cut her one song and made her share a tiny dressing room with Julie Newmar and Tina Louise, who had smaller roles. Charlotte thought they were idiots and tied a rope across her corner of the room and hung a blanket from it. She left instructions at the stage door that visitors were to go directly to her dressing room. She wanted everyone to witness her humiliation. I was embarrassed because she was insulting these broads, but she was right. She refused to leave for a long time, but finally she couldn't stand it anymore, and they got Billie Hayes. She was wonderful, but I can't say she was any better than Charlotte."

Such were the knocks that made so many female performers tougher than their male colleagues. In general, however, Rae was nobody's fool. "This is a strong woman," says Bagley. "If you cross Charlotte you'll be on her shit list forever, and she's going to behave in a very nasty way." "She was hard as nails," says one producer. "She told me once, 'I don't have any friends and I don't want any.' She hated other woman performers, and they hated her." Onstage at the

Bon Soir, Bibi Osterwald had her say about a routine in which Rae pulled a sequin off her dress, licked it, stuck it on her décolletage, and winked. "You think that's funny, you think that's class, right? Honey, that is *disgusting*!"

"One day," according to Bagley, "Charlotte approached Bea Arthur at a rehearsal of *Threepenny Opera* and said, 'Tell me your troubles, dear. I can see you're a very troubled woman.' Bea said, 'Oh, fuck off! Just fuck off!' "

Bud McCreery, who wrote a delightful monologue for Rae entitled "We Who Are About to Diet," recalls that "Charlotte seemed to worry a great deal about what 'the other girls' were doing. Pat Carroll was at One Fifth Avenue, and Charlotte asked me if Pat's act were anything like hers. I assured her there would never be any conflict, and she seemed somewhat mollified. But then she added, squinting in the classic manner of Maggie suspecting that Jiggs might be sneaking out for corned beef and cabbage, 'Well, she'd better not get in *my* way!' "

Rae's fans were sometimes dismayed to meet the woman who displayed such good-natured warmth onstage. "She had no time for admirers who approached her between shows or on the street to tell her how wonderful she was," Bagley says. "We were in a bakery once, and when she got to the counter the woman began to tell her how much she'd enjoyed her performance in some TV show. Charlotte said, 'Just give me the bread, please.' I was so embarrassed."

Just as comedy was generally seen as a man's field, café singing, with its tender expressions of vulnerability and longing, remained feminine territory. Men usually sang in quartets such as the Four Lads, who made their New York debut at the Ruban in 1950. Later they were signed by Columbia Records and cut two of the biggest hits of the '50s, "Standing on the Corner [Watching All the Girls Go By]" and "Moments to Remember."

Being a pianist, Julius Monk had a special fondness for singers and liked them to wear black dresses with pearls or a rhinestone brooch, to pin up their hair, and to sing Rodgers and Hart or Jerome Kern under a pale pink spotlight. One of his better canaries was Ellen Hanley, who in 1951 began a tempestuous marriage to Ronny Graham. A tall, willowy blonde, Hanley used her silvery soprano for a repertoire of mainly lesser-known Kern, Porter, and the like. An even finer voice belonged to June Ericson, an exquisite soprano whose high *pianissimi* in such ballads as Rodgers and Hart's "The Blue Room" and "A Ship Without a Sail" brought the room to a hush.

The apparent glamour of this vocation led many an unglamorous girl to try it herself. It looked so easy—most of the time you just sat on a stool or leaned against the piano. Even male comics were a little jealous. As James Kirkwood complained to Lee Goodman, "Jesus, they come out with their tits hanging out, all made up, in lovely gowns, with this beautiful background music, but *we* really have to work!"

So no one could blame a few future comediennes for trying their hands as chanteuses. One of them was Beatrice Arthur, whose fame as the star of television's *Maude* and *The Golden Girls* eclipsed any memories of her brief career in clubs. "She came in as an ofay Lena Horne," says Julius Monk. "After two weeks I said, 'You're perfectly wonderful, but it has not been successful and I've got to fire you. And I recommend you do comedy." (Arthur's brown taffeta evening gown with ruffles, probably one of the ugliest outfits ever worn on a café stage, may have influenced his decision.)

He cured the same identity crisis with Dorothy Loudon, whose long career in clubs and shows peaked with a 1977 Tony Award for her portrayal of Miss Hannigan in the musical *Annie.* Loudon auditioned for Monk as a stand-up singer after many months spent as a saloon singer-pianist. She arrived in a red knit suit with matching beanie. Recalls Monk, "She opened—I thought mistakenly—with

It cost me a lot
But there's one thing that I've got
It's my man . . .

"I fell out of my seat. Dorothy almost had a stroke. She meant it seriously. And it was almost second to Bea Arthur. I screamed with laughter."

Today Loudon says, "When you're in Claremont, New Hampshire, where I grew up, you look at movies and see women sitting at bars with a drink in one hand and a cigarette in the other, talking very intimately with someone. And suddenly the lights go down, and someone comes out in this gown and sings *one* song, and it's always something like 'My Man.' I thought, 'Well, that's what they want to hear.' "

Monk hired her that day to do comedy, not torch singing, so she had to prepare an act. "Don't worry about anything," Norman Paris told her, "we'll fix it." Paris not only assembled her act but also became the immediate love of her life. "While I was in college my roommate had taken me to the Ruban, and that's when I first heard him. I'd never heard *anything* like that trio. Accompaniment is an art, and Norman was an artist. He looked like a little toy. He had great big hazel eyes and this angelic smile, especially when he was playing." Unfortunately their love affair did not culminate in marriage until 1971. For the sake of his children Paris told Loudon he would not get a divorce until his youngest daughter had graduated from high school.

Her act combined lighthearted pop tunes such as "True Blue Lou" and "You Make Me Feel So Young" with corny turn-of-the-century or vaudeville ditties—"A Bird in a Gilded Cage," "I May Not Be a Real Old Red Hot Mama (But I'm Getting Warmer All the Time)"—that she made gleeful fun of. Her Rabelaisian sense of humor transformed those creaky numbers into high camp, and eventually she devoted most of her act to them.

That disdainful, sarcastic style gave a clear reflection of her personality, in and out of character. Ben Bagley recalls a party of tourists who came into the Ruban in the middle of her act. "When she finished Dorothy said to them, 'Now, if you're going to leave, leave now. Whatever you do, don't get up and go while I'm doing my next show. I hate to see people's backs. I've got a whole new show—stay, you'll love it.'

"Well, they didn't seem to like Dorothy too much, so they stayed for the other performers and then tried to leave before she came on again. But they had trouble getting a waiter to take their money, and sure enough, Dorothy had already started when they got up to leave. She let them have it. 'Oh, God, there they go! I knew it! Where are you people from? You're from out of town, right? I wonder how I knew that!' And on and on. You just don't treat an audience like that. Julius was standing on the side looking up to the heavens."

No such arrogance came from one of Monk's most prized "discoveries," actress Pat Carroll, whom he groomed as a singer-comedienne. During the '60s and '70s this bright, articulate woman appeared frequently as a game show panelist, in lieu of the theatre work that eluded her and many other middle-aged female performers. "Very few producers are interested in an aging, overweight actress," Carroll said. So in 1979 she commissioned her own one-woman play based on an artist she admired, *Gertrude Stein Gertrude Stein Gertrude Stein*. The show, which opened off-Broadway, toured the country, and was televised by PBS, presented Stein in an intimate, ruminative autobiographical monologue, showing a national audience that Carroll was not only erudite but a sensitive actress as well.

Her early training in this sort of one-to-one communication came at the Ruban, when the future "dowager queen of the game shows," as she called herself, was slim, petite, and looked like a girl scout. Born in Shreveport, Louisiana, in 1927, Carroll moved to Manhattan in 1950 to become an actress. That year she won a role in *Talent '50*, a revue with sketches by the young Michael Stewart.

"Julius Monk came to see me," says Carroll, "and asked me to come to the Ruban Bleu. I didn't understand a thing any performer was doing—it was all so chic and grandiose. But I realized Julius was offering me a job."

Carroll called upon Stewart and Jim Wise, a young teacher and songwriter who later composed the score for Broadway's *Dames at Sea*, to write for her. Carroll loved material with an intellectual theme, but most of her numbers—"My Best Girlfriend's Very Best Boyfriend's My Best Boyfriend Now," "Look *Vogue*, Look *Glamour*, Look *Harper's Bazaar*"—were just the opposite, and on opening night she bombed. Uneasy in her new role as nightclub entertainer, the rather grand young lady amused nobody but Monk. "I saw myself as an actress, working in the *theatah*," she admits. "I assembled my act out of sheer ignorance."

Monk diplomatically suggested that she polish her act out of town. "An agent booked a roadhouse in Worcester, Massachusetts, where I had played stock, so I thought I was queen of the ball," she says. "I brought my own accompanist and ended up giving him most of my salary. The hook-nosed chap who owned the place said, 'Hey gal, you'll be the emcee.' I'd never emceed anything but varsity shows at Immaculate Heart High School, but I thought, 'I know how to do that.' Well, I was so grand and so non-emceeish that they threw dinner rolls at me. Boy, did I learn fast!" Humbler now, she moved on to Boston for a booking in a club across the street from the Copley Plaza, where Hildegarde was appearing. "She was billed as The Incomparable Hildegarde, so I called myself The Inconsequential Pat Carroll."

She returned to the Ruban, this time to better response. Her colleagues adored her, sensing that beneath her uneven act lay a uniquely gifted actress-comedienne. Her best material put these skills to work. For a takeoff on Edith Sitwell's *Facade*, Carroll played a recording of William Walton's score, chanting a funny spoof of the poet's facile exercises in polyphony and internal rhyme. Her most memorable moments came in a Mike Stewart monologue based on the O. Henry short story "The Gift of the Magi." Stewart transposed the tale to Brooklyn with a veneer of high comedy, but as it progressed Carroll drew her listeners into a serious and touching mood. She told the story in the first person, as the girl who shears her flowing hair to buy her husband a watch fob—unaware that he has sold his watch to buy her a hair clip. "I had this beautiful long golden hair that went all the way down to the floor. And my father always said to me, 'Della, the man who marries you will never go without cigar butts!' "

Even after several years in New York, Carroll still retained much of the Louisiana-bred childlike naïveté that gave that portrait its vulnerability. In those days it was still possible to live in New York a few years without losing all of one's small-town attitudes. Carroll recalls her Mike Stewart monologue in which Mae West tells the Rapunzel story. The girl asks the witch (West) to take out her dirty Scrabble board, and they begin to play. The piece closes with the line, "Sit down here, honey, and close that window. It's colder in here than a witch's . . . Your move, honey."

To this former English major, Rapunzel was a lot more familiar than Mae West. "Ellen Hanley came into my dressing room and said, 'Pat, may I ask you something? You don't really know what you're saying in that last part of Rapunzel, do you?'

"What do you mean?"

"What does 'witch's . . .' mean?"

" 'Witch's . . .?' "

"Why do you pause after that word and say, 'Your move, honey?' "

"Because it was on the piece of paper."

"You really don't know that comes from a saying, do you—'It's colder in here than a witch's tit'?"

"I started to blush. I never thought to ask what that pause meant."

Before the earthy Village Vanguard audience, Carroll did not fare as well. "For six weeks I walked off to no applause. Finally I got mad and took two belts of brandy and told them who was boss, and it got better." At the Blue Angel, Herbert Jacoby hired Ben Bagley to liven up her repertoire. "Pat had all these terrible songs that weren't funny and had no payoffs, but she owned them and insisted on using them. Eventually I said, 'Pat, the only way you can save this act is by coming out at the beginning and announcing, 'Hi, my name is Pat Carroll—a lot of charm and no laughs.' And I think she actually did."

Gradually she moved into television, winning regular spots on *The Red Buttons Show*, *Your Show of Shows*, and *Caesar's Hour* starring Sid Caesar, which earned her an Emmy as best supporting actress. "I was thrilled to make a living doing only TV, because I never really felt that I fit into clubs. By this time I was engaged and I did not see a life of playing saloons. I knew it was not a commercial act. Years later I tried it again at a club in south Philadelphia, and they threw things at me. It reminded me of the roadhouse in Worcester. As my fiancé said, I probably had the worst act in the history of show business, but I seemed to enjoy it so much. He said, 'Audiences liked you because you looked like you were having such a good time.' "

High spirits could not salvage every act, even that of Jane and Gordon Connell, one of the most consistently employed couples in the theatre as well as one of the longest wed (since 1948). In 1966 Jane carved her own niche in Broadway history when she created the role of Agnes Gooch, a prim spinster housekeeper persuaded to kick up her heels, in *Mame*.

The Berkeley-born couple spent the late 1940s and early '50s working with the Strawhatters, a San Francisco revue group. Jane acted and sang, while Gordon arranged, played the piano, and acted in a few sketches. When the group came to New York in 1953, the Connells decided to stay. She got a survival job as a cashier at the Pottery Barn; he became a toy-store salesman—professions for which they at least looked the part, Jane with her short, wispy blonde hair and solicitous smile; Gordon with his teakettle ears, square jaw, and fatherly grin. "We went to all the nightclubs to investigate what was happening," says Jane. "We heard Alice Ghostley and G. Wood, and Charlotte Rae—we thought she was magnificent. I wrote asking for some of her numbers, and she wrote back, 'Darling, I'd sooner give you my husband than my material.' "

They went home in January 1954 to perform at San Francisco's Purple Onion, for which they threw together a makeshift act. It was made up mostly of Gordon's material, including Jane's portrayal of a hoydenish clubwoman giving a Wagner appreciation lecture, as well as "Boston Beguine" from *New Faces of 1952*—a number that outshone most of their own creations. After it received a huge ovation, Jane turned to Gordon on the stand and said, "Now why can't we write anything like that?"

Nevertheless they had a warmth and flair for entertaining akin to that of a suburban California couple in their own home, and they stayed a whole season. "We got into a coupe with a rumble seat and drove into North Beach every night," says Gordon. "It was the environment for the likes of a black folk singer by the name of Stan Wilson and a rising crazy with some pungent and savvy things to say about the political and social scene. He wore a sweater and was clinging to some collegiate image, and that was Mort Sahl.

"On the bill with us was Maya Angelou, who was singing a series of Caribbean songs and calypsos—'Sitting by the Ocean,' 'Shame and Scandal in the Family'—with great dramatic moves and lighting. She was wearing a Trinidadian sort of outfit—the skirt looked like a sheet with the side cut out, and it allowed her to flash an extraordinary set of limbs. She was six feet tall in her bare feet, and they were bare. She had close-cropped hair, and one hoop earring, a bracelet, and arms bare in a tank-top sort of blouse that allowed her to do those marvelous moves."

"Maya meant a lot to us," says Jane, "because it was the first time we'd ever been close to a black person. I had never been south, I had never known a Negro. At that time Berkeley was mostly lily-white. We were with Maya when the desegregation laws were passed, and she and Odetta toasted them at the bar.

"Pat Carroll saw us at the Onion and talked us into going back to New York. She thought Julius would want us. Some friends took up a collection of three hundred dollars to get us there. We left our baby with her grandparents and came back on spec. Pat was going on her honeymoon, and she told us we could stay in her apartment. I remember looking at her pad near the phone and there were things such as 'NBC-ten o'clock,' New York–type of things. This was only the second time we'd been to the city. I was walking once behind a woman whose kid was walking along the curb, one foot up, one foot down, and thinking of my little child at home. The woman said, 'I'm gonna cut off your foot if you don't stop that!' Then I'd see a bum sitting on the street and think, 'My God, there's Gordon in a couple of years!' "

"We went over and auditioned for Julius," Gordon says. "Pat arranged it. We were about two-thirds of the way through, and he said, smoothing his mustache, 'Would you like to have a little tea?' We said yes. 'Do you think you could be ready by Thursday?' "

"Julius said, 'Darlings, you're going to turn New York upside down!' " remembers Jane. "It was all very romantic. I walked down Sixth Avenue and passed a fancy clothing store, and I thought, 'I can buy that! I have a job in New York!' We were shocked and absolutely giddy.

"After Pat came back we had to look for our own place. Keith Rockwell, co-owner of the Purple Onion, recommended a hotel across from the Winter Garden—a house of ill repute is what I think it was. We had a room for about seventeen dollars a week. A black woman down the hall practiced voodoo and used to leave her door open. I peeked in once, and she accused me of dropping powders by her door."

Their booking at the Ruban, unfortunately, was not a success. "We failed miserably there," Jane says. "The San Francisco audiences were more indulgent than the New York audiences. When we brought that material to the Ruban, our batting average dropped to zero. We knew about timing and about handling the material, but we weren't loose enough. We didn't really let the audience dictate the show as you're supposed to do in a club. We didn't sense the audience and realize that we couldn't do *this* number but we could do *that* number. A real club performer sculpts the show right there. It's entirely different from a theatrical presentation.

"But what loyalty Julius had! The Meles were complaining, but it was hard for him to fire us. He took it personally. He told them, 'You can have my notice if they go!' "

But go they did, never to return. Jane won a job as understudy to Dody Goodman, Beatrice Arthur, and Dorothy Greener in Ben Bagley's *Shoestring Revue*, and Gordon returned to the Strawhatters to help prepare their next revue. In 1958 they reunited with Monk to appear in several of his revues at the Upstairs at the Downstairs.

Such experiments made Monk's loyalty even better known than his taste, but sometimes both were unfathomable. Occasionally he took a chance and failed; at other times he allowed friendship or loyalty to cloud his judgment. An example of the latter was brunette bombshell Penny Malone, a would-be comedienne whom Ben Bagley calls "one of the worst acts I've ever seen. A Murray Grand double-entendre song was the highlight, 'I've Got It Hidden,' which he wrote for Gypsy Rose Lee:

I've got it hidden
I've got it tucked away
I've got it hidden
It's for a rainy day . . .

"Penny decided to stage it as a courtroom scene:

> If it pleases your honor, I should like to call as my next witness Miss Angelina Sincere, who has been accused by the state of unlawfully exhibiting in public sections of her anatomy, for the purposes of mass seduction . . .

"She played Angelina as a stripper, and since Penny herself was a tough bimbo it was right in character. She was chewing gum, and she pulled it out of her mouth in a long string and got it caught in her hair—which was supposed to be funny. I said, 'My God, how do you get that out?' She said, 'Oh, it's really a wig, and I just take scissors and cut it out.'

"I was with her in a coffee shop, and I said, 'Penny, you look depressed.' She said, 'Well, gee, two months ago my husband left with the garbage.'

" 'What?'

" 'My husband left to take out the garbage and he never came back.'

" 'Well, that's a joke, isn't it?'

" 'No, he never came back. I stayed home the whole next day and he never showed up. Then I had to go out for my voice lesson, and when I came back all his clothes were gone.'

" 'Well, maybe he'll come back.'

" 'No, there's no chance of that. He took all his stuff.' "

Such missteps were easy to overlook in that marvelously sophisticated atmosphere. Naturally, most of Monk's performers were fiercely devoted to him. "The Ruban spoiled people," says Marshall Izen, "because Julius coddled his talent." Monk always introduced them by saying, "Ladies and gentlemen, may I direct your attention and applause to . . . ," an assurance that the upcoming act did indeed deserve attention and applause. Acts were reluctant to leave, even if this meant passing up better opportunities. Michael Brown began at $85 per fourteen-show week; eventually this rose to $125, or less than $9 a performance. Monk himself fared little better. "He was a salaried employee just like us," says Brown. "He was paid very little. But the rest of us were so happy to have a job in such a prestigious place that we never complained."

Despite occasional crossovers, the Blue Angel and Ruban contingents generally stayed faithful to the club that had launched them and thought less of the other. Michael Brown echoes the Ruban partisans: "The Ruban to me was a friendly room. The Angel was not." Monk aired his own feelings frequently. Marshall Izen approached him backstage one evening with a tape recorder:

> IZEN: Now, say something dirty, Julius.
> MONK: Quail shit.
> IZEN: Nah, Julius, say something really dirty.
> MONK: Goddamned mother-fucking son of a bitch.
> IZEN: Aw, come on, Julius, say something *really* dirty.
> MONK: Herbert Jacoby.

Ben Bagley's opinion was a popular one for Jacoby's club: "The Blue Angel was where you went to have fun. When you went to the Ruban the most you could hope for was that one act out of four might be amusing."

Monk took great pains to keep his crowds quiet and respectful, either chiding them at the microphone ("This is by no means a competition!"), "shhh"-ing them, or asking them to leave. But as with any establishment predicated on booze sales, the club had its share of sots and hecklers. Disruptions most often occurred on nights Monk was not there. Wrote Tim Taylor in *Cue*, "Proprietors of nightclubs owe an obligation to sober patrons to squelch (and, if necessary, eject) those vulgarians who shout, 'You stink!' and similar jabs at performers trying to entertain. Two loudmouths got away with such behavior the last time I was at Le Ruban Bleu, and I can't imagine why the management didn't persuade the bums to take their business elsewhere."

One reason is that Tony Mele, eager to keep the cash register ringing, was reluctant to alienate paying customers, leaving performers to deal with the problem in their own ways. One evening a drunken woman at ringside stretched out her legs and rested them on the stage during Irwin Corey's act. "Oh, darling, darling, darling, what *beautiful* legs," he said. "Do they go all the way up?" Or to a heckler, "All the world's a stage—but you ain't got yer part yet! If you did have a part, it would probably be a tertiary part at that. And tertiary comes from the Greek meaning 'that which is terd!' "

On rare occasions this could lead to violence, as James Kirkwood learned in 1952. "One Friday night about two A.M., Lee and I were doing a number based on 'That Old Black Magic.' He sang the song, while I sat on the piano with a basket of props to distract the audience. I had a little toy fire engine, for example, with an incredible siren. When he turned around I'd hide them. I had just gotten off the piano and raised the top when a full beer bottle flew right by my ear and smashed on the piano. Lights up, and there was a guy standing back there and a girl saying, 'Please! Please don't!' "

"About four of us jumped on the guy," says Ronny Graham, who was also on the bill. "He was threatening us all, saying he was gonna have us shot."

"He had picked up this girl, and he was a little drunk," says Kirkwood, "and apparently they were going to a hotel. While we were on she kept saying, 'Isn't he cute?' The guy said, 'Which one?' She said, 'The little one.' People used to call me 'the little one' because I was six feet and Lee was six-two. With that he picked up the bottle and threw it right at my head.

"The Meles didn't want any scandal. They wanted to let the guy go, but we wanted to press charges. Julius was outraged. 'I shall go down to the police station and file a complaint against this ruffian!' A couple of policemen came and said, 'Look, you weren't hurt.' When we got to the station the cops said, "Go back there and go in that door to the left.' I did, and the next thing I knew, the door opened and in came that guy. He picked up a chair and threw it across the room. I ran out and said, 'Jesus Christ, what are you people trying to do to me?'

"It turned out that he had been in a mental institution. I remember being a bit disenchanted with the Meles, because all they cared about was keeping it out of the papers."

HISTORIANS HAVE PAID little attention to club comics of the early and mid-'50s, simply because they made few topical inroads. Most of them treaded as carefully upon the topics of the day—the cold war, the H-bomb, racism, McCarthyism—as if they were walking on a minefield. As Douglas Miller wrote in his critical history *The Fifties: The Way We Really Were*, "It was more an era of fear than fun. The bomb, communists, spies, and Sputnik all scared Americans. And fear bred repression, both of the blatant McCarthyite type and the more subtle, pervasive and personal daily pressures to conform."

Intimate clubs bred no more prototypical comic than Orson Bean, a crew-cut Vermonter who gave gentle, good-natured chucks under the chin to atomic research funding, space exploration, Mark Twain, and George Washington. He closed the act with a demonstration of how to make an eight-foot eucalyptus tree out of a rolled-up newspaper.

Wally Cox graduated from the Vanguard and the Angel to his own niche in the golden age of television as Mr. (Robinson J.) Peepers, the midwestern science teacher in the eponymous NBC series. Cox fit that Caspar Milquetoast character to a T: a meek, round-shouldered nebbish with glasses and a soft, slightly lisping voice that murmured as if he were talking to himself. He created a gallery of neighborhood characters: a grade school teacher, a prissy scoutmaster exhorting his troop to chop wood, a soda fountain clerk, and Dufo, a Greenwich Village delinquent. Cox fleshed them out vividly but with few jokes; when the audience didn't laugh at a line he thought funny he glared at them until they started to chuckle. He opened his 1948 Vanguard debut with his hands folded in front of his tweed jacket, a blank expression, and a deadpan delivery: "I shall begin my sociological lecture by recalling some scenes from my childhood experience, placing emphasis on the prenatal influences in connection therewith."

More pointed topical humor came from Ronny Graham, a tall, saucer-eyed singer-songwriter-pianist from Philadelphia with curly black hair and a gravel-edged voice. His act ranged from a parody of lyrics based on the titles of '50s movies ("Quo Vadis / That's what I said the night we met / Quo Vadis / Means whither goest thou, my pet?") to a lambasting of Freudian psychoanalysis, a trendy subject of the day. Psychotherapy was still considered laughable alien territory by a nation reluctant to analyze its ills; hence the giggles when Graham sang, "You left me with an unfulfilled libido / And a complex of inferiority / You left me here a pinin' till my ego needs relinin' / Poor unsublimated me!"

But Irwin Corey was not afraid to be blasphemous, rude, or long-winded to get his own, more scathing points across. In 1943 Corey introduced his famous "Professor" character, a blustery old pedant whose every thought splintered into a pile of digressions, contradictions, and non sequiturs. He entered to *Pomp and Circumstance*, wearing a baggy white shirt, a long string tie, a frock coat, and dirty tennis sneakers. Rearranging his notes while considering his first words, he made several false starts before clearing his throat and saying: "HOWEVER . . ." His stream-of-consciousness "lecture" slipped from pompous professorial tones into his native Brooklynese, into a mock British accent or Irish brogue, and even into fluent French. "Ah, yes! Sir Isaac Newton and the law of gravity. There he was walking through his apple orchard, and he saw an apple falling down from a tree, which amazed him. Because up until that time—until the law of gravity was passed—all apples fell up!"

In a discourse on *Hamlet*, Corey intoned, "You, like many others whose folly is seeking merriment, have made willing fools who strive to give others happiness pay the price . . . Made that up m'self!" Mixed in with these "seminars" were flashes of his personal credo. "I have a philosophy which is simple and poignant and to the point. Point blank. Unsubtle. Simple. Poignant. My philosophy is . . . you can get more with a kind word . . . and a gun . . . than with just a kind word."

The "Professor" was, at his best, a brilliant indictment of dogmatic authority, and like all great satire was just a few degrees removed from reality. Unfortunately, his allotted twenty minutes or so at the Vanguard or the Ruban often stretched to forty, and it was difficult to get him off. He shared one Vanguard bill with the legendary pop-jazz singer Lee Wiley. Wiley built her reputation through radio and recordings, since her discomfort at live performing approached Anita Ellis's. She also drank excessively, as folk singer–guitarist Will Holt, who opened that roster as part of a square-dance troupe, remembers. "We did our ten or fifteen minutes, then Professor Corey went on, and on, and on. Lee finally went to the bar and said, 'Gimme a drink.' By the time she went on she was smashed. Corey just didn't care."

In an atmosphere based on booze, performers faced all kinds of challenges while staging shows known for their apparent ease and machinelike efficiency. Because so many of Jacoby's customers drove in from faraway cities, he vowed never to cancel except in the direst emergency. He also hated to lose money, believing that anyone on his payroll had better be prepared to work. "The Blue Angel made you go on no matter what," says Kaye Ballard, "even if there was a blizzard and it was ten below and there were four people in the audience."

Jacoby was always a bundle of nerves before showtime, snapping his long, bony fingers and roaming around to see that everything was running on schedule. He made everyone twice as nervous, as did Max Gordon in his unassuming way. "Max worried if there were too few people," says Will Holt, "and if the place was full he worried about the fire laws." Bart Howard did most of the actual work. "Bart was sometimes like a schoolmarm," Holt says. " 'It's time to go on. Let's get moving. Don't forget this. You've got to do that.' I knew he was under Herbert's orders, but he could be terribly rigid."

At the foot of the back staircase leading from the dressing rooms to the stage were two buzzers, with which Howard signaled acts five minutes before showtime. Upstairs that harsh, squealing sound made people even tenser. The men's dressing room was as large as the average kitchen, and all the male performers changed there, including the musicians. Certain acts associate it with the plight of Reyneaux, a suave magician who appeared in white tie and tails. Reyneaux used white doves in his act, and one night before his entrance one escaped from its cage. Several bystanders conducted a quick search, until one of them glanced underneath a chair in the dressing room and saw it lying there dead. Someone suggested stuffing it and hanging it backstage as a mascot for all the acts who had died at the Angel.

But even though the men's dressing room had a dirty floor and graffiti, Jacoby saw no reason to spend money on something he considered unimportant. He felt the same about lighting. On a board near the buzzers were controls for one pinspot, one body light, two backlights, and a few colored gels. "Whatever good lighting there was Bart was responsible for," says Dorothy Loudon. "Poor Bart stood in this tiny cubicle working what few lights there were. And there was a little switch underneath the piano that the pianist could turn off and on, and that controlled another light. It was like the switch a hostess uses to summon the maid. Well, I never knew which light was which."

Occasionally lights burned out during acts or did not work at all. Performers complained to Howard, to alternate emcee and pianist Otis Clements, or (as a last resort) to Jacoby, who was the most skillful at cutting them off. He was too busy fussing over other things. The crackle of tension on a busy night affected him like the push of a gas pedal. "When Herbert saw that the room was full and they were all having a good time," Clements says, "he'd want to move the show faster, and we had to do what he said. The waiters would all be bitching because they had no time to take orders and get the drinks in. You'd hear them screaming at Herbert, and he'd scream back, and I'd be buzzing for the next act to come downstairs. Well, sometimes they wouldn't be ready because they expected a longer intermission. Then the chain of madness would go on. Herbert would scream, 'WHERE IS EVERYBODY?' And we'd say, 'Herbert, you're rushing things!' "

No such chaos plagued the Ruban Bleu, but neither was Monk's guiding hand so forceful, especially in the early '50s, when his tendency toward drink had developed into alcoholism. "He was a trial to everyone," says Michael Brown, "and as much as we liked him we were contemptuous that he embarrassed us sometimes. Some of his introductions were so slurred that no one in the room knew what was about to walk onstage." Eventually he went on the wagon with the aid of a psychiatrist and switched to black coffee. Several of his acts had alcohol problems of their own. One was Jonathan Winters, who arrived at the Ruban in 1953 after trying unsuccessfully to break into TV. Even in his first engagement, however, he showed a remarkably finished talent and a masterful knack for sound and characterization. With his flair for American dialects he created an array of figures that the whole country recognized: farmers, gas station attendants, construction workers, general-store owners, and various men in the street. His most famous alter ego was Maude Frickert, an elderly lady with a hip, liberal, acerbic view of contemporary society and a fierce empathy for the young at heart. Winters was also famous for his ability to imitate everyday sounds using the microphone as an instrument. His re-creations of planes taking off, speeding cars, dripping water, animal noises, and so on brought his monologues vividly to life.

Away from the stand Winters seemed exactly the same. He was "on" constantly, joking, trying routines, making sounds. *Time* magazine (October 13, 1958) reported that "As long as someone laughs, Johnny is on. And someone is always laughing. Johnny was 'on,' " it continued, "the night he toured Manhattan bistros with an empty hand grenade (pulling the pin, he would cry: 'Everybody goes when the whistle blows'). He was 'on' when he panicked a staid hotel lobby by turning to a friend and barking in a loud, serious tone: 'We should never have operated in a hotel room. Granted he's alive, but you shouldn't have let that brain fall on the rug. Next time St. Vincent's.' "

Winters and comic Pat McCormick also liked to enter a crowded elevator pretending that they were robbers on the getaway. "You don't think we tied him up too tight?" But all this role-playing was clearly a camouflage. Winters admitted that he was "bombed most of the time" in his nightclub years, a problem that also plagued his father. "He later stopped," Winters told Cleveland Amory in the *Daily News Parade* (December 20, 1987), "but before he did, it cost him his marriage, his work and very nearly his life." The comic's eccentric behavior peaked at a time of severe overwork in 1959. Midway through a show at the hungry i in San Francisco he launched into a long, unamusing monologue on Alcoholics Anonymous. Many customers jeered him or walked out. The second show was worse. As the *New York Post* reported, "Winters again broke the format of his act and told no stories or jokes. He talked . . . about the Marines and a broken cigarette holder given to him by a friend.

"When more of the patrons left and others heckled, he broke into tears and left the floor. A friend accompanied Winters from the club to a nearby coffee shop while he regained his composure, then to his hotel . . . The friend remained with Winters, then went to the lobby to make a telephone call. When he returned to the room, Winters was gone."

The next day the *New York Journal-American* wrote,

> Winters was taken into protective custody yesterday on trying to board the old sailing ship, Balclutha. Ticket taker Julius Larsen, 79, called police, due to incoherent remarks, and Winters was persuaded to leave.
>
> Returning in half an hour, Winters said, according to Larsen, "If I knock your block off, you'll let me aboard, won't you? I want to climb the rigging, slide down the anchor chain and jump overboard."
>
> Police returned, whereupon Winters said:

"I'm John Q—what's it to you—I'm in orbit, man! I'm a mooncat, on Cloud 9, from Outer Space."

Refusing to leave, he was handcuffed. He refused to enter the police car. A station wagon took him to San Francisco General Hospital.

Although Winters has denied this widely reported episode, he admitted that "everything had closed in on me, and the whole world was disintegrating in front of me, and I was alone. When they told me they wanted to send those electric bolts through my head, for the first time in my life there was no place to hide." Occasionally he joked about the breakdown but accepted few other club bookings, always speaking bitterly of his café years. "Most club audiences ignore you," he told the *New York Daily News* (January 12, 1969). "They're either part of the Virginia Woolf crowd that's always playing games, or they're sauced out of their heads. But even if everything went perfectly inside a club, I'd still hate it. Clubs are boring and they keep you away from your family. I'm one of those guys who enjoys staying at home."

KIRKWOOD AND GOODMAN'S partnership came to a violent halt in 1954. Kirkwood's explosive temper and deep-seated resentment of his easygoing partner's abilities had continued to erupt in frightening ways.

"There was a table backstage where we used to sit and have a cup of coffee," Goodman recalls. "I was wearing my white dinner jacket and having a piece of strawberry shortcake. Jimmy was late. He'd been to a party and gotten sauced. I saw him coming up the stairs with that evil look in his eye. He came over and said, 'Gimme some of that.' He was like a mean little kid. I said, 'No, this is mine. They'll give you a piece.'

" 'No, I want some of yours.'

" 'Well, you can't have it. Go in and get yourself dressed.'

" 'You mean you're not gonna give me any?'

"I said no. With that he put his hand in the plate and rubbed the cake all over me."

Goodman finally struck back in 1954. "Everybody was waiting for Jimmy to get it. One night we were doing a number called 'Downy Little Brownie Man,' based on a terrible old art song. I played Mrs.

Stankey, the narrator, and Jimmy was my son, who accompanies me on the glockenspiel. I was introducing the number onstage, wearing a hat with feathers. On the left side of the stage was a little room hidden by a blue curtain, where Frank Cerchia kept his guitar amplifier. We stored our props in there, and Jimmy went in to put on his little collar and beanie hat. I was talking onstage and the next thing I knew there were birdcalls coming from the room. Well, it had been building up for too long. I stopped and said, 'Would you excuse me?' I went over and pulled aside the curtain. I couldn't even see him. I went, WHAM! Right in the face. It was like Fibber McGee's closet. Half the keys fell off the glockenspiel. The audience was gone. Norman Paris was lying on the floor next to the piano bench, his feet up in the air kicking. Then just when you thought everything had quieted down, one more key fell off. It was classic.

"I went back and finished the introduction, and out he came. He was ready to kill. The glockenspiel was destroyed, his collar was all twisted around, the propeller was smashed. We just about got through the number, and I was afraid to turn my back on him. But as soon as we went backstage he grabbed a wooden hanger and chased me around with it. The waiters were all frightened because they knew I'd turned. They held me and said, 'Don't fight him!' Bibi Osterwald was standing on a chair screaming, 'DON'T KILL HIM! DON'T KILL HIM!' She always overemphasized everything. 'Oh my God, oh my Jesus, good heaven!' And Jimmy was banging me over the head with the hanger. I had double vision for a week.

"That's when I decided we had to break it up. It's painful when you don't know why you're getting it, and he was very hurt when I decided to break up the act. Columns were carrying lines like, 'What comedy team is trying to kill each other onstage?' Our agent at MCA said, 'Lee, you've got bookings.' I said, 'I don't care.' "

AN OFT-HEARD PHRASE in 1950s New York, anywhere from eleven at night to four in the morning, was "Let's go to Mabel's." Not "to the Byline Room," the forty-or-so-seat club above the Show Spot Bar on East 52nd Street where Mercer sang from 1949 until 1955, and certainly not in later years "to the Pin-Up Room" or RSVP or the King Arthur Room. Hence the title of her best Atlantic album, "Midnight at Mabel Mercer's."

Mercer became a fixture in all these rooms, as she had at Tony's, and left the Byline Room only after it burned down, forcing her to relocate for several months to the dingy Pin-Up Room on 34th Street and Lexington Avenue. But her followers didn't care. In *Down Beat* (January 27, 1966) Nat Hentoff wrote fondly of her "somewhat cracked voice that has long chronicled the losses and transient expectations of city nights." Mercer herself cherished the fact that her admirers knew where to find her.

By now her voice had taken on its trademark sound: frail, pinched, no longer steady or melodic, but highly dignified in its precision. With that deterioration her artistry reached its full flower, for it focused all her attention toward lyrics and away from the smooth vocal effects that once came so easily. As Buddy Barnes suggests, "I have a feeling she thought of herself as a not-so-interesting mezzo-soprano and a more-than-interesting diseuse." That tradition of singing, mainly French and German, was also practiced by Greta Keller and Lotte Lenya, and denoted a singer of flawed vocal abilities who acted her songs. Why this happened to Mercer at the relatively young age of about fifty is open to speculation. Some say that it resulted from a bad tonsillectomy in the late '40s; others suggest that the smoky nightclub environment, coupled with her dislike of microphones, ravaged an already fragile voice.

Now she had become a true cult singer, often compared to caviar, champagne, and black olives. As Hentoff wrote, "There are some who find Mabel Mercer overstylized and otherwise regard those of us drawn to her singing as mesmerized without musical cause. I was one of the unconverted for a while." Certainly those who favored a strong, tuneful voice and valued music as much as lyrics were not her fans. They ranged from jazz singer Anita O'Day ("Man, this chick has got the weirdest fucking act in show business!") to Cole Porter himself. In spite of widespread claims that Porter worshiped Mercer, his musical tastes—as well as the recollections of Lew Kesler, his longtime rehearsal pianist, notator, and friend—indicate otherwise. Porter shuddered at deviations from what he had written and sent withering letters to Frank Sinatra, Ella Fitzgerald, and Lena Horne criticizing their renditions of his songs. One singer he did admire was Doris Day, whose recording of "I Love Paris" prompted him to say that it gave him the feeling that she loved Paris as much as he did, and that he wished she would perform more of his work.

But Kesler remembered a time in the '50s when Mercer told him she was singing Porter's "Ours" at RSVP, and asked him to tell the composer. Porter rolled his eyes and said, "God, that woman couldn't sing when she was young, and she can't sing now that she's old!"

Her lyrical skills, though, were infinite. Unmellifluous though it was, her voice had a comforting, mature sound, and her sympathetic presence was a balm for the deepest heartaches. Even in lyrics as tragic as Bart Howard and Ian Grant's "If You Leave Paris" or Maxwell Anderson's "Trouble Man" (written with Kurt Weill for *Lost in the Stars*), she revealed reserves of strength that would see her through the pain, as well as a hard-earned wisdom that taught her it would soon pass. For the vulnerable of any age, that was a priceless kernel of truth.

And few voices could communicate romance so directly and powerfully, not so much from her to her listeners as from lover to beloved. Wrote Victor Lownes III in *Playboy* (December 1955), "The song is hers, but the sentiment becomes your own, and as she sings a love lyric by Cole Porter these seem to be the very words you would use to express your state of heart to the girl sitting next to you. And funny, when you squeeze her hand, your companion seems convinced that *you* are saying these wonderful things, too."

The converted in those years included Harold Arlen, Leonard Bernstein, and Alec Wilder, who called Mercer "the guardian of the tenuous dreams created by the writers of songs." During the same period Frank Sinatra made his oft-quoted comment that she had taught him everything he knew.

Mercer spent Sunday, her day off, at her thirty-acre estate in East Chatham, New York, returning to her apartment on 110th Street in Harlem the next day. Then she began another week of singing in rooms that became homes-away-from-home not only for her but for a body of listeners who looked upon her as an anchor in that most turbulent of seas.

The popularity of New York's late-night hideaways peaked in the mid-'50s, as did the number of TV appearances, recordings, and theatrical "big breaks" achieved by their alumni. All this, combined with relatively affordable rents, inspired dozens of would-be entrepreneurs to create their own little havens for night people. Even without much money for promotion or decent decor, a few rooms caught something of the Blue Angel's style of elegance; others were seedy holes-in-the-wall—or ground—sometimes opened to launder Mafia money.

In either case, the variety of places to drink and unwind after 10 P.M. or so became so vast that most local residents took them for granted. As writer Ron Diamond stated in his liner notes for a Portia Nelson album of Bart Howard songs:

> In every great cosmopolitan city—be it San Francisco or Paris, New York or London—there are night spots where the frantic day can be brought to a restorative end with good food, drinks to hold hands over, and a little night music. Call them clubs, *boites*, or bistros, the central ingredient is the after-dark poetry of musicians with quiet pianos, singers with persuasive but uninsistent voices, songs that somehow become as personal as memories.

One of them was the Left Bank at 309 West 50th Street, a cocktail lounge and jazz room owned and operated by Richard Kollmar, husband of Dorothy Kilgallen. Best known for his chatty morning radio show with Kilgallen, *Breakfast with Dorothy and Dick*, Kollmar also acted, produced, and ran a small art gallery. He decorated the club with paintings from his own collection and with models of human hands, one of his quirky passions. Visitors felt as if they had unlocked the door to the basement of a museum. The Left Bank was mainly an arty nest for midnight conversation and romance, although it featured first-rate jazz pianists and trios, a slick vocal quartet led by singer John LaSalle, and some surprise guest appearances, as Tim Taylor reported in *Cue* (March 3, 1957): "Each banquette in the softly-lit room is equipped with a plug into which a table microphone can be set at a moment's notice. The night I dropped in, Judy Holliday obliged with a tune from her hit musical, *Bells Are Ringing*. It made my steak sandwich taste just a little bit better."

Across town on East 53rd Street was the Cameo Club, a sprawling room that usually presented voices that could fill its farthest corners, such as Frances Faye, Mel Torme, and Buddy Greco. But the room is best remembered for a rare New York club engagement by Julie London. A luscious blonde with a knockout figure and a breathy, jazz-tinged singing style, London had worked mostly as a film actress until 1955, when she broke into the recording field with her hit single "Cry Me a River." A long series of albums for Liberty Records boasted some daringly sensual cover photographs, a lush, romantic repertoire, and a silky voice that captured the essence of '50s seduction. Disc jockey William B. Williams estimated that her recordings were on the turntable (or car radio) during more deflowerments than those of any vocalist besides Frank Sinatra.

At the Cameo she simply sat on a stool and sang to the accompaniment of jazz pianist–songwriter Bobby Troup, whom she married in 1958; nothing more was needed to lull listeners into a dreamy state. Short on breath and range, London's singing sounded like whispered words of postmidnight passion, a quality her liner notes exploited:

> The lights are dim . . . and by chance, it's the maid's night off. The radio plays softly and out of a fragrant haze of perfume, she whispers . . . "Make Love to Me." So steady the trembling hand, pour the martinis—let your imagination go . . .
>
> *If I Could Be With You*, she pleads—and you answer, "You can, you can . . . anywhere . . . everywhere . . ."

On the San Francisco Waterfront she sighs, *It's Good to Want You Bad*... You cling to her... to the mood, to the magic... don't lose her in the mist...

I Wanna Be Loved, she taunts... and in wild anticipation you'll follow her... to Madrid, to Siam, to the moon!

Many people regretted that she didn't sing in clubs more often, but London's stage fright made her tremble even at the sight of a recording microphone. A prominent jazz pianist who recorded with her claims it was necessary to get her high or tipsy to make her calm enough to sing; some albums were even taped in her living room. The mellow mood they capture was not simulated.

Other clubs—the Red Carpet, the Tender Trap, Arpeggio, Quadrille, La Commedia, Chi-Chi, the Living Room—are notable mainly for keeping such singers as Bobby Short, Matt Dennis, and Sylvia Syms continually employed in the '50s. The Den in the Duane, beneath the Duane Hotel on Madison Avenue and 37th Street, had the distinction of hiring Lenny Bruce in his first New York engagement in 1958, as well as Nichols and May and a number of other gifted comics and singers.

One of the latter was Jeri Southern, a large-boned, rueful blonde who usually performed at jazz clubs such as Birdland or the Village Vanguard. Southern began as a pianist, adding vocals in 1951 to make herself more marketable. As a singer she recorded several best-selling singles, among them "When I Fall in Love" and "You Better Go Now," as well as a superb series of albums. At the Den in the Duane, as elsewhere, she began with a slow love song—a courageous practice that many attributed to Barbra Streisand years later. Her deep, velvety voice, serene style, and thoughtful, unforced musicality were matched by the sparest gestures and movements; most of the time she seemed lost in a private, bittersweet world that she longed to escape into. Indeed, friends report that she found singing painful. Beneath the surface of even her upbeat numbers lay a dark angst that gave her work an understated sadness. "It was as if she had looked into the heart of some American dream and seen the outlines of a nightmare," wrote Colin Butler in his annotations for a Southern collection.

But her insecurities were mostly personal, rooted perhaps in such trials as a 1956 Carnegie Hall concert in which she appeared with Sarah Vaughan, Joe Williams, and the Count Basie band. Scheduled to perform early in the show, Southern emerged in a strapless purple velvet gown trimmed with white ermine. Her opening ballad evoked immediate hostility from an audience eager for a night of powerhouse singing and playing. They began to hiss and gradually drowned her out. Southern's eyes filled with tears, and she walked off without finishing her song.

Southern performed and recorded sporadically until the early '60s, when she suffered a nervous breakdown and decided never to sing again. She concentrated on coaching until her death on August 4, 1991, one day before her sixty-fifth birthday. Recalls a singer friend, "I would always say, 'Jeri, sing this phrase. I want to hear how it should sound.' She never would."

Over at 55th Street and Sixth Avenue, the Baq Room took exclusiveness to new heights. A dark, dank little box in the back of a rowdy Irish pub called the Midtown Bar, the Baq Room seemed like a deliberate attempt to segregate the cognoscenti from the hoi polloi. No matter that it consisted of only a battered baby grand and a bunch of crowded black tables and chairs, and smelled like a beer cellar (courtesy of the bar outside).

The hostess and featured singer was Janice Mars, a short-haired brunette in her thirties who dressed in simple black. Another diseuse, Mars allied her nasal, bleating voice to a "method" acting approach intended to illuminate an esoteric repertoire of story-songs. Her minor performing credits included a replacement role in the Broadway musical *Little Mary Sunshine* and a small part in Tennessee Williams's *Orpheus Descending*. Thus she became known as an "undiscovered jewel" and as "one of New York's best-kept secrets." Mars's idiosyncratic style endeared her to the theatrical community, particularly members of the Actors Studio. On a single night in 1957 one might have spotted Maureen Stapleton, Susan Strasberg, Marlon Brando, Siobhan McKenna, Richard Burton, Adolph Green, and Tennessee Williams listening raptly. Williams, along with Brando and Stapleton, had given Mars the necessary $1,900 to open the Baq Room. "Janice possesses a quality that is absolutely unique," he said, for a hand-lettered flier printed in 1958 for limited distribution.

When columnist Joe Hyams of the *New York Herald Tribune* visited the club and announced his intention to do a story, he found himself about as welcome as a cattle rustler in Texas looking up into the barrel of a shotgun (December 12, 1957):

The people at our table were horrified. "If you give this place publicity it will be spoiled!" they said.

We asked Miss Mars how she felt about a story.

"I'm in a spot," she said. "We haven't advertised because the place is sort of homey now, and I'm afraid once people start coming in off the street it'll be spoiled. People out of show business don't understand how actors enjoy themselves, and it would take only a few gawkers to spoil everything."

Then you don't want a story about you and the club?

"I guess maybe it's almost imperative that we get some publicity. Only, if you write about the club, don't make it seem as though there's any fancy atmosphere, because there isn't. There's only me and I'm not really much of a singer.

"Things go wrong with my voice and I act like it is pure emotion. I get phlegm in my throat and it comes out like I'm overwhelmed. But people seem to enjoy it."

Mars's magnetism was an even more acquired taste than Mabel Mercer's, and when Buster Davis brought Ethel Merman into the Baq Room Merman bluntly summed up the dissenting school of thought. As he recalled, "Janice had just finished singing 'This Is the Winter of My Discontent,' an obscure Alec Wilder song, and Ethel leaned forward as if she were about to whisper something in my ear. 'CHRIST!' she said, in a whisper that almost broke my brandy glass, 'it sounds like she's got the microphone up her ass!' "

The art of the diseuse also flourished in Greenwich Village, where a ramshackle club called the Duplex gave free reign to the imaginations of an adventurous group of youngsters. The room, which in 1989 celebrated its fortieth anniversary, was founded by an Italian immigrant named Jimmy DeMartino. He purchased a two-story building on Grove Street, making the lower level a bar and the upper a restaurant with piano music. Gradually the local residents turned it into a pickup place. By the mid-'50s the second floor, now known as Upstairs at the Duplex, began to feature casual entertainment; acts performed there virtually for free to get experience.

During 1955 it was dominated by actor Hal Holbrook, who used it to develop his remarkable Mark Twain impersonation, and by a tall, sylphlike, and utterly gorgeous singer named Lovelady (Lovey) Powell. Powell chose the most recherché songs she could find—Jimmy Shelton's "Lilac Wine" from *Dance Me a Song*, a short-lived Broadway revue; Johnny Mercer and Harold Arlen's ballad of disillusionment "I Wonder What Became of Me"; Noel Coward's "If Love Were All"—singing them in a style so intense that many found it unintentionally hilarious. Serious love songs as well as lighthearted tunes were punctuated by gasps of emotion, quizzical giggles, and heavy emphasis on words such as "but" and "just." Audiences preferred to tune out her high, quavering voice and drink in her hypnotic doe eyes, short Audrey Hepburn–styled hair, and fashion model's face, dusted with rice powder makeup.

Powell was hardly unaware of her visual splendor, as Ben Bagley remembers. "Her dresses were so tight, you thought if she took one deep breath the waist would break and her tits, small as they were, would pop out. While she was singing she would cross her legs and dangle one high-heeled shoe on her toes. It would swing back and forth, back and forth, and you would see everyone's eyes follow. Men were crazy about Lovey and made passes at her all the time. They knew she couldn't sing, but nobody cared." Gordon Connell, who with his wife Jane appeared with Powell at the San Francisco Purple Onion, adds, "Between songs she talked a lot about what she did that day, about people she met in department stores, with an audience who had just happened in off the street. In a sense she was re-creating a genuine living room feeling where nobody was barred from coming in and having a drink."

This was always the atmosphere at the Duplex, which seated only fifty-six between its bare walls and which had no stage, only a piano in the back corner. But in the '50s, when small artistic efforts of every sort—poetry, plays, obscure jazz vocal albums, recherché nightclub acts—were given attention that they had seldom received before, the merely eccentric was sometimes mistaken for genuine artistry. It was easy to believe that a singer's or writer's misguided efforts were too special for mass appreciation. Consider the liner notes of Powell's 1956 album "Lovelady":

> The Duplex has a Parisian-paradise-lost quality, being reminiscent of the Rive Gauche bistros where young American expatriates in their—and the century's—twenties smouldered in determined disenchantment.
>
> In this age of anxiety, disillusion seems almost an unaffordable luxury. But at the Duplex, three unique individualists cherish and

minister to the cause of lost and dimming illusions—pianist Brooks Morton, Hal Holbrook and the goddess-songstress of the cult—Lovey Powell, whose songs of unfulfillment are in this album.

A nod to Brooks, and she sings. Her eyes sweep the room, so luminous and compelling the songs seem to radiate from those eyes rather than the throat. Yes, she is an actress—and an enchantress—which only means that she is an artist.

Listening to this, her first recording, is hearing the prelude to a legend.

Lovey's voice is a black opal, with flashing depths and sudden fire. A jewel requires a jewel. Put a diamond needle to her record.

For every club with scheduled entertainment there were three or four piano lounges, which *Time* (March 24, 1967), called "refuges for the bewitched, bothered, bewildered and just plain bombed." And for every polite listener there were ten drunk, loud, or sloppy ones—a guaranteed occupational hazard for these most abused of entertainers. Cy Walter thwarted sing-alongs by changing keys so often that participants grew dizzy and, when hit with a lousy request, would fracture it beyond recognition. More timid players such as Forrest Perrin dealt with these problems in their own ways. When a cantankerous woman tottered over and asked, "When's the music start?" he answered, "As soon as I finish typing this letter."

Nonetheless the names of these rooms conjure pleasant memories of huddled, hushed conversation, clasped hands resting on tables, knees touching beneath them: Toni's Caprice, Malmaison, Celeste, the Café de la Paix of the Hotel St. Moritz, Gatsby's, the Hotel Earle's Waverly Lounge in Greenwich Village, and the Café Carlyle, years before it became Bobby Short's bailiwick. The Drake Room, by now synonymous with Cy Walter, would outlast almost all of them. And at the Composer at 68 West 58th Street, a more jazz-oriented club, a young pianist and fledgling songwriter named Cy Coleman won many of his earliest fans in the late '50s.

Pianist-singers found the inattention in these rooms especially maddening. One of the most frustrating spots was the Beverly Club of the Beverly Hotel at 50th Street and Lexington Avenue, noteworthy only for having given Bobby Short his first New York job in 1956 after his return from several years in Hollywood and Europe. A cavernous room filled with pillars that blocked most sight lines, it caused sound to bounce from wall to wall and ceiling to floor, leaving listeners cross-eyed.

No such distractions marred the breeziest piano hangout of the '50s and '60s, Goldie's New York, which columnist Jack O'Brian called "the New Yorkiest spot in town." He was not speaking for those who equated New York with long-stemmed roses, pearls against black velvet, or Cartier lighters, however. A bar-restaurant, Goldie's offered as its only regular entertainment the piano duets of Goldie (Louis) Hawkins, the club's Alabama-born owner, and partner Wayne Sanders. The bustle of their twin uprights, playing showtunes that ranged from a driving arrangement of Cole Porter's "Ace in the Hole" to a medley from *Gypsy*, welcomed patrons down three steps into the lower level of a brownstone at 232 East 53rd Street. That sound lifted spirits higher than the Stork Club's most expensive champagne and proved even more addictive to the people who came back night after night.

At the door they were greeted by Effie, known as the oldest and most charming hatcheck girl in town. During breaks Goldie himself whisked them into a small room with hardwood floors, red and orange walls, lots of little tables (capacity was sixty-eight), a bar, and two uprights facing each other in the back. The menu, with such entrees as Turkey Goldie and Spaghetti Goldie, was a bargain by any standards—a point that appealed not only to the general public but also to the club's earthy celebrity regulars, among them Ethel Merman, Lucille Ball, Judy Holliday, Julia Meade, Betty Comden, Adolph Green, and musical comedy actress Benay Venuta, a chum of Merman's. As soon as they walked in, Hawkins gave them a fanfare of their signature songs. Wrote Arthur Gelb in the *New York Times* (December 15, 1960), "Goldie seems to populate his room exclusively with close friends. He creates this impression by personally greeting all of his customers; the least ceremonious and the most approachable of hosts, he is apt to be on a first-name basis with you before you have finished your first drink . . . It's hard not to fall in with the illusion that you are participating in a big, happy, informal house party."

Hawkins first became known as the proprietor of Goldie's Fire Island, an Ocean Beach club that existed from 1952 until 1974. After playing at several New York cafés and restaurants he bought a room at 302 East 58th Street for $6,000 and opened the first Goldie's New

York, before relocating to his more familiar East 53rd Street location. In the first six months his guests included Marilyn Monroe and Ronald and Nancy Reagan, which helped word of mouth spread quickly. "People come where celebrities are," he explains, "and celebrities go where other celebrities have been written about." All of them appreciated having an alternative to the starchier, more expensive clubs. "To me," Hawkins says, "the reason Goldie's was so popular was that anything went. But I had complete control. If it went too far I told them to stop. Everybody had to act like ladies and gentlemen. We had no pickups at the bar. And the girls there—most of them were like models, they were so gorgeous: The guys went crazy."

He considered his club a place to eat, drink, and shoot the breeze as loudly as you wanted, with a rollicking two-beat soundtrack provided by Sanders and himself. He had no pretensions about reverent listening and discouraged casual drop-in singers from taking the stand. "I hate singers in nightclubs," he says, "because they interrupt you. You don't go to hear singers in places like this. You go to talk!"

Even so, Merman sang there on many occasions, Jule Styne played most of his score for the Broadway musical *Do Re Mi* before it went into rehearsal, and Jason Robards recited Shakespeare. On one memorable night actor Sydney Chaplin brought in Gene Kelly and Fred Astaire, whom Hawkins acknowledged with a medley of their hits. "The first thing I knew," he told Gelb, "Fred and Gene began singing at their table. There were only about twenty customers, and some of the tables had been pushed back against the walls. Suddenly Fred was on his feet, doing a tap dance up and down the aisle. He got a standing ovation."

A close friend of Hawkins's for many years, Merman was the celebrity many hoped to see when they went. Approaching her, though, was usually a mistake. "Everybody knew when she was there," says Hawkins, "but she didn't want them to know it, because she hated when anyone she didn't know came over and spoke to her. She'd look up as if to say, 'Get the hell away from me! What do I want to talk to you for?' "

Most of the time she came late at night, when she was well in her cups and likely to try even Hawkins's boundless Southern hospitality. "We had a Mr. and Mrs. Blackstone from way out in the west," he recalls, "and every time they came to New York they came to us.

They'd say, 'Goldie, we love this place so much. The other night we went to the Copacabana and we just couldn't wait to get back here.'

"One night Mrs. Blackstone came in with her two daughters and their husbands. I seated them, and a little later I went to their table and said, 'Is everything all right, Mrs. Blackstone?'

" 'Oh, I'm just so disappointed. I told Jennifer and Mary and Sam and Bob that we'd see celebrities here, and there aren't any.'

"I said, 'I can't make 'em come, it just so happens that they drop in sometimes.' Well, I looked up, and in were coming Merman and the songwriter Jimmy Van Heusen. As they came in the door so did Art Carney and his wife Barbara. Then a trumpet player named Jim Perry, who was a friend of Ethel's, came in with a date of his from the cast of *Gypsy*. All of them decided to sit together. I said, 'Now, Mrs. Blackstone, here are some celebrities right now. There's Ethel Merman, and there's Jimmy Van Heusen, who wrote almost everything Bing Crosby ever sang, and here's Art Carney. Would you like to sit at the table next to them?' They were thrilled. 'Why, *yes*! How sweet of you, Goldie!'

"*Big* mistake. I didn't realize that Ethel and the others were as drunk as they were. Art was on the tube, Ethel was bombed, Jimmy was always drunk, and Jim Perry egged everybody on.

"I brought them over, and to keep it from looking strange I sat down with them. Just as we were settled in, Art Carney looked up and said to Merman, 'I DON'T CARE WHAT YOU SAY, ETHEL, BENAY VENUTA IS A C---!' I thought, oh, Jesus Christ, I gotta stop this. I said, 'Jimmy, are you still in Palm Springs?' I didn't know what else to say. He said 'Oh, hi, Goldie. Yeah, I'm still in Palm Springs.' 'Are you still raising horses?' 'Oh, yeah, I'm raising horses.' Ethel said, 'Jimmy? How do horses fuck?'

" 'Well, they fuck just the way you do, Ethel.'

" 'Oh, do they go GRRRONNNG, GRRRONNNG?'

"I left the table. I thought, 'I can't get out of this.' "

Downtown at the Bon Soir, the outrageous was a nightly custom thanks to either Mae Barnes and the Three Flames or Kaye Ballard, an institution there by the mid-'50s. Fans were never surprised to see her enter, lie on her back on the piano, and chatter away as if the audience were on the ceiling. Ballard introduced new material constantly, leaving top writers such as Fred Ebb, Murray Grand, and Herb Hartig furious because she didn't pay them. The spendthrift comedienne was always in debt, even though she eventually commanded the highest fee of any Bon Soir act. "They said they couldn't make any money when Kaye was there," according to Ben Bagley, "but they kept inviting her back because she attracted crowds and kept the place on the map."

Nancy Andrews enjoyed playing the club, for she could uncrate the dirty jokes and songs that Herbert Jacoby forbade. If she spotted anyone who looked a little too sensitive, she took joy in reddening his face. When a student group from Yale sat ringside, she responded by singing "Renoir, Degas and Toulouse," a Bud McCreery number from *Shoestring '57* about a Paris model's saucy experiences posing for artists. Out dancing at the Moulin Rouge, she discovers that she is "zoooo tall, and he is zooo small" that it was "eazzzy to lose Toulouse-Lautrec." Andrews turned around on the bench and looked between her legs, as if Lautrec had escaped up her dress. Seeing how embarrassed the boys were and egged on by the entire room, she zeroed right in. "I could have gotten a diploma at Yale," she called out, "but I decided I wanted to make a living instead!"

Thelma Carpenter was one singer who knew how to quiet things down—even, she says, at the expense of such a crowd pleaser as Ballard. "Even though Kaye did mostly comedy, she's also a great singer. I usually went on first, and one day I heard her complaining that I mesmerized the audience and it was hard for her to do comedy. So being a bitch, sometimes I'd go out there and do a little comedy. Well, it was competition, and I loved competition. Avon Long and I were in a show together, and he tried to upstage me. I said, 'How dare you!' He said, 'Just remember one thing, Carp, I'd step on my mother's tits onstage!' "

Prima donnas did not survive long at the Bon Soir. The husky jazz-tinged voice of Sylvia Syms resounded with powerful authority, underscored by her girth as she wiggled between the twin pianos. For several years Syms's career was limited mainly to New York jazz clubs, but her 1956 hit recording of "I Could Have Danced All Night" helped change that. "Sylvia was a bitch on piano players," says Tiger Haynes, leader of the Three Flames, "because she likes her music a certain way. She made a wreck of Harold Fonville at Number

One. She couldn't get away with that at the Royal Roost, because the bop players were the stars there and nothing would upset them . . . Sylvia *who*?

"Then she has a big hit, and she is now a big recording star. They wanted her back at the Bon Soir, and now she has to make demands. One of them was that they get a new Steinway grand for her. Ernie Sgroi said, 'Tell her to go fuck herself!' She came back, and there was no new Steinway grand."

Some time later Sgroi ran into her. "So how much are you getting now?"

"For singing or fucking?" she asked.

The demonstrative audiences at the Bon Soir helped ease Anita Ellis's stage fright, for the singer was at her loosest there, telling Rita Hayworth and Vera-Ellen stories that led up to a piece of special material called "I Was the Girl Behind the Girl That Put the Blame on Mame." She wore her hair in a bun, parted severely down the center. During the number she turned upstage, pulled out the pins, did a quick turn, and down it tumbled. Then she peeled off one of her long gloves and twirled it, looking for all the world like Hayworth, and launched into a smoldering "Put the Blame on Mame."

In view of such attractions all over town, it isn't surprising that the ultragenteel Ruban Bleu began to decline by late 1955. Julius Monk himself yearned for a change. Starting in the late '40s he had spent several summers at a Provincetown club, presenting Dorothy Loudon, Kirkwood and Goodman, Nancy Andrews, and others in a loose revue format. In the summer of 1953 he took another group of players, including Bibi Osterwald and Alice Pearce, to Bermuda for a revue entitled *Stock in Trade*. He wanted to present one in New York, but the Ruban's postage-stamp stage would not accommodate it.

Nevertheless it was a shock when his tenure there ended abruptly around the beginning of 1956. According to Ronny Graham, "Julius always got along with Al Mele, Tony's older son, and he sort of ran the room with Julius. Al was wise enough to know that Julius was a prize, and you don't get this kind of guy often. But Tony was one of those old Italian men who felt the children should take over the business when he left. He opened a place in Long Island and moved Al out there, and Lee, the younger son, took over the Ruban. But this boy knew nothing about the business. Julius would come back from a short vacation and find people on the bill who were ludicrous." Tony Mele, however, felt that once his son got a feel for the job things would improve. Near the holidays, Monk was let go.

The Ruban declined steadily for its remaining year and a half. Of Monk's regulars only Bibi Osterwald, Irwin Corey, and two or three other performers remained. The other acts were a mixed bag. The better ones included folk singer Josh White, singer-actress Rosetta LeNoire, and standup comic Don Adams, future star of television's *Get Smart.* The big surprise was an appearance in November 1956 by Ethel Waters, whom theatre and movies had long forgotten. She accepted this booking and another at the Bon Soir because she was broke. By now Waters had found God and sang mostly spirituals and gospel numbers—a disappointment to those hoping to hear "Am I Blue?" or "Happiness Is a Thing Called Joe." Tired, immensely overweight, and frail of voice, Waters was no happier with the engagement, which she considered a humiliation. Recalls Bibi Osterwald, "She would come out and do her heavenly blessing, then go over to the cash register and say, 'Where the fuck is my money?' "

"She was very bitter," remembered Nancy Andrews, who shared the bill with her at the Bon Soir. "I had her over to dinner one night. I wanted to do something nice for her, because she had been so great and had fallen on hard times. I guess I felt sorry for her. This was Hate Whitey Week for her. We got to be pretty good friends, but it didn't last."

The Ruban was spared from inevitable bankruptcy when, near the start of 1957, the Meles received notice that the building had been slated for demolition that spring. Corning Glass planned to build its local headquarters there. The same fate would befall many nightclubs from the late '50s onward, as Big and New began to replace Small but Quaint. "It had nothing to do with beauty," says Bibi Osterwald. "It was money." The news saddened Monk and his alumni but mainly for nostalgic reasons; the time had come to move on. Little did he realize that he was on the threshold of a success that would outweigh any that he had known at the Ruban.

SOME NIGHTCLUBS were run by men with a sincere love of the profession, others by businessmen out to make money. Irving Haber, who owned four—the Playgoer's Club, Jorie's Purple Onion, the Downstairs Room, and Upstairs at the Downstairs—belonged among the latter. Haber was an accountant, well accustomed to counting income down to the penny. He owned his firm, Irving Haber and Company, for four decades, as well as a delicatessen, at least one bar, and a chain of tearooms called the Gypsy Tea Kettle, one of which still exists, left to his widow, Doris. Haber was hard-nosed, extremely tight with a buck, always looking to cut expenses, and not too concerned about employees, who complained constantly about his cheapness. Whenever possible he hired people for less than they were worth or tried to lower their salaries later. His small empire made him very wealthy, but he seldom acknowledged that fact. "You think I'm making any money out of this?" he would ask the young performers who worked in his clubs. "Forget it! I'm only doing this to give you kids a break!"

Haber's first nightclub venture was the Playgoer's Club, a cellar on 51st Street and Sixth Avenue where the Time-Life Building now stands. He owned a deli at street level and in 1945 turned the basement into one of the city's most popular boîtes. The featured act was comic Morey Amsterdam, remembered from television's *Dick Van Dyke Show*. Amsterdam kept the club packed for three seasons. As interlude pianist Audrey Pohlers recalls, "The capacity was officially about ninety, but most nights it was so crowded that I literally had to climb over people to get off the piano bench. Mel Torme was there a lot, Robert Young of *Father Knows Best* was a big fan, Milton Berle was always there, Merman came in several times, and so did Vic Damone.

"To get in you had to walk down a stairway on 51st Street under the deli. There was a flight of very narrow, steep steps leading into a tiny area, which was the entrance to the checkroom. That was the only staircase, and there was no emergency exit. Morey went on at ten o'clock and again at two, and people started lining up at eight-thirty, all the way to the top of those stairs and three across, so there was no room for people to come up. A fire would have been a disaster.

"The decor was strictly functional—it looked like every other tacky nightclub. Inside there was a small stage with space enough for the trio, and Morey worked in front of it. Food wasn't served at all, but in those years the Alcoholic Beverage Control Board insisted that there be food in addition to liquor. They had a kitchen downstairs, with one token sandwich in the refrigerator to show the inspector if need be. When it began to turn green they replaced it with another sandwich."

Amsterdam was anxious to break into the more lucrative and respectable fields of television and theatre. He considered nightclubs low-class and seldom mentioned the Playgoer's Club in later interviews. In 1948 he left to open in an unsuccessful Broadway revue entitled *Hilarities*. Shortly afterward Amsterdam began his TV career and gave up clubs entirely. Jackie Miles and other comics stepped in at the Playgoer's, but the room was so identified with Amsterdam that it faltered rapidly and eventually closed.

Thereafter the deli upstairs became a sleazy bar frequented by neighborhood prostitutes and drunks. The cellar stood vacant until 1954, when Keith Rockwell, a young entrepreneur from San Francisco, and a statuesque comedienne named Jorie Remus took it over. Rockwell was familiar in San Francisco for having opened the Purple Onion there in 1953. That club got off to a slow start and nearly closed until he found Remus, whom he calls "the best act we ever had"—this in a room that helped introduce Phyllis Diller, the Smothers Brothers, and the Kingston Trio. Like most club owners, the blonde, mousy, thin Rockwell seemed like an odd candidate for the business. "Keith had been a chicken flakker in East Oakland," says Gordon Connell. "What's a chicken flakker? Probably everything you can do to a chicken that you wouldn't want to think much about." (He sold the results door to door.)

Remus resembled an over-the-hill *Vogue* model. Fortyish, with a fabulous body and a face that she described as "interesting" rather than pretty, she looked as if she had enjoyed the high life a little too long. But she had not lost her allure. Seated on the piano for much of her act, she held a running discourse on the challenges that a modern girl faces once she lets the wolf inside the door. Her shoulder-length brown hair tumbled across her eyes, revealing a blonde streak that won her the nickname the Streak. Around her neck hung the longest feather boa ever waved around in a nightclub. It became an extension of her body, underlining every acerbic observation. "Have you ever known one of those years," she asked, "when everything seems to go all wrong? You wake up in the morning on the wrong side of your *life*. The first thing you discover is that your husband has run away with your best friend . . . and you miss her."

Remus was like a combination of Tallulah Bankhead and Dorothy Parker—a beat-up broad who did not always come out on top but could pinpoint the absurdity of any situation with a snappy wisecrack. Her low, husky purr resulted from constant smoking, which made her singing voice a croak. Except for her trademark, a piercing ballad she wrote herself entitled "You Know Where the Door Is," she used it to spoof torch singers of the Helen Morgan variety. "I detest people who become victims of love," she once said. She found some of the new canaries just as ridiculous. "Have you ever noticed," she asked a reporter, "that all stool singers, those sweet youngsters who wear Peter Pan collars and sing sitting down, always sing 'My Funny Valentine'? Well, it's my theory that the words bubble up out of the stool. They never have to learn the lyric; it jumps into their heads and pours out of their rosebud mouths whenever they climb up on their high chairs."

"Jorie was an extraordinarily creative comedienne," says Murray Grand, who accompanied her at Haber's club. "She really was the forerunner of Joan Rivers and Phyllis Diller. Phyllis copied her point-blank after hearing her at the San Francisco Purple Onion—and admits it."

The daughter of a dentist, Remus was born in New York as Marjorie Ramos. Her singing career began in Cannes in a tiny café called the Candlelight Room. One night she came as a guest, and the owner overheard her serenading some friends and offered her a job. "In those days," she said later, "I sang seriously the songs I now satirize. But anything I did brought smiles instead of swoons. I don't know what it was, but every number had 'em laughing. I had designed an all-white wardrobe for myself, and the gown was so tight I couldn't sit down. There were candelabra on the piano, and one night in the middle of a torchy chanson I got too close and my hair caught on fire. From then on no one has taken me seriously."

After appearing in Paris, London, and the Far East, Remus returned to America for a long engagement at the hungry i before moving across the street to the recently opened Purple Onion. Rockwell played the bass there and operated the club along with his family, a group of middle-class suburbanites who ran it like a general store. "Ma Rockwell was the ticket-taker," says Gordon Connell. "She had a permanent and wore a sweater, with glasses on a chain behind her neck. Behind the bar was Bud, who was married to Virginia, Keith's sister. Later they took over management of the place when Keith left the empire."

The hungry i monopolized the local business, and the Onion nearly went bankrupt until Rockwell brought in Remus. "Nothing much happened right away. Friday was our only busy day. We charged a quarter to get in and forty cents for beer and wine. After Jorie opened, Herb Caen of the *San Francisco Examiner* came in, and he had to sit on the steps and never even got served. The following Wednesday he wrote a big article about Jorie, and before long we had lines waiting to get in. After a few months we were out of debt, and I had ten thousand dollars in the bank and gave everybody two-hundred-dollar bonuses. Herbert Jacoby wanted Jorie at the Blue Angel, and Jorie asked me to come to New York with her.

"She had a two-week contract at the Blue Angel, but Jacoby renewed it for eight weeks. Jorie wanted us to open a place in New York, so every day I went out and got loaded talking to this bartender and that bartender, trying to find a place. I was told to go to the police department to get my nightclub license, and Orson Bean was on line in front of me. He said, 'There's a little place down on 51st Street where Morey Amsterdam used to work. It's just sitting there vacant. Why don't you go talk to the owner?' "

Haber agreed to hire Rockwell and Remus on a percentage basis, allowing them to manage the room and book acts. After what little redecoration Haber would pay for, they opened in 1954 and called it Jorie's Purple Onion. Once again they faced potential disaster. "It was a real struggle," says Rockwell. "No one was coming down. Then one day I heard that Popsie Whitaker of the *New Yorker* wanted to review us. The show started at nine o'clock, but he got there at six thirty to have dinner. Well, our dinner consisted of practically nothing. There was a young woman who made a pile of rice and put something different on top of it every night. We called it the All-Nations Dinner Hour. Finally the show started, and there were about twenty-five people there, as usual. But he gave us a very nice paragraph the next week, and from then on we were busy as hell."

Thereafter Remus took charge. The club reminded her of some of her seedier haunts on the Left Bank—the dominant feature of its decor was a Cocteaulike series of mannequin arms holding light globes—and had a no-holds-barred atmosphere well suited to her brand of comedy. "The clientele couldn't afford the Angel or the Ruban," says Grand. "A lot of college kids—not a hip crowd but very intellectual. They read the *New York Times* and *Time* magazine, but they weren't chic. After all, the place looked like the pits of hell."

On the minuscule budget that Haber allowed Remus, she could not afford top acts. "It was mostly people who would work cheap," Grand says. "If you got thirty-five dollars a week you were lucky." But even at that price there were many interesting acts available. The club opened with Remus, Will Holt, and nineteen-year-old Barbara McNair, a high-spirited, giggly youngster with a lovely voice and a girlish sense of humor. "She did mostly ballads like 'When I Fall in Love' and 'My Foolish Heart,' " says Grand, "with a couple of up-tunes, and she was absolutely wonderful. Then there was Cynthia Gooding, whose husband, Jac Holzman, owned Elektra Records. She was about six feet two and wore huge dangling earrings. She sat on a stool, playing the guitar and singing the most boring songs, like 'I Gave My Love a Cherry that Had No Stone.' "

Remus also featured Dolly Jonah, a redheaded singer who later married Will Holt. Jonah was, to put it mildly, an unfinished talent, as a fellow performer remembers. "One night Murray started the vamp to Matt Dennis's 'Will You Still Be Mine?' Dolly said, 'Wait a minute, I wanna talk first. Now, I'm gonna explain. I remembered there was a third chorus to this song, so I went to Schirmer's for the sheet music, but they said, 'No, honey, it doesn't exist.' I couldn't get it anyplace, and I happened to be sitting in the ladies' room of Bonwit Teller's—' Murray was trying to vamp her into the song. 'Wait, Mur, wait,' she said. 'All of a sudden I thought of the words, so I reached over for a piece of paper and I wrote them down. So when I look at these sheets, you'll know why.' " Such repartée tried even the Purple Onion crowd. One night Jonah stopped short in the middle of a monologue and glared into the crowd. *"Who threw that seeded roll?"*

The sublime took its place alongside the ridiculous when the young duo of singer Jackie Cain and pianist-singer Roy Kral appeared in 1955. Married since 1949, the couple developed a jazz-inflected style of club singing, characterized by bop-inspired harmonies and improvisations, scat fills, and difficult unison lines sung with perfect precision. They introduced a vast catalog of vocalized jazz instrumentals and shed new light on even the most familiar Gershwin and Rodgers and Hart standards.

In a field where musical values usually take a backseat to dramatic or comedic ones, Jackie and Roy (as they are commonly known) have continued to bring a rare level of musicianship to café singing, especially Cain with her pure, uncannily accurate intonation and ability to sculpt a ballad with loving concentration. Unlike most jazz singers they exude a flair for performing that has made them as pleasurable to watch as to listen to. Throughout their sets Cain, with her silky blonde bangs, delicate cheekbones, and svelte figure, gives frequent and affectionate glances toward the man at the keyboard. The couple has straddled the difficult border between jazz and café singing with ease, their painstaking arrangements sounding remarkably fresh and spontaneous.

A former band vocalist in her hometown of Milwaukee, Cain met Kral in Chicago, where he had played the piano with various orchestras and jazz groups. Admirers of Gene Krupa vocalists Buddy Stewart and Dave Lambert (later of Lambert, Hendricks and Ross), who originated a style of wordless unison bop singing in the mid-'40s, they decided to team up and do the same. At Jump Town, a Chicago jazz club, disc jockey and future television host Dave Garroway heard them and began to plug them on his radio show. This helped lead to a two-year stint with saxophonist Charlie Ventura's renowned orchestra. From there they branched into non-jazz rooms (they made their New York club debut at the Blue Angel in 1954), where they added such show and movie songs to their repertoire as "Mountain Greenery," "The Continental," "Lazy Afternoon," and Ira Gershwin and Yip Harburg's "Let's Take a Walk Around the Block." They also took pride in introducing songs by such young writers as composer-pianist Tommy Wolf and lyricist Fran Landesman, premiering that duo's "Spring Can Really Hang You Up the Most," the hippest torch song of the day. In 1991 they celebrated their forty-fourth anniversary as a musical duo, looking and sounding not much different than they did in 1947.

Remus also featured the comedy team of Igor and H: writer Herb Hartig and actor and future film director Paul Mazursky. Classmates at Brooklyn College, they had come separately to New York—Hartig to write for nightclub comics and singers, Mazursky to act. Mazursky won a role in Stanley Kubrick's first film, *Fear and Desire*, but by 1953 wound up working in a health food shop. He asked Hartig to write an act for him, then suggested they form a team. Mazursky called himself Igor because of his party impersonation of the character from *Frankenstein*. They auditioned for Remus and were hired in 1955. "I think the AGVA minimum at the time was one hundred and seventy-five dollars an act, or eighty-seven fifty per person," says Hartig. "Irving said, 'Fellas, I can't afford to pay you that. I gotta give you eighty-seven fifty on the books, but you gotta give me back fifty dollars each.' And we were grateful to do it. Irving was a decent guy, I thought, because he was a scoundrel but you knew where you stood with him. He was very up-front, which Julius was not always. Julius could harbor a grudge and you wouldn't know it, but you'd suffer a thousand deaths."

Their act consisted of high comedy with an intellectual touch, brightened by impersonations of prison wardens, aging surgeons, Sherlock Holmes, and a variety of other characters. In a piece entitled "Great Moments in Motion Picture History" Hartig explained how American movies saved you time. "If you happen to come in a little late you don't have to stay to see the beginning again, because there's usually one bit of dialogue which not only sums up the whole plot, it gives you the producer's IQ as well."

> "Say, gang! There must be *some* way to raise money for the new football stadium!"
> "Say, gang! *I* know! Why don't we put on a Big Broadway Musical?"
> "Swell! And my Dad's a Good Egg: He'll let us use his old Hippodrome!"
>
> *
>
> "But perhaps the murderer had his reasons, Doctor?"
> "Reasons? Could any 'reasons' justify such bestiality? No, no, no, my dear friend, we're dealing with a homicidal schizophrenic."
> "A . . . homi . . . cidal schizophrenic, but . . . to conceive and . . . perpetrate such crimes, a man would have to be a GENIUS! Don't you think?"
> "Genius? No, a MAD DOG—who must be hunted down and DESTROYED! . . . You *must* let me look into those headaches of yours, they seem to be getting *worse*."

They also examined the lines used by men to get "object of emotion X into position Y"—some direct ("A girl *your* age? What are you *saving* it for?"), others circuitous: "Life . . . is meaningless. Man . . . flung into a forgotten corner of Chaos . . . creeps toward the polarity of Woman, to find . . . in her briefness . . . a momentary warmth, and the illusion of Belonging. [PAUSE] So what about it?"

But Remus was the star of the show, each night dispensing words of experience in a voice that had not lost heart even if she had lost her illusions. She concentrated on practical subjects, such as how to send the insistent gentleman on his way tactfully. "I didn't tell you I was writing a book, did I? Well, everybody else is writing a book so I thought I should too. My book is a book for women. It's called *Men: How To Say No To Them, or What To Do Until the Police Come* . . . Let's pretend you've spent the evening with someone you like very much, and now he brings you home, and though it was a lovely evening it's very late and you're very tired and you want to go to bed. And so does he. Well, you don't want to be harsh with him because you'd like to keep him around, perhaps for future reference, and after all this is your first date with him. You might tell him that. You might say, 'This is our first date!' Well, he doesn't care about that. Well, then you say—pleading sort of pathetically—'I thought *you* were different!' Well, he wasn't. As a last resort, you say, 'Why, sure! Why don't you make yourself a drink while I slip into something comfortable, and then perhaps we can talk this over . . . [SCRATCHES HERSELF NEAR THIGH] Oh, this? I don't know exactly *what* this is. It's some sort of rash, I guess. Doctors don't know either . . ."

As a running gag, she answered a ringing phone near the piano and talked to one of her suitors, an ungrateful bunch of losers who continually tried to get the better of her. "Hello? Oh, yes, I was just going to call you to tell you that I'm not coming over. Yes, I know you're expecting me, but I'm not coming over. Now, just listen to me for a minute. I'm tired, and I'm sick, and . . . What do you think I'm made of? *Steel?* Look, let's get this straight once and for all . . . *You have tortured me for the last time!*" [SLAMS DOWN PHONE] Then, matter of factly to the audience, "I just canceled an appointment with my dentist."

But sometimes Remus was the loser, as with Reginald, who "supported me in a manner to which I never thought I'd grow accustomed—poverty. I began to get suspicious," she confided. "I began to notice little things. I went to him, I said, 'Reginald, Reginald, don't you love me anymore? Tell me the truth—give it to me straight!' Well, I shouldn't have said that. As soon as I was able to walk—

with crutches—I went to him again. I was tired of playing games. I wanted to know the truth. Well, I wish I'd kept my big mouth shut. I wouldn't have lost quite so many teeth. I decided to give him one last chance. I went to him, I said, 'Weginald? Weginald? Don't you wuv me anymaw?' He said, 'Naw! You don't have any teeth!' "

There was a kernel of truth in these monologues, for insecurity and self-destructiveness plagued her. She was addicted to alcohol as well as cigarettes, and drank before and after shows. It never interfered with her performances, but offstage it contributed to a sad, brooding manner. "Before the shows," Grand says, "she sat in her tiny dressing room for hours applying all this makeup. She had very bad skin, and she knew it. Then she'd look in the mirror and say 'Ecccch!' and take it all off again."

Remus later married photographer Allen Murray. "They were drinking buddies," says Grand. Murray often humiliated her in public and in private, but Remus had a certain masochistic streak, and the marriage lasted. Her lack of motivation hindered her career, causing her a lot of bitterness over missed opportunities. "She was her own worst enemy," says Keith Rockwell, "the opposite of Phyllis Diller, who practiced positive thinking. Somebody important would want to see her backstage, and she wouldn't come out. She didn't do anything to promote her career as she should have."

Her heart lay in the theatre. Asked what she wanted to do next, her answer was always the same: "Stage, stage, and more stage!" She was a skillful and charismatic actress but always seemed to land in regional or off-Broadway shows that closed quickly, and many parts that were promised to her never even materialized. After *New Faces of 1956* Leonard Sillman offered to cast her in his next revue, but by the time *New Faces of 1962* opened (and bombed) Remus had moved to San Juan. In any case, she was in her mid-forties by then and would no longer have been a new face.

Jorie's Purple Onion began to crumble in 1955 when Rockwell suddenly departed. "The better we did the more Irving Haber kept bringing up petty expenses, so we never made much ground. I'd been away from San Francisco for two years, and I was kind of homesick. I had a terrible fight with Jorie, so I told her I was taking a couple of weeks off and going back. When I arrived I got to thinking: I didn't own the license, I didn't own the lease, I didn't own anything. I called

Jorie and told her I was giving her my half of the club and that I wasn't coming back."

Relations between Haber and Remus had always been strained, but with Rockwell gone there was no one to play peacemaker. They had several ugly arguments, mostly about money, and Haber knew how to play upon her insecurities. Remus took a leave of absence to costar with Kaye Ballard and Josephine Premice in a revue called *Pleasure Dome.* The cast looked forward to an off-Broadway opening, until one of the producers allegedly skipped town with the funds. After so many similar disappointments, Remus was shattered. Unable to bear the thought of returning to Haber, she disappeared. No one at the Onion knew where to reach her. When it became apparent that she would not return, Haber appointed Murray Grand as manager.

Most of the regulars were Remus fans, and when they learned of her exit, attendance fell sharply. Nevertheless Grand kept the club running for several months, renaming it the Downstairs Room and hiring some bright, appealing acts, none of whom, unfortunately, could take Remus's place. Grand decided to team actor-comic Jack Fletcher with comedienne Dody Goodman, known to TV viewers as Jack Paar's late-'50s sidekick and, twenty years later, as Martha Shumway, the mother of *Mary Hartman, Mary Hartman.*

A redhead with befuddlement written all over her face, Goodman spoke in a nasal twang through which the most innocent reflections emerged as hilarious. She came to New York in the late '30s to be a dancer but didn't make a name for herself until 1955, when she appeared as a singing comedienne in *Shoestring Revue.* The year before, she had accepted a hasty offer from Max Gordon and assembled a slightly bizarre act for the Village Vanguard. Its centerpieces were a "dramatic" reading of E. B. White's poem "The Song of the Queen Bee" and an original poem, "I Am a Shepherdess," performed in a long white gown with a bow. "I didn't audition for Max," she says. "If I had he probably would never have wanted me. I guess he just needed someone to fill in for two weeks. I don't think I ever really wanted to do nightclubs. I didn't like the smoke, and I don't drink. And I don't think the audience at the Vanguard knew what I was doing at all. It was really a jazz place, and there at that time was Enid Mosier and her Trinidad Steel Band. It was loud, and they stayed on forever. Then I came out with a shepherd's bow, and they didn't know what that was. I had written to White and asked for permission to do his poem, but then his wife came and didn't like the way I was doing it. I did it like a Marilyn Monroe bee, and she felt I should do it like a Bea Lillie bee, so I just cut it."

Goodman was reluctant to return to nightclubs, especially with a cohort she didn't know. "I met him one night and said, 'I don't want to have an act with anyone.' Fletcher said, 'I don't either. I don't want to have an act with you.' " But Grand persuaded them to try it, and although it ran only two weeks their show created a last spurt of enthusiasm at the failing room. "We split the proceeds," Goodman says, "and it seems to me I got forty-five dollars. I can't remember if that was for the two weeks or for one."

That act inspired the first legitimate café revue in New York City. Walter Winchell dropped by and was so delighted that he suggested that Grand expand it into a revue. Grand liked the idea but was not sure he could do so alone, so he called Julius Monk, then in San Francisco. Monk had reached one of the lowest points in his career. After his dismissal from Le Ruban Bleu he took a job at the hungry i as a talent adviser and, according to some, a glorified maître d'. Monk had dreamed of producing a nightclub revue since seeing the Revuers, and he flew back to Manhattan immediately.

Grand posed the idea to Irving Haber, who had never heard of a revue. "I said, 'Well, instead of having one act come out after another and introducing them, we'll combine them and turn it into a little show.' I told him Julius Monk was here, and since he'd never heard of Julius all of us met at the Gypsy Tea Kettle. Julius was a wreck. He didn't have a job and didn't know what he was going to do with his life now that the Ruban was finished. Anyhow, we decided then and there to do a revue."

Eager to give the club a fresh start, Haber closed it with little notice and allowed everyone about two weeks to create a new show and to get the room in shape to reopen. Monk organized the renovation, enlisting an artist friend named Milton Marx to paint a set of celebrity caricatures along the staircase walls. Other friends repainted, built a makeshift stage, and tried to make the dilapidated club a bit tidier.

In the meantime, Grand struggled to assemble a show in almost no time. At Monk's suggestion he hired June Ericson and comic Gerry

Matthews, both Ruban alumni and great favorites of Monk's. Beyond this, Grand took charge. He had time to write only a title number, drawing the remaining material from Goodman and Fletcher's collaboration and from the trunks of colleagues. Along with arranger and second pianist Stan Keen, Grand and the cast rehearsed in his apartment for thirteen days, then went to the club for a hurried runthrough. John Heawood, who had choreographed *The Boy Friend* a year before, offered some direction. Monk looked on and made a few minor comments.

Four Below, as the show was called, opened on March 4, 1956. That afternoon Grand arrived at the club to begin preparations. "I looked up at the marquee, and it said in big letters: JULIUS MONK'S DOWNSTAIRS PRESENTS FOUR BELOW. My name was nowhere to be seen. I was livid. I said, 'This show's not opening until I get my name up there!' Then I saw the program, and my name wasn't mentioned at all. There were no composer credits on my songs. I made such a fuss that Julius had my name painted on the marquee in small letters and added it to the program, but he still screwed me.

"It was all so tacky. He didn't do anything on the first show. *Nothing.* During our rehearsal at the club he said, 'Now, dahlings, move this here and that there.' We just did what we had done eight million times before and gave it a running order."

To everyone's surprise, Grand's little revue became the hit of the season. "Who knew it was going to turn the town upside down?" says Grand. "We were just doing it to collect the salaries." Raved *Cue* (March 17, 1956): "Along comes that touring boulevardier and *conferencier par excellence*, Julius Monk, and with the wholehearted cooperation of a gaggle of extraordinarily talented people, he has brought in a gusher of sophisticated entertainment . . . easily qualifies as the best nightclub fare in town." The *New York Journal-American*'s John McClain wrote, "There's a pleasant lack of pretentiousness about the whole thing and it has the same charm that can be found in only, as far as I know, those little joints in Paris . . . And I know absolutely nothing about any of [the cast] beyond the fact that they're gay and talented."

Nearly every review extolled Monk as the mastermind of *Four Below*, as did the liner notes of his future revue albums. Only the cast, it seemed, knew the truth. "Julius didn't seem to like to give other people credit for anything," says Dody Goodman. "He did have a big following, and that may have been why we had such a big hit, because he was known to have quality material and good taste. But his work on the first show was minimal—'Why don't we do this a little faster and that a little slower?' And he didn't find any of the material. Murray arranged the whole thing."

"Dody wasn't speaking to him," Grand says, "and I didn't talk to him for about five years. He kept saying, 'Well, dahling, your sister died and left you money and I don't have any money. I've got to protect myself.' I thought, oh, fuck you! Protect myself!"

Since it was assembled hastily *Four Below* lacked the smooth flow of the later shows that Monk did direct. But the material, written by Grand, Michael Brown, Tom Jones and Harvey Schmidt, G. Wood, Herb Hartig, and others, was consistently brighter and funnier than that in Monk's revues, and never would he have a comedienne of Goodman's calibre. "Nothing like Dody has ever been seen before or since," says Bud McCreery. "Her voice, her expressions, even her slightly slouched, wavering stance—like a puppet without strings—were all hilarious."

Goodman appeared in every other piece and stole the show. The highlight was a Herb Hartig takeoff on Tennessee Williams entitled "Southern Belle." "So! You're a travelin' salesman, and you would like a night's lodgin'? . . . Well, now, I don't know, Sir, truly I do not. You see, I'm a young lady all alone here. No one for miles and miles. You could take me in your manly arms an' molest me, and carry me upstairs an' have your way with me, an' nobody would hear my screams for help. But you wouldn't take advantage of a young lady like that, though, would you, Sir? . . . Oh. You wouldn't. [PAUSE] Well, then, let me put it to you another way—"

Elsewhere in the show June Ericson sang the Jerome Kern–Leo Robin ballad "Up with the Lark," looking like a dream café singer and sounding as light and wistful as the lark itself. The cast joined for "The Third Avenue El," a nostalgic Michael Brown requiem for the recently demolished structure that had long submerged Third Avenue in shadows and mechanical clatter and that was now strangely missed.

Despite Monk's touch-ups the club still looked like the cellar it was. "By that time," says Gerry Matthews, "it was like Berlin after the war. It stood among a block of old apartment buildings that were ready to be demolished to make way for the Time-Life Building. People kept coming down the outside stairs looking for the subway. Cats lived in the basement and used the club as a bathroom. The stage had been built by a drunken young friend of Julius's. It was supposed to be a semicircle, but he had used an electric saw and cut it crooked. The room was painted battleship gray, and the ladies' room was right next to the doorway to the stage, so we heard flushing toilets all through the show. People walked up onstage and strolled right past us to get to the ladies' room. Rita Hayworth was in the audience one night, sitting up front next to the right wall. Some woman fan walked over to accost her and threw up right next to her on the floor. One of the waiters came over and swept that deposit under the little curtain at our stage entrance, and one of us came offstage and slipped and fell right in the mess."

"The greenroom was painted black," adds June Ericson, "and whoever got to the club first kicked the dressing room door to get the rats out."

"The dressing room was about the size of a closet," Dody Goodman remembers. "June dressed in there, and so did Stan, Murray—everyone. I had nine different costumes, and after a while they all smelled like cats. We supplied the costumes ourselves—the cats certainly supplied the odor. At first we did shows at ten-thirty, twelve, and one-thirty, which meant I had to do twenty-seven costume changes a night in that little room."

And yet this close, huddled feeling was part of the club's charm. The Downstairs Room had an exciting sense of exclusiveness that year, before it became nationally publicized. For now the atmosphere was much simpler. Eighty people cramped together in a basement shared an evening that seemed intended only for those as serendipitous as themselves. But *Four Below* and its sequel *Son of Four Below* were refreshingly free of the precious material and snobbish tone of Monk's later revues. They seemed like parlor shows, with four likable young performers singing and clowning in someone's tenement living room. Everything moved as swiftly as a fall breeze. No sketch or song ran longer than five minutes, and if any piece failed on a given night another followed quickly. And although it was a challenge to rise from the table without spilling at least two drinks, audiences enjoyed the novelty of seeing a show in the genial atmosphere of a nightclub, with no obligation to sit in silence.

Four Below ended its five-month run in August 1956, and Irving Haber was anxious for a follow-up. To no one's surprise, Grand and Goodman would not be part of it. Haber believed that Monk's reputation and flair had made *Four Below* a smash, and saw no reason to reengage Grand. "I was offended when Murray wasn't asked back," says Goodman. "They asked me back, but I wanted to do the second *Shoestring Revue* with Ben Bagley so I turned them down."

And so the Downstairs Room became Julius Monk's terrain. For *Son of Four Below* he kept Fletcher, Matthews, and Ericson, replacing Goodman with singer-comedienne Ceil Cabot, another Ruban alumna. Cabot had gained some national celebrity through a thirteen-week stint on the Robert Q. Lewis television show. With her short red hair, saucer eyes, impish grin, and squeaky voice Cabot had the same sort of outlandish charm as Goodman, and sparked Monk's shows for the next six years.

Monk hired Bud McCreery to help in choosing material. McCreery would contribute some of the wittiest numbers to Monk's revues and provided *Son of Four Below* with a special standout, "Guess Who Was There," a satire on the East Side pseudosophistication that would, ironically, dominate Monk's future shows. It recalled Noel Coward's "[I Went to] A Marvelous Party":

Elsa and Noel, Tallulah and Cole
And ev'rybody was there!
The host in a toga was practicing yoga
And floating twelve feet in the air
All the women were dressed
In their newest and best
And babbled with great incoherence
Dear Elsa, they said,
Stood all night on her head
Which greatly improved her appearance . . .

Five numbers came from lyricist Tom Jones, with and without Harvey Schmidt, his partner and future collaborator on off-Broadway's legendary *The Fantasticks.* Jones and Schmidt had met nine years before at the University of Texas but went their separate ways upon graduation, Schmidt into the army and Jones to try his fortunes in the theatre. Once in New York he met Gerry Matthews, a former classmate, who asked him to fashion a comedy act for him and an out-of-town actor friend from Chicago named Tom Poston. Jones combined some of his own tunes with sketches that Matthews and Poston had performed in *Talent '54*, an annual showcase produced by New York's stage managers, and they auditioned at the Vanguard. "Max said we were too big for the room," says Matthews. "Then we auditioned for Jorie Remus at the Purple Onion and flopped. After that Julius, who had heard us in *Talent '54*, booked us at the Ruban for a month."

Gordon was right, however. Like many stage-oriented performers, the team had trouble scaling down their work for a tiny club. "The customers didn't know what we were doing," Matthews admits. "Vernon Rice of the *New York Post* came on opening night and wrote a column championing Tom and me. He died after handing it in. Julius didn't want to tell us, but Norman Paris said, 'Boy, you really killed old Vernon, didn't you?' That hit us like a sledgehammer. One night some drunken man in the back of the room announced in a stentorian voice, 'YOU WILL DIE!' He said it several times, until Julius finally turned up the houselights and lectured him. But it was prophetic. We did die."

Monk wanted them to stay their full month, but the Meles insisted they leave after two weeks. "The act just fell apart," says Matthews. He managed to line up a few TV appearances. After Poston was signed by Jack Rollins, he won a regular spot on the *Steve Allen Show* as "The Man in the Street" and went on to a lengthy career as an actor, comic, and television writer. Jones stayed in New York until Christmas. "I had dreamed of becoming a successful director, and it all collapsed. At the end of one full year, I went back to Texas to lick my wounds and figure out what I was going to do." When Schmidt left the army soon after, he and Jones moved to New York and began contributing to Monk's revues. They wrote two-thirds of *Demi-Dozen*, his fourth show, and in 1960 The *Fantasticks* opened at the Sullivan Street Playhouse in Greenwich Village. In 1991 it was still in residence, the longest-running musical in theatre history.

The success of *Son of Four Below* inspired Monk and Haber to try a second nightclub venture. On April 10, 1957, they created the Upstairs at the Downstairs by converting the upstairs bar into a café for singers and instrumentalists. "Julius wanted to protect us from the old clientele," says Matthews. "It was all drunks and prostitutes." According to a press release:

> The room, furnished in Early American Kemtone, seats a tidy thirty-five, with a standup bar for a like number, and has been opened primarily to comfortably take care of the overflow waiting to see the intimate revue "Son of Four Below" which is still playing to turnaway crowds downstairs.
>
> Entertainment is continuous from 9:30 P.M., and a menu, replete with Sandwiches du Jour, is available. Minimum charge during the week is $1.50 per person, with $2.50 on Friday and Saturday.

That room is fondly remembered for the partnership of Blossom Dearie and Annie Ross, two singers who have earned a permanent place in jazz vocal history. In 1958 Ross became the female third of Lambert, Hendricks and Ross, a vocal trio who sang original lyrics based on instrumental jazz solos. With her short red hair, tailored, understated attire, and frosty voice Ross typified the best '50s jazz singers—a group who limited their emotional display to a tantalizing undercurrent and who outwardly were pictures of musicianly authority.

Singer-pianist Dearie's dulcet, girlish voice projected a grown-up wisdom and sophistication but refused to raise itself above the crowd. As Whitney Balliett wrote in the *New Yorker* (May 26, 1973): "Without a microphone, it would not reach the second floor of a dollhouse." With it went a delicate piano style that swung infectiously, packing some extraordinary rhythmic and harmonic invention into a few well-chosen notes and chords. Her blonde pageboy bobbed up and down as she surveyed the keyboard with the concentration of a country girl giving a church recital.

She was born in East Durham, New York, in the Catskill Mountains. "I was born in April," she told Balliett, "and the day I arrived a neighbor brought over some peach blossoms, and when my father saw them he said, 'That's it. We'll call her Blossom.' " She stubbornly kept that name, even against the advice of one agent who felt that in keeping with the trend for '50s jazz canaries to have either masculine-sounding first names (Jo, Chris, Bobbe, Pat) or names ending in "i" (Jeri, Teri, Lori, Vicki, Wini) she should change hers to Toni Grey.

Her act with Ross couldn't have been simpler. Dearie took her place at the piano, and Ross entered. "Hi, Blos. How are you doing?"

"Just fine, Annie."

"You wanna sing some songs?"

"OK, Annie."

The songs included "Love Is the Reason" from the Arthur Schwartz–Dorothy Fields musical *A Tree Grows in Brooklyn*, the Gershwins' "Nice Work If You Can Get It," and Rodgers and Hammerstein's "It Might As Well Be Spring," which Dearie translated into Berlitz French as a nod to her years spent in Paris in the early '50s.

Ross kept the duo earthbound, which was not easy, for along with Dearie's unique musical personality went one of the most eccentric natures in nightclubs. As Murray Grand remarks, "I think Blossom went into a little room somewhere when she was a child and never came out." Audiences who dared talk or clink their silverware while she was performing got a hint of this. Dearie never accepted the fact that nightclubs were not concert halls and that customers sometimes came for reasons other than music. Wrote Tim Taylor in *Cue* (July 17, 1957):

> During a stop-in at the Upstairs the other night I witnessed a show of temperament which both astonished and annoyed me. A gal named Blossom Dearie, who sings and plays piano (she's a pretty fair cocktail pianist) finished her first song and then asked a tableful of patrons if they'd please be quiet "while I sing." In the first place, the customers weren't particularly loud and, in the second, I've always thought it was a performer's job to capture—not demand—our attention and applause. Come off it, dearie.

Prior to the Upstairs, Dearie and Ross had teamed at the Mars Club in Paris and at the Embassy Club in London. The French were appreciative, but at the Embassy they faced a snobbish, unresponsive audience. On the first evening of their two-week booking hardly a soul applauded.

Afterward Ross said, "Blossom, we really died in there!"

"Oh, Annie, no we didn't. The English are just so undemonstrative."

At that moment the owner walked over. "Well, ladies, you can make it easy and quit right now."

"We can't quit! We have a two-week engagement!"

"All right, then you'll have to show up fully dressed every night. I may decide to put you on at twelve o'clock. I may decide to put you on at eleven-thirty. Or I may decide not to put you on at all."

They were staying at a cheap hotel some distance from the club. Their booking coincided with one of the thickest fogs London had seen in years. It was impossible to get a cab, so every night they had to walk to work—no mean feat, for they could hardly see a foot in front of them. By the time they reached the club each evening their hair and clothes were soaked—and to little avail, for on all but two or three nights the owner chose not to use them at all. They were not asked back.

Reserved as English audiences are, this gives another indication of the rarified character of so many New York acts, even those as straightforward as Ross and Dearie's. The charm of a Manhattan repertoire often eluded those in other cities, who did not understand the local references or the urbane quality that held so much appeal at clubs like the Upstairs. That is why most café performers were relieved to come back to New York, where worthy acts seldom went unapplauded, even if only by aficionados.

MONK'S NEXT REVUE, *Take Five*, opened on October 10, 1957, and put him and the Downstairs Room on the national map. It may have been the finest of his career, largely due to its star and principal author, Ronny Graham. With this show Graham returned to nightclubs after a troubled and mostly inactive year. In 1956 he had become a patient of Max Jacobson, the notorious "Dr. Feelgood" who prescribed amphetamines and cortisone to countless celebrities in the '50s and '60s as "cures" for a variety of emotional ills, real or imagined. "Alan Jay Lerner recommended him to me because he had used him when he had a writer's block once. He suggested that I sign myself into a psychiatric institute, and I stayed there for seventy days. During 1956 I did hardly anything at all."

Ben Bagley paid one visit to Jacobson. "He was mad as a hatter. When I walked in Henry Fonda was the receptionist. The regular girl was out sick and Fonda had volunteered to answer the phones. I went inside Jacobson's office, and he didn't even ask for my medical history. His nurse started to prepare an injection. Something seemed fishy to me, and I said, 'What you're giving me doesn't contain cortisone, does it?' I was severely allergic to cortisone. Their jaws dropped. Jacobson said in his German accent, 'Well, yes it does, but I can give you something that doesn't.' Can you imagine? That stuff would have killed me. I don't know why I stayed, but I did. As the nurse mixed up a potion he said, 'Now, these are vitamins that are going to give you a lot of energy, and since you're a creative person they'll make you accomplish twice as much.' Within minutes I was so full of energy I walked twenty blocks, but by evening I felt completely drained. I also noticed that I had a strong foot odor, and I never have that problem. I took a long bath and went to bed. The next morning when I woke up, the odor was back. That's one of the things amphetamines do.

"The next week Jacobson's nurse called me and asked when I was coming in for my next treatment. I said, 'Well, they cost thirty-five dollars each and I really can't afford it.' A lot of famous people could, though, and went to him week after week until they were hopelessly addicted to the stuff."

Take Five's cast also included Ellen Hanley, comedienne Jenny Lou Law, Gerry Matthews, and Ceil Cabot. It was directed by Irish stage actor Max Adrian, who had costarred earlier that year as Dr. Pangloss in the original Broadway production of *Candide*. The show featured some of the boldest (for its day) and funniest material that Monk would ever use. Two songs about unlikely seductions were penned by comedy lyricist Steven Vinaver and composed by Jonathan Tunick, whose exceptional arranging and conducting talents would contribute greatly to the success of Stephen Sondheim's shows. In "Pro Musica Antiqua" Ellen Hanley sang of a maiden's ruin at the hands of a supposedly respectable gentleman whom she had met at a concert at the Cloisters:

He invited me to his flat
For a cup of tea and a chat
For he said he had a batch of recordings to play
Of Dufay and Després
So what could I say but yes?

What a fool I was to go
What an idiot from tippy-top to toe
For I knew from that lovesick look in his eye

He could lay me low with a single sigh
Well, he laid me low and he laid me high
At the Pro Musica Antiqua . . .

And Jenny Lou Law sang "Gristede's," a beguine set in the expensive East Side supermarket:

Gristede's
We were both in Gristede's
I was looking for Wheaties
You were looking for Kix . . .

Vinaver satirized beat poetry in "Poet's Corner," a panel reading by three prototypical bards of the day. Graham portrayed the Angry Poet:

> We are the youth! We are the drivers of the trucks, we are the drivers of the slag. We toil from dawn till dusk till dawn, till dusk till dawn. And you think you can lick us? Well, that's where you're wrong, you lousy fascists. You call yourselves Big Business? But you don't fool me, 'cause I don't scare so easy! And I'm gonna get ya, you crummy bastards! I am the voice of my community and I got a song to sing and I'm gonna sing it! And my song goes: YOU CRUMMY BASTARDS, I AM YOUTH!

In addition to excellent reviews in *Variety* and local newspapers, *Time* devoted a full page to the Downstairs Room:

> There are no leg irons in the walls, but otherwise it is the sort of place the Count of Monte Cristo might have tunnelled from . . . What brings full basements (legal limit: 80 customers) to the Downstairs these nights is a small, eccentric troupe of humorists who put on one of Manhattan's first successful nightclub song-and-satire revues in fifteen years, recalling the Village Vanguard's famed Revuers with Judy Holliday.

Next came several syndicated reviews and a *Life* magazine spread, and within weeks *Take Five* had become Monk's biggest hit to date. The press touted him as the epitome of urban sophistication, if of an eccentric sort (*Time* called him "a mustached, elegant North

Carolinian . . . who dresses like an under secretary at the foreign office, struts a pea soup-thick British accent, and floats out an occasional sowbelly vowel"). His vocabulary, demonstrated in his nightly introductions, suited that accent perfectly:

> Ladies and gentlemen, good evening. And thank you so much for coming downstairs to join us in our third subterranean spelunking season. By this time we believe it is a complete and general consensus that an actor will *abso*-lutely *destroy* himself—if encouraged by applause. May I have the privilege of directing yours to our new cabaret concept. Why not be prudent? Why not indeed—Take Five!

As he called their names the cast poked their heads through slits in the curtain. And no one but Monk could have written the program notes:

> PORTOFINO—Words and music, Michael Brown. A Mediterranean melange made manifest by the troupe, *prego*, *prego*!

These capsule summaries were no more comprehensible than his speech, but Monk's idiosyncrasies carried with them a mystique that made anything he did seem like New York elegance personified. This would play an important role in the success of his later shows, where chic prevailed at the expense of wit.

But no one could deny the authority that he brought to all his revues. "Julius told us at the beginning that our role in a particular sketch could change," says Graham, "and we had to take it on faith that he knew what was best for us. And by God he did. I wanted one piece so bad my teeth ached, and he said it was just not right for me. He gave it to Gerry Matthews and he was absolutely right."

Take Five ran until the summer of 1958, and everyone shared in the excitement of watching their little revue achieve the commercial success that they could never have predicted. No longer was the Downstairs Room a local secret, a fact that some cast members regretted. "There used to be parties at Irving Haber's tearooms," Graham says, "and everybody came, because they were like family affairs. Julius would be there, and Bruce Kirby, one of our waiters, brought all his kids. It was very warm and close then. We used to go on treasure hunts after the show. We'd go in the old deserted brownstones on 51st Street with Xs on the windows, and take marble covers off the fireplaces and use them as benches at home."

Monk tried to preserve this family feeling by using the same fifteen or so players for most of his revues. They included George Furth, later librettist of *Company*, *Merrily We Roll Along*, *The Act*, and other Broadway productions, and a film and stage actor in his own right; Bill Hinnant, a pint-size, sandy-haired actor known in the '60s for his portrayal of Snoopy in the musical *You're a Good Man, Charlie Brown*; Jane and Gordon Connell, who had grown into expert singer-actor-comics since their Ruban days; Rex Robbins, a tall, attractive graduate of the Yale Drama School who later rubbed dramatic elbows by night with Laurence Olivier and John Gielgud and, by day, enjoyed a lucrative career in TV commercials; and actress-comedienne Mary Louise Wilson, whose no-nonsense manner helped keep the increasingly lofty proceedings earthbound. Monk also began a tradition of hiring handsome out-of-work actors as waiters. Several achieved solid show business careers, notably Robert Downey, director of the film *Putney Swope* and father of film idol Robert Downey, Jr.

Early in 1958 Monk and his company's euphoria fell with a crash when they learned that they had to vacate the premises. Every month another brownstone or small business fell victim to an office building, and the wrecker's ball was about to strike at Sixth Avenue and 51st Street to make way for the Time-Life Building. With great serendipity Monk and Haber found a dream location, John Wanamaker's former mansion at 37 West 56th Street, between Fifth and Sixth avenues. Just a block from the defunct Ruban, this duplex brownstone had housed a series of failed restaurants. Its present owners and occupants were the Dooley Sisters, two charming gray-haired ladies who had once been a popular singing team. Now retired, they could no longer afford their palatial home. Haber negotiated a low purchase price, and on July 3 it became his property.

The duplex setup allowed them to reopen both nightclubs. The new Downstairs at the Upstairs was on street level. Decorator Tom Harris's design included forest green walls with white globed sconces, gaslight style; blue banquettes; and a crystal chandelier that had once hung in Grace Vanderbilt's Fifth Avenue mansion (Harris found it in an antique shop for eight dollars). In front was a small circular stage;

on the far right a doorway led to the bathrooms and kitchen. For identification purposes a stained-glass figure of a small boy urinating was placed above the doorway.

The Upstairs at the Downstairs was designed by actor James Karen and his wife Susan Reed, a harp- and zither-playing folk singer who had performed at the Ruban and other clubs. They gave the room burgundy carpeting, red plaster walls, and a small "Pollack Penny-Plain Tuppence-Coloured Stage," Victorian-style, with a painted wooden backdrop simulating a heavy red fringed curtain.

For the next six years Monk's evenings enjoyed amazing commercial success and sparked a citywide vogue for nightclub revues. There was still an enormous thirst for chic in New York, and the more Monk's revues exploited it, the more popular they became. Soon their freshness and spontaneity would almost vanish, but it took the public several years to notice.

AFTER THE DOWNSTAIRS ROOM had crumbled into dust, many of its old regulars thought fondly of the days when they could hear Jorie Remus on that site for the price of a drink. In 1956 Remus resurfaced in New York to appear at the Bon Soir and in a few minor plays. Four years later she and Allen Murray opened a nightclub in San Juan called the Gilded Cage, and over the next two years she returned occasionally to the Bon Soir and the hungry i. But since the club circuit had started to dwindle and her acting career had never taken off, she became largely inactive by the mid-'60s. Her bad habits began to catch up with her, and she suffered a stroke. People were saddened but not incredulous when Dorothy Kilgallen reported in 1965 that Remus had died. She had not died—she was living in Los Angeles with Murray—but Kilgallen never retracted the error, and many who knew Remus believe it to this day.

Shortly before Kilgallen's notice, Laurie Brewis, an English pianist who played at the Waverly Lounge of the Hotel Earle in Greenwich Village, had died of a ruptured appendix. Someone mentioned this to Dorothy Greener, star of the *Shoestring* revues and, like Remus, a comedienne whose personal life was touched by tragedy. A tomboyish but vulnerable personality of enormous depth, Greener displayed a temperament that made her nearly unemployable, and she lapsed into severe alcoholism. In the '60s she took a job as a hatcheck girl at the

Five Oaks, a Village piano bar–restaurant that still exists. Greener spent most of her breaks at the bar, but occasionally someone recognized her and asked her to perform "Grace Fogerty" or "Roller Derby," two Mike Stewart monologues from Bagley's shows. One evening Bagley came in for drinks with a young singer. "We were about to leave when she spotted Dorothy at the bar. 'Look!' she said. 'There's Dorothy Greener! Will you introduce me to her?' I brought her over and tapped Dorothy on the shoulder. 'Dorothy? There's a young lady here I'd like you to meet, a talented newcomer you've probably heard about. Her name is Barbra Streisand.' Dorothy turned her head, mumbled something incoherent, and passed out on the bar."

According to Murray Grand, on such an evening Greener heard about Laurie Brewis's death and confused her with Jorie Remus. She called about a dozen people to break the news: "Oh, my God! Jorie Remus is dead!" Leonard Sillman heard the rumor and called Kilgallen, who printed it without checking.

In 1969 Grand visited Los Angeles, and on a scorching day stopped in a bar on Ventura Boulevard to cool off. "This face looked up at me, and I thought, 'Oh Christ, I'm seeing things!' It was Jorie. She said, 'Murray, what are you doing here?' I said, 'Well, what are *you* doing here? You're supposed to be dead!' She had never heard the story."

Around that time she appeared at a San Juan club run by singer Louise Ogilvie, but her stroke had impaired her timing and the booking was a failure. She and Allen Murray moved to Honolulu, where in the '70s and early '80s she played a few minor roles in films and in TV shows such as *Hawaii Five-O*. The only published souvenir of her nightclub work is a long-unavailable album on the obscure Everest label entitled "The Unpredictable Jorie Remus." Like so many masterful club performers, her heyday passed with the era, remembered only by those who happened to have been there.

Throughout the late '50s, more and more middle-class families were finding television the cheapest, safest, and most entertaining way to spend an evening. In fact, it was becoming the primary constant in their lives, as it remains today. The postwar mania for normalcy, for a serene existence governed by trust in family, God, government, and the bomb, had given way to a pronounced uneasiness over the fact that our traditionally invincible nation could now be destroyed at the touch of a button. National self-confidence received a further blow in October 1957 when the Soviets launched the first sputnik, knocking the United States off its pedestal as the world leader in space exploration. Teenagers, never before a powerful independent buying market, were propelling rock and roll into a multimillion-dollar industry. For the first time they had their own music—music their parents neither liked nor understood—which immediately made them a subculture. They began to create their own places to enjoy it in, and the more dissimilar they were to the nightspots that older folks attended, the better.

Max Gordon knew that jazz, though not a universal favorite of youth, appealed to far more of them than the chicest chanteuse or hippest comic. Unwilling to waste Vanguard space on the offbeat acts that had given the room its character but had, of late, left a lot of tables empty, he announced a change in policy. As of June 10, 1957, there would be no more Shakespeare recitations, no more harpists intoning Elizabethan verse, no more beat poetry, no more singing comediennes. On that date the Vanguard became a jazz room. "The whole operation had become weary, stale, flat and unprofitable," he explained in the *New York Times Magazine* (June 19, 1957). "I had to give young people what they want. They want jazz. The older ones all grew up, got married, moved to Great Neck and dance to Lawrence Welk."

But the Blue Angel would remain in its prime until about 1961. The unknown and still-unrecorded Johnny Mathis passed through for four weeks in the spring of 1956, making a pleasant but not outstanding impression. Still believing himself a jazz singer, Mathis had come to singing only the year before, after a humble San Francisco rearing. His father was a valet-chauffeur, his mother a maid to a wealthy family that had endowed several colleges and offered Mathis a scholarship to any of them. Both in high school and college he was a star high jumper and hurdler, and seemed to be headed for the Olympics. A casual interest in singing bore fruit unexpectedly in 1955 when Helen Noga, manager of the prominent San Francisco jazz room the Black Hawk, heard him sitting in at a local club and hired him immediately. George Avakian, a Columbia Records executive, saw Mathis in a subsequent engagement and signed him, sending his company the following telegram: "Have found phenomenal 19-year-old boy who could go all the way. Send blank contracts."

Mathis left for New York to sing at the Vanguard and at the Angel for four weeks starting in March 1956. "When Mathis came to the Blue Angel," says Bart Howard, "his style hadn't matured at all. He was the cutest, sweetest little boy, with a good education, and he liked me. I realized he wasn't able to go to many restaurants because of his color, so I invited him to eat at my apartment a lot." That month Mathis recorded his first album for Columbia Records, a collection of standards with top jazz accompaniment, and it was released in July to only fair response. In a field crowded with great jazz singers, Mathis's nasal head voice did not stand out. Mitch Miller, Columbia's head of Artists and Repertoire, wisely guided him in another direction. In the fall he gave him a pair of pop ballads to record, "Wonderful! Wonderful!" and "It's Not for Me To Say," thus launching a staggering lineup of hits and a career that rapidly left both jazz and the Blue Angel far behind.

The same could not be said of Dorothy Loudon, a longtime favorite in the Angel's latter years. Between 1956 and 1962 she played fourteen engagements, some as long as three months. She debuted there with a similar edition of her Ruban Bleu act. Because her lover Norman Paris still played at the Ruban, she now had to perform with Jimmy Lyon and his trio. Though a deft, sensitive accompanist, Lyon could not read music, and Paris's intricate arrangements terrified him. On opening night Paris sat in the audience to cheer her on. As the minutes before showtime ticked away, everyone grew concerned that Lyon had not shown up—and with good reason. He was down the street at P. J. Clarke's, drunk and petrified to go on. So Paris walked up to the piano and the show went on.

Even with his expert touch, Loudon flopped. Numbers that had worked so well at the Ruban did not impress the tougher Blue Angel audience, and Jacoby almost gave her no second chance. "Herbert didn't like her material," says Ben Bagley. "It was all old cornball songs like 'Some of These Days' and 'You've Gotta See Your Mama Every Night,' and the audience didn't want a whole show of that. They expected witty special material, but Dorothy didn't want to spend any money." Jacoby did not want to rehire her, but in a rare show of stubbornness Bart Howard told him, "You've got to let her come back and give her the confidence to know she can do it."

Loudon gathered some comedy songs by writers the Angel audience loved, such as Sheldon Harnick, Michael Brown, and Bud McCreery, combining them with the better numbers from her older repertoire, among them "I Like a Hungry Man" and "South Rampart Street Parade." Now, however, she unleashed all the broadness that became her trademark, and gleefully turned the songs into high camp. She returned in January 1957 and tore the place apart.

From then on Loudon shot arrows at a wide range of pretension and absurdity, much of it feminine, from Scarlett O'Hara–style Southern affectation to tone-deaf female jazz singers to Abbe Lane. Her most popular number was a spoof on "Mobile," a down-home tune recorded by Julius LaRosa. Loudon took it for a death ride, singing it in an expert Southern twang:

They saw a swallow buildin' his nest
I guess they figured he knew best
So they built a town around him
And they called it Mobile . . .

WHERE'S THAT? [*asked the trio*]
Alabama . . .

"It gets much worse," Loudon says. "It's like 'Birth of the Blues,' only really rotten."

A Bud McCreery arrangement of the Vincent Youmans standard "[There's Gonna Be a] Great Day!" spoofed the endless finales of '40s Broadway musicals. Loudon tossed out a huge accordion stack of sheet music, announcing, "This next song is a production number. It calls for a cast of thousands, but I have lots of teeth and I move very quickly and my eyes dance."

Such exuberance did not come easily. "Much of Dorothy's material wasn't funny in itself," says Ben Bagley, "and she had to put everything but the kitchen sink into it to make it work. There were no jokes in 'Mobile,' for example. It needed a lot of funny looks and gestures and vocal tricks. That's why material that worked one night could bomb the next. If she was in a lousy mood or felt uninspired, she'd throw the whole thing away." Loudon herself felt the tension of keeping people laughing. "Every comedienne I've known has been a comedienne offstage as well as on, and I think it's boring," she told the *New York Journal-American* (April 16, 1963). "It's work for me to be funny, and I work hard enough up there on the stage."

More than any other intimate room, the Blue Angel placed this burden on its acts, who struggled to please not only Jacoby but also an audience that had seen the best and expected nothing less for its $6 minimum. "It was a scary thing," Bagley says, "to stand up in a place like that with a top reputation and a show-me audience. In the '50s the customer was God. Doormen opened doors, and waiters were subservient. In a bank you could be fired if you didn't smile all the time. Usually if the Angel crowd didn't like you from the start you were out on your ass."

Few acts have forgotten Jacoby's withering glance of disapproval when a gag misfired or an ambitious choice of material left customers cold. "Herbert had a definite sense of how to structure an act, so you had to choose your material very carefully," says Will Holt. "If you did an up-opener you did a ballad second, then a bright piece of material, then a really solid ballad, and finally a big up-tune to get you off. You could set your watch by that formula. It discouraged a lot of us from experimenting. Opening nights at the Angel horrified everyone I know, because God forbid you strayed too far from what you were expected to do. When the tension broke—when Dorothy really let loose, for example—you had the illusion of a carefree, happy place, but I don't think it ever was. I think Dorothy felt the necessity to always be on, like her old boss Ted Lewis—'Is everybody happy?' I don't think she ever allowed herself the luxury of singing a ballad. I doubt I changed more than five songs in my own act for two years. I remember trying 'There's a Boat Dat's Leavin' Soon for New York' from *Porgy and Bess* with guitar. It went okay, and I walked off. Now if Herbert wanted to see you he somehow met you just as you were coming down the back stairs to do your second show. He stopped me and said, 'That's a Negro's song!' I got the message."

Rigid as it seemed, that obsession with taste and consistency ensured that acts would rarely fall below a respectable level. Even when the material or its execution failed, the presentation as a whole looked professional. But Jacoby's judgment was far from flawless. He booked several acts that made audiences wonder if he had lost his mind, and he rejected others that seemed ideal. Like most club owners he hired performers for reasons besides talent: as a favor to influential friends, for example, or in later years because he could not find anyone better. He sometimes used acts that he hated, among them Mort Sahl and Lenny Bruce, because they packed the room. His record of "discoveries" becomes less impressive in view of the fact that he seldom took chances. Julius Monk hired many unknowns simply because he believed in them, but the Blue Angel was bigger-time. Jacoby had to struggle constantly to uphold its reputation and attendance, and he could not afford to gamble too often. Most of the performers he introduced are forgotten, whereas Pearl Bailey, Nichols and May, Harry Belafonte, and other stars drew such publicity at the Angel that people mistakenly thought that he had discovered them.

"Julius found people, picked songs for them, chose their outfits, and nurtured them," says Ben Bagley, "but Herbert seldom did that. I remember hearing June Ericson at the Ruban, and I thought she was terrific—a pretty, round-faced blonde with a beautiful voice. I recommended her to Herbert and he auditioned her. The next day he snarled at me, 'That girl has a face that looks like it's been run over by a Mack truck!' But I guess he changed his mind, because he hired her in 1960.

"One of Herbert's backers made him use a woman who was

ghastly. She did a song she wrote herself called 'The Brooklyn Mambo' during which she performed a full mambo. It was her second number, and the poor idiot was out of breath for the rest of her act. She was short and squat, with jet-black dyed hair, and looked like a dumpy housewife. She ended by saying it was her great dream to appear at the Blue Angel, and she'd finally made it, but that she wouldn't forget her old friends who helped her on the way up. Right after the show I called Sheldon Harnick, because he collected wretched performers who did awful songs. My deal with Sheldon was that he would give me first crack at material he'd written, providing that whenever I heard anyone who was rotten I'd call and tell him to come. I was afraid she'd be fired during intermission, but she wasn't. She was there two weeks, because the backer insisted.

"Then there was Helen Halpin, a singer-impressionist who worked there in the early '50s. I guess Helen was too cheap to buy good material so she wrote her own routines, including an impression of Rosemary Clooney. She held a match to her lips and sang, 'If you loved me halFFFFFFFFFFFF as much as I love you' and blew the match out. That was supposed to be funny. I always thought that it was an act you would have had trouble finding outside a bowling alley."

Jacoby made graver mistakes than these. Says Kaye Ballard, "He told Lena Horne to get out of show business, and he fired Sarah Vaughan. He hated the way she went all around the melody."

An avocational hazard for clubgoers of the '50s was the ubiquity of a pretty blonde singer named Isobel Robins. Inexplicably she kept appearing at the Blue Angel, One Fifth Avenue, the Bon Soir, Le Ruban Bleu, and Downstairs at the Upstairs, singing off-key with questionable comedic timing and little charisma—failings evident on the 1958 album "The Saint and the Sinner," which she shared with her close friend, comic Henry Morgan. Also a chum of *New Yorker* reviewer Rogers Whitaker, Robins was nicknamed the Messy-Soprano by Herbert Jacoby, as Buster Davis recalls. "I asked him once, 'God, Herbert, why are you booking Isobel again?' He frowned and said, 'You know why!' Of course, I have no idea what he meant by that."

Did such missteps damage the Angel's reputation? Not at all. Jacoby could not have afforded the sparse attendance that a bad notice might cause so, like other nightclub entrepreneurs, he bribed most of the local reviewers with money or liquor when necessary. He found club critics easily corruptible. Some earned ten dollars a review or less, and since few were syndicated they needed an additional source of income to survive. Virtually the only publication that Jacoby could not pay off was the *New York Times;* nearly all the others resided safely in the palm of his hand, where there was enough cash to go around.

FORMAL ENTERTAINMENT in the main room of the Angel ended by about one-thirty. The houselights were raised, and the remaining customers paid their checks and filed out into the lounge, filling their lungs with that smoky but cooler air. Most got their coats and left, but a few lingered, hanging out near one of the spinets in the back, where the show went on. For eight seasons the vocal-instrumental duo Martha Davis and Spouse alternated between the lounge and the main room. A short, stout black woman with tiny hands and fingers, Davis looked like a little pillow as she sat at the keyboard and played in a style reminiscent of Fats Waller at his best. Spouse was her husband, Calvin Ponder, a professorial-looking bass player whose big eyes focused on Davis from behind a pair of thick tortoiseshell glasses, as they sang standards by Waller, Duke Ellington, and others.

Around 2 A.M. the relaxed atmosphere reached its peak, and propriety sometimes faded away into an alcoholic haze. Says Bud McCreery, "Sally Benson, who wrote *Meet Me in St. Louis* and all those heartwarming stories of innocent childhood, used to come into the bar and end up spread-eagle on the floor. I hope this doesn't sound meanspirited, because I'm one of her admirers, but from her writing I'd never associated her with the face on the barroom floor."

The club closed at four, but performers were so accustomed to late hours that many had no desire to go home until the sun rose. The feeling that the world had gone to sleep and left them the whole city as their playground was intoxicating in itself. A favorite early-morning hangout was P. J. Clarke's, which was always crowded with celebrities such as Frank Sinatra, Montgomery Clift, Henry Fonda, Rita Hayworth, and Truman Capote. Bud McCreery recalls unwinding there with Lyon and Loudon. "We often refereed fist fights between Ben

Gazzara and Elaine Stritch. I thought they were married—they acted as if they were—but it turns out they were only lovebirds."

Another habitué was then-Senator John F. Kennedy, who brought prostitutes but behaved with greater decorum. Kennedy was a good friend of Jacoby's and spent a lot of time in and around the Blue Angel in the late '50s and early '60s. Ben Bagley recalls that around 1961 "Dorothy Loudon asked me to work on her act with her. I came into the club for rehearsal, and Herbert said, 'Now, there's going to be a friend of mine here while you're rehearsing, a senator from Massachusetts, in the dressing room upstairs. You'll have to answer the phone for him.'

"Well, the phone would ring and ring and ring. Only myself, Dorothy, and her accompanist were there. I'd answer the phone, and it was for Senator Kennedy. Up I'd go to the dressing room, knock on the door, and find him inside with the ex-wife of a famous black singer-dancer who has since died. Kennedy would be winking at me, and putting on his pants, and zipping his fly. Dorothy was furious. 'I'm paying you all this money and you're spending half the time answering the phone for this senator!'

"On her opening night Herbert said to me, 'Senator Kennedy requested that you sit with him and be his guest. Now I want you to be polite, because this is a very nice man, no matter what you think.'

"First I went back to see Dorothy. She said, 'Do you know that man is married?' That upset her greatly.

"I went over to sit with Senator Kennedy. He loved Dorothy's act, and he'd seen my *Shoestring Revue* and asked me all sorts of questions about it—did Dody Goodman really talk that way?—and so on. He was so desperate to get laid that his legs were going a mile a minute under the table. There were always whores in front of the Waldorf, where he was staying, so I said, 'If you're that hot, why don't you pay for it?' He said, 'No, I would never do that again. One of them gave me syphilis once, and it was very embarrassing for my wife.' He made me go to a pay phone and call Dody to see if I could fix them up, but since it was the middle of the night I got her answering service. Then he wanted me to call Bea Arthur. I told him that Bea was married to Gene Saks and living way out in New Jersey. He said, 'Well, if she's that far away she's never gonna drive in.' The fact that she was married to Gene didn't even register—and knowing Bea, I don't think she would have treasured that call, because he wasn't the President yet. He even asked me if I thought Dorothy would be interested, but she wouldn't come near him. 'That son of a bitch. What a creep!' I said, 'Just come over and say hello, then tell him it's getting late and you have to go home.' She said, 'I will not! If you introduce us I'm going to give him a bill for all the time he wasted!' It got to be four o'clock and they were closing—the waiters were putting the chairs up on the tables. He said, 'Don't leave me.' He was a very lonely man. We went to P.J.'s and talked until six in the morning. Finally he said, 'I think I'll go home and get an hour or two of sleep.' This man existed on no sleep. So he went back to the Waldorf, and I never saw him again.

"After he became president, Herbert used to say to me, 'Do you realize we could commit murder and he'd get us off?' "

IN THE MID-'50S a new wave of young comics began to emerge, most of them college-educated and not content to limit their observations to the corner drugstore or the PTA. Both the targets and the level of ferocity had changed. They fixed their keen eyes on the hypocrisy in current events and attitudes, on national and urban politics, as the *Christian Science Monitor* noted (February 7, 1961):

> Just when comedy was solemnly being declared obsolete—who can laugh in the shadow of the nuclear stockpile?—a new kind of comedian has emerged in the United States to twang laughs from the tensions that were supposed to silence him.
>
> Phase No. 1: Our hero first appears on the scene as a cult comedian in small but hip clubs appealing to the far-out public that likes its jazz avant-garde.
>
> Phase No. 2: He makes a recording of his monologues—sophisticated, acidulous, intended for the cultural minority group to which he feels he belongs. The results are astounding. It seems that a mass audience, glutted on blandness, has just been waiting for the bite of satire. The records are snapped up by the millions.

The earliest of these comics was Mort Sahl, the acknowledged pioneer of social and political standup comedy in the '50s. Sahl first came to attention in 1953 at the hungry i, where his jabs at McCarthyism, the Eisenhower administration, the H-bomb, and other topical issues contrasted starkly with the much safer house-and-garden humor that audiences were used to. In a much-quoted moment of rhetoric in that first hungry i engagement he asked, "Have you seen the Joe McCarthy jacket? It's like an Eisenhower jacket, only it's got an extra flap that fits over the mouth."

Though he may not have been a great wit, Sahl's political candor was unprecedented and quite daring. In the company of the hip, socially conscious hungry i audience Sahl was in his element. He looked the part of a nonviolent, intellectual rabble-rouser, with his dark, wavy hair and wide eyes that spotted every shifty glance at a press conference or between-the-lines nuance in *Time* magazine. He dressed it too, strolling onstage in slacks and a crew-neck sweater, with a rolled-up newspaper under his arm—this at a time when even the crassest Borscht Belt comic performed in a dark suit or tuxedo. Opinionated, brash, but never venomous, Sahl chattered as if he were a headstrong undergrad political science student holding court after class with friends.

Shelley Berman was often branded an intellectual comic, although he argued that he was simply a spokesman for the family and personal trials that haunt us all. Skinny and green-eyed, with an ever-furrowed brow and pained expression, he looked as if life's frustrations might at any moment drive him either to pull out a gun or burst into tears. Not a topical humorist, Berman focused on the red tape of day-to-day home and community life. "What he communicates," the *Christian Science Monitor* (February 7, 1961) wrote, "is the private nightmare of a slightly overfastidious young man coping with an untidy and hostile world in which black specks appear in your milk and refuse to be removed; small children answer your phone calls and decline to summon Mommy; your date breaks her heel before the evening has fairly begun; and you slam a cab door with the handle still in your pocket."

Berman had been an actor and could inject a serious note into his monologues, giving the act a dimension lacking among most humorists. He staged many of his routines as one-sided telephone conversations, perched on a stool with an imaginary phone to his ear. The idea came to him in his days with the Compass Players, a Chicago-based improvisatory group that also included the still-unknown Nichols and May. "While Mike and Elaine could play lines against each other, I had no one," he told *Cue* (May 31, 1958). "So I thought of using the phone as a dramatic device."

In one monologue he portrayed a father struggling to explain the facts of life to his teenage daughter just before her first date.

> There's something I want to talk to you about, Annie, uh . . . shame it has to be on the phone, but I'm stuck here in his office and I won't be home in time . . . It's a little something I should have talked to you about a few years back. Actually your mother should have talked to you about this subject, but she doesn't believe in it . . . Now, uh, Annie, here's the thing. Now don't rush me, honey, I'm trying to think of the right way to say this . . . clean. Now you're a big girl, you're not a baby, if you were in India you'd be a mother by now . . . of course, a lot of girls in Chicago *think* they're in India . . .

As with Sahl, the controversy over such material may seem hard to understand today, but respectable comics in the '50s rarely delved into the facts of life. Berman's detractors used the word "tasteless" again and again, apparently content for comedy to remain at a squeaky-clean standstill forever. The *New York Journal-American's* Jack O'Brian complained (August 15, 1962):

> Berman somehow reverts, and we're certain it is consciously, to too many tasteless words, phrases and ideas . . . In cafes and on TV, he has evidenced an odd affection for many fairly repellent notions. One for instance he has leaned on all too frequently is a four-letter word meaning a nasal mucus, found mostly in sick crossword puzzles but rarely in polite circles . . . Last night Berman interspersed his hour-long monologues with such unnecessary shock words and phrases as bad breath, stinky, assorted hells and damns, rotten, bedamned, a discourse on functional irregularity, an unzippered fly joke, pimples, throwing up, broad (for girl), a nose-blowing jape and more.

But the public succumbed happily to Berman's "repellent notions." Many people first heard him at Mister Kelly's in Chicago, an engagement that led to a TV appearance with Jack Paar in August 1957 and then to a six-show contract with Ed Sullivan. From then on Berman became highly visible on television and in the most prestigious nightclubs, particularly the Blue Angel. In 1957 he also signed a recording contract with Verve Records, which would release his Grammy-winning first album, "Inside Shelley Berman," and several other bestsellers. In 1956 he could not afford a winter coat; two years later his annual income had risen to $500,000. Berman's new sense of self-importance led him to behave arrogantly and offhandedly toward the Angel staff, who remember him sourly, but his unique performing gifts were never in doubt. "In the first year that I have money I am an egregiously disgusting *nouveau riche,*" he told *Time* (January 12, 1959). "I'm being a sport. The other day I slipped an aunt a hundred-dollar bill and said, 'Buy yourself a hat, honey.' Most important is the feeling of strength. The feeling that I've got money in my jeans, and if you don't want me here, I can go elsewhere."

Characterization comedy may have reached its peak with the emergence of Mike Nichols and Elaine May, whose brilliant portraits of contemporary life ranged from a cozy chapter in the home life of a German scientist who spends his days accelerating the arms race to the trauma of a man who loses his last dime in a pay phone and must beg for help from a machinelike operator. Although famous for improvisation, they performed mostly set pieces with extemporaneous touches; only in their finale, when they created a skit based on audience suggestions, did they throw all planning to the winds. Both partners had a remarkable ear for the speech patterns and, more important, the thought processes, hangups, and quirks of their characters, whether an executive putting the make on his mousy secretary, a snooty French art gallery owner displaying her overpriced originals, or a pair of teenagers exploring the limits of first-date decorum inside a parked car. Nearly any of their famous routines makes it clear why Jack Rollins, the agent who launched their careers, says that he has twice had the privilege of working with genius: with Woody Allen and with Nichols and May.

Each of the duo had a vivid background to draw upon, especially Nichols, who was born Michael Igor Peschkowsky in Berlin. His mother was the daughter of a leading Social Democrat, Gustav Landauer, whom Nichols reported was the first Jewish victim of the Nazis. His father, a Russian physician, fled with his family to America in 1939 but died only four years later, leaving them broke. Nichols went to a series of schools in New York, Connecticut, and elsewhere on scholarships and loans. Quiet and introverted, he made few friends and bore the jeers of his classmates because of a childhood bout with scarlet fever that had caused him to lose his hair. He spent most of his time observing people.

At the University of Chicago he encountered true animosity in the person of Philadelphia-born Elaine May. The daughter of Yiddish actor Jack Berlin, May ceased her formal education at fourteen, after three weeks in high school. "I really didn't like it," she told the *New York Times Magazine* (May 24, 1959). "The truancy people came around and threatened to take me to court, but I called their bluff. I sat around the house reading—mostly fairy tales and mythology. After three years I thought I would go to college and become extremely educated. I didn't actually enroll, but I dropped in on different classes for a couple of years. I first saw Michael in a university production of Strindberg's *Miss Julie.* I laughed all the way through it. We loathed each other on sight."

"I was very bad," Nichols later admitted to *Newsweek* (November 14, 1966). "One night in the audience a dark-haired, hostile girl was staring at me. I knew she hated it and I hated her because she was right. Then [*Chicago Sun-Times* critic] Sydney Harris wrote a rave review of the play. Holding a copy, I was walking down the street and I passed a friend with this hostile girl next to him. I showed him the review and she read it over his shoulder and said 'Ha!' and walked away."

Nichols next saw her sitting on a bench in the Illinois Central station. He walked over and said in a Nazi spy accent, 'May I zit down?'

" 'Eef you vish.'

" 'I beg your pardon. Vould you have a light?'

" 'Of course. You are . . . Agent X-9?'

It was their first improvisation. They did not team up, however, until both joined the Compass Players, whose members improvised scenes based on words and phrases from the audience. The Compass visited St. Louis on tour, planning to hit New York soon after, but Nichols and May were so eager that they left the group early and arrived in Manhattan in 1957 with only $40 between them. When they called their producer from an Esso gas station, he broke the news that the group would not be coming to New York after all. Nichols borrowed money from a friend, and he and May decided to try putting together an act. They learned about Jack Rollins, who invited them to lunch the next day at the Russian Tea Room. "We walked in," Nichols told the *New York Morning Telegraph* (June 9, 1961), "and had a scoop of borscht while wildly improvising a set of ad-libbed little skits we not only had never rehearsed but had never even thought of until that desperate minute. When the coffee came he signed us to a management contract. I remember with some relief that he not only signed us but also sprang for the lunch check. That had us pretty worried until he grabbed it."

Rollins arranged a Sunday night audition at the Angel, and Jacoby booked them to open in ten days. When Nichols asked, "How do we eat for the next ten days?" Max Gordon sent them to the Vanguard, where *Variety* gave them their first review (November 13, 1957): "Mike Nichols & Elaine May are hipsters' hipsters. Their thought patterns are Cloud No. 7 inspired and their comedic routines are really far out. It's an act that requires plenty of 'digging' on the audience's part. In a setting such as the Vanguard with its hip music policy, the duo is in a favorable environment . . . However, in average exposure spots the act will have trouble finding its mark."

At the Angel, they made that critic eat his words. Shortsighted as ever, *Variety* forgot the appeal of intellectual comedy in that room. Audiences were never at a loss when asked to call out opening and closing lines for the team's final improvised sketch, and to dictate its literary style (Shakespeare, Hemingway, Dostoyevsky). Wrote Douglas Watt in the *New Yorker* (December 21, 1957): "Mr. Nichols and Miss May . . . carry on little dialogues . . . with something of the same delightful interplay characteristic of that splendid vaudeville team the Lunts . . . On one of my visits they took off Euripides (with no props at all), and I'm sure that the Greek theatre was never more fun."

"There were lines outside the club within two weeks," says Rollins. "They were the hottest thing in the city." It was a triumphant time for two young people who had been outcasts for most of their lives. Nichols found the recognition especially gratifying. "There was one guy at Cherry Lane High School [in Connecticut] who used to hold my head under the water," he told *Newsweek.* "He would stand on it." One night he showed up at the Blue Angel. "You don't remember me," he said to Nichols.

"It was as if I had been waiting for that moment for fifteen years. I said, 'Your name is so-and-so and you were a son of a bitch. What are you doing now?'

" 'I'm selling used cars.' "

" 'I'm so glad.' "

Their best dialogues, many recorded for Mercury Records, pointed up our own behavior through only the slightest exaggeration of its absurdity. In one sketch they portrayed two young would-be intellectuals having a pretentious postcoital discussion on literature, science, and music as they listened to a Bach recording:

WOMAN: There is, always, another dimension to music. And it's apart from life. I can never believe that Bartok died on Central Park West.
MAN: Isn't that ugly?
WOMAN: Ugly, ugly, ugly . . . Oh, I *love* this part!
MAN: Yes, here, here, here.
WOMAN: [HUSHED] Yes, yes, yes.
MAN: Almost hurts.
WOMAN: Yes. Beauty often does.
MAN: What a shock when I discovered Nietzsche, and he said that in a way.
WOMAN: In many ways, when I read *Thus Spake Zarathustra* a *whole world* opened for me.
MAN: [EXCITED] I know exactly what you mean!
WOMAN: Do you know what I mean?
MAN: *Exactly!*
WOMAN: Oh, did that happen to you?
MAN: I know *exactly* what you mean!
WOMAN: Oh, I had never known such things *existed*!

In another piece a bereaved man answers a *TV Guide* ad for a sixty-five-dollar package funeral for a newly deceased loved one—a slap at a society grown so greedy that it thought nothing of treading on that sacred ground. It anticipated Jessica Mitford's best-selling 1963 expose *The American Way of Death* by at least two years:

WOMAN: Charlie, I'm Miss Loomis, your Grief Lady.
MAN: Hi.
WOMAN: Well, Charlie, that will be sixty-five dollars.
MAN: Thank you, I have the check all made out.
WOMAN: Oh, before you go, I was just wondering . . . would you be interested in some extras for the loved one?
MAN: What kind of extras?
WOMAN: Well . . . how about a coffin?

Filial woes also received their due when Nichols portrayed an astronaut's guilt for not calling his mother. "Arthur, I sat by that phone all day Friday. All day Friday night. And all day Saturday. And all day Sunday. Your father said to me, 'Phyllis, eat something, you'll faint.' I said, 'No, Harry, no. I don't want my mouth to be full when my son calls me!' "

They became regulars on the NBC radio variety series *Monitor,* where they performed true improvisations from only the barest outlines. Most are surprisingly weak; some of the better ones, centering on the medical profession, are collected in their album "Mike Nichols and Elaine May Examine Doctors." But *Monitor* did produce a few other gems, notably "Culture and Cooking," in which May played the vapid hostess of a women's radio talk show "dedicated to bringing you the best in culture . . . the best in cooking . . . for all women." She struggles to interview her guest, Professor Heinrich von Rieft, author of *The Theory of the Universe*:

MAY: It is a mag*nifi*cent book, ladies—seven volumes.

NICHOLS: Have you read it all?

MAY: Uh, I've *skimmed* most of it, uh, and I find, uh, the chap—the *illustrations,* I think, are particularly lovely, and—

NICHOLS: They're not mine.

MAY: No, well, but they do so well *illuminate*— uh, your wonderful th—the professor has a marvelous theory of the universe that I think we should all know, umm—how did you happen to come onto this particular theory?

NICHOLS: It just struck me as ze truth.

MAY: [PAUSE] I see, I see—very good, very fine . . .

NICHOLS: You're referring of course to ze theory zat ze universe iss *whirling* away from us.

MAY: [PAUSE] Uh, well, that too—uh, I think that that's *terribly* interesting, I think that we have all felt that at one time or another. Uhh—could you go into it for just a few minutes for the girls, Professor?

NICHOLS: [INTONES] If you remember ze first writings of Ptolemy, and how angry he was with all of us for not realizing zat ze stars turned and ve didn't . . . How ve laughed at Ptolemy, and how surprised ve all are now to learn zat he was absolutely right!

MAY: Oh, wonderful, Professor, wonderful, yes, I think that's a lesson . . .

NICHOLS: Not finished.

MAY: . . . to all of us. Oh, will you excuse me for just one second, then?

NICHOLS: Yeh.

MAY: Girls, our universe is big. But sometimes a housewife's universe is a little smaller. Sometimes a housewife's universe . . . is her kitchen. And in our universe, shouldn't we have a kitchen that is well ordered? A universe that doesn't *whirl* away from us? For the kind of universe that you and your loved ones would like best, let me ask you to stock Recessed Cookbooks, Recessed Refrigerator, Recessed Stove, and Recessed Cabinets. On sale now at your nearest Recessed store.

NICHOLS: [READING] And—I vould—just like—to mention—ladies—zat my little woman Fricka—*swears*—by her Recessed kitchen.

But it was the TV series *Omnibus* that put them on the national map. Shown on Sunday afternoons, *Omnibus* was a showcase for music, comedy, documentary, and anything else its producer Robert Saudek found educational and entertaining. The team was invited to appear on a January 1958 comedy episode, "Suburban Revue," starring Bert Lahr. Rollins bargained for fifteen minutes of airtime, allowing them to do two full sketches. Not even the Angel could have brought them such widespread and instant exposure, which explains why more and more young performers headed straight for TV. "Mike and Elaine were getting very hot," says Rollins, "and they could have gone anywhere, but without *Omnibus* it would have taken much longer."

Thereafter Rollins asked for and received $5,000 for all TV appearances. Even at that price they appeared regularly on Steve Allen, Jack Paar, Dinah Shore, and a dozen other programs. On Allen's show in 1958 they performed one of their best-known sketches, about a dumb movie starlet interviewed by a name-dropping disc jockey on her new film, *Two Gals in Paris* ("It is the life story of Gertrude Stein"). He interrupts her constantly to mention his close friendships with Bernard Baruch ("a hell of a good kid"), Bertrand Russell, Ernest Hemingway, and Albert Schweitzer ("I told him, Al baby, you're wrong, there's no money in Africa"). A sketch that mentioned Baruch, Russell, Hemingway, Schweitzer, and Stein within five minutes and brought a sackful of fan mail may indicate how far network television comedy has sunk in years since.

Nichols and May went on to perform at the Den in the Duane, at the Mocambo in Hollywood, and at Mister Kelly's in Chicago, and returned to the Angel in July and October 1958 to fulfill their return option. The next year they booked New York's Town Hall for a pair of sold-out evenings, followed by a concert tour that culminated in their smash show at Broadway's John Golden Theatre in 1960, *An Evening with Mike Nichols and Elaine May.* They found Broadway far preferable to any nightclub. As Nichols told the *New York Times* (December 18, 1960):

> People have been asking us whether we didn't find it difficult working to a big theatre full of people sitting there cold and sober as critics, all lined up in deadly neat rows and separated from us by the stage. They talk as though working in a nightclub were like getting up at a party, with your friends clustered close around you, all warmed up by a couple of drinks and a general ambience of let's-have-fun. Let me tell you, it's anything but . . . [people] go there to drink, or to impress a girl or client—a lot of reasons that have nothing to do with the show. They're terribly distracting places to work in. The waiters are always bouncing crockery around. Nobody's paying attention.

Not surprisingly, the duo format cramped two such enormous talents, and in 1962 they had a stormy breakup. Colleagues wondered what would become of Nichols, feeling that May was the true creative talent behind the team. As it happened, the decline of their partnership suggested the direction in which each would go alone. Nichols discussed it with Barbara Gelb in the *New York Times Magazine:*

> Several things happened. One was that I, more than Elaine, became more and more afraid of our improvisational material. We never wrote a skit down the first time, we just sort of outlined it: You be so-and-so, I'll be so-and-so. I'll try to make you, or we'll fight—whatever it was. Elaine was always brave. But I became more and more afraid. And we found ourselves doing the same material over and over, especially in our show for Broadway. This took a great toll on Elaine. And I nagged the hell out of her. I was always saying,

"Can't you do that any faster?" and "You're taking too long over this."

She'd fill things, I'd shape them. She had endless capacity for invention. My invention was not endless. But it taught me about beginnings, middles and ends. I had to push the sketch ahead, because I couldn't invent as she could.

Elaine wrote a play called *A Matter of Position* [in which Nichols starred in 1962], and that's what fractured our relationship. I was onstage, she was in the audience watching me, judging me . . .

As soon as we weren't in balance . . . equals on the stage . . . great angers . . . and things . . . arose. We flew apart.

It took years for Elaine and me to come back to each other after that. And what happened in those years was that we became two individual people, rather than Nichols-and-May. When she became wholly Elaine May and I became wholly Mike Nichols, we became the dearest of old friends.

WHILE NICHOLS AND MAY were soaring to fame, another career was in the making in New York and San Francisco clubs. Phyllis Diller was a rarity: a female stand-up comic whose act consisted not of material by other writers but of a barrage of self-deprecating one-liners from her own pen, punctuated by her famous cackle. But audiences were not impressed in the beginning. "At the Blue Angel she bombed, bombed, bombed, night after night," says Will Holt. "After every show she would go back to her dressing room and pore over each piece of material—why this didn't work, and what went wrong with that. And she got better and better. But she faced such failure—hostility, even."

Diller was a staunch advocate of positive thinking, however, and once she made her rather late start nothing could deter her. Born in Lima, Ohio, in 1917, she found herself at age thirty-five a housewife with five kids and no money, living in a San Francisco housing project and holding down a series of odd jobs in order to help make ends meet. Her home was ever in danger of foreclosure, the phone was frequently turned off, and she even sold her mother's diamonds. Her husband, Sherwood Diller, knew how much she enjoyed making people laugh, especially at her looks. At Bluffton College in Ohio, Diller amused her roommates by walking the dormitory halls completely nude, except for a belt around her waist, curlers in her hair, and a rose in her teeth. He convinced her to try an act, and she quit her job as a radio copywriter and forged ahead. "My boss wanted me to take a leave of absence," she told Nora Ephron in the *New York Post* (September 1, 1963). "I said forget it. It was my grand affirmative gesture. I was going to all these places trying to sell my material, trying to get my act on. I realized I couldn't go as an employed copywriter, I had to go as an unemployed comic."

To get a better idea of club performing, Diller saw acts at the hungry i and the Purple Onion, among them Jane and Gordon Connell. "She came backstage," recalls Jane. "Her comment to us was, 'Gosh, if you can do it I can do it!' " In 1955 Diller got a job at the Onion for forty dollars a week and elicited mostly groans. In one bit she played a gun moll: "All right, you guys. We're heisting an underwear factory tonight. I don't want no slips."

"Gordon played for her," Jane says. "She seemed to pattern a lot of her stuff after ours. She would take off Eartha Kitt, singing 'Monotonous' while slithering all over the piano. But she was out to kill. She was going to do it."

"She worked at it until two or three A.M.," adds Gordon, "then she was up again in the morning, trying this, trying that. Conversations with her were never conversations in those days. She was always honing material with us." "If Gordon said something funny she'd write it down," Jane says. Gradually she became more competent and stayed for a staggering eighty-nine weeks—a vote of confidence that also indicates the patience of club owners in those years for artists with potential.

Diller faced far less indulgent audiences in New York, even at One Fifth Avenue. "We saw her there," Jane says, "and there were about three people in the house. Talk about rejection! I would have given up right then, but she went full steam ahead." Fortunately for Diller, Herbert Jacoby also recognized her talent and gave her a break that no one understood at first. *Variety* sneered (March 12, 1958): "Phyllis Dillen [*sic*] manages laughs with her rather forced comedy material."

Diller wrote a report for the *San Francisco Examiner* on her New York City adventures (May 25, 1958):

> Each night I became Cinderella and went over to the East Side, which is solid platinum. The people there flock to the Blue Angel and dine on sow belly en brochette, snails soaked in garlic and other rare delicacies.

Celebrities by the hundreds flow through the portals of the Blue Angel: Bob Hope, Herman Wouk, Grace Metalious, Miss Sweden, Gladstone Chilblain, Celeste Holm. Many of these people spoke to me, plying me with questions like, "Where's the powder room?" and "May I please have my check?"

Going cross town in a taxi is like riding a turtle. You get in a cab and have the feeling you're backing up because the people on the sidewalk are passing you so fast.

Winter in New York is strictly a black and white movie. Everything becomes drab and soot works through the walls like magic. Window sills look like coal chutes.

The native San Franciscan misses the technicolor vistas he is accustomed to and so spoiled by. New Yorkers, whether they admit it or not, get edgy for lack of nature's closeness. They miss trees and flowers. In the dead of winter a piece of parsley on a luncheon plate can send one into transports of joy.

Amidst it all is the siren call of the fast buck, the sudden turn of events and the endless opportunities with which the streets are paved. It's a fast track and every day there's a winner. It's a town full of gamblers, or at least people who like the race. But this filly will be happy for a chance to return for a breather to the green pastures by the Golden Gate.

By 1959 Diller had hit her stride. Her routines were dotted with images that Edward Albee, an avid fan, felt bordered on the surreal: "Oh, I've got a greasy sink. I have watched bugs slide to their death."

Through 1962 she played regularly at both the Angel and the Bon Soir, often tearing the latter to shreds. "They invited me here in hopes I might be able to bring up the *tone* of the place. HAHAHAHAHAHA! So you *know* we're never gonna get it up to street level! You know if they put down a new rug they think they've done their part. And they didn't do it right, they just slapped it down over everything. And there're some big lumps that I *know* are people. And there are some little tiny lumps that are still moving . . . Incidentally, watch out for that waiter. He's *very* nervous. You'd be nervous too if you were stealing."

Hers was a world plagued by domestic woes—a wife's, mother's, housewife's, and woman's—where even the best intentions met with disaster. It started with her looks, which were so awful that she simply gave in to them. From the short, scraggly blonde wisps on her head

("You probably think this is hair. Oh, you're sweet. These are nerve ends!") to her heavy jeweled collar ("I made this in beadcraft"), satin gloves, tacky fur scarf, long cigarette holder, and high-heeled rhinestone shoes, Diller drew laughs as soon as she walked onstage. Her analyst, she explained, had traced a lot of her problems to her childhood: "When I was three years old my folks sent me out to buy bubble gum. And while I was out they moved." She entered marriage with dubious credentials and never advanced much farther: "My husband said, 'I want a little old-fashioned housewife, and we'll start off by your dressing a chicken for Sunday dinner.' HAHAHAHAHAHA! It took me three weeks to make the blouse!"

Dining out in restaurants was just as risky: "I ordered a steak a couple of nights ago. Rare. With a little care this thing could have recovered!" Field trips were a mistake, because her driving was a hazard to the community: "I have called home so many times that my husband can tell by the way I say 'Hello, sweetie' what make and model I hit. The other day I said, 'I've had a little accident at the corner of Post and Geary.'

"He said, 'Post and Geary don't cross.'

"I said, 'They do now!' "

With all this, it was no wonder that "Fang" fooled around with other women, especially foreign ones: "I warned him about foreign women. I told him if something goes wrong with a foreign woman, parts are hard to get"—and so on, in staccato manner, for up to an hour.

There was still plenty of good silly fun of a more offbeat variety at the Angel. An agile young man named George Matson brought a lot more imagination than usual to the old formula of pantomiming in costume to popular recordings. For "The Man in the Flying Trapeze" he rigged up a swing and soared back and forth over the front tables, tossing out pebbles that landed with a plop in people's drinks. And for an Yma Sumac takeoff he lit a fire inside a big cauldron, narrowly escaping a reprimand from the fire department.

Also popular was T. C. (Thomas Craig) Jones, a female impressionist who had first come to attention in *New Faces of 1956*. Jones gave campy impersonations of Louella Parsons, Tallulah Bankhead, Bette Davis, and other familiar subjects, seldom descending into bad taste. Offstage he resembled a bare mannequin, with plain features and a shaved head as shiny as glass, but with an endearing manner and warm smile. Like many homosexuals Jones was married, and lived happily with a rather eccentric wife and a little dog named Angel. Recalls Will Holt, "T's wife was backstage once with me and my wife, Dolly, and she looked worried. 'Angel has a headache,' she said.

" 'Oh, that's too bad. Did you give him aspirin?'

" 'No, he doesn't like aspirin.'

"Later Dolly said to me, 'How does she *know* that Angel has a headache?' "

In the summer of 1957 came the Blue Angel debut of a headstrong twenty-four-year-old named Carol Burnett. She began her brief club career at the top and within two years had conquered theatre and TV as well. After growing up in Texas and California, Burnett moved to New York in 1955 under alleged circumstances that sound like a press agent's fantasy. According to her story she and her husband, actor Don Saroyan, performed a scene from *Annie Get Your Gun* at a party. One of the guests, the millionaire head of a construction company, loved them so much he gave them each a thousand-dollar check to start their careers. "There were four provisions," Burnett told columnist Earl Wilson. "We mustn't tell his name. It was a five-year loan to be paid back without interest. It must be used to go to New York. Afterward, we must help others as he'd helped us."

Jobs were few during her first year. She longed to work at the Blue Angel, but when Jacoby heard her at Tamiment in the summer of 1956 he found her unpolished and crude. She won a costarring role in *Stanley,* a new NBC-TV series, as the girlfriend of star Buddy Hackett. The show lasted only five months, and subsequently Burnett began rehearsals for Ben Bagley's *Shoestring '57*—an experience she later claimed to have forgotten. "Nothing else mattered to her except her determination to make a million dollars and become the biggest star in the world," Bagley recalls. "I had heard her at Tamiment and thought she was much too broad, but I believed we could get rid of that. We couldn't. There was no way of controlling her; she knew everything. I had a sketch by Herb Hartig about two strangers meeting in a coffee shop who utter all the clichés people say at a first encounter. Carol loved it, and that's what got her excited about the show. There wasn't much else for her to do in it. I told her she should play it straight in order to make it more realistic, but she insisted on camping it up, crying big sobs, and exaggerating every line. Finally I told her, 'If you cross your eyes one more time in that sketch you're through.' By now we were two weeks into rehearsal, and I was afraid we wouldn't have enough time to break in someone new. I gave the sketch to Fay DeWitt, which left Carol only with bits. 'Well, then, I want to get out,' she said. But according to Equity rules, after two weeks of rehearsal a performer could not quit until after the show opened. Carol was very upset. She said, in a loud voice, 'Wouldn't it be awful, Ben, if I got sick on opening night and couldn't show up!' John Bartis, one of the male stars, was my Equity deputy, and he overheard this and reported it to Equity, where it was placed on file. But I was worried she'd really do it, so I had no choice but to let her go and hire someone else."

Luckily for Burnett, Jacoby had decided that he would now take a chance on her. Burnett went to work with composer Ken Welch and prepared for a June 1957 opening at the Blue Angel. In an effort to give her a tasteful appearance, Jacoby arranged to borrow a gown from an expensive East Side boutique named Martha's. To his horror, Burnett spilled something on the dress on opening night.

Her act was generally well received, even though she compensated for her youthful lack of artistry by mugging outrageously, sticking out her tongue, and again crossing her eyes. The material included "Puppy Love," a paean to rock and roll romance; a routine about a young singer performing "My Romance" on TV while greeting, by gestures, a large array of family and friends at home; and a parody of a club performer who tries to milk every drop of applause from an audience even though the houselights are raised, the trio has walked off, and the microphone is carted away. Her numbers were often amusing in concept but fell flat in execution, and since Burnett worked frantically to get laughs the results were wearying.

But she became a sensation due to one number, a Welch original dedicated to the secretary of state entitled "I Made a Fool of Myself Over John Foster Dulles":

The first time I saw him, 'twas at the UN
I never had been one to swoon over men
But I swooned, and the drums started pounding, and then
I made a fool of myself over John Foster Dulles . . .

She corrals him at Newark Airport and clutches at his sleeve but grabs his briefcase by accident; unable to convince the FBI that she is not a spy, she lands in the clink for seven years. The song is a banal example of the type of material that passed for daring in the '50s, but since Dulles was very much in the news that year, and since his stern, grandfatherly persona seemed like such an unlikely subject for a crush, the number drew phenomenal attention. Burnett sang it on Jack Paar's TV show that August and repeated it by popular demand on Paar and Ed Sullivan. It rankled James Reston, the crusty Washington correspondent of the *New York Times,* who called it "a lyrical propaganda campaign"; but Dulles himself was flattered and requested a recording of the song to enjoy at his leisure.

The doors that opened for Burnett because of that song were extraordinary. In 1959 she starred in Mary Rodgers, Jay Thompson, Marshall Barer, and Dean Fuller's musical *Once Upon a Mattress,* based on "The Princess and the Pea." Later she divorced Don Saroyan, married a rising young television producer named Joe Hamilton, and became one of the nation's highest-paid comediennes—a surprise to some of those who remember her from the Angel. "It was just another act," says Will Holt, who shared the bill with her in 1957. "She was a nice singer, a sort-of-funny girl, but there was nothing that wonderful about her. Then she did that song on Jack Paar, and it was incredible what happened. Carol has made a brilliant career for herself, but she never had the impact of Dorothy Loudon in that room. Dorothy was like a terrier there. She could shake that room apart.

"Again, what Carol did was just right for Herbert. It was specifically tailored material, honed to a T. I never would have thought she'd become a star, but that's what happened."

NOW THAT JULIUS MONK and his revues were the talk of the town, a flurry of competitors began to open shop. The most prominent was the Showplace, a nightclub-theatre that helped launch Jerry Herman, Estelle Parsons, Dom DeLuise, Ruth Buzzi, Warren Beatty, "Mama" Cass Elliot, Charles Nelson Reilly, and Joanne Worley. Its founder, actor-model Jim Paul Eilers, had such a passion for fledgling writers and performers that he kept it open for seven years at a frequent loss.

The Showplace occupied the first two floors of a five-story brownstone at 146 West 4th Street, in the heart of the West Village. During Prohibition the building had housed a speakeasy called the Pepper Pot, where Al Jolson allegedly sang for tips and Norma Shearer worked as a waitress. Around 1931 another speakeasy, the Chantilly Club, took its place but closed after a gangland murder. In the '50s a new Chantilly Club opened there but came to a similar fate, which allowed Eilers to step in. He had long dreamed of owning his own off-Broadway theatre, particularly so his friend Rick Besoyan, a young composer, would have a forum for his work. Besoyan was then writing *Little Mary Sunshine*, a successful off-Broadway and Broadway musical. In order to afford a theatre Eilers turned to modeling, for which his matinee-idol looks more than qualified him.

Finding a site was difficult. "I looked uptown, downtown, East Side, West Side for a place I could afford. One night I was visiting Rick in his apartment in the Village, and I came out onto West 4th Street. There were police and ambulances in front of the Chantilly Club. I said to a cop, 'What the hell's going on here?' He said, 'Someone was just shot. We're about to take the body out.'

"I went right to the phone and called Besoyan. 'We've got the place! Someone was shot at the Chantilly Club, and tomorrow they're gonna want to get out, because they're gonna lose their liquor license.' "

Eilers leased the entire building for less than $1,000 a month, signing an agreement whereby he would pay the taxes and provide maintenance. He used the first two floors for the Showplace, rented the third and fourth, and moved into the fifth, the upper half of a duplex that once belonged to Mayor James J. Walker, who had designed it as a hideaway for himself and his mistress, Betty Compton. Huge and sumptuous, it featured multicolored skylights above the bedroom and living room, an enormous working fireplace, and a shower big enough for six.

The first level became a bar and the second a performance room. Long, narrow, and black, it had little charm; wrote Rogers Whitaker in the *New Yorker* (August 30, 1958), "So thin is this upstairs playhouse that nearly every seat is on the aisle." But it had an adequate stage, dressing rooms (entered only by way of the stage), and rudimentary sound and lighting systems.

In October 1957 the first revue, Besoyan's *In Your Hat,* opened with a cast of five and with staging by Christopher Hewett, later famous as television's *Mr. Belvedere.* Despite pleasant reviews it floundered commercially; customers remarked how almost every night was like an off-night. The Showplace gained little attention until *Nightcap*, a revue with music and lyrics by the twenty-four-year-old Jerry Herman. Just a few years from a string of Broadway successes that would include *Mame, Hello, Dolly,* and *La Cage aux Folles,* Herman occupied his evenings by playing cocktail piano at RSVP and other clubs and spent his days composing. His wealthy family helped support him in his early years in New York, enabling him to rent an apartment on West 10th Street that many struggling young composers envied. Eilers hired him during the run of *In Your Hat* to work in the "Speakeasy," as he called the downstairs bar. After glimpsing the poor houses upstairs he would say to Herman, "Boy, you better get some stuff together, because this show is not gonna last long."

So Herman assembled sixteen of his songs into a revue. Eilers gave him full artistic control, extending to direction, designing the printed program, painting a sign, sewing curtains, and hiring a staff that included future Broadway actress-singer-dancer Phyllis Newman as choreographer. The cast consisted of Australian singer Fia Karin; handsome actor-singer Kenneth Nelson; comic Charles Nelson Reilly; and Jane Romano, who later earned a footnote in theatre history by subbing for the notoriously healthy Ethel Merman for two weeks in *Gypsy.* Later in the run actress Estelle Parsons would replace Romano.

They rehearsed in Herman's apartment and opened in May 1958. *Nightcap* was not the work of an innate revue composer; most of the songs sounded like outtakes from a second-rate musical comedy. But the cast sang them with gusto, and *Variety* delivered the following valentine (June 4, 1958):

> The Sardi set and a lot of the wise music publishing boys have been streaming downtown to this small Greenwich Village nitery because word has gotten around that cleffer Jerry Herman is a comer. Herman, still in his 20s, shows in this intimate revue (which he directed as well as wrote) that he's got a big potential and if properly disciplined and directed could develop into a potent writer for Broadway and the music biz.

Consequently *Nightcap* fared better than any Showplace revue and sold out in its early weeks. When attendance dwindled, however, Herman recruited busloads of family and friends from Jersey City, and sometimes he and the cast would go out on the street and flag passersby, telling them, "There's a great show in there!" Herman's father reportedly poured money into the revue to keep it running and helped finance *Parade,* the off-Broadway adaptation of *Nightcap* produced two years later at the nearby Players Theatre. *Parade*'s notices, however, were not as good as its predecessor's. The Showplace's "let's put on a show" atmosphere had given Herman's uneven material a youthful, ingenuous feeling; in a more formal theatrical setting it seemed, as the *Village Voice* put it (January 27, 1960), "merely ambitious, avaricious, forced, pushed and, worst of all, tailored carefully to the trim of every other revue ever launched before us."

On opening night, Walter Kerr of the *New York Herald Tribune* (January 21, 1960) detected Herman's flair for self-promotion. "The assembled customers thundered approval of the three-piece orchestra, stomped for the solo dance routines, whistled for the couples singing ballads to one another, and shouted 'Bravo!' until it seemed as though the McDougal Street walls would crack under the salvos. If any of the material had been especially entertaining, I dread to think what might have happened."

Nevertheless *Parade* attracted producer Gerard Oestreicher, who asked the young composer to write the score for *Milk and Honey,* Herman's Broadway debut and the beginning of a truly golden career in American musical comedy. "Being seen—that's how it all began," said Herman. "Whenever people ask me how you get started, the only answer I have is to get your work seen. I don't care if it's a workshop, or a nightclub, or on a street corner. You can't say, 'I'm talented and no one knows it.' Knocking on the door of the Showplace is the reason I'm here today."

None of the revues that followed won any comparable notice, although two are fondly remembered. *The Prickly Pair* showcased the gifted comic-singers Marian Mercer and R. G. Brown in an evening of sketches by Brown and haunting songs by composer-pianist Baldwin Bergersen. *Stewed Prunes,* featuring Richard Libertini, MacIntyre Dixon, and Linda Segal, won a spread in *Life* magazine and the admiration of Samuel Beckett, Mike Nichols, and Norman Lear.

But the room stood in the shadow of the more auspicious uptown clubs, particularly the Upstairs at the Downstairs, which had reached its peak. The Showplace was considered an amusing hangout at best, its shows ranked inferior to Monk's. To make the room appear full Eilers sat life-size cardboard cutouts of people on the chairs. There was

Between 1958 and 1962, when Julius Monk's revues occupied the Upstairs at the Downstairs, newspapers proclaimed him the greatest discoverer of talent in show business. *Life* magazine published photo spreads of several of his shows; the *New Yorker* extolled them all as masterpieces of the genre. With Leonard Sillman's best work behind him, Monk took his place as the acknowledged master of the revue.

On July 22, 1958, Alice Ghostley launched the lower level, the Downstairs at the Upstairs. Then, on October 11, the Upstairs at the Downstairs premiered *Demi-Dozen*, a showcase for the work of Tom Jones and Harvey Schmidt. To Monk's delight, SRO audiences crowded the club.

The staggering popularity of his revues depended mostly on his skill at packaging a brand of snobbery that made them seem like a celebration of self-flattery for everybody involved. New Yorkers have always prided themselves on sophistication, and the city teemed with genuinely elegant and savvy people, as well as many others who wanted to be. Tourists visited the Upstairs and felt like Manhattan highbrows, while New Yorkers had the chance to rub elbows with what many thought was the crème de la crème.

However, nonresidents who revealed an ignorance of local ways were quickly brought down to size. One Upstairs performer recalls walking through midtown with a group of actors. A confused-looking tourist couple stopped them and asked, "Excuse us, where can we find East of Bway?" (They pronounced Bway as in "bwana.")

"East of Bway?"

"Yes," the husband said, taking a pair of tickets from his pocket. "This says the theatre we're looking for is 'East of Bway.' "

"God, you mean east of *Broad*way!" one of the actors said, as the group burst into mocking laughter. The couple slunk away, humiliated.

So it was at the Upstairs, where audiences could look down their noses at everything from Lincoln Center to children's TV variety shows. Social and political issues, when touched upon at all, were reduced to the level of cocktail chatter.

But Monk at least found a few players capable of bringing the material to life. In *Pieces of Eight*, his 1959–1960 revue, he introduced the splendid comedienne Mary Louise Wilson. A young brunette from New Orleans, Wilson came to New York in 1953 to become an actress. With no trouble she found a fifth-floor apartment on West 4th Street—"three rooms with slanting floors," says Wilson. "I paid thirty-seven fifty a month, which was ridiculously low even then. Friends had to use a crowbar to get me out of there." Between secretarial jobs she won her first role, one spoken line in a Circle in the Square production of *Our Town*, and later succeeded Beatrice Arthur as Lucy in *The Threepenny Opera*.

"I kept reading the *New Yorker* squib about the Upstairs at the Downstairs, and that to me was the acme of wit and sophistication. It took me years just to get a date who could afford to take me there. One day George Furth came into my apartment and said, 'Jane Connell is leaving *Pieces of Eight* to do *Threepenny Opera* on the coast. You've got to go audition.' I said, 'I can't, I can't! For Julius Monk?' I had just gotten the part in *Threepenny*, and I couldn't see leaving it. Finally he bullwhipped me into going. I sang 'Something Wonderful' from *The King and I* for Julius and the cast, and I knocked an entire pitcher of water into the piano. Julius took me aside and began to talk, and I didn't know what he was saying. Finally I realized I'd gotten the job."

With an air of comic bemusement, Wilson conveyed a sense of landing in the middle of one unearthly situation after another, attempting to stay calm while making it clear that *she* couldn't make head or tail of it either. *Cue* magazine called her "as stylish a comedienne as there is around and one whose mere presence touches any setting with class."

Also for *Pieces of Eight* Monk hired William Roy, an expert young pianist and musical director who had accompanied Portia Nelson, Mary McCarty, and other singers. Roy had worked extensively as a child actor on such radio programs as *The Lone Ranger* and *The Green Hornet* and in an illustrious series of '40s films that included *The Corn Is Green*, *Passage to Marseilles*, and *It Happened in Brooklyn*. In 1953 he made an ill-fated venture onto Broadway as the composer of *Maggie (What Every Woman Knows)*, a musical version of J. M. Barrie's comedy. *Maggie*'s failure submerged a charming, tuneful score, and Roy soon moved to California to accompany singer John Walsh, formerly of the Café Gala. In 1959 he returned to New York and went to work for Monk for seven seasons, playing the piano, arranging, and contributing many original songs. Recalls Mary Louise Wilson, "I didn't realize until I'd left Julius what an education I'd gotten from Billy. He made very sophisticated harmonies seem so simple. He'd give us the first three notes of a song, and we'd say, 'How am I going to remember that?' He'd play them again, and tell us, 'Just think of "Home on the Range." ' "

Roy was the only person Monk consulted while choosing and adapting material. "The writers came to Julius's apartment, sat at his little upright, and played and sang for him. We had several writers who couldn't play the piano or write things down musically, so they'd just sing or hum them. Julius would say, 'Make a setting for this. Put it in a style.' "

Monk wanted each song and sketch to represent a chic and timely New York outlook, often by dropping the names of local celebrities, places, and shows. Just as important, he insisted that all his material be in "good taste," offensive to no one. His pieces never stung; at best they delivered a gentle slap on the wrist. Mild double entendres were permissible, but never anything more explicit. In 1961 he told the *New York Herald Tribune*, "We are more witty than iconoclastic, and we proceed with great caution. No one has a Pollyanna fixation around here, but we do respect civilized propriety. The entertainment here is as guileless as a children's pageant, which is our idea of sophistication. Any policy of sharp political satire would be defeatist, like trying to make Kafka into a Broadway show. I don't really understand the propensity for people to be evil on stage."

But this cautious approach prevented most of his attempted satire from hitting center and gave a sense that the writers were walking on eggs. Ronny Graham remembers "Barry's Boys," a Barry Goldwater lampoon written by June Reizner from *Dime a Dozen*, and *Baker's Dozen*, Monk's first two revues at the Plaza Hotel, where he relocated in 1962. Gerry Matthews, Jack Fletcher, and Rex Robbins sang and danced this lighthearted tune:

GM & RR: Why does a chicken cross the road?
JF: To get from the left to the right.
GM & RR: Right!
ALL: Alla Kanee Kanak Kana
Let's investigate the PTA!
JF: Roses are red
GM: Violets are blue
RR: Walter Lippmann's a pinko too!
JF & RR: Barry, Barry, make your bid
GM: I love John Birch, but oh, you kid!

"I thought, God, there's more to dig into here that's more savage," Graham says. "This is just name-dropping. It was such a mild piece." When Monk received an amusing song or sketch that had what he deemed objectionable content, he laundered it in a way that made it innocuous or even nonsensical. "We can't do that here," he would declare. "We don't say that in this room. Highly incendiary." Ben Bagley, who succeeded Monk briefly when he left for the Plaza, remembers, "There was a song Jane Connell sang in *Ten-ish, Anyone?*, a Downstairs revue, called 'Festivals.' It was a gem by Jack Holmes, one of Julius's best writers, but Julius ruined it. It was about a lady musician who performs in national music festivals, and the whole idea was sexual innuendo:

To all you horns at Juilliard, your technique will develop
Chin down, cheeks out, don't puff too hard
And never let me catch you with your bell up!
Practice makes perfect; now don't evade
To be a good musician, you must work years
But perfect you will all be made
I was last year in the Berkshires . . .

"It was a filthy song, but wonderful. And Julius cut out all the sass so that it didn't make any sense. Why he took this material in the first place, I don't know."

Monk usually avoided the problem altogether by choosing pieces on safer subjects such as Con Edison, Radio City, Kabuki theatre, and the *New Yorker*. He altered even these in any way he felt necessary. "Julius angered a lot of writers," says William Roy, "because we had very private rehearsals and they weren't invited. During that time he often restructured things and put the back on the front or whatever."

Rehearsals lasted about six weeks, and never in their careers did many in the cast endure such grueling hours. "Julius loved rehearsals," Roy says. "He lived only for the Upstairs at the Downstairs or the Plaza and hated having to go home. Equity or AGVA rules about rehearsals were never enforced. I don't remember ever taking more than a five- or ten-minute break, and even then he would always come over and say, 'Dear friend, will you come and try this piece out, and Celia, would you come and sing it?' It was outrageous. We had a few twelve-hour rehearsals. I even remember arriving one day at ten in the morning, and at midnight Julius came over and said, 'Dear friend, will you try this piece for me?' I picked up the entire score and threw it across the room. It was the only time I showed any anger toward him. Irving's brother Hy was in the kitchen, and he would set up lunch for us: a couple of cans of sardines, a couple of slices of cheese, mustard, and some bread and butter. We had sardine sandwiches until we could have swum to Europe and back.

"One year Julius called a Christmas Day rehearsal during previews. He was three hours late. Finally he arrived and began rehearsing us, and it was about an hour and a half before the performance. I said, 'I beg your pardon, but I haven't had anything to eat, and I don't wish to do the preview without having something in my stomach.'

"He said, 'Excuse me, cast, we will now dismiss because Mr. Roy insists upon having some food!' "

Monk assigned material on the first day of rehearsal. Since many cast members were newcomers and happy to be working, they accepted whatever he gave them. In any case, Monk was not interested in their opinions. "Julius was approachable but difficult to communicate with," says Mary Louise Wilson. "If we complained about a number he'd get angry. I was a complete brat. I never felt the material was good enough. I always thought Ceil Cabot got the best material. I spent a whole day lying under the piano in the rehearsal room of the Plaza crying, because Julius had given me a song I hated. It was about Leonard Bernstein—'Is it Bern-*steen* or Bern*stine*?'—and I thought it was the dumbest song I'd ever heard. He'd always look at me to see my reaction when he brought me a new song."

"We were always a little surprised the way some of the stuff went over," says Gerry Matthews. "We would drag our feet and complain about some of the things we were asked to do, especially the ensemble numbers. Other things I was delighted with, and it was a big competition over who was going to get what. We never had any say about it, of course. We had devious ways of trying to get out of things: we just wouldn't learn them."

Monk's gentlemanly demeanor crumbled when his taste was questioned. "Once we were in rehearsals," says Roy, "and there was a number practically everyone in the cast had tried and hated. Julius gave it to Jamie Ross. We were running through it, and Jamie said, 'Isn't this awful?'

" 'It's ghastly,' I said.

" 'Well, what should I do?'

" 'Just go in the dressing room and tell him you don't want to do it.'

"Julius answered, 'We've been waiting for your charm to come through for three years and it hasn't shown yet!' "

Adds Rex Robbins, "Julius would say, 'I'd be less of a friend if I didn't tell you . . .' and say something evil. Once at the Plaza he said to [cast member] Susan Browning, 'Now, Miss Browning, I'd be less of a friend if I didn't tell you . . . when you make that face, you are grotesque!"

Starting with *Pieces of Eight* Monk engaged a choreographer named Frank Wagner to devise elaborate movements for his players. The cast punctuated almost every phrase with some gesture, creating a whirlwind of action. "He choreographed our little fingers," Mary Louise Wilson says. "And I've got two left feet." "We called Frank 'Pick-Pick,' " says Robbins, "because he was so picky about everything. You had to do exactly as he said."

There were other matters for Monk to attend to, such as costumes. Wishing them to be as simple and versatile as possible, he barred plunging necklines or any other distracting styles. "I think flesh is destructive to revue material," he said. Usually the men dressed in tuxedos or dark suits throughout, the women in black gowns to which a scarf or gloves might be added. The women's clothes were seldom truly elegant, for usually they were made cheaply from poor materials. Charles Blackburn, who designed the costumes for *The Fantasticks*, made his professional debut in New York with *Pieces of Eight*. "Julius gave me two hundred and fifty dollars and said, 'This is the money you'll use to make the costumes, and the rest will be your salary.' "

Each show had a week of previews, when Monk exercised his extraordinary skill at pacing and editing. "Julius had a set of note cards with the names of each number written on them," says Wilson. "During the show he'd move them around, adjust them. If something didn't work in a certain place he'd put it somewhere else. That was his art. If a number got too much applause he was intimidated, because it brought the show to a halt. It was all flow and rhythm, and everything had to keep moving. If a waltz didn't work he'd try it as a tango, or he'd use marimbas."

Monk had other, less orthodox ways of pulling a show into shape. "When we were in previews," says Roy, "he'd come backstage between acts or at the end with his producer, Tom Hammond. He always looked as if we had all gone out on stage and deliberately done something to hurt him—we had all trampled on his lovely little show. And after the terrible rehearsal hours, people went on for the opening like zombies. We had worked so hard and were so tired that we couldn't have written a grocery list, but we could have easily done any of those sketches in our sleep."

No one, of course, could argue with the notices or sold-out houses, or with the fresh, youthful appeal of many of the performers, whose sincerity touched audiences even if their technical skills fell short. "Oh, those people thought they knew us," says Wilson. "And when I say people, every celebrity in town was out there looking at us darling kids, as we were called. I was pushing thirty."

Moreover, those evenings spotlighted the work of many fledgling writers and occasionally uncovered some gems, although most of them are unmistakably of their day. Two of Tom Jones and Harvey Schmidt's fine numbers from *Demi-Dozen* were special favorites. Wearing a long blonde wig decorated with flowers, Jane Connell satirized an arty folk singer in "The Race of the Lexington Avenue Express," performed in the galloping rhythm of singing bandleader Vaughn Monroe's hit recording "Riders in the Sky." It told of Mervyn

Schwartz, a motorman on the East Side IRT subway line who, accused of moving his train too slowly, challenges the Brooklyn BMT to a midnight race:

The train was pretty old, lads
As old as it could be
It was up against the very best of the Brooklyn BMT
He slammed the doors at Union Square
And threw the throttle wide
Then he shouted to his passengers,
By God, you're gonna get yourself a ride!

As the train barrels up Lexington Avenue toward the Bronx, Mervyn picks up enough speed to win but finds himself moving too quickly to stop. And so the race—and Mervyn—come to an end at the last station: Woodlawn Cemetery.

In the same show Gerry Matthews recited a "parable with music" entitled "The Holy Man and the New Yorker," about a more serious demise. This touching example of early Schmidt and Jones captured the ambivalence of late '50s New York life, in which a sense of boundless opportunity vied with the tensions of a city that had begun to enclose itself in mortar and steel.

The number told of a vagrant living on a street corner near an empty Gristede's packing case. Passersby call him a religious freak when he tries to point out the vestiges of nature that they are too busy to spot: the sky, the sun, the earth peeping through from beneath the pavement. Finally he persuades a skeptical man to pause:

The New Yorker, ready to dare it, looked straight up and saw the sky
He saw two clouds like angel's wings as they drifted slowly by
He saw the blue of the heavens through the burning tears in his eye
Son of a bitch! the New Yorker yelled
God bless you! came the Holy Man's reply

And now they were both of them weeping
From the mysterious joy of life

All of them clouds! the New Yorker cried
Just wait till I tell my wife! . . .
There were tears that blurred his vision
Making rainbows in his eyes
As he took his leave from the Holy Man he looked straight up at the skies
As he stepped down off the curbstone
His eyes were seen to flash
Then someone cried:
My God, there's a taxi! Wait!
And then there came the crash . . .

Bill Dana contributed "Conference Call," probably the first anti-smoking sketch in comedy. In it a group of ad agency executives discuss the failure of cigarette filters to prevent cancer. "You know how they test the little mousies to see if they get you-know-what? The lab looks like they bombed Disneyland!" Dave Garroway thought so highly of the sketch that he fought successfully with his cigarette sponsors to have it performed on the *Today* show.

For *Pieces of Eight* Dana's "Conversation Piece" spoofed pseudo-intellectual talk shows, a TV staple that had begun to replace meaningful conversation in the living room. In this sketch the target was *Open End*, David Susskind's panel discussion show. "David Somekind," the host of *Open Mouth*, welcomes Bernard Bastille, "famous analytical economist and ex-jaywalker," Gerald Breen, "noted sexologist," and Fern Beatty, "noted leg":

BEATTY: I hope, Mr. Somekind, that you're not calling on me first out of some outdated feeling that there's a moral obligation that women should go first.

SOMEKIND: Now we're getting someplace!

BASTILLE: But are we really? I mean, try to look at this sagely and obtusely, for God's sake.

SOMEKIND: Well, let's see if I can draw this thing into focus for us. What you mean is that sometimes the funniest things are said in jest?

BASTILLE: That, and the realization that there's a basic quality of unity that is untouched. And until that is weened and unfettered, we're not going to be able to stand apart and say, "This is our planet. This is our world. This is a planet and a world of ours."

BEATTY: I think a case in point could be the example we get from Julius Caesar, Abraham Lincoln, and recently James Dean.

SOMEKIND: Well, what exactly?

BEATTY: How things happen in threes.

SOMEKIND: Of course!

The highlight of *Dressed to the Nines* was William Roy's "Billy's Blues," a sassy declaration of independence sung by comedienne Pat Ruhl:

The first guy who gave me a bad time
From lookin' at too many women and hittin' the booze
Was sorry he said that he had time
When I sang him the love-me-the-way-that-I-wanna-be-loved-or-go-pack-your-pajamas-and-get-the-hell-out-of-here-blues . . .

And Jack Holmes contributed "Names," a piece of shameless silliness sung deadpan by Mary Louise Wilson:

If Conway Twitty would marry Kitty Carlisle
Then Kitty Carlisle would now be Kitty Twitty
If Phoebe Snow had run after Lucius Beebe
Just think, we might have wound up with Phoebe Beebe . . .

The possibilities were endless, but Holmes had the sense to limit them to about a minute and a half of clever quatrains.

Two charming numbers brightened *Ten-ish, Anyone?*, a Downstairs revue with Jane Connell and Jack Fletcher. "Thor" by Jack Holmes spotlighted the fictitious creator of a new antiballistic missile, a normally laconic man who, when called upon to make an acceptance speech for a Congressional Award of Honor from the president, confirms a widespread suspicion about the leaders of the arms race:

Why do I call it "Thor"?
Thimple—I like the thound of it!
I'll never forget how embarrathed I wathe when the Thor exthploded

It thpluttered and thplattered and thertainly
made me thore!

Most Upstairs alumni have a common favorite: "Daisy," written by G. Wood. Touchingly sung by Connell, it tells of a woman's memories of early childhood after her mother, a Ziegfeld showgirl, returned home after work. Tucking her into bed, she would "sing me a song from her show, a song I still adore / As she took off her clothes exactly the way she'd done / Less than an hour before":

When men with homes in which to dwell
Register in a hotel
Their wives don't know and I won't tell
And that's why they call me Daisy
Men say the only thing that settles whether love is true
Is to remove a daisy's petals, which they do
In life the girls who get ahead are like flowers, it's
been said
Transplanting well from bed to bed
But some of us are limited
You have to pay the price for orchids' lovely bloom . . .
For lily of the valley, with her delicate perfume
But just for something colorful to decorate the room
Call up Daisy . . .

Monk usually included at least one nostalgic ballad about the New York of long ago, and for *Seven Come Eleven* (1961–1962) Michael Brown wrote a superior one entitled "New York Has a New Hotel." It described the opening of the Summit Hotel at 51st Street and Lexington Avenue—another "place of glass and steel," Miami Beach–style, with every modern convenience but without the charm of simpler hostelries. Far from being a world-weary grumble, it expressed a heartfelt regret at the commercialization of every last trace of the city's Old World heritage:

But when I look at it, nostalgia overcomes me,
I long for marble in the place of tile,
The gleam of all the chromium benumbs me,
When did oak with velvet fade from style?

Most of the other material sank far below this level, overburdened with inside references and condescension. The name-dropping snob appeal of the shows is epitomized by Dion MacGregor and Michael Barr's "The Hate Song" from *Dressed to the Nines,* in which psychiatric patient Bill Hinnant visits analyst Ceil Cabot and airs his hostilities at breakneck speed:

HINNANT: Hate Virginia Bruce
CABOT: Hate Virginia Bruce . . .
HINNANT: Hate Anita Loos
CABOT: Hate Anita Loos . . .
HINNANT: Hate Dolores Gray
CABOT: Hate Dolores Gray . . .
HINNANT: Hate Nanette Fabray
CABOT: Hate Fabray . . .
HINNANT: Hate Patricia Neal
CABOT: Burt and Harry Piel?
HINNANT: No, I'm fond of them . . .

Such list songs were a trademark of Monk's revues. Says Tom Jones, "Julius would say to Harvey and me, 'We need dem bones':

DA-da-da-da-da-da—Cole Porter!
DA-da-da-da-da-da—Elsa Lanchester!

"We'd just drop these names over a rhythm section. The audience had the illusion they were being titillated by great wit."

All this bustle helped camouflage the true quality of the material. "It all went by so fast," says Rex Robbins, "and that was its saving grace. If you slowed it down and heard what was being said, you'd realize that most of it wasn't really that witty."

Yet audiences roared with laughter at every punch line and came away raving. "In some fantastically instinctive way Julius made the shows work," William Roy says. "He took material that Leonard Sillman couldn't have made anyone yawn at, and made it funny." But Ben Bagley, whose own revues could never be accused of prissiness, questions their actual wit. "You'd say 'Bonwit Teller' and everybody would laugh. Then you'd say 'the Plaza' and everybody would laugh. There was no real humor or satire here—just a lot of people being snotty about everything."

A crucial factor in Monk's success was the support of his friend Rogers Whitaker, whose *New Yorker* nightclub reviews were regarded as gospel by most cafégoers. Early in the run of every show Whitaker, a gruff curmudgeon of late middle age, would drop by with his notebook, take his seat, then fall sound asleep within the first ten minutes. Two or three issues later a rave review would appear in his "Tables for Two" column.

Such celebrities as Judy Garland, Bette Davis, and Charlton Heston enjoyed the shows, but others were mystified by all the hype. As Montgomery Clift watched *Seven Come Eleven*, he counted the sketches and songs that remained, and left at intermission. Ethel Merman walked out of *Demi-Dozen* after comedienne Jean Arnold's performance of Cy Coleman and Carolyn Leigh's "You Fascinate Me So," bellowing to her young companion, "That bitch looks like a female gas station attendant!" On more than a few evenings the audience sat in perplexed silence, unaware that certain lines were supposed to be funny. That this happened so seldom is another indication of the vogue for Monkian humor in late '50s and early '60s New York.

As in all nightclubs, the great leveler was alcohol. "We all know that a drinking audience is not necessarily a listening audience," Gerry Matthews says. "Diana Barrymore came in one night with Tennessee Williams, and they were sitting in what we call the nostril seats, all the way up front in the center. They drank themselves blind and were falling down on the floor, making noises and yelling at us, grabbing at our feet and putting their drinks on the stage. It was infuriating."

"People seemed to be throwing up all the time," Matthews adds. One winter night actor Jim Sheridan, one of Monk's "custodians of the rope," stood downstairs by the reservation desk while the show was in progress. Down the curving staircase tottered an inebriated Joan Crawford, wearing a full-length mink and looking queasy. She grabbed Sheridan's arm and started to mumble.

"Errr . . . excuse . . . my dear . . . where . . ."

"Yes, Miss Crawford? Can I get you anything? Would you like to sit down?"

Still holding on to him, Crawford managed only to ask "Where is . . ." before turning her head and throwing up on the reservation book.

Monk was not always around to quell these disturbances, though.

"After the show opened he'd go off to Mexico for a month or six weeks," says Matthews. In any case, that job fell to maître d' Bruce Kirby. Most of the time he managed this with relative grace, but grace sometimes failed, as actor Brandon Maggart, a longtime waiter at the club, recalls. "One evening a guy onstage said, 'And now I'd like to do a number that's been requested.' Two guys were sitting together in the audience, and one of them called out, 'Nobody requested you to do anything!' Instead of ignoring him the actor said, 'Well, you're about to be requested to leave!' Bruce was downstairs, so there was nobody to do that. It was a stalemate—the actor wouldn't finish his number. So I got Bruce, and we went over to ask the guys to leave, but they wouldn't budge. So we physically insisted they leave. There was a back stairway, and customers would often skip out on checks that way—you'd see waiters chasing them down 56th Street. And we were required to pay those checks. I had one guy behind me with a full nelson, and the other guy took a swing at me. I picked them both up, and I had one in one hand and one in the other as I headed down those steps. It was like a western. I was going to throw them out the swinging doors into the street. I reared back and got ready to toss them, and I forgot that the doors swung in but not out. So their faces smashed against the doors as they fell to the ground. In my mind the director was yelling, 'CUT! CUT!' "

In contrast, certain customers were sober, appreciative, and tasteful—but not in the conventional sense, as Gerry Matthews relates. "There was a well-known transvestite from Chicago, a businessman who loved the shows and came regularly. He called himself the Duchess. He always came in a tiara and an elaborate sequined gown with matching shoes. He was a great big man and made no effort to change his voice. He would write ahead to reserve a specific table in the back, with room for his valet and handmaiden—two black servants dressed in livery. And there were to be certain flowers on the table. The waiters loved him because he was a big tipper. He came backstage, and we were all gathered to pay homage. The Duchess said, in his baritone voice, that it was a lovely show and thank you. Then he swept out of there."

Monk himself was tickled by such guests, and it seemed ironic that this terribly genteel man should privately rejoice in the risqué and have such a ribald sense of humor. "Julius was the wittiest, most flamboyant man I have ever known," Matthews says. "His appearance was so grand and proper, and yet he'd get really scatological."

A lot of this escaped casual listeners, however, because Monk's speech, with its hybrid Southern-British overtones and oatmeal diction, was still unintelligible. Not wishing to offend him, those at the club pretended to understand but sometimes wished they had an interpreter. "Marilyn Child was understudying Judy Holliday in *Bells Are Ringing*," says Brandon Maggart, "and one night she came into the Downstairs at the Upstairs. Julius had a little table outside the door where he sat with friends, and he could see the acts through the glass partition and hear them on the speaker. Marilyn and Julius sat there talking, and Marilyn kept saying, 'Uh-huh, uh-huh.' Julius got up, walked through the packed house, and got onstage, and all of a sudden he was introducing her. She had agreed to sing and hadn't the faintest idea of what she'd done. So she got up there and sang."

The situation was far more trying for those who worked there. Writers had an especially hard time following his specifications. Says Louis Botto, one of Monk's best, "Many times we'd ask one another, 'Do you understand what he's saying?' The consensus was only half the time, so you just nodded and hoped you write the number he wanted. It was either pretention or just his eccentric character. At the club he would make pompous announcements: 'While you're having your libation, do enjoy William Roy and Carl Norman at the tandem pianos.' "

The toughest job remained for the cast, who had the double burden of deciphering his directions as well as their own material. "Once during a rehearsal," Matthews says, "Julius called out from the back, 'Well, it's any more than Wimbledon, my dears' and got up and left. We were totally mystified. The next day I said, 'I know what he means. He wants us to trade lines back and forth as if it were a tennis match.' I had been with him so long that I could sense what he wanted, without ever really understanding him."

"Once Julius took an actress aside and began talking to her," says Roy. "She just smiled and went on her way. The next night she showed up for work, and one of the waiters said, 'What are you doing here?' Julius had fired her the night before."

Jack Holmes was one of the few who ever heard what lay beneath Monk's cosmopolitan accent. "One night we were sitting at the bar and he got completely bombed with me and lost that accent completely. He began to talk half as fast, and he sounded like a lazy Southern boy. Finally I knew what he was talking about."

It was ironic that all the metropolitan savoir faire in Monk's shows should be spouted by youngsters from Pipestone, Minnesota; Eldred, Pennsylvania; Montgomery, Alabama; and Greenville, Texas; and who were anything but sophisticates themselves. One of these was Fredricka Weber, a cute blonde from Beardstown, Illinois, whom Monk introduced in a Downstairs edition of *Dressed to the Nines.* Her father ran a tavern, and her mother's family owned a restaurant called Mother's Grill. As a child Weber showed musical promise. Her Aunt Jimmy taught her to play the ukelele, and soon after she won a contest for her self-accompanied rendition of "Blue Pacific Blues." Later she worked as a local band singer and, while attending Northwestern University, played the piano and sang at Chicago's Sheraton Hotel. "I wanted to be a serious singer like Eydie Gorme, but whenever I tried to sing serious songs people would laugh. I had a couple of funny ones too, and people would say, 'You're just so funny, you belong in New York!'

"One day I got mad at my boyfriend and threatened to get a job in New York and leave him. I got a copy of the *New Yorker* and saw a listing for Julius Monk's Upstairs at the Downstairs. I had no idea who Julius Monk was, but I called the number and said, 'Hello, Julius? Julius Monk, please.' They didn't even ask me who I was. He got on, and I said, 'Hello, my name is Fredricka Weber, and I would like to know, are you auditioning anyone soon? I'm from Chicago, and I've been told I belong in New York.'

"I could hardly understand a word he said. 'Well, Miss Webah, I'm overwhelmed. When do you want to come in?' This was Tuesday, and we agreed on Friday. So I got a flight, and the Sheraton put me up because I worked for them. I took a cab to Julius's and never saw another thing in New York. I sat at the piano and played and sang for three hours. Julius laughed and laughed. Then he brought everyone in, and they all laughed too. I didn't know what was so funny—I thought I was being real serious. Finally he got up and walked over to the bar, so I ran over and said, 'Julius, I play the trumpet and whistle, too.'

" 'Well, Miss Webah, I'm not surprised.'

The Revuers in "Baroness Bazooka," an operetta takeoff, ca. 1939. *Left to right:* Adolph Green, Betty Comden, Alvin Hammer, Judy Holliday, John Frank. (*courtesy of Betty Comden*)

Spivy's Roof by day, 1940. Note the celebrity caricatures on the walls, including Martha Raye at far right. (*courtesy of Marsha Harkness*)

ABOVE LEFT: Actress-comedienne Paula Laurence in her Ruban Bleu headdress, ca. 1940. (*photo by George Platt Lynes; courtesy of Paula Laurence*) ABOVE RIGHT: Daffy diseuse Alice Pearce with accompanist Mark Lawrence, 1946. (*author's collection*) LEFT: Pearl Bailey, ca. 1944. (*author's collection*)

Pianist Cy Walter holds forth at the Drake Room of New York's Drake Hotel in the company of a few colleagues and friends, 1947. *Left to right:* Fellow keyboard artists Ted Straeter, Stan Freeman, Alex Fogarty, Lester Crosley (hidden); Cy Walter; singer-pianist Walter Shirley; pianist Jacques Frey; songwriter Johnny Marks; pianists Abram Chasins and Roger Stearns. *Foreground:* Maurice Chevalier. (*photo by Fritz Henle; courtesy of Cam Walter LaGianussa*)

ABOVE: The Blue Angel goes to the movies: a scene from the 1948 United Artists murder mystery *Jigsaw*, with Jean Wallace onstage. (*author's collection*)

RIGHT: Two A.M. in the Blue Angel lounge with Portia Nelson and composer-pianist William Roy, 1952. (*courtesy of William Roy*)

LEFT: Composer Bart ("Fly Me to the Moon") Howard in his East Side apartment alongside Viennese chanteuse Greta Keller, 1946. (*courtesy of Bart Howard*)

BELOW: At Bricktop's in Rome, 1953: chanteuse Simone Gallos with Murray Grand at the piano. Bricktop is reflected in the mirror. (*courtesy of Murray Grand*)

Imogene Coca lampoons a female trombonist in the mid-'40s, during her peak nightclub years. (*author's collection*)

Pat Carroll in 1951, looking more like a Girl Scout than the self-confessed 1970s "dowager queen of the game shows." (*author's collection*)

This page and next: singing comediennes of the café years

ABOVE: Bart Howard with the greatest café singer of them all, Mabel Mercer, in 1947. The scarf on the piano bears the words and music of Howard's "You Are Not My First Love," which Mercer introduced. (*photo by Ray Long; courtesy of Bart Howard*)

RIGHT: Mercer leans against the piano at Tony's West Side, her 1940s headquarters, in 1946. (*courtesy of Donald Smith*)

Kaye Ballard, onstage at the Bon Soir, as a self-enamored starlet serenading her own reflection, 1958. (*photo by Peter Stackpole; courtesy* Life *magazine © 1958 Time Warner Inc.*)

Dorothy Loudon, best known for her Tony-winning portrayal of Miss Hannigan in Broadway's *Annie*, in a 1951 RCA Victor Records publicity shot. (*author's collection*)

Three café songbirds of the 1950s. RIGHT: Anita Ellis, the ghost voice of Rita Hayworth and other movie stars. (*courtesy of Anita Ellis*) BELOW LEFT: Felicia Sanders. (*courtesy of Irving Joseph*) BELOW RIGHT: Broadway's Barbara Cook, later the star of *Candide, The Music Man,* and *She Loves Me.* (*author's collection*)

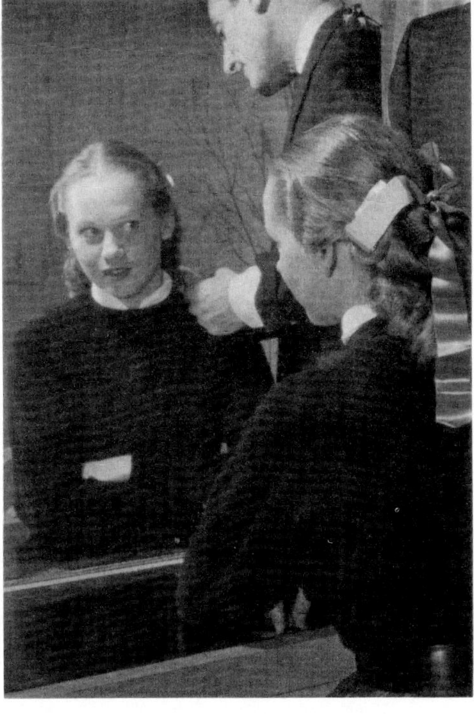

Lee Goodman and James (*A Chorus Line*) Kirkwood, Jr., in 1950, during their violent seven-year collaboration. (*courtesy of Lee Goodman*)

"Igor and H": comedy writer Herb Hartig and future film director Paul Mazursky, 1955. (*courtesy of Herb Hartig*)

This page and next: 1950s café duos

Musical comedy mainstays Gordon and Jane Connell, 1955. (*courtesy of William Roy*)

Onstage at the Blue Angel: Elaine May as a crotchety telephone operator crossing swords with exasperated caller Mike Nichols, 1958. (*photo by Peter Stackpole; courtesy of* Life *magazine © 1958 Time Warner Inc.*)

RIGHT: "Professor" Irwin Corey, ca. 1950. (*author's collection*)

BELOW: Orson Bean, ca. 1951. (*author's collection*)

RIGHT: Eartha Kitt onstage at the Blue Angel, 1952. (*photo by Ernst Haas; courtesy of Magnum*)

BELOW: Resident bon vivant Mae Barnes onstage at the Bon Soir, 1956. (*photo by Fotiades-Knudsen; courtesy of Mae Barnes*)

Goldie's New York, home away from home for Ethel Merman and many other stars, moves to 232 East 53rd Street in 1956. *Left to right:* Pianist-proprietor Goldie Hawkins, Jayne Mansfield, Portia Nelson, Cy Walter, TV and stage personality Kyle MacDonnell, Elaine Stritch, Ben Gazzara, and Mansfield's dog Philip on piano. (*photo by David McLane; courtesy of the* New York Daily News)

Bobby Short, 1956. (*author's collection*)

Jazz vocal duo Jackie Cain and Roy Kral at the Embers, Indianapolis, ca. 1959. (*photo by Jerry Wright; courtesy of Jackie and Roy Kral*)

Dan Dailey with ex-vaudevillian and Little Club owner Billy Reed.

Pianist Cy Walter with the great pop-jazz stylist Lee Wiley.

Singer-comedienne Bibi Osterwald.

Pianist Ralph Strain with singer Sylvia Syms.

This page and next: late nights at Dottie's Sutton Tap Room, a favorite East Side hangout for café folk, 1955 (*all photos courtesy of Cam Walter LaGianussa*)

Husband-and-wife piano team Eadie and Rack.

Lena Horne with arranger-conductor husband Lennie Hayton.

Jazz songstress Stella Brooks admires a photo of composer Alec Wilder.

Bon Soir emcee Jimmie Daniels with Blue Angel co-owner Herbert Jacoby.

ABOVE: *Four Below. Left to right:* Dody Goodman, Jack Fletcher, Gerry Matthews, June Ericson. (*courtesy of June Ericson Gardner*)

RIGHT: *Take Five.* Ronny Graham, Gerry Matthews. (*courtesy of Gerry Matthews*)

Son of Four Below. Left to right: Jack Fletcher, Ceil Cabot, Bud McCreery, Gerry Matthews, June Ericson. (*courtesy of June Ericson Gardner*)

Julius Monk's Downstairs Room, 1956–1957

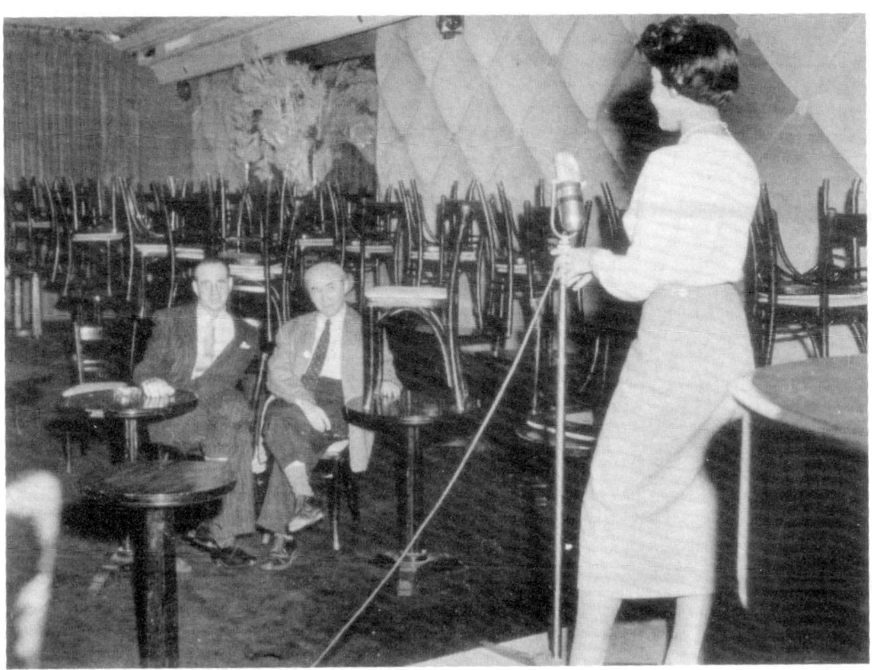

Afternoon auditions at the Blue Angel: singer Carleen Fitzgerald smiles gamely for Herbert Jacoby and Max Gordon, 1957. She didn't get the job. (*photo by Tom Watson; courtesy of the* New York Daily News)

Jacoby in the Blue Angel lounge with resident vocal-instrumental couple Martha Davis and Spouse, 1957. (*photo by Leonard Detrick; courtesy of the* New York Daily News)

Backstage and onstage at Jorie's Purple Onion, 1955: comedienne Jorie Remus, who combined a tongue in cheek, over the hill glamour with a devastating sense of the ridiculous. RIGHT: Remus in her nightly struggle to beautify a face that never responded as she hoped it would. BELOW: The results.

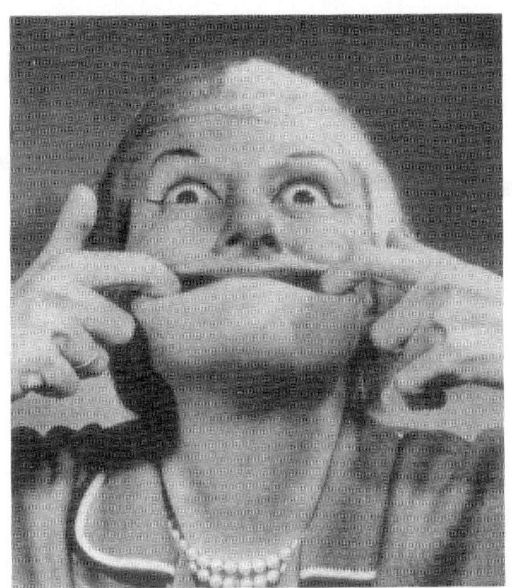

LEFT: Phyllis Diller, on whom Remus was an important influence, displays none of the same insecurities, 1961. (*photo by John Duprey; courtesy of the* New York Daily News)

BELOW: Feather-voiced, madly eccentric singer-pianist Blossom Dearie, 1960. (*author's collection*)

Two vocal and visual objects of many a late-night fantasy, both in 1957. LEFT: Julie Wilson, who fogged the bifocals of countless tired businessmen at the St. Regis Hotel's Maisonette Room. (*author's collection*) ABOVE: Julie London, whose sensual half-whisper heated up a sultry selection of ballads. (*courtesy of the* New York Daily News)

ABOVE: Joanne Beretta at the Showplace, 1962. (*courtesy of Joanne Beretta*)

LEFT: Lovelady Powell, Upstairs at the Duplex, 1955. (*courtesy of Lovelady Powell*)

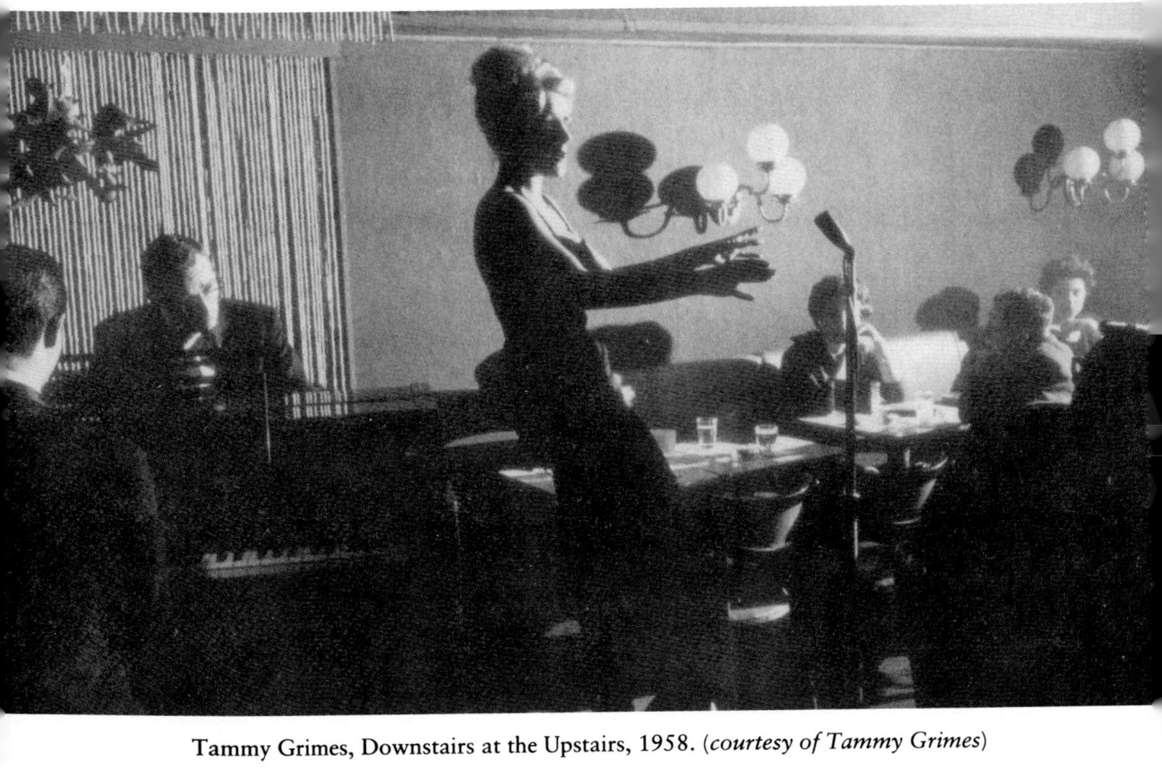

Tammy Grimes, Downstairs at the Upstairs, 1958. (*courtesy of Tammy Grimes*)

Three café chanteuses in performance

RIGHT: Social and political satirist Mort Sahl onstage at the Village Vanguard, 1958. (*photo by Peter Stackpole; courtesy of* Life *magazine © 1958 Time Warner Inc.*)

BELOW: Woody Allen in his standup comedy days, ca. 1965. (*courtesy of Jack Rollins*)

Opposite page:
ABOVE AND BELOW LEFT: In the Greenwich Village apartment of nightclub and stage singer-actor Barry Dennen and his 1959–1960 roommate Barbra Streisand. (*photos by Barry Dennen*) BELOW RIGHT: Streisand and Phyllis Diller in the Bon Soir's dressing room, 1962. (*photo by Bob Schulenberg*)

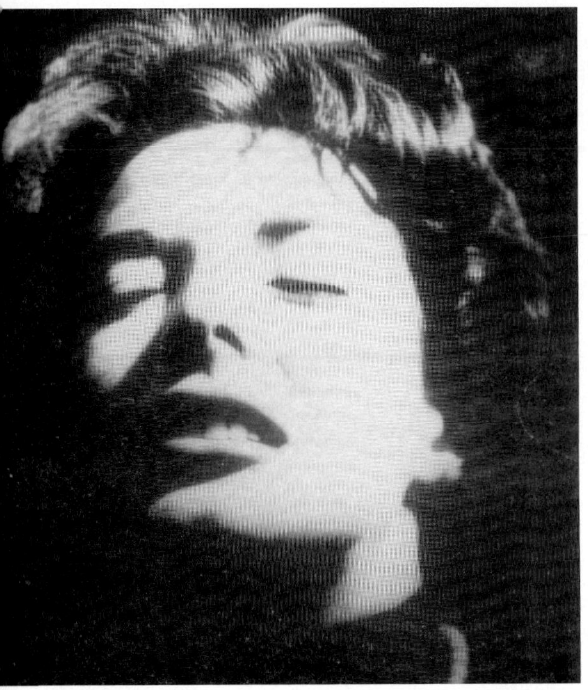

An impassioned moment at the Little Club, ca. 1960: ex–Benny Goodman vocalist Jane Harvey sings Jule Styne and Sammy Cahn's "Guess I'll Hang My Tears Out to Dry." (*photo by Robert Saffir; courtesy of Jane Harvey*)

Johnny Mathis, 1957. (*author's collection*)

From Julius Monk's *Dressed to the Nines,* 1960: a Kabuki takeoff on "Casey at the Bat." *Left to right:* William Roy, Pat Ruhl, Gerry Matthews, Bill Hinnant, Mary Louise Wilson, Ceil Cabot, Gordon Connell. (*photo by Walter Daran; courtesy of William Roy*)

Two scenes from Ben Bagley's Upstairs at the Downstairs revue *No Shoestrings,* 1962. LEFT: "Good Book and Lyrics," a musicalization of the Bible with melodies from *The Music Man. Left to right:* Danny Carroll, Patty Regan, Bill McCutcheon. RIGHT: Woody Allen's "Dr. Schweitzer," on the doctor's hidden yearnings to become a ventriloquist. *Left to right:* Regan, McCutcheon, nurse Jane Connell, Larry Holofcener. (*both photos by Werner J. Kuhn; courtesy of Ben Bagley*)

Julius Monk plays charioteer outside the Plaza Hotel for the cast of his PLaza 9- revue *Dime a Dozen,* 1962. *Left to right:* Monk, Mary Louise Wilson, Rex Robbins, Susan Browning, Gerry Matthews, Ceil Cabot, Jack Fletcher. (*courtesy of Gerry Matthews*)

Julius Monk's *Struts and Frets* at the White House, 1963. *Left to right:* Sandy Suter, June Ericson, Skip Hinnant, Monk, Nagle Jackson (hidden), President Kennedy, Delphi Harrington, Jamie Ross, Charles Kimbrough, Mary Jane Kimbrough, Frank Wagner, William Roy, Elman Anderson. (*courtesy of William Roy*)

From the cast of *The Game Is Up*, Downstairs at the Upstairs, 1966: Betty Aberlin, Richard Blair, and Linda Lavin, later famous as TV's "Alice." (*photo by Werner J. Kuhn; courtesy of Richard Blair*)

ABOVE: *Mixed Doubles*, Downstairs at the Upstairs, 1966. *Left to right:* Madeline Kahn, Robert Rovin, Janie Sell, Gary Sneed, Judy Graubart. (*photo by Werner J. Kuhn; author's collection*)

RIGHT: Lily Tomlin as Laverna, a disastrous computer date, sizes up costar John Paul Hudson in the revue *Two Much*, Madeira Club, Provincetown, Massachusetts, 1967. (*courtesy of John Paul Hudson*)

LEFT: Composer-pianist-singer Michael Brown at PLaza 9-, 1967. (*photo by Robert Parent; courtesy of Joy Brown*)

BELOW LEFT: Broadway's Dolores Gray at Brothers and Sisters; William Roy at the piano. (*courtesy of William Roy*)

ABOVE: A quartet dubbed "The Summit" at the wedding reception of Dorothy Loudon and pianist-arranger Norman Paris, 1971. *Left to right:* Herbert Jacoby, Rogers Whitaker of the *New Yorker,* Bart Howard, Julius Monk. (*courtesy of Bart Howard*)

Mabel Mercer greets old friends Bricktop and Jimmie Daniels, 1974. (*courtesy of Donald Smith*)

A Cole Porter birthday gathering at the Algonquin Hotel, 1982. *Left to right:* Composer Kay Swift, Celeste Holm, Paula Laurence, Steve Ross, singer-actress Taina Elg, Kaye Ballard, Benay Venuta, Dolores Gray, Mabel Mercer, actress Carole Shelley, singer-actress Leigh Beery. (*courtesy of Steve Ross*)

ABOVE: Michael Feinstein at New York's Town Hall, 1989. (*photo by Maryann Lopinto*)

RIGHT: Karen Mason at Town Hall, 1989. (*photo by Maryann Lopinto*)

ABOVE: *Forever Plaid*, an affectionate sendup of '50s vocal quartets, at Steve McGraw's, 1991. *Left to right:* David Engel, Guy Stroman, Jason Graae, Stan Chandler. (*photo by James Gavin*)

LEFT: Ann Hampton Callaway at Battery Park, New York, 1990. (*photo by Maryann Lopinto*)

" 'When will I know if I have the job?'

" 'Why, Miss Webah, you *have* the job.'

" 'Oh, I didn't know that.'

" 'Well, yes. How could I *not* give you the job?'

"He invited me to see the show, and I sat there like a local yokel. I did not understand a word. It was so fast, and all those names—designers, stars—I'd never heard any of them. As I was going down the curving staircase I stumbled, and I thought, 'I'm so awkward, why does he want me?'

"I asked him, 'Why do you want me to work for you?'

"He said, 'My dear, because you have a malocclusion, and because of your diffidence.' He meant my shyness and humility. And I noticed that all the actors had buck teeth."

"Julius didn't like conventional types in general," says William Roy. He viewed his shows as ensemble efforts, and if one cast member outshone his colleagues it might throw things off-balance. No one could be too prepossessing, vocally alluring, or dynamic. Not surprisingly, he turned Barbra Streisand down flat, later pronouncing her crude. But he would regret hiring another performer who was anything but crude, future Broadway actress-singer Nancy Dussault, whose lovely voice and fresh ingenue looks stole too much attention from her fellow players in *Four Below Strikes Back*. It infuriated Monk when *Life* magazine proposed a spread on Dussault that would cover him and the show only peripherally, and he vowed not to use her again. This attitude produced a general mediocrity among the cast, but Monk wanted viewers to be able to identify with them. "They are conceivably the man and woman next door, which is their potency. It is the potency of the huckster on television."

Monk directed the cast to focus all their attention on the customers, forbidding them even to look at one another during a sketch. "This is one of the major reasons his revues worked," says Mary Louise Wilson. "He made us establish a line of contact with the audience and never break it. Eventually I longed to turn and look at my fellow actors, because I found eye contact with the audience extremely frightening."

So did some of her colleagues, especially Ceil Cabot. "Somebody told Ceil that Bonita Granville [star of *Hitler's Children* and other Hollywood potboilers] was in the audience, and she went completely to pieces. We didn't think anybody would care. Another time somebody said 'Tennessee's out front,' and she fell apart because she thought it was Tennessee Ernie Ford."

Cabot had an unfortunate problem: nervousness or tension often caused her to giggle uncontrollably, making her lose bladder control. "Ceil could be funny with the worst material," says Ben Bagley. "She'd pull out all the stops, make funny faces and sounds, and Julius knew audiences would laugh at her no matter what. So he gave her a lot of rotten things to perform. She didn't know how to tell Julius she didn't want to do it, so she'd start laughing and lose control."

Rex Robbins recalls an evening early in the run of *Dime a Dozen*. "We were doing a number called 'Marching for Peace.' All six of us marched in place shoulder-to-shoulder, and at one point we had to separate and join hands. I was a step behind Ceil, and she put her hand back to grab my hand, and she grabbed my joint. That struck her as amusing, and she started to laugh. Phil Bruns was on the other end, and whenever anything dirty happened he wanted to know about it. He stuck his head out to watch Ceil, and after that it just went up for grabs. Ceil pissed all over the floor. The audience was wondering what the hell was going on. None of us could stop laughing, and as soon as somebody tried to sing we all exploded again. Julius wasn't there that night, thank God."

Lovelady Powell performed in Monk's revues only as a replacement or standby but never failed to make a memorable impression, as Mary Louise Wilson recalls. "In *Pieces of Eight* she had a number with Gordon Connell about *Lady Chatterley's Lover*. She wore a breakaway skirt that revealed mesh tights underneath. During one show the skirt broke away, and she wasn't wearing any panties." Her vocal solos also caused a stir. "Jimmy Sheridan, one of our maître d's, used to say, 'Lovey's brought out her flatware tonight.' She'd come to the end of a number and hit a note that was slightly to the left or right of what it was supposed to be. Instead of trailing off she'd get louder and louder, as if to say, 'I insist this is the note!' As the lights went out, she'd shake her head and growl."

Then there was a problem that often came at the end of a season of perfect performances. "After three months you're making grocery lists," says William Roy. "Then you get to that awful point where you begin to forget what you've been doing for ages." As Wilson says, "By the eighth month I'd begin having memory problems with some of those patter songs. It took me forever to learn 'Names.' One night late in the run I started, 'If Conway Twitty would marry Kitty Carlisle—' I just went blank. The audience all said 'Awwwwww . . .' in unison. I started again, 'If Conway Twitty would marry Kitty Carlisle—' I just couldn't remember the next line. There was a lot of thumping backstage, as they realized I wasn't going to finish and they'd have to start the next sketch."

Despite these demands, the cast never made much money. By the early '60s they earned about $125 a week, a reasonable salary for the time, but some resented having to give ten physically challenging performances a week to SRO crowds for this comparatively small sum. Writers earned five dollars a week per sketch, five per lyric, and five for music. For William Roy, who worked longer and harder on the shows than anyone, including Monk, the pay seemed meagerest of all. "For *Dressed to the Nines* I did the musical direction, wrote the vocal and two-piano arrangements as well as five songs, played the piano, and appeared in one sketch for which I got nothing. My salary was one hundred and fifty dollars a week—plus my five-dollar royalties." Then why did so many artists, including Roy, stay for years? In the first place, the shows brought them remarkable exposure. Top New York casting agents came to the club, as well as endless celebrities. Advertising representatives showed up nightly, leading several cast members to lucrative careers in TV commercials. And the Upstairs was a steady, long-term job at a guaranteed weekly salary. "What a life!" Mary Louise Wilson says. "We had a job for nine months, and we were free all summer, with unemployment. We didn't make a lot of money, but we were in the hottest show in town." Writers were happy to see their work run an entire season, with their names printed in a program read by thousands. Like the performers, they were reviewed by the major journals and were often singled out for their contributions.

But somehow all of this mattered less to them than the presence of Monk himself, whom many regarded as a father figure. Despite his insensitivities, no other theatrical entrepreneur took as much personal interest in his players or, most of the time, instilled in them such pride and confidence. He resented the fact that he, along with all his nice young actors, had to be fingerprinted in order to get a cabaret license—a legality inspired by the long history of organized crime in nightclubs. "It is a shame that one's artistic proclivity hangs on a liquor license," he said. "It's as if we were all kleptomaniacs and nymphomaniacs and worse."

Addressing the cast as Mr. Robbins and Miss Dussault, he made them feel like ladies and gentlemen as well as artists. No wonder so many were reluctant to move on when a show closed. According to Estelle Parsons, who appeared in *Demi-Dozen* and *Pieces of Eight* before beginning a film and stage career highlighted by her Oscar-winning appearance in *Bonnie and Clyde*, "It was so unlike any of that group to leave Julius. They were all devoted to him, and he was so fond of thinking he'd presented them in a successful show. They felt like his children. I had great confidence in his decisions. They were tasteful, and the people you worked with were very gifted. More often than not in the theatre you work with people who aren't very good. Bad taste and wrong decisions—that's mostly what the theatre is about. I felt terrible when I left Julius. It felt like home.

"Julius hired a guy named Leonard Elliott for *Pieces of Eight*. He wasn't right for the show, and Julius fired him a few days before we opened. During a rehearsal this guy got temperamental and started to criticize people. And Julius got up and gave this big passionate speech in front of all of us, saying he would not tolerate this man insulting us. It was really why I loved Julius, because he acted as if everyone there was an artist, and nobody was going to hurt them."

Some of this loyalty, however, eventually began to diminish. In interviews Monk always boasted of the performers and writers he had "introduced," leading some to resent the credit he took for their success. Stephen Sondheim was infuriated to be included in a list of writers "we helped launch"—and rightly so. Only one Sondheim number appeared in a Monk revue, "Pour le Sport" from *Take Five*. "It was written for a never-produced show called *The Last Resorts*, which Hal Prince and I were working on," Sondheim says. "Sheldon Harnick heard the song and asked if he could give it to Julius Monk, which he did. Mr. Monk in no way 'helped discover' me, although I attended most of his shows."

In 1961 Dorothy Loudon struck out at Monk after reading a newspaper interview in which he described himself as her "mentor." Ben Bagley visited the Downstairs at the Upstairs that spring with Loudon and a pianist friend. Loudon had had several drinks and created an embarrassing scene. "The three of us stood in the waiting area outside the club," says Bagley. "The door was closed, and the show had started. Julius walked up to us, and immediately Dorothy screamed, 'My mentor! This is my mentor!' Everyone at the bar turned and stared. 'MY MENTOR! MY FUCKING MENTOR! I'd be nowhere without you, without you I'd be nothing! I'd be dirt! MY FUCKING MENTOR!' People inside the club could hear all this, and Julius said, 'Oh, please be quiet, Dorothy, there's a show going on!' But she kept yelling. 'Oh, my fucking mentor! Where would I be without you? Out on the street?' " He couldn't shut her up, and it went on and on. Julius was mortified, and I felt sorry for him. The next day he said, 'Please don't ever bring her here again!' "

Not all the writers tolerated Monk's harsh editing or having their material dropped without notice. One of them was Herb Hartig. "I stopped writing for Julius because all the material was becoming homogenized. He would impose his own personality on it." Monk made things more complicated by avidly pursuing many of the men who worked for him. Some were heterosexual and were either amused or embarrassed by his advances, while others led him on in hopes of winning better exposure in the revues.

"You would go to Julius's apartment and he always seemed to be taking a shower when you got there," says Louis Botto. "He'd come out in this very fancy bathrobe with nothing on underneath, and of course the bathrobe would fall open. I thought it was my imagination, but I'd talk with the other writers and they'd say, 'Don't worry about it. The same thing happened when I was there.' "

USUALLY THE ENTERTAINMENT on the tiny semicircular stage of the Downstairs at the Upstairs outshone that above it. There such singers as Blossom Dearie, Portia Nelson, and Susan Johnson sang for up to forty minutes—a luxury not allowed them at the Angel or the Bon Soir, which limited them to twenty. In 1959 the gravel-voiced Ronny Graham followed in their footsteps by opening with "I Enjoy Being a Girl" from Rodgers and Hammerstein's *Flower Drum Song*. But the Downstairs is best remembered for the nightclub debut of a twenty-four-year-old singing actress named Tammy Grimes. If ever a voice and appearance were suited to a midnight café, they were hers: a slim blonde poured into a black satin dress, with a mass of uncombed hair pinned atop a head tilted slightly to the rear. Her eyes seemed to focus on a spot above the audience's heads, as her clenched fists reached out toward them. Her throaty voice still had a youthful sound, but her interpretations of Cole Porter and Lorenz Hart were remarkably mature.

Grimes had won the praise of Walter Kerr and Brooks Atkinson in a handful of off-Broadway shows, notably *The Littlest Revue*, but the public at large would not discover her until 1960, when she starred on Broadway in *The Unsinkable Molly Brown*. Most interviewers failed to evoke her distinctive looks and personality. Wrote Robert Wahls in the *New York Daily News* (December 22, 1957): "A featherweight blonde, Tammy affects an ashen makeup and pink lips. Her eyes, she insists, are sea green. In profile, she looks like Marilyn Monroe. In full face, she could be a Kaye Ballard."

Grimes offered little in her conversation to illuminate them. As *Time* magazine wrote (December 29, 1958):

> At 17, Boston-bred Tammy came out of the Brookline (Mass.) Country Club. "All those other debs look exactly alike," says she. "And all of them knit." It seems a shame to Tammy that people can no longer live like F. Scott Fitzgerald's flappers, "bang, bang, bang, without worrying how it will all come out." The trouble is, she complains, "people are so wriggly about things. I don't say I was naughty, but I've been in swimming pools that didn't have any water in them."

Nor could she shed much light on her roles, as Wahls found:

> Currently, Tammy's projecting "The Flounder" in Marcel Aym's *Clerambard* at the off-Broadway Rooftop Theatre.
>
> "The Flounder?" she mused. "Well, she's the town prostitute, you see. But she's not all good, and not all bad. It depends on how you come in contact with her."

Monk saw the show and decided Grimes would make a good nightclub chanteuse, even though "The Flounder" was a nonsinging comic part. She opened in December 1958. Recalls Gary Haber, the older son of Irving Haber, "My uncle Hy worked as day manager. He called my father on the intercom and said, 'That's it, Irving. Julius has really gone out of his mind now! He's hired this woman who I swear to you sounds more like a man than a man!"

But Monk knew what a uniquely gifted performer he had found.

For Grimes he chose a program of mostly obscure songs by the masters, including "I Loved Him" from Cole Porter's *Wake Up and Dream*; "Shoein' the Mare," a Harold Arlen–Yip Harburg–Ira Gershwin collaboration from *Life Begins at 8:40*; and "Take Him," a ballad from Rodgers and Hart's *Pal Joey*. Grimes had never heard them, so the experience was like learning a new role—or a dozen—on short notice. But even though she calls the Downstairs "the most marvelous room I shall ever work in," it was still a saloon, and the conditions backstage were hardly glamorous. "I dressed in a cold, damp little room in the basement, at the bottom of a long, curving staircase." On her first two nights she ascended the stairs to discover audiences that included Cecil Beaton, Roddy McDowall, and Myrna Loy, seated in frightening proximity for a performer accustomed to the fourth wall of the theatre. "My knees were shaking, I was so frightened."

She spoke not a word onstage. "It was much easier for me. To this day it scares me to death." In any case, there was no time for chatter. Monk had imposed some uncomfortably swift tempos upon her and pianists Stan Keen and Carl Norman, with minuscule pauses between songs, so that fifteen numbers flew by in slightly more than a half-hour. Even so, the results were so beguiling that Grimes won full-page features in *Life* and *Time* as well as the admiration of some of the most distinguished actors of her time. "All these people embraced her," says Ben Bagley, "because she was so special—winsome, and glamorous. This was a woman who did everything with a flair—a *je ne sais quoi*, as the French say."

One of her admirers was Noel Coward, who visited her dressing room. After praising her act he said, 'I have a play that I'd like very much to show you. If you like it perhaps you'll consider appearing in it."

"I'll do it."

"You'll do it?"

"Yes."

"Now, I really think you ought to take the play home and read it first," Coward said. "Then you can give me your answer."

Look After Lulu opened on Broadway in 1959 and closed quickly but established a friendship that would again bear fruit in 1964 when Coward cast Grimes in *High Spirits*, a Broadway musicalization of *Blithe Spirit*. In the meantime Grimes had won stardom in *The*

Unsinkable Molly Brown, once more affirming Monk's uncanny gift for spotting the unusual, when he chose to exercise it.

THE BANE of Monk's existence was his employer, Irving Haber. From their first meeting Monk regarded the accountant as low-class and "venal" and made his feelings obvious. "They hated each other," says William Roy. "They were civil, but I'm sure Irving thought that Julius was just a foolish old faggot, but as long as he was making money for him, what was the difference." Although their duties were quite separate—Monk handled all artistic matters and Haber managed the business—Monk did nothing to discourage the common misconception that he owned the club and produced the shows himself. The latter was the job of Thomas Hammond, Monk's business manager. Hammond acted as a buffer between Haber and Monk, and as Monk's henchman, breaking unfortunate news to cast members or making announcements that Monk preferred not to deliver personally.

Monk met him while still operating the Downstairs Room. "Before that time," says Ronny Graham, "Julius hadn't put any money aside. When the possibility loomed to move to the new club Tom said, 'I want everything handled right for you, and I want to fix it so whenever you are through with this business you have enough money to live comfortably for the rest of your life.' " Hammond induced Haber to pay Monk the then-exorbitant salary of $1,000 a week, $500 for emceeing and $500 royalties for the revue. (In the '50s and '60s Monk also worked as a model for Hathaway shirts and other clothing lines and products, earning $40 and up per hour.) A common tenet at the club was that everyone made money but the actors. Most blamed Haber, but a few resented that Monk and Hammond never fought to get them raises.

"Irving looked like a gangster," Bagley says, "fat, with an enormous potbelly, and very loud and coarse." "He would throw Christmas parties," says Gerry Matthews, "where he would get onstage and dole out cheap presents to everybody—Big Daddy Irving. Some of the waiters liked him a lot, but I didn't care for him because he was so cheap. Julius went off to Mexico after one of the shows opened, and Irving tried to cut our salaries. He wanted us to take less money for the first few weeks to cover the cost of the production. I said, 'We won't do it, we won't play here then.' He said, 'All right, it's fine with me. I don't make any money here anyway, I only do this for you kids.' "

A few at the club found Haber quite jolly and amiable, and he sometimes displayed uncharacteristic generosity, lending them money to help them out of financial holes. Also, few knew Haber the family man, who cherished his children. But most of his employees either mistrusted him or found him downright repellent. "One night," says Ronny Graham, "Bruce Kirby was furious at Irving and said, 'If I could only find his neck I'd choke him to death!' "

Another prominent figure at the Upstairs was Doris Dreyfus, Haber's secretary and close companion. Haber was still married during this period, and not until his first wife died in the '60s did he marry Dreyfus. Even though she had little dealing with the cast, many of them suspected her of being a spy for Haber.

Monk and Haber began to clash seriously in 1961 during *Seven Come Eleven*, when Monk hired a wardrobe mistress. "She was about six feet tall," says Bagley, "with a hook nose and skinny as a bean pole—a smelly, snotty dike. Now, they didn't need a wardrobe woman. The girls had only one costume, with maybe a cape or something. Julius informed Irving and Doris that he had hired this woman, and they had to pay her. The girls in the cast didn't want her in the dressing room. Irving said, 'I have to get rid of her, Julius, because your cast is afraid of her.' Julius supposedly said, 'She's necessary, because a button might pop off, and she'll be there to sew it back on.' And that was their first altercation, because Irving went ahead and fired her."

Monk considered matters intolerable and vowed to relocate. Luckily the Plaza had just come under new management, and the hotel decided that nothing would be nicer than to present his revues in its Rendezvous Room, soon to be gutted and redesigned. One source claims that the new manager attended *Seven Come Eleven* and adored it, especially Michael Brown's "New York Has a New Hotel," which contained the line "Oh, the Plaza, the Plaza / For this I'd go eyeless in Gaza!" (This ancient method of torture was used in Arab countries against homosexuals and other criminals. Their eyes were plucked out and they were forced to walk along the Gaza Strip, a long stretch of desert, where they soon died of thirst and starvation.) Monk was thrilled at the prospect, and he and Hammond began private negotiations in March 1962. His contract with Haber would expire on July 2.

Eager to have a Monk revue that fall, the Plaza accepted all of Hammond's financial demands.

When Monk gave notice at the Upstairs, Haber flew into a rage. Realizing that he was about to lose an enormously lucrative series of shows, he doubted that he could ever replace Monk. Haber took the cast members aside one by one and offered them more money to stay. Most refused, feeling as Fredricka Weber felt: "I couldn't do it. I didn't want to stay without Julius."

Newspapers began to report Monk's imminent departure in mid-April. Wrote *Variety* (April 18, 1962):

> Irving Haber, owner of the twin niteries, Upstairs at the Downstairs and Downstairs at the Upstairs, N.Y., and Julius Monk, who produces the revues at these boites, have agreed to sever their partnership arrangement following a disagreement on policy. Monk will not renew his contract which expires in June [sic] . . . Haber is currently auditioning producers and directors as successors to Monk.

The successor was Ben Bagley, who arrived in May amid mounting hostility. "Julius had just ignored Irving; it was as though he didn't exist. He had been so rude and officious to him over the years that it just built up. One night after I was hired Julius had an awful fight with Irving and was ordered to leave—'Get your ass out of here, you fucking fag!'—that kind of talk. Luckily I wasn't there that night, but Jane Connell phoned me and said, 'You should know that Irving has thrown Julius out. I just wanted to prepare you.' "

About a week after Haber put Bagley in charge of *Seven Come Eleven*, Monk returned to the club. "There was a big portrait of Julius hanging in the area leading to the toilets," Bagley says. "You went through a little alcove to get to the kitchen and rest rooms, and there was Julius. There was also a beautiful Harvey Schmidt watercolor of the old Downstairs Room hanging in the spot where the maître d' sat. Julius claimed that Harvey had painted it for him, and that it was his possession. [Schmidt confirms this.] Irving said it was painted for the club. Julius tried to grab it, and they started pushing and shoving. Julius tried to run back to get his full-length portrait, and Billy Haber jumped out from behind the bar and held him back. While they were going after Julius, Tom Hammond ran out into the street into a cab with the Schmidt painting. Irving put the portrait downstairs under lock and key."

The period was a living nightmare for Monk. "My life was threatened," he now says. "It was a horrible time." According to Bagley, "Practically overnight Julius became an old man. His hair turned white from shock, from Irving's threats and abuse." Then came another blow. Wrote *Variety* (June 27, 1962):

> A $210,000 damage suit against cafe producer Julius Monk has been filed in N.Y. Supreme Court by Irving Haber, owner of the Downstairs Restaurant, Inc., which operates Upstairs at the Downstairs and Downstairs at the Upstairs, N.Y. where Monk produced shows for the past four years.
>
> Haber asks $75,000 for Monk's alleged refusal to get started on material for the cafe's new revue slated for September although it was part of his contractual duty.
>
> Haber wants another $25,000 for Monk's asserted walkout on May 18 though his contract was not over until July 2, and he has not returned to the cafe where he is supposed to be nightly. Haber also demands $100,000 for Monk allowing publicity to be placed regarding his new affiliations.
>
> In addition, the suit seeks $10,000 for material okayed by Monk for future use with his imprint on them. These items include ashtrays, napkins and advertising material.

How Monk could have worked out his contract after Haber threw him out is unclear, but it does attest to their ugly impasse. When *Seven Come Eleven* and *Dressed to the Nines* closed, Bagley faced the task of compiling, casting, and directing two complete revues. If he expected to fare any better than Monk he received a rude awakening.

"On my first night there, after negotiations, Bruce Kirby asked me, 'Are you happy?'

"I said, 'Not quite.'

" 'Well, then you shouldn't work here, because you know as well as I do that if you're not happy it's not gonna work out.' Did I have cause to remember that! I was signed for a year, and they were so cheap they tried to pay me only $250 a week after giving Julius $1,000. I got it up to $400. Irving said, 'The first year we pay you badly and we'll see how everything goes. The second year we'll pay you what Julius got.'

"My contract said I had to stay in the club from six until closing, which was four in the morning, and then Billy Haber would drive me home. Then I'd get to sleep, and at eight or nine in the morning Irving would call me and ask what happened and how everything went. My Upstairs show was in rehearsals, and that was driving me crazy. But after rehearsals, when everyone went home, I had to go downstairs and work there as host. This was three years after my bout with tuberculosis, and when I left the sanatorium the doctors told me that if I took my life carefully I might have seven to ten more years. I thought, what kind of a life is this?

"Before Julius left the club he came over to me one night and said, 'Need for law-yay. Imperative need for law-yay. Trust not here. Integrity, values gone, diminished. Need for law-yay.' I had no idea what he was talking about, so I got Fredricka Weber to translate.

" 'He means to tell you that these people are crooks and corrupt and to get a good lawyer.'

"When I began working there Irving said, 'There are only two people I don't want you to ever hire here. You can have carte blank, but you can't hire Jorie Remus 'cause she's a bitch, and you can't hire Kaye Ballard 'cause she brings in the fags.' Jorie I would have had, but Kaye would never have worked for that money in that room.

"I wanted to call my Downstairs show *Ben Bagley's First Edition*, but Irving insisted we use the old title *Seven Come Eleven*, which was ridiculous because it was almost entirely new. People didn't come because they thought they'd seen it already. But Irving hated Julius so much that he wanted to infuriate him by using his title. He wanted the whole show to be as Julius had done it, and I didn't do it as Julius did. I wanted everyone to laugh—not just Julius's in-crowd. I wanted ordinary people out for a good time to have a good time."

Bagley's edition of *Seven Come Eleven* opened on July 11, 1962, and shattered the mold of Monk's revues. Its subtitle, *Something New, Something Novel*, did not begin to prepare audiences for Bagley's sassy material. For political satire he offered "Auf Wiedersehen" by the British team of Stan Daniels and Ray Jessel, drawn from the West End revue *Intimacy at 8:30*. In this number a pair of Nazi officers sing and dance a toast to the German government:

What is this slander about there being anti-Semitism
in Germany?
Anti-Semitism in Germany?
That's just a lot of lies put out by the Jews!

Louis Botto collaborated with Arthur Siegel, the show's pianist and arranger, on "After Burton, Who?" Written just after Richard Burton was preparing to divorce his wife Sybil to marry Elizabeth Taylor, the song pondered which marriage Taylor would break up next:

After an actor which type will she choose?
Will she make Prince Rainier fall out of Grace?
From Natalie would she snatch Warren, alas
Just to experience splendor in grass?
One thing is certain, I'll wager my life—
It won't be Rock Hudson—he hasn't a wife.

Bagley's Upstairs revue, *No Shoestrings*, continued his campaign of irreverence. Patti Regan lampooned Shirley Temple in "Lollipop Lane," another Bud McCreery gem. As the pianist began the intro to "On the Good Ship Lollipop," Regan stumbled onstage reeling from a sugar hangover:

. . . Here's the magic soda fountain
Drink a big giant glass
Gee whiz!
Listen to it fizz!
Bbbbbbllllll . . . rrrppp! It's a gas!
There's a breakfast snack of Cracker Jack
with Delaware punch
But look in back—caramel crunch
For sure enough, yup, it's lunch
Comin' right up . . .

In Michael McWhinney's "Little Girl Blue" Danny Carroll depicted the plight of a decoy cop:

I've been sitting on this park bench for six hours upon end
And I haven't seen a rapist or a mugger or a friend

My brassiere has come unfastened and my bun has come undone
A policeman's lot is not a happy one!

Peter Myers and Ronald Cass, another British team, attacked racial prejudice in "The Ballad of Beauregard Green," about a Ku Klux Klansman who uses too much tanning dye and is mistaken for a mulatto. His landlord evicts him, a local restaurant turns him away, his girlfriend departs, and he suffers the scorn of society until finally the color wears off:

It took three whole days for him to erase
The effects of that bottled tan
By the time it was purged he had emerged
A sadder but wiser man
He no longer traps frightened colored chaps
For their skin's a thing they can't choose
That's how Beauregard Green learned what tolerance can mean . . .
Now he only beats up Jews.

Also in that show Bagley was lucky to engage the services of Woody Allen, then working as an NBC-TV staff writer. One of Allen's sketches, "Dr. Schweitzer," opens with a serious enumeration of the great humanitarian's achievements and then gives an imaginary glimpse into his true ambitions:

ASSISTANT: Dr. Schweitzer, Dr. Schweitzer, what is it? Something's on your mind. You've been pacing like this all night. People will be here any minute . . . I know you're working out some problem. Tell me, what's troubling you? What's on your mind?

SCHWEITZER: Well . . . I've been thinking it over and I want to become . . . a ventriloquist.

ASSISTANT: Please, Dr. Schweitzer—what is it?

SCHWEITZER: Listen, last night when everyone was asleep I sneaked downstairs . . . I put a little dress on a potato . . . oh, you're gonna flip over this—(GETS PUPPET)

ASSISTANT: Dr. Schweitzer, what's troubling you?

SCHWEITZER: Wait here. I'll get it. You're gonna be amazed really.

ASSISTANT: Sir, please!

SCHWEITZER: (WITH PUPPET) Watch this. Tell me if my lips move. (IN PUPPET'S VOICE) Hello. My name is Johnny. My name is Johnny.

Nothing can deter him—not the arrival of a doctor from Vienna with news of a new vaccine, not even a scheduled Bach recital. He tries to sing "Rag Mop" while drinking a glass of water, and calls Paul Winchell to ask his secret: "Let me tell you, when you make that Jerry Mahoney's head turn around, I scream!"

At that moment the "archbishop of Brancusi" enters for his appointment with Schweitzer, and the hapless assistant leads him in, where he witnesses the doctor's behavior. The end of the sketch was Bagley's: The archbishop says, "You think that's good? Wait till you see this!" He opens his mouth, and an egg falls out.

Both shows opened to good notices. The *New York Times*'s Milton Esterow wrote of *Seven Come Eleven* (July 13, 1962): "Upstairs, downstairs, inside or outside, it is a bright and witty show . . . most of the sixty minutes are droll, fresh or poisonously joyful." Of *No Shoestrings*, *Variety* stated:

> It's a bright and literate money's worth. What's more, this show seems to make an attempt to widen the audiences for intimate revues with a broader base of humor. The laughs don't have to be searched out, a lot of obscure and inside humor has been removed and it's possible even that the westsiders, who have long shunned this entertainment form, will see its humor.

"Anything that Ben ever did was *terribly* funny," says Jack Holmes. "He was a wonderful director, and he loved outrageous things. He'd have a man come out and sing a ballad, and two little people would come out and slowly wind gauze around his body until they reached his head. Then just as he's about to sing the big note the tape goes around his mouth and they carry him off. This was so much more amusing than the sort of things Julius liked to do. I thought Julius's material was awfully chichi, and I guess that's what turned me off to so much of it."

Bagley clashed even more explosively with Haber than Monk had. "Irving *hated* my choice of material. When he heard 'Auf Wiedersehen' he started screaming, 'We can't use that! People don't want to hear the word Jew in this club!' I said, 'Why, Irving? Is that a dirty word?' He yelled, 'I give you carte-blank here, and you take my chic place and turn it into a White Rose Tavern!'

"He did everything he could to be impossible. I came in once with a gray shirt, and he said, 'Look at you! That shirt is so filthy it's gray!'

" 'It *is* gray!'

" 'Go home and change that shirt!'

" *'This is a gray shirt!'*

"I made the lighting man turn up all the lights onstage, and I dragged Irving up there to look at my shirt.

"He would always tell me, 'You ain't got no decorum' and then start these screaming fights with me at the bar during the happy hour. Customers sat there watching the two of us yell insults at each other.

"As if this weren't bad enough, I had to bear the resentment of all the waiters, because every single one of them wanted to be in my show. Julius had promised several of them parts in the next show, but now he was gone and I had already chosen my cast. I had a real hatred for Sidney Armus, the Downstairs maître d'. Once Louis Botto and I went to the country for the day. I came back with a tan, and Sidney said, 'It's been reported that you're wearing liquid leg makeup on your face.' Nobody reported that—it was his idea. He said, 'Grooming is very important here, and everybody can see that's liquid leg makeup.' That was something women wore in the '40s—you couldn't even get it anymore. I showed him my arms and neck, and said, 'Do you see any liquid leg makeup?' He said, 'No, I guess you're right.' But every night as I passed he'd say, 'I still think that's liquid leg makeup.' So I did a lot of snotty, arrogant things to make him feel like the servant of the world. He loved Julius as a friend and resented my replacing him. And Sidney, who had a potbelly even then, wanted very much to be in my show. He said, 'I can do anything Cy Young and Hal Buckley can do.' I said, 'Not with that stomach!'

"Then I learned that the pay phone downstairs, which we all used, had a direct line to Irving's office, so he could listen to all our calls. I was desperate to leave, but my lawyer said, 'You've got to figure out a way to make Irving fire you. If you quit he can run your work as long as he wants, and pay you nothing.'

"One night Carol Channing came in with her husband Charles Lowe and with Charles Gaynor, the author of *Lend an Ear*, which helped launch her. She had a big hat on, with flowers and feathers, and it blocked the view of everyone sitting behind her. A young man got up and said to me, 'You know, my wife and I drove all the way in from Connecticut for this show, and we can't see anything. Would you ask Miss Channing if she'd mind removing her hat?'

"Now, protocol was that I should have asked Bruce Kirby to go talk to her. But I thought, I'll fix these shits, because Irving's whole life was the fact that stars came there. The minute a celebrity walked in Bruce would call Irving at home and say, 'Guess who's in the club tonight!' So Irving knew she was there. I went over and said, 'Miss Channing, you'll have to remove your hat.' She said, 'I can't remove my hat, because my hat is attached to my hair, and my hair is a wig.'

" 'Well, then, you'll have to leave.'

"Charlie Gaynor said, 'You can't mean that!'

" 'I certainly do. This is ridiculous—people can't see.' And the show was in progress—people were singing onstage. She said, 'I didn't know it was gonna—'

" 'Get out of here! GET OUT!' I was outraged. So they got up. Charles Lowe wasn't going to pay, but on the way out he said to Bruce, 'I'm sorry, I really should pay for this.' Bruce said, 'No, I'm sure everything will be okay. We don't want you to pay. I'm terribly sorry.' It was a mess. Bruce said to me, 'You're gonna be in a lot of trouble when Irving finds out about this!'

" 'No I'm not, Bruce, because no one would dare tell Irving!'

"Well, at four-thirty in the morning the phone rang, and Irving was in a state of shock. 'YOUR DAYS ARE NUMBERED!' he screamed. I said, 'Thank you! I hope so!'

"Well, Irving didn't fire me for that, but a few weeks later I figured a way out, thanks to Doris. The waiters were setting the tables up, and the cast was backstage. Doris was bugging me. 'You're always complaining about money! You're always arguing about money! That's all you do. I don't know why you're so worried. You artistic people have so much fun doing your work, you shouldn't expect to be paid!' Well, I had my in. I said, in a voice that could break glass, 'WELL, DORIS, YOU ENJOY *TYPING* WITH IRVING IN HIS OFFICE SO MUCH, YOU SHOULDN'T GET PAID EITHER!'

"She walked right out of the room in deep humiliation and went into the basement to cry. She called Irving and said, 'I want him out of here! I will never come back to this place unless he's out!' So Irving fired me after about four months, and he had to pay me for a whole year. But he took great advantage of this. Ronny Graham came in next, and Irving said, 'I can't pay you anything at all, Ronny, because I'm paying Ben Bagley a fortune.'

"Then Rod Warren came in. Rod told me he got about one hundred and fifty dollars a week for two years, because Irving said, 'We're still paying Ben Bagley off on his five-year contract.' It wasn't a five-year contract, it was a one-year contract. That's the kind of man he was."

Shortly before Bagley left the club, Monk and Hammond retaliated against Haber. As the *New York Times* reported (September 7, 1962):

> Julius Monk, the cabaret impresario, charged in a $2.5 million lawsuit yesterday that his name and show material were being illegally exploited by the split-level nightclub, Downstairs at the Upstairs and Upstairs at the Downstairs.
>
> Mr. Monk, who left the club last spring after creating and producing musical revues there for seven years, said his replacement, Ben Bagley, had copied acts from his show *Seven Come Eleven*. The suit, filed in the State Supreme Court, also sought an injunction to bar the club from using his name in the advertising, and demanded that the names Downstairs at the Upstairs and vice-versa be changed.
>
> Defendants in the action are the Downstairs Restaurant, Inc., Irving Haber, its president and sole stockholder, and Mr. Bagley.

The preposterousness of Monk's suit is obvious, and on September 24 Supreme Court Justice George Tilzer denied the injunction. Says Gary Haber, "I remember my father saying to me, 'Look at this! Look at the money I'm worth! Where the hell is the goddamned money?' "

By the time Monk began rehearsing his Plaza show that fall, any attempted legal action on either side had evaporated. "Nobody was successful in the lawsuits," Gary Haber says. "These are the kind of things that happen in the heat of the moment. When you have a bad breakup, a love affair or an intimate business relationship, a lot of accusations get flung around when people are hurt. Courts in general are loathe to enforce personal service contracts. If you want to leave, you leave. If someone is injured financially we'll figure out how much it's worth."

That fall Haber and Monk settled out of court. Reportedly neither paid any monetary damages, but time would reveal just how harmful the breakup was for both. The freer, more permissive revues that followed Monk's at the Upstairs were more in keeping with the '60s, but none won the acclaim or attendance of Monk's. At the Plaza, Monk would cling to the increasingly antiquated values that characterized his work; eventually this would spell an end to his career. Meanwhile, he and Haber went their separate ways. According to friends of both, they never exchanged another word.

Chapter EIGHT

By 1959 Herbert Jacoby was having trouble booking acts. Many of his past headliners now earned up to five times their weekly Blue Angel salaries for a single TV appearance. Young performers did not seem to need the room anymore; it had become small-time. They too headed for television, a higher-paying and more prestigious talent mill that snapped up the best immediately. Those unable to break in—often the second- or third-rate—came to the Angel. No longer could Jacoby be as selective as he wished; now he was forced to hire a distressing number of folk singers and mediocre comics. "Whenever we got an act that was really good it went on television," says Bart Howard. "The next time we wanted them they wouldn't play the room. We couldn't afford them."

Howard was about to move on as well, thanks to Johnny Mathis. In 1957 Columbia Records released his smash LP "Wonderful! Wonderful!" which included three Howard songs. After twenty-five years of composing with only nominal financial returns, Howard earned $200,000 from that album alone. Over the next three years Mathis recorded eight more of his songs, and eventually Howard realized that he no longer had to work as a nightclub emcee.

The end came in 1959, his ninth year at the Blue Angel. Stepping onstage to introduce an act, he heard a woman's voice: "My God, is he still here?"

"I thought, 'That's it! I'm quitting!' "

A few weeks later Otis Clements took over as full-time emcee. After that Howard composed hardly another song. Ironically, though, his greatest success lay ahead of him. Peggy Lee sang "In Other Words" on Ed Sullivan's show in 1961 and soon after mentioned plans to record it on her Capitol album "Pretty Eyes."

"But please," she said, "no one asks for it under that title. They all ask for 'Fly Me to the Moon.' Why don't you change it to that?"

"At that time," says Howard, "all the big artists were watching what Peggy did, because she was so successful. And I had a hundred big records of my song after that. Then, after the moon shot, every country in the world did it in another language." The royalties supported him for decades—a happy ending of sorts, but not for those who loved his writing and regretted seeing him give it up so soon.

In 1960 the perennial Portia Nelson flew to California to compose and to appear in films. "It was in the wind," she says. "The small voice was dying out for all sorts of reasons—rock and roll, television, the fact that the quality of music went downhill, and people wanted to hear the rock singers and the noise and something they could shout along with. Being still, quiet, just went out of fashion. Nobody wanted to cry in their beer anymore. They wanted to get up and do it themselves."

The changes in the wind were most obvious to Jacoby. Not only had the Angel failed to attract a young crowd, it had also lost much of its older one to the suburbs and the TV set. In an effort to bring them back he hired comic Jack E. Leonard, an enormous favorite from the glory days of the Copacabana. He paid Leonard a starting salary of $2,500 with no options, the handsomest deal a Blue Angel act had ever received. Pitched for the farthest reaches of the Copa, Leonard's rumpus-room delivery bounced off the much closer back wall of the Angel with a resounding thud. "He brought in the Copa crowd," says Otis Clements, "and the Angel regulars didn't like that. 'What's happening to this place?' they asked. There were complaints about it, because they were no longer getting to discover new faces who surprised them." Jacoby rebooked as many Blue Angel favorites as possible, among them Robert Clary, Herb Hartig, Jorie Remus, Irwin Corey, and Kaye Ballard. But even they demanded higher fees, and profits continued to drop.

The most controversial hiring of his career came in February 1960, when he booked a comic whose explosive, profane observations had sent shock waves throughout much of the nation. Brooklyn-born

Lenny Bruce had spent six years working a series of sleazy Mafia-run "toilets" (as he called them) in Chicago, Miami, Pittsburgh, Detroit, and San Francisco. People who had never heard him knew that he examined religion, sex, blacks, Jews, and homosexuals in language that comedians simply did not use. Many listeners could not hear past the profanity, while others enjoyed him because it was exciting, at least for a couple of years, to hear a comic use dirty words in public.

His growing following heard something revolutionary and brilliant underneath. Buddy Hackett, an early influence on Bruce, recommended him for a job as a 20th Century–Fox scriptwriter. San Francisco columnists Herb Caen, Ralph Gleason, and Pauline Kael heard him at Ann's 440, a lesbian dive run by singer Ann Dee, and became his biggest early boosters. Such jazzmen as Jack Sheldon, Herb Geller, and Terry Gibbs loved him because they found his delivery like a jazz player's—improvisational, daring, and constantly creative. Bruce took a chance in every phrase, and even a failed attempt could be fascinating. Indeed, Max Weiss and Saul Zaentz of Fantasy Records, a California jazz label, heard him at Ann's and signed him immediately.

Some of Bruce's material was just what his detractors called it: obscene and tasteless with no apparent substance to justify the profanity. On less inspired nights he fell back on shock value alone to rouse audiences. At his best, however, Bruce was a natural innovator who, more than any other comedian before him, helped crack open the shell '50s America had built around itself: a shell composed of conventional values that he hated. Under a veneer of prosperity and productivity he spotted something hypocritical and riddled with bogus morality: in the self-serving television preaching of Norman Vincent Peale, Oral Roberts, and Billy Graham; in organized religion itself (he liked to say how happy he was to see people "leaving the church and going back to God"); in sexual standards that he felt bred fear and repression; and in traditional nightclub comedy, which he thought prissy, self-absorbed, and unrelated to the times. He called clubs "the last frontier" of uninhibited entertainment, the only arena that gave him total freedom of speech. He had not begun to do concerts and had to expurgate his TV routines; even his early albums were censored. No one imagined that in 1964 he would get busted at the Café Au Go-Go in Greenwich Village and jailed for four months; evidently no place was permissive enough for Bruce.

In the late '50s, when he first became famous, it was still easy to shock; and since he aimed to shock, his timing was right. Like many new comics he considered himself not just an entertainer but a social commentator. He wanted to shake audiences out of their apathy, to make them conscious of (and angry about) the appalling problems that affected them in ways they did not realize. As a result he was hailed as the sickest of "sick" comics, a group so christened by the establishment for daring to comment on anything taboo. Nichols and May, Shelley Berman, Mort Sahl, and Jonathan Winters had all, at various times, been placed in this company.

Bruce examined the issue on his 1959 public television special "The World of Lenny Bruce":

> Most of my humor lies in the ludicrous, or, you know, being just out-and-out irreverent. Sick depends on what your point of view is. And it concerns John Graham Green. John Graham Green blew up a plane with forty people on it and his mother. And for this he was sentenced to the gas chamber, proving that the American people are losing their sense of humor. When you think about it for a minute, anybody who blows up a plane with forty people and their mother can't be all bad.
>
> You would say a bit like that is in *horrendous* taste. And it is. But there's a thing about comedy that a lot of people never realize. Actually there's very little comedy that's in—that semantic beartrap again—good taste. Anything you satirize was, at one time, uncomfortable to someone. When you satirize any tragedy, if you do it later enough people aren't concerned with it. To satirize Napoleon, who was a heinous figure and perhaps had millions of people killed, you'd never get a bad review, because he was in another era.
>
> Here's another example. If I ever did—and I don't—satirize any physical handicap—this you could never do anywhere, on a nightclub stage or television. You'd have people saying, that's terrible! And yet—a severe handicap is alcoholism. And if any of you people have ever known a guy that gets juiced every day—it's a sad kind of thing, the whole family is goofed up. And yet guys do drunks on every television show. It's a terrible disease, worse than many others. So to satirize anything, unless we satirize cement, you gotta alienate somebody.

Bruce spoke onstage the way he spoke off, with a high, nasal, slightly sibilant delivery and a vocabulary peppered with "right," "man," "you know," and—away from television—every four-letter word in the language. Today fans remember the charged, "inside" feeling that he generated—a sense that they were all sharing something forbidden, outrageous, and antiestablishment that no one had dared say before. After his first arrests, when his monologues became more scathing than ever, an aura of danger added to the excitement.

Bruce made his New York debut at the Den in the Duane in 1959. Just thirty-five feet long and with a legal capacity of eighty, the room had all the looks and ambience of the basement it was. A musty smell greeted the employee who unlocked the front door every night; there were no windows and the circulation was poor, producing a claustrophobic feeling on crowded nights. Yet the little cave intrigued Bruce, who knew instinctively that its remoteness, lack of a traditional East Side clientele, and overall seediness would work for him. He even accepted scale—$125 a week—plus each night's five-dollar cover charges. Within a week demand for admission was so high that the owners bribed the police into allowing them to seat an additional forty per show, earning Bruce nearly $1,000 a night. Steve Allen fought successfully to have Bruce on his show twice, making the comic a national celebrity.

When he returned to New York in 1960 he could have played almost any room he wanted. His backers encouraged him to try the Blue Angel, but everyone was skeptical. Although the prestige would put him in a better bargaining position with other owners, Bruce doubted that the conservative Angel crowd would understand him. Jacoby feared the scandal that "Dirty Lenny" would cause in his sophisticated room; Gordon, ever practical, worried that the $3,500 a week Bruce demanded would wipe out profits. He and Jacoby agreed on one condition: they could fire Bruce after a week if he didn't draw.

Opening night was a sellout, as was every night of his two-week engagement. His fans did not mind the $7 minimum, and in fact this booking had a special interest for them. They may never have gone there before, but they knew the room's reputation. How would this audience react to "Father Flotsky," his takeoff on 1940s prison-break movies in which a warden informed his frustrated inmates, "We'll meet any reasonable demands—except the vibrators"? What would they think of "The White Collar Drunk," his imitation of a whining, effeminate East Side WASP alcoholic—a type so often present at the Angel? Or "How to Relax Your Colored Friends at Parties," his depiction of a drunk suburban building contractor telling a black guitarist at a party how much he admires colored people? "You had anything to eat yet? I'll see if they have any fried chicken or watermelon . . . I don't care what a guy is, long as he keeps his place . . . You know Paul Robinson? Aunt Jemima? What about the guy on the Cream of Wheat box?"

The opening night audience included Mel Brooks, Buddy Hackett, Milt Kamen, and Shecky Greene. Wilt Chamberlain and Sammy Davis, Jr., also showed up, willing targets for his racial jokes, and Bruce's fans were everywhere. Albert Goldman, in his 1974 biography *Ladies and Gentlemen—Lenny Bruce!!*, called them "night people, inside people, hipsters . . . some strange-looking women with tough, ballsy voices. Diesel dykes with their femme friends. Some wild-looking hookers . . . cramped up front with their sharp-looking pimps. After the show, they'll work the bar."

Hostile stares bore into them as the Angel regulars filed past the bar on their way to the main room. First up were Robert Clary and singer Pat Scot. Bruce's followers barely concealed their impatience. After about forty-five minutes he made his entrance. From his opening line—"Looks like some faggot decorator went nuts in here with a staple gun!"—he gave them what they wanted. The audience clapped in recognition at the start of several routines: the White Collar Drunk, Lawrence Welk auditioning a black junkie musician, and particularly Father Flotsky, which he had recorded. Flotsky quit the priesthood because he found confessions so boring: "One out of fifty is sexually stimulating, but the rest—whew! It's the same trite crap over and over, week after week." He closed with "Colored Friends." Most of his characters spoke with his diction and vocabulary; usually he mimicked only one or two obvious mannerisms. He was more interested in getting inside their head, capturing their quirks and prejudices, so that what they said sounded authentic.

But the Angel's regular clientele—about half those present—did not have a clue what he was doing. After five minutes the walkouts began, leaving his fans to cheer him on all the more triumphantly as Bruce drove the old crowd out of their own room.

Jacoby was appalled, pacing back and forth in the rear of the room, snapping his fingers, and barking at waiters who dared approach him. He glared resentfully at Gordon, seated at a back table, who seemed less disgusted than Jacoby thought he should be. Gordon was thrilled by the attendance and thought the publicity might boost future business, but Jacoby saw crashing down around him all the standards he had built up over seventeen years. On her way out Dorothy Kilgallen said, "If that act isn't out of here tomorrow I'll never mention this place in my column again!"

But the club made a small fortune. Reviews such as *Variety*'s achieved just the opposite of what they intended:

> Why a personable young man of 34 . . . should labor under some warped impression that a stream of non-sequiturs interlarded with back-fence language qualifies as humor is one of those intangibles.
>
> Bruce's bad taste doesn't end there. His stream-of-consciousness brand of humor (?) is unconscionable in its repetitive usages of stereotyped language. The ugliest of phrases applying to minorities are interjected for no good purpose. That somewhat bewildered-looking young colored guitarist (Eric) must need his stooging job very badly to stand up as a foil for the cliche insults, humorous though they may be intended.
>
> Bruce is on for over an hour. It's a mad melange of yakity-yak which just borders on avant-garde effectiveness and then veers alternately into the gutter and boredom.

Bruce cared little about critics, though, as did his fans. His mother, Sally Marr, recalls an episode from that period. "I brought up Lenny's daughter, and in the house where we lived in Hollywood we had a retaining wall around the whole place. It rained heavily, and everything was covered with dirt and mud. I sent him a letter in New York while he was appearing at the Blue Angel, and he wrote back, 'Dear Mom: I wish I had a mother who couldn't speak English so I wouldn't have to listen to these complaints.'

"I wrote him another letter:

> Dear Lenny Bruce,
>
> If you had a mother who couldn't speak English you'd be waiting on line like a schmuck paying a seven-dollar minimum to see a guy named Lenny Bruce and you wouldn't know one thing he was saying.
>
> Your mother,
>
> also known as Sally Marr."

The rest of his stay was just as memorable as opening night. "He would get up there and be one of the most fantastic things I ever saw,"

Anita Ellis recalls. "He became a black guy serving a party in the South, and then he'd become the Southerners who would call him names and tell him what to do and lash him with a whip if he didn't. One woman in the audience became hysterical. She stood up and went absolutely crazy. 'YOU ARE GOING TO BE JAILED! WE ARE GOING TO BLOW YOU UP! AND IF PEOPLE WERE EVER HUNG FROM A TREE NOW YOU KNOW WHY! YOU SHOULD BE HUNG FROM A TREE!'

"He said in a big drawl, 'Well, tell me more, darlin'! You're full of shit! Fuck you, and I know no one has *ever* fucked you, so you'd be happy if they did!' "

On another night Ethel Merman sat at a front table with a chorus boy from *Gypsy*. Bruce was mimicking the aged Sophie Tucker, by now a pompous self-caricature, talking to Manuel, a busboy. "Now, come here, Manuel. I'm an old lady and I want you to think of me as your mother. Get down on your knees and stick your tongue out and find the little pink slit. Mother needs some energy, she's got to go on soon. C'mon, dear, keep trying." Bruce caught sight of Merman and her escort as they rose and struggled through the maze of tables toward the exit. "And there's another old has-been," he announced. "She does the same thing, probably. What's wrong, you old cow?"

"The way was blocked," says Ben Bagley. "The place was just packed. The fire laws were always broken when he was there. There were people standing against the walls, and they put extra tables in, and the waiters all wanted to see what he was doing so every bit of help in the place was standing there. Ethel couldn't get out, so she had to hear all this. He said her breath smelled like it came out of her ass."

After two weeks Bruce moved downtown to the more relaxed Village Vanguard. "Too many straight people come to this place," he told Gordon before leaving the Angel. "I need a place of my own, where my kind of people can come to see me—me alone."

After Lenny Bruce, fewer New Yorkers regarded the Blue Angel as a home of polite sophistication. A comic named Ted Markland appeared that December, attacking phony piety in a routine about the return of Christ. If Jesus came back today, he said, he wouldn't be crucified; instead he'd be electrocuted, and people would wear tiny electric chairs around their necks. More boos and more walkouts, especially when Markland made the sign of the cross on his exit.

Not every new wave humorist was as incendiary. Nineteen sixty-one saw the Angel debut of Dick Gregory, whose incisive comments on the problems of being black *or* white made him, according to *Time* (February 17, 1961), "the first Negro comedian to work his way into the big time." Gregory was best known for his monologues on integration and civil rights, although he also dissected the arms race, nuclear fallout, urban crime and poverty, and other life-threatening issues. He was not an "angry" comic and avoided haranguing listeners or even lecturing them. His casual delivery softened even the most caustic material. Writing in the *New York World-Telegram and Sun* (September 15, 1961), Robert Ruark placed him "in the best classic tradition of the late Will Rogers."

Many of his monologues were based on personal experience. The second of six children, Gregory was born in St. Louis in 1932 and grew up on relief. He began doing stand-up comedy in the mid-'50s and after five lean years broke through with a booking at Chicago's Playboy Club. Engagements at the hungry i and other top rooms culminated in his Angel bow on March 17, 1961. Gregory had such an amiable manner in those days that even the following monologue did not seem out of place there:

> I go south every now and then. About six years ago I went home for my brother's funeral. He messed up—driving a pickup truck, went right through a red light into a Ku Klux Klan parade. I was there, and I started drinking heavy, and I walked into the wrong restaurant. I sat there, and a blonde waitress walked up to me. I said, "Would you bring me two cheeseburgers, please?" She said, "We don't serve colored people down here." I said, "I don't eat colored people nowhere." Just about that time these three big brothers walked in. And if you've ever been to Mississippi you know what three brothers I'm talking about—Ku, Klux, and Klan. Big one walked up and kicked my chair. Said, "Boy, you know damned well you can't eat in here." I said, "Just for that, bring me a whole fried chicken." He said, "Boy, you can't eat that fried chicken in here, and whatever you do to that chicken we're gonna do to you." Twenty minutes later the waitress brought the chicken out, put it in front of me. They said, "Boy, we told you whatever you do to that chicken we're gonna do to you." I was feeling so good, I looked at 'em and told 'em, "You all line up," and I kissed it.

Despite surprises like Gregory, both the Angel and the Bon Soir seemed to be too past their primes to uncover another superstar.

Occasionally a soon-to-be-familiar face passed through, among them comic Pat Harrington, Jr., at the Angel and actress Renee Taylor at the Bon Soir, then trying her hand as a singing comedienne. But Taylor's moments of humor were mostly unintentional, as illustrator Bob Schulenberg recalls. "She was singing this song about wanting to be a Tennessee Williams heroine, and she started to sound a little strange. She turned her back to the audience, and got down on her hands and knees, and began groping around on the floor. We thought, what's this all about? She finished the song and smiled, then went into a ballad, and she had a slight sibilance. Suddenly her bridge started coming out, and she put her hand up and slapped it back in. People were whispering, 'It was her teeth!' "

Outstanding young singers had become few. Yet in 1961 along came the nineteen-year-old Barbra Streisand, who once and for all wiped out the stale image of the prim café chanteuse. With her antique wardrobe, and a repertoire dotted with such surprises as "Who's Afraid of the Big Bad Wolf?" and her ballad version of "Happy Days Are Here Again," Streisand made a triumph of individuality over convention.

It started with her wide-ranging, sweet-and-sour voice, which combined a pronounced nasality with a throb of emotion that came straight from the heart. Like Judy Garland and Edith Piaf, Streisand sang as if her life depended on it, a spine-tingling urgency behind every note. At dramatically heightened moments she could become strident and braying, but even when overwrought the effect rarely sounded untrue.

Streisand came to nightclub performing through the encouragement of Barry Dennen, a gifted actor-singer who performed a funny, fast-paced vocal-comedy act at the Duplex and Showplace and later starred as Pontius Pilate in *Jesus Christ Superstar* and as the emcee in the London production of *Cabaret.* According to Schulenberg, a friend of Streisand's in the early '60s, "Barry really formed the whole act that she did at the Lion. Barbra wants people to think she did it herself, but she didn't—it was Barry."

A UCLA graduate, Dennen left a comfortable family existence in Beverly Hills to assume the role of struggling actor in New York. "I associate being in New York with being poor. Things were cheaper then, but you were earning less. When Barbra appeared at the Blue Angel I could only afford to go once, and when she appeared at the

Bon Soir I had to pay to get in. We used to stand at the bar, but even then you had to buy a drink."

Dennen and Streisand had met as cast members in an off-Broadway production of Josef and Karel Čapek's *The Insect Comedy*, in which they played butterflies. By day Streisand took acting lessons and worked as a receptionist, secretary, and printing company clerk, jobs she hated and left as soon as possible. (She told friends she grew her trademark fingernails in order to discourage typing.) Her constant auditions usually met with failure, mainly because of her large nose, homeliness, and Jewish-Brooklynese mannerisms.

Streisand occasionally sang a number or two at Village piano bars such as the Ninth Circle and the Showplace, and had already created enthusiastic word of mouth among the gay public. But she considered herself an actress rather than a singer, balking when Dennen suggested nightclubs. "I told her, 'Look, you can continue your acting classes and still do this, and you'll get seen, you'll make money.' "

Across the street from Dennen's Village apartment was the Lion, a gay bar that smelled of beer and urine but that had a piano in the back and held popular talent contests. Owner Burke McHugh awarded winners a weeklong engagement and, through his friendship with Jimmie Daniels, an opportunity to audition at the Bon Soir. "I agreed to assemble an act for her," says Dennen, "if she agreed to physically walk across the street and sign up for the contest at the Lion."

During this time Streisand camped out wherever she could, a thrift-store skunkskin coat around her shoulders. "Barbra traveled around with a foldup cot," says Schulenberg. "Sometimes she'd stay in my apartment, since she didn't want to go home to Brooklyn and her mother. At one point she lived in a publicity office owned by some friends of hers on East 53rd Street. She couldn't come in until about seven at night, and she had to be out by eight-thirty the next morning. Finally she moved in with Barry when she was at the Bon Soir."

Dennen had a large collection of old recordings by Fanny Brice, Helen Morgan, and other vocalists, which became the source of much of Streisand's early repertoire. "We were the only people I can remember at that time," says Dennen, "who were actively enthusiastic about old Shirley Temple movies or Astaire-Rogers. We would tape all this stuff off television and trade the tapes back and forth."

With Harold Arlen and Truman Capote's "A Sleepin' Bee" from *House of Flowers*, Streisand auditioned and won easily. At this time her wardrobe was at its most outrageous, with junk clothes from Brooklyn antique stores and Victorian-style lace-up boots, but rarely if ever had audiences seen such an obvious star in the making. She auditioned at the Bon Soir, once more with "A Sleepin' Bee," and began there in the summer of 1961.

From the beginning Streisand was drawn to songs that allowed her to assume characters, especially scorned or lovesick ones. "Cry Me a River," "Have I Stayed Too Long at the Fair?" Rodgers and Hart's "Nobody's Heart (Belongs to Me)," and other laments filled her early repertoire. Her slow, deliberate tempo in "Happy Days Are Here Again" made it clear that although everything had ended on a quiet, confident note of triumph, sad times were not far behind her. Between songs she spoke little, except to introduce her musicians in a Mae Westian purr ("Weighing in at 183 pounds . . . in black trunks"). With the help of Schulenberg, Streisand had refined her makeup and thrift store garb and wore a few pieces that were perversely elegant, among them an antique velvet jacket and a striking pair of '20s high-heeled pumps. But she was still clearly a misfit, which helped make her songs of unrequited love or the sudden, surprise discovery of romance so effective.

As her confidence grew, so did her onstage authority, which came in handy at the loud Bon Soir. "At one time," recalls Dennen, "she said to me, 'What do I do? They're making a lot of noise.' I said, 'Stare them down. Stand there and think, 'Shut up! Listen to *me*! Look at *me*!' One night after she finished an up number, Peter Daniels [house pianist at the club and Streisand's early musical director] began the intro to 'Sleepin' Bee,' and Barbra simply stopped singing. Peter kept noodling while she waited for the audience to be quiet. Then you heard a couple of people going, 'Shh! Shh!' The house quieted down and she began the song."

Ben Bagley, who met her around the time of her first Bon Soir engagement, recalls a steely confidence exceeded only by chutzpah. "She'd call me up at eight in the morning and say, 'So, what are ya gonna do for me today?' 'Am I any good or do I stink?' "Got anything in mind? If I'm so good why can't you help me?' I sent her to one prominent nightclub agent, who had no use for her. 'She's got a wonderful voice,' he said, 'but she's so ugly no one could use her on anything but the radio, and no one wants radio singers these days.' I called Barbra and said, 'He already has too many girl singers, but he was very impressed with you.' She said, 'What an asshole. He's making the biggest mistake of his life.' "

Late one night during the same engagement Bagley joined Streisand and Schulenberg for cappuccino at Rienzi's, a coffee shop near the Bon Soir. "Barbra said, 'You know, I think the *New Yorker* comes out tonight.' She went to a newsstand and got the magazine, and there was the first review this girl ever got in her life, by Rogers Whitaker. It said, 'Barbra Streisand, singer—file and forget.' Instead of being upset, she was irate. 'That old fart!' she said. 'What does *he* know?' Didn't deter her for a minute. The average person would have been devastated.' "

But Whitaker was in the minority. Among the singer's most avid early boosters was Harold Arlen, who invited her to his apartment and played and sang hours of his songs for her. Thereafter she performed and recorded many, including "Down with Love," "Right As the Rain," "I Had Myself a True Love," and "Any Place I Hang My Hat Is Home." For the moment, however, Streisand was still obscure and quite broke. "Usually at the end of an engagement," says Tiger Haynes, "the performers gave the musicians a gift. I got tons of cuff links and cigarette lighters from Kaye Ballard, Phil Leeds, Danny Meehan, and Phyllis Diller. Streisand was so poor that she gave each of us a package of cheese in little wedges. Stamped in purple on the back was ninety-nine cents."

Herbert Jacoby went to the Bon Soir to hear her and cringed at her wardrobe, her sometimes gauche stage mannerisms, and her still undisciplined singing, but sensed her star quality and booked her at the Blue Angel for three weeks in November–December 1961. He paid her $200 per week, with an option that allowed him to bring her back twice at a predetermined pay increase.

Streisand was frightened to move from the loose, informal Bon Soir to the stiffer Angel. The Village club felt like home to her largely, Bob Schulenberg believes, because of the enthusiastic gays at the bar. "I have a feeling that Barbra, like Bette Midler later on, felt like a social outlaw, and that's why she identified with them. And Barbra had almost exclusively gay friends in those days."

And as Bagley adds, "One reason why performers liked the Bon Soir was that whether they were good, bad, or mediocre the bar was always supportive. That was nice, but not the acid test. Streisand was phenomenally successful at the Bon Soir, but it was very frightening when she went on to the Blue Angel, because there was no gay bar there. She had a very conservative audience, a typical Blue Angel crowd, and they loved her." Jacoby told her she had to dress more tastefully, and thereafter she appeared in several lovely dresses, one in black chiffon. He also asked Bagley to help her with repertoire. "Herbert said, 'See if you can find her some lovely songs, some showtunes of the past—maybe a nice medley of Rodgers and Hart.' I wanted her to do a medley from *I Married an Angel*, but Barbra had definite opinions as to what she liked and didn't like. She said, 'It's nice, but it's not me. There's only one thing in it that I like, 'I'll Tell the Man in the Street.' Later she recorded it for Columbia Records.

"Herbert was alarmed about her because she was not grateful. He could be very generous when he believed in someone, like Carol Burnett. He thought she was very sincere. But nothing impressed Barbra." Nor did he have any control over her punctuality. "She was never on time, through the whole thing," says Otis Clements. "The show began at nine-thirty, and she'd walk in at nine twenty-five and go up to her dressing room for a half hour."

Otherwise, things happened fast. Marty Ehrlichman, her first agent, heard her there, as did Broadway producer David Merrick, who signed her for the supporting role of Miss Marmelstein, a harried secretary, in Harold Rome's musical *I Can Get It for You Wholesale*. Streisand would alternate between the Angel and the Bon Soir until 1963, doubling at the latter club for late shows even while she was stopping the show nightly on Broadway. "I'm doing it because I can sing the way I want to sing there," she told the *New Yorker*. "I can't do that in the show. I see the part differently from the way it was written and directed, and I'd like to do it differently, but I can't."

By now she had received fabulous press from Dorothy Kilgallen, Walter Winchell, and nearly every other columnist. Wrote *Variety* (May 30, 1962):

> 20-year old Barbra Streisand returns to Gotham's intimate nitery circuit with the assurance of a performer who knows that the road ahead is strictly upward . . . Especially good are an excerpt from Leonard Bernstein's "Songs for Children," Harold Arlen's "I Had Myself a True Love," and a humorous item salvaged from the past season's off-Broadway musical entry "An Evening with Harry

> Stoones" [a bomb in which Streisand appeared] called 'I'm in Love with Harold Menkert' . . . At 20, she may be considered a show business natural, but even if it is calculated for maximum impact, it works, and that's what counts.

Even Rogers Whitaker begrudgingly amended his appraisal. "The cynosure of all eyes is Barbra Streisand," he wrote, "who hasn't yet decided whether to sound like a million far less accomplished singers or whether to be absolutely the most stirring soprano since Anita Ellis." "Beautiful"—a word one had never dreamed would be used to describe her—came into use more and more often. In an interview published during the run of *Wholesale* the *New Yorker* called her "an animated, poised, and unconventionally beautiful young woman, with an aquiline nose, great big soulful eyes and great big soulful eyelashes." Her own comments were amazingly free of ego, in view of the Streisand to come. "I was given sort of a good voice," she told them, then allowed, "I suppose I'm going to be famous." Her greatest concern seemed to be food, a luxury she could now afford to wallow in:

> "I often go to Chinatown to eat late at night. You get wonderful white hot breads with the center filled with shrimp at the little coffee shops there. Only ten cents! I love food. I look forward to it all day. My body responds to it. Everything else seems so nebulous. I love broiled mushrooms and watercress. The best fried chicken I know of comes with a TV dinner. I like interviews—they're still a novelty—but by the time they appear they look funny to me, because my attitude changes from week to week."
>
> "Your attitude toward what?" we asked.
>
> "Oh, toward smoked foods, say," she replied, and we rushed to the phone to file our copy.

In 1962 Columbia released her debut LP "The Barbra Streisand Album," but that was not her first recording. In 1961 she had cut an audition demo for RCA Records, ten songs from her club repertoire with piano accompaniment by RCA staff arranger Marty Gold. She re-recorded all of them later for Columbia with the exception of "At the Codfish Ball," an old Shirley Temple number from Dennen's collection. RCA, of course, never signed her.

Her first official recording project was to be an album of rare John

Latouche songs funded by his protégé, poet-lyricist-playwright Kenward Elmslie. Ben Bagley was set to compile the disc, which would also feature Carol Channing and Jerry Orbach. This enterprise was nipped in the bud by Elmslie's lawyer Robert Montgomery, Jr., currently head of the Cole Porter trust, who told Elmslie he would never get his $8,000 investment back.

Around the time *Wholesale* opened, Streisand appeared on the Columbia cast album as well as an LP re-creation of *Pins and Needles*, Harold Rome's 1937 revue about the garment industry. Her first solo album was to be recorded live at the Bon Soir. Reported *Variety* (November 14, 1962): "Columbia Records brought its engineering crew down to this Greenwich Village cellar Monday [November 5] to record an album titled 'Barbra Streisand at the Bon Soir.' Miss Streisand's stint is well-worth preserving and the LP should serve as an excellent launching pad for her new career as a Columbia discer."

"They brought in a paid audience," says Tiger Haynes. "Streisand had the engineers and technicians come down and record her first show for the rest of the week, through Saturday. Same musicians, same songs, every night. And then Columbia scrapped the whole bunch of tapes and did a studio album instead. But she made sure we got paid."

In 1963 she made her final nightclub appearances at the Angel, the Bon Soir, Mister Kelly's in Chicago, and San Francisco's hungry i. A tape recorded at that last club surfaced in the mid-'80s as a bootleg album entitled "Barbra Streisand—Live, 1963," until the singer slapped a blistering lawsuit on its producer.

Once she became a Broadway, film, and recording superstar her nightclub career faded into relative insignificance and was hardly mentioned, least of all by her. "She claims not to remember," says Schulenberg. "And yet whenever anybody says anything, she seems to have it all right there. It's always the same story, about how she did it all herself."

Streisand became notorious for burning those early bridges, but as a close friend from those years says, "I don't think it's so much a question of burning bridges as it is of cutting out of her life people who were not directly relevant to her success. I don't think Barbra wants to acknowledge that in her early years she had a lot of people to be grateful to. I was astonished when somebody told me years later that Barbra's published position was that she listened to her 'voices,' and her voices told her what to do. It had nothing to do with that; she had *people* with voices telling her what to do. People who were helping her with her hair, her makeup, her shoes, her dresses, the material, and her direction. I think it makes her feel guilty and uncomfortable that she's never been able to find it inside herself to repay this in any way. And that's between her and her conscience."

Around 1975 Ben Bagley ran into Streisand and her agent Sue Mengers in a Beverly Hills restaurant. He greeted Mengers, then said, "Barbra? Hi, it's Ben Bagley." Streisand never looked up from her spaghetti. "Oh, hi, how ya doin'," she said in a flat voice. Bagley's position? "Some people may think she's the biggest bitch in the world, but she is also the biggest talent in the world. This is an enormous talent that can reach out and touch the heart."

Schulenberg is another who remembers her only with fondness. "She was the funniest person I've ever known, the brightest, the cleverest. I think nightclubs were the closest she came to really dealing with people. Later when she started doing movies and Broadway there was so much at stake that she would come on ready to kill. But in nightclubs she felt that whatever happened on stage had to be true; the acting technique, the gestures all had to be real. She felt that if something went wrong it would just be another part of the show. They'd be seeing another aspect of the young woman on the stage. With the orchestrations that Peter Matz wrote for her Columbia albums she had to pump it up, which destroyed a certain spontaneity she always had at the Bon Soir with Peter Daniels. She started creating the emotion, instead of letting it happen."

Streisand and later Woody Allen were Jacoby's last major newcomers. He was sixty-one now and disillusioned with the whole business. He tried lowering the minimum, and that cut profits without attracting a larger crowd; raising it only discouraged his remaining regulars. Bobby Short and his trio, performing in the lounge, were one of his only dependable draws, even with a $2.50 minimum (Short did not come cheap). Why struggle to seek out new talent when audiences could discover the best in their living rooms for free? Now Jacoby had to feature a folk act almost every week, even though he hated folk music. In December 1961 he and Gordon booked Peter, Paul and Mary, whose recording of Will Holt's "Lemon Tree" had become a hit. Rogers Whitaker, who loathed folk music from the first acoustic triad he heard, echoed Jacoby's feelings when he called them "a flock of tongue-in-cheek folk singers who may be the beginning of a new trend or the end of the whole damn business." In a sense he was right on both counts, but Gordon thought they might attract a lot of kids, and they did.

Nineteen sixty-two began with a violent winter, and as business at the Angel came to a halt, Jacoby's spirits dropped to their nadir. His mood always influenced the room, and during those weeks the staff dreaded coming to work. He was not angry or surly; instead he sat in his office and brooded. On a gray, bitingly cold day in February he headed upstairs to Gordon's cluttered office. Stale cigar smoke met him at the door, as it had every day for nineteen years. The papers at the bottom of the stacks on his desk might well have been there that long, shuffled around but never filed. Gordon was on the phone, his brow furrowed, wearing his typical worried look. When he hung up, Jacoby announced as tersely as ever that he had decided to leave the club and needed to work out the specifics. Gordon took the news calmly. He had no intention of doing the same, so he would have to choose between finding a new partner or carrying on alone. For the moment, they settled on a price of $30,000 cash. Jacoby wanted more, but had to agree that 50 percent of a nearly bankrupt club was not worth much. The sale would take place on June 30, 1962, his last day.

Gordon invited bids for Jacoby's shares. Chicago nightclub entrepreneurs Oscar and George Marienthal offered him $50,000. Another bid came from Nat Sackin, who owned London House, Mister Kelly's, and the Happy Medium in Chicago and had recently purchased the Bon Soir. But Sackin wanted Gordon's shares as well, and when he refused, the offer was withdrawn. By June 30 Gordon had decided to carry on alone.

The 1962–1963 season began on September 1 with Phyllis Diller, The Folksters, and comic Vaughn Meader, whose album "The First Family," a satire on the Kennedys, had made him an instant celebrity. That bill, unfortunately, kicked off the dullest season in Angel history. Gordon booked a few good comics, including Wally Cox, Nipsey Russell, Jackie Vernon, and Don Adams, and some singers of note, among them Georgia Brown, Felicia Sanders, and Streisand, but most of the other acts were forgettable.

April 17, 1963, marked a shaky twentieth anniversary for the Angel, and Gordon's associates arranged a celebration. Two hundred friends, celebrity acquaintances, ex-employees, and reporters gathered at the club, and several alumni came to perform, mostly comics. The truly stellar graduates were absent, but Vincent Sardi, Jr., sent a birthday cake, which Gordon sliced before the cheering crowd. The most touching moment came when Gordon spotted a welcome guest, Herbert Jacoby, who walked over and shook his hand.

Jacoby sat discretely at a table as Tom Lehrer, Milt Kamen, Henry Morgan, Orson Bean, and Henny Youngman saluted Gordon, as if he alone had made the club a show business landmark. Irwin Corey ended his roast with a much-quoted assertion: "The Blue Angel is indestructible. It will be here long after most of us don't care."

The next morning a heavy feeling hung in the air amid the smell of stale smoke, as Gordon again faced the problem of how to bolster business. Most shows were drawing 40 percent capacity or less, and sometimes only twenty people sat in the room. Night after night acts faced the disheartening sight of a near-empty room; the handful of customers felt self-conscious and embarrassed.

Bobby Short left on July 10, and Gordon hired Dudley Moore to play his Erroll Garner–style piano with a trio. But Moore worked there for less than three weeks, for Gordon closed the season on July 30. He spent the rest of the summer consulting friends on changes in decor, menu, and entertainment. He held auditions and discovered almost no one.

When he reopened on September 2, Jimmy Lyon's trio was gone and Otis Clements had been replaced. Gordon had a "new operation" in mind. He wanted Bobby Short desperately, but Short had already signed with a new room, the Café Ambassador in the Sheraton East Hotel. The opening bill consisted of Woody Allen, ragtime pianist Max Morath, and singer Emily Yancy. To everyone's delight, the show was a hit. "IT'S SRO AT THE BLUE ANGEL," raved Gene Knight in the *New York Journal-American* (September 4, 1963). But when Allen moved to the Bitter End three weeks later, the crowds followed, leaving business at an all-time low. Gordon had to borrow money to stay afloat and finally made a last-ditch effort to save the club, calling in Stewart Chaney to redesign it completely. Gordon decided to break down the middle partition, creating one huge room with the stage center right so that customers could sit at the bar and watch the show for the price of a drink. He would charge a nominal table fee, maybe $2. A group would play until midnight, then a single headliner would take the stage for an hour.

Announcements of the proposed changes brought a wave of protest from agents and managers. Wrote *Variety*, "Not only was the spot intimate enough to reveal every attribute of a performer, but it was a room in which the talent had the audience directly in front of them and not to the side or to the rear." The renovations never happened. On April 17 Gordon filed a bankruptcy petition, listing liabilities of $126,230 and assets of $36,446. He told the press he blamed television; the New York World's Fair, which was just about to open; and the fact that people weren't staying out as late as they used to.

Even then he refused to give up. Vaughn Meader began a five-day engagement on April 28 for $100 instead of his regular $3,000 a week. As he told John S. Wilson of the *New York Times* (April 29, 1964), "I got my start on the nightclub circuit when Max Gordon gave me a break when I needed it. That was before the First Family album. The Angel is one of the few remaining places where a new act can be seen that is a respectable room, not just a hole in the wall . . . It's important to show business that it be kept going."

Unfortunately President Kennedy's assassination had also spelled death for Meader's career. He tried to carry on with a new, mostly nonpolitical act, but the national tragedy was too fresh in the country's mind, and no one wanted to hear from the former Kennedy lampoonist again.

Gordon was sure he would do well with actor-comedian Godfrey Cambridge, already acclaimed for his commentary on the middle-class Negro, but he was wrong. By 3 A.M. on Sunday, May 24, 1964, word was out that the Angel was about to close forever. Gordon stood by with a cigar, wearing one of the rumpled suits he had owned for years, and shaking the hands of consoling friends and patrons. But he was philosophical: rock and roll, jazz—that's where it was at. He still had the Vanguard, of course. Things became quite sentimental, but by four o'clock it was all over. Newspapers carried only minor notices, and the *Times* blurb appeared, in all places, among the TV listings. Gordon sold the club to hotel entrepreneur Ed Wynne, who planned to convert it to a restaurant.

Jacoby's and Gordon's paths seldom crossed after that. Early in 1964 Jacoby began a disastrous partnership with Bobby Short, opening a club called Le Caprice on East 52nd Street with Short as the featured act. Jacoby put most of his savings into the room, believing Short could draw enough high society to make it a success. But after a festive first night, attendance sank steadily, and Le Caprice closed in a few months. It was simply too late in the day for such an enterprise. Caprice was perhaps the nadir of Short's career in the '60s, a decade when most café singers took on the status of antiques.

For Jacoby, however, it was the beginning of the end. Caprice's failure left him broke, and he was forced to become "manager" (in truth, maître d') of a rock club on Second Avenue called Wheels. He hated the job but had no choice. By 1969 he and Gordon had fallen out of touch. "He used to come to the Vanguard," Gordon said. "He'd always have free entrance. After all, we were partners. That was the last place I ever saw him. In the early '70s I wrote him a letter. I wanted to see him, but he wouldn't answer." The letter arrived after Jacoby learned that he had developed terminal cancer. By then he had lost contact with nearly everyone. Bart Howard was among the last to see him.

"There was nothing left of him. He was very upset because his sister was supposed to come and feed him and she hadn't arrived. I said, 'Well, Herbert, I'll feed you,' and I did. Finally she came, and he told her in French how much he liked me. He didn't know I understood French. He said all these wonderful things about me. He'd never said them before."

When he died in November 1972, "We knew an era had ended," as Jimmy Lyon said. But Max Gordon would become one of the hardiest survivors of all. Twenty-five years after the Blue Angel closed, his Village Vanguard continued to thrive, secure in its position as the oldest and most respected jazz room in Manhattan. Patrons who phoned on a typical afternoon to make a reservation were answered by Gordon himself. When he died on May 11, 1989, at age eighty-six, the club showed no signs of decline.

In 1959 a matronly young woman named Jan Wallman had taken over management of the Upstairs at the Duplex, saving it from imminent bankruptcy. Heavy, with an ash blonde wig and a mature look that changed little over the years, Wallman ruled the club with as firm a hand as any of her male colleagues. Decades after most of them had died or retired, she continued to run her own New York room, her love for young performers keeping her wedded to a business that barely supported her. Today dozens of them recall with gratitude her encouragement at a time when they needed it most.

Wallman brought the Duplex some of the respectability of the uptown clubs, even though it lacked such niceties as a telephone in the beginning. But many youngsters, particularly those from other cities, found in that small, shabby room the essence of everything they had hoped New York would be. Its look did not matter—they were in Manhattan, in a club that they had read about in the *New Yorker*, one that was cheap enough for them to afford. Major reviewers sometimes dropped in, so a new star could be discovered at any time. With all the optimism of youth, they felt that the future was theirs.

The club had an erotic magnetism as well, with its large following of people in their twenties thrown together in this most liberal of cities. Even though the sexual revolution was in its infancy, Manhattan seemed like a playground compared with the rest of the country, especially for homosexuals. As singer-actor John Paul Hudson says, "There was always the flirtation across the room, from the very first night I went into the Duplex. We were sitting in this little black boîte where everyone was locking eyes, and it all seemed like the pinnacle, the reason I left Missouri."

Under Wallman's aegis the Duplex became a launching pad for performers headed for the Bon Soir and the Blue Angel, and sometimes for stardom. The most prominent of them was Woody Allen, who until then had made his living as an anonymous comedy writer. Allen sold his first quips to newspapers during high school, then got a job in a public relations firm writing jokes that were then attributed to clients in columns. In 1955 Allen joined NBC television as a staff writer for Sid Caesar, Pat Boone, Art Carney, Garry Moore, and others.

Around 1960 he sought out Jack Rollins. "Woody was the shyest little bunny that ever was," Rollins remembers. "He came and asked if he could possibly be considered as a writer for Nichols and May. I told him no, because they did their own writing. He thanked me, and shuffled out of the office. Later he came back and said, 'Would you consider managing me?' At that time we managed only performers, but we agreed to look at his material. Well, we howled with laughter. We decided to work with him for six months to see what we could do." Rollins felt that Allen should try performing the material himself to see if he had any flair for stand-up comedy, and Rollins convinced Jan Wallman to present him at the Duplex. "I thought the material was absolutely brilliant," Wallman says, "but I thought his delivery was dreadful. He was a scared little mouse, but he developed."

Allen hated the process. "At the Duplex they put on *anyone* who's not a catastrophe," he told Cleveland Amory in the *Newark Evening News* (February 18, 1968). "At eleven at night I'd get a cab in the freezing cold and go down there and perform for five or six people. Twelve was a big night."

During this period Allen met his second wife, Louise Lasser, whose ambitions would lead her toward a career in films and as star of television's late-night comedy serial *Mary Hartman, Mary Hartman.* Their courtship is still vividly recalled by the old Duplex staff. "She broke up his marriage," says Wallman. "It was one of the most frightening things I ever saw. I was very fond of Woody's wife, who was so supportive and used to show up every night, and all of a sudden she's supplanted by this weird girl. Louise had been brought to me by two writers who had given special material to a lot of my acts for practically nothing. They said they had this rich girl, the daughter of J. K. Lasser, the tax expert, and could we try her. The girl could sing, I have to say—she had a big belt voice. And she could act. And you could see her acting onstage. It was totally phony. She just took Woody over."

Rollins next arranged a Sunday night audition for Allen at the Blue Angel. Customers watched with bemusement as the short, red-haired, bespectacled young man stuttered through his routine, knees visibly shaking. But Herbert Jacoby trusted Rollins's instincts and hired Allen for $350 a week.

The first night was especially bumpy. "He was terrified," says emcee Otis Clements. "He came down the stairs white as a sheet, and he was shaking. 'I'm not used to standing up in front of an audience,' he said. 'I just write.' " "He recited the material like a six-year-old doing show-and-tell," Rollins says. "People looked at this gaunt, bony weirdo and didn't know what was going on. He was the worst comic you've ever seen for the first year and a half. But Herbert sensed there was something here, so he gave him the chance."

Allen specialized in one-liners and short bits on subjects close to home: domestic and neighborhood troubles, his family, growing up, and relationships, particularly his first marriage. His ex-wife was indignant at being the butt of so many jokes. "I had a rough marriage," he said. "My wife was an immature woman . . . well, that's all I can say. See if this is not immature to you: I would be home in the bathroom taking a bath, and my wife would walk right in whenever she felt like and sink my boats." Or, "The Museum of Natural History found her shoe. Based on the measurements they reconstructed a dinosaur."

Ultimately, though, most of his gags were targeted at himself. "Honeymooning . . . I was fabulous. You would have adored it. I was on water skis, stripped to the waist, skiing fast on top of the surf. My hair back. I oiled my muscle. Holding on with one hand. My wife was in the boat ahead of me, rowing frantically."

His slumped, nebbish appearance, combined with a deadpan, Brooklynese, nasal delivery gave his self-deprecation a ring of truth, and even at the Duplex it was hard not to like him. (The polish and confidence that he had acquired by the mid-'60s would make that persona less believable.) Even though his material seldom strayed from walking distance of his neighborhood, it had a cerebral quality typical of his mature film work: a sardonic, bitingly honest feeling that was also sympathetic, without ever taking itself too seriously. "I was captain of the Latent Paranoid softball team. We used to play all the neurotics on Sunday morning . . . the Nailbiters against the Bedwetters. And if you've never seen neurotics play softball it's really funny. I used to steal second base, then feel guilty and go back."

Allen's Blue Angel booking helped pave the way for five years of nightclub work. In 1962 he spent several weeks at the Bon Soir and later that year performed at the Bitter End, a Greenwich Village coffeehouse. In the *New York Times* (November 21, 1962) Arthur Gelb called him "the most refreshing young comic to emerge in many months . . . He is a Chaplinesque victim with an S. J. Perelman sense of the bizarre . . . Mr. Allen will be at the Bitter End five weeks for anyone who is interested in watching a rising young comic develop into an established young comic."

Other acts at the Duplex in the early '60s included future film star George Segal, an astonishingly handsome young man who played '20s tunes on the banjo; vocalist Patricia Scott, ex-wife of actor George C. Scott; and a profoundly moving singer named Joanne Beretta, a large young blonde from San Francisco. A minimalist performer, Beretta usually wore black and sang with only a pinspot illuminating her face, her shimmering mezzo-soprano underscoring a lyric intensity that younger clubgoers found as mesmerizing as Mabel Mercer's. Beretta's offbeat repertoire included not only such seldom performed theatre songs as "One Hand, One Heart" from *West Side Story* and "You Have Cast Your Shadow on the Sea" from Rodgers and Hart's *The Boys from Syracuse* but also "I Left My Heart in San Francisco," which she introduced at least two years before Tony Bennett's hit record.

Beretta came to New York in 1959. "The city was huge, and it seemed ugly to me. It was hot, and the air was dirty. People were rude and I wasn't used to it. In San Francisco at the time, a cab driver would get out and open the door for you. If I went to the supermarket he would come into the store, put everything in the trunk for me, take it to my elevator, and say something sweet. Then I came here. I was sitting in a cab after I paid, and the driver turned around and said, 'What the hell are ya sittin' there for?' I got out and started to cry. I'd never had a stranger talk to me that way."

But such naïveté had its rewards—perhaps for the last time in the city's history—helping to make New York seem, in retrospect, like a storybook place. "I was living in the East 80s and taking cabs to the Village to sing, which cost about two seventy-five. A friend had an apartment on MacDougal Street that he wanted to get rid of, but he said, 'You wouldn't want it, it's terrible.' It *was* terrible, but there was something I liked about it so I just moved in, bag and baggage. The next thing I knew there was an eviction notice on the door, because his rent check had bounced. I called the landlord and said, 'I spoke with Mr. Milner, and he said the check was all right.'

" 'Well, who are *you*?'

" 'I'm Miss Beretta.' "

" *'Yes?'*

" 'I moved in.' "

" *'You moved in?'*

" 'Yes, I liked the apartment, so I moved in.' "

" 'Young lady, you don't just move into an apartment because you like it!'

" 'Well, can I stay?' "

" 'Yes, you can stay.' "

Every new generation that came to Greenwich Village—indeed, to any part of Manhattan—mourned the era it had missed, then later looked back on its own as a never-to-be-recaptured golden age. But the '60s were perhaps the last blossoming of the freethinking creative atmosphere that had distinguished that area for decades. Housing had not yet reached a premium; even a young out-of-towner could usually find something affordable. Nor had big business taken over. Small esoteric shops still flourished, along with a community diverse enough to support them. "It's true that when you cross 14th Street it's a whole other world," Beretta says. "I used to love the wonderful old antique shops, jewelry shops, family-run places—mom and pops, as we called them. But they don't exist anymore. They can't afford to. What was the Pioneer Grocery Store is now Banana Republic, and they pay thirty thousand dollars a month rent." Most sorely missed is the community feeling that made the Village a true microcosm, and that vanished in the wake of an ever-rising crime rate. "Everybody knew everybody," says Jerry Herman. "When I walked out of my apartment I said hello to fifteen people on my way to the supermarket."

The same warmth sparked the Duplex in the '60s. The Showplace had it as well, but it had fallen onto rocky ground. Jim Paul Eilers's humble "Mickey and Judy" operation, as he called it, was going nowhere, and he had begun to buckle under the strain of running it almost single-handedly, as he felt he had to do. Eventually he suffered a heart attack. "Everybody had their job. Mine was the shit detail. I'd arrive at nine in the morning, go to the bank, get change, make orders, do chores. During the day I had to look for talent for the next show. I closed up, counted the receipts. These were things nobody else could do. I couldn't afford a staff. At four or five in the morning I'd go to bed for three or four hours, then get up and start the whole thing over.

"You had to check everything. One night I had tickets for the opening of *Camelot*, and I left another guy in charge. I got back and said, 'God, there are hardly any receipts!' Well, somebody ratted on him, and I found out that an attractive girl had come in. He asked everybody to leave, closed up for an hour, and went back and laid her in the kitchen."

Worse still was the legal corruption that Eilers encountered, a problem that plagued Village clubs. "Everybody was looking for payoffs—the police, detectives, the building inspector. They'd take you back in the kitchen. The garbage can would be covered, and they'd say, 'We're gonna have to give you a citation.' I'd say, 'Why?' They'd take the lid off and say, 'Your garbage can is uncovered.' Or they'd take you into the men's room and put the soap in their pocket and say, 'You don't have any soap.' But I never gave them money. I'd go to court. Some days all I did was go from one place to another over some stupid, trumped-up charge because I wouldn't pay somebody fifteen dollars, twenty-five dollars, a hundred dollars. I had enormous legal fees because of it."

In 1961 Eilers hired Jan Wallman away from the Duplex to manage his upstairs room. "Jim Paul gave me a budget and a salary, which he said I could use on the shows if I wanted, so I did." Again she succeeded in injecting some life into the faltering club. She replaced the revues with solo acts, among them Joanne Beretta; jazz singer Mark Murphy; singer-comedienne Linda Lavin, later the star of television's *Alice*; future film director Tom O'Horgan, who sang comedy songs and accompanied himself on the harp and various rare instruments; and Joan Rivers in an awkward and rather vulgar version of an act that she later polished to a gleam. Rivers used the Showplace as a workshop, talking extemporaneously on any subject that came to mind. Her shows were a blast of frantic energy; tapes of her early performances reveal a comedienne chattering as if on speed, laughing more at herself than anyone in the audience. At that time she attacked mostly easy targets, especially Jews and homosexuals. (Later she would devote a large portion of her act to Mr. Phyllis, a scathing caricature of a gay hairdresser, and record an album titled after it.) Remarking one evening on the sparse audience, Rivers mentioned two boys who came in earlier only to leave during her show. They might have stayed longer, she mused, if she were a dike and had come out snapping her suspenders.

But her drive to succeed was overwhelming, as with most performers who achieved superstardom. "You knew they had to make it," says Joanne Beretta, "because if they didn't they'd kill themselves. I went to the Lion once, and Bette Midler was sitting on the piano. 'She's gonna be a big star,' I said. You could smell the desperation in the air."

Most of the Showplace's business came from the downstairs bar, a teeming hangout for showbiz-loving youngsters as well as for some remarkable contemporary and future stars. Checking coats was an enormous young woman named Cass Elliot, soon to become Mama Cass of the Mamas and the Papas. Elliot settled against the elbow of the piano and sang whenever she could leave her post for a few minutes. The presence of celebrities caused her to squeal like a midwestern teenager who had crashed the Academy Awards. "Oooh, when is George Grizzard coming in?" she would ask Beretta. "I've got such a crush on George Grizzard!"

On several evenings Barbra Streisand climbed up on the piano and sang. Eilers remembers standing in the back of the room thinking, 'Sing, honey, 'cause you're so ugly you'll never make it." The piano was played at various times by entertainer Bert Wallace; John Wallowitch, a devilishly clever songwriter, coach, and accompanist for Beretta and other singers; Jack Holmes; and even Warren Beatty, whose competent playing kept him employed between acting jobs. Commonly acknowledged by Showplace regulars as the handsomest pianist in any New York bar, Beatty reportedly entertained all the propositions from female customers he could handle, rebuffing male customers.

Among the comics who tried out material there were Joan Rivers, Woody Allen, Robert Morse, Charles Nelson Reilly, and Ruth Buzzi, who supported herself by cleaning apartments, including Eilers's. Other visitors included film actor Farley Granger, a decade after his smash appearance in *Strangers on a Train* but still handsome and quite the star. "Farley asked me to play for him once while he sang," remembers Jack Holmes. "Very little sound and tones of questionable pitch came out, but his companions applauded wildly and he sang several encores. He was sweet and gracious, but when I saw him in his only Broadway musical, *First Impressions*, I was not surprised that he spoke all his songs."

Another regular was three-foot-tall actor Michael Dunn, with "a huge chest, a normal-size head, and a giant's capacity for drink," says Holmes. "When he had enough pints, up to the piano he'd come. I'd lift him up on the stool, and he would sing." Dunn had a booming bass voice, and though acting roles were naturally limited, he enjoyed a successful career, appearing on Broadway in *The Ballad of the Sad Café* and in the film *Ship of Fools*. His frequent visits inspired someone to write on the men's room wall:

Paul Lynde lived a few blocks away and dropped by often, usually after midnight when the room had become more or less a gay bar. Lynde's bitchy-funny-sarcastic persona, introduced on Broadway in *New Faces of 1952* and later familiar to millions of TV viewers of *Hollywood Squares*, was no fabrication. "That *was* Paul Lynde—sober," says Holmes. "Drunk, he was ten times more bitchy, cutting, and unforgivably rude. Bartenders, waiters, pianists, customers would all gently move right, left, go upstairs, into the kitchen, the bathroom—*anywhere* to avoid him. Every word out of his mouth was venomous, with a sting that really hurt, into every unexpected vulnerability a human being might have. He could rouse a sane, normal person to instant fury."

Alcohol caused other Showplace customers to lose control. Regulars still tell of a visit by actress Colleen Dewhurst, who, after several drinks, reportedly became infatuated with the handsome downstairs bartender Alan Derrick. "We had a terrible time getting her out of the place," says Eilers. "She pulled the brass rail off the bar. So she was banished. Well, at four in the morning after everyone had gone, I walked over to the glass door to get to my apartment, and there was Colleen standing on the sidewalk. It was starting to snow. She pantomimed wanting to be forgiven so she'd be allowed back in. I shook my head, and she started to disrobe, and became very disrobed. But I still wouldn't let her come in again."

Although such scenes tended to outshine the entertainment, they illustrate the giddy atmosphere of the Showplace, which customers missed when it came to an unexpected end in 1964. Eilers had never purchased the building, although he had many opportunities. Eventually it was bought by a businessman whose interests included an allegedly illegal export of U.S. grain to India. When Eilers's lease expired, his new landlord raised his rent to a then-unaffordable $1,200 for the two floors of the Showplace alone.

Eilers had no choice but to turn the premises over to two specialists in the city's declining gay bar circuit. They converted the Showplace into one of these at a dangerous time, for the law had begun to crack down on these establishments as ceremoniously as possible. Within a few weeks there was a "raided premises" sign on the door and a slew of arrests. The liquor license was revoked, and in order to prevent any renewal the city called on an old law that now came in handy. As Jan Wallman explains, "When Prohibition was repealed the dries managed to get a law passed that you could not obtain a liquor license within two hundred feet of a church or school. The Showplace was within two hundred feet of the Washington Square Methodist Church. Now the Washington Square Methodist Church couldn't have cared less, but that was the law." Although Eilers succeeded in renewing the license after the previous owners had lost it, the scourge against gay bars had become so severe that 146 West 4th Street lost this privilege permanently.

The situation typifies New York's homosexual climate of the mid-'60s, when one's presence in a gay or mixed establishment was a frequent invitation to arrest. These rooms ran the gamut from the raunchier bars on Third Avenue, rife with male prostitutes and transvestites, to dance bars that warned of potential raids with a flashing red light, to more elegant spots such as the Regent's Row, an East Side bar-restaurant whose older clientele dressed in dark suits and behaved with great decorum. Virtually all of these rooms had to pay off the police; those that did not, or met with the rare honest cop, were usually shuttered. Employers and families of those arrested in a raid were often notified—a tragedy for men who happened to be married.

Eilers and Wallman experienced a problem that plagued any bar or club with a homosexual following. Says Eilers, "Plainclothes detectives used to come around to try and entrap people. If they could get you to have a conversation and leave with them, they would say you had propositioned them and arrest you. The phone at the Showplace would ring, and it would be Burke McHugh, who owned the Lion, or some other friend. 'Eilers, the guy's out tonight, and we heard he's coming to your place.' I would actually have to step between people who were getting friendly at the bar and say, 'Gee, you look familiar, I think I've seen you here before—*Are you a detective?*' They were supposed to tell you, and that would blow it for them. It protected the other customer.

"Anita Bryant was in one night with a press agent. He went to the john, and the next thing I knew, two plainclothesmen were leading him out. She said, 'What the hell's going on? Why isn't he coming back?' He was being arrested for allegedly propositioning someone."

show called *Bravo Giovanni* that ran about four months. I'd had an affair with one of the dancers, and Ellen found out. We were in the midst of breaking up, and neither of us was in any condition to be in a show. We were behaving badly, shattering morale, and it drove the other actors crazy. One day I demanded an extra number, so Ellen demanded one too. We talked with Tom Hammond, who discussed this with Julius. Tom came over and said, 'I don't know how to tell you this, but Julius says you're both fired.' I didn't talk to Julius for a long time, but now I know he was right. I wish he'd done it himself, but he didn't know how to do that."

Nevertheless opening night ran with mechanical ease, and the next mo. ning Monk rejoiced in the greatest raves of his career: "One of the funniest shows in town . . . a gay, irreverent, satirical revue . . . Monk does it again!" *Dime a Dozen* would play a spectacular 728 performances over its fourteen-month run. The show was typical Monk, a collection of domestic and cultural trifles with such titles as "Cholesterol Love Song," "Ten Percent Banlon," "Bless This School," "Ode to an Eminent Daily," and "H.M.S. Brownstone." But now the inadequacies of material seemed to sink away into the most luxurious setting a nightclub host could envision. From its red velvet, gold-fringed-and-tasseled stage curtains to its feather-soft banquettes, PLaza 9- was the room that Monk had always dreamed about, and it provided the finishing touch in his formula for manufactured chic.

Naysayers, however, found just as much to criticize. They traded barbs on Frank Wagner's overchoreography; on the unflattering black gowns by designer Donald Brooks, whose services Monk was thrilled to have; and even on the cast. On opening night John Paul Hudson sat at the table of famed theatrical producer Cheryl Crawford. "She was really a tough dike. I was awed by her presence. After the first number she took a look at all those babes onstage and said, 'Doesn't Julius ever hire a woman who doesn't have a mustache?' "

As before, the critical raves attracted many customers who sat mystified for ninety minutes, resentful that the show seemed pitched above their heads. Out of boredom they sat and drank, sometimes abandoning decorum. The twin uprights stood amid the front tables on either side of the room with no guardrail behind them, an oversight that William Roy came to regret. "One night during the last song in Act I I felt something pressing against my back. I turned around, and there was a man with a very sick look on his face. He let out a groan and threw up all over my jacket. As soon as I played the last note I tore it off and ran backstage to Julius and Tom Hammond. 'THIS IS VOMIT!' I said. I changed and went back for Act II, and the man was still there, sitting with two ladies. 'Alvin, what a good sport you are to stay. Now, there are only a few more numbers. Just relax.' "

Other customers passed the time in ways equally inappropriate at the Plaza. "Once I heard a strange noise coming from the banquette behind me," says Roy.

Mmmm . . . mmmm . . .
Shhh! Shhh!
Mmmm . . . mmmm . . .
Shhh! Shhh!

"I looked over my shoulder, and a woman on the banquette was jerking off the man sitting next to her. He, of course, kept going 'Mmmm . . . mmmm,' and she was trying to quiet him down. 'Shhh! Shhh!' "

Monk soon began receiving offers to mount revues in other cities. He agreed to try Chicago, and in the winter of 1963 started preparations. The chosen site was peculiar, a former Abyssinian church at 56 West Huron Street, in a shabby neighborhood one block from a stretch of strip joints and seedy bars. Into this setting workmen came to build a club whose lushness would rival PLaza 9-'s. The location was chosen for its relatively low rent and quick availability, but even so the project cost well over $200,000. Most of the funding came from the Abbey Corporation, a production company headed by Ed Gardner, husband of the show's star June Ericson.

Monk used mostly old material and rounded out the cast with seven newcomers: Delphi Harrington, Skip Hinnant, Nagle Jackson, Charles and Mary Jane Kimbrough, Jamie Ross, and Sandy Suter. Entitled *Struts and Frets*, it opened on March 9 with all the fanfare of a visit from the royal family. Many Chicagoans felt that New York snobbery had reared its ugly head, especially when Monk discussed his reasons for coming to the city. Wrote Austin C. Wehrwein in the *New York Times* (May 11, 1963): "Boston is out, [Monk] said, because people there don't go in for entertainment. And so is Philadelphia, he added, because everyone in Philadelphia goes to New York for fun . . . But he is sure that as New York went, so will go

Chicago . . . This is all to the good for a city in need of more sophistication."

Chicago audiences, however, decided that they were not in need of this revue. It contained only one new gem, William Roy's touching "Chicago, Illinois," sung beautifully by June Ericson:

> *I know that sometimes it's called the Windy City*
> *And sometimes just Chicago, Illinois,*
> *But I say heaven is what you call Chicago*
> *'Cause anytime that she is there*
> *The only place to be is there . . .*

The other attempts at local material woefully missed their mark; a description of Marina City, for example, a pair of cylindrical sixty-story apartment buildings, as "twin salt-and-pepper shakers" did not amuse many Chicagoans.

Attendance was poor, leaving the producers little money for promotion—a problem compounded by Monk's insistence on receiving his customary $1,000 a week. But *Dime a Dozen* continued its smash run, and on May 24, 1963, Monk honored an invitation to bring his cast to perform for President Kennedy at a White House correspondents' dinner. Instead of taking his veteran Manhattan players, he brought the Chicago company, an about-face that alienated the faithful group back home.

Struts and Frets closed on August 10 at an enormous loss, leaving Monk determined never to do another revue outside New York. He went home to begin plans for *Baker's Dozen*, his next Plaza show. As in Chicago he featured only one alumnus, in this case Gerry Matthews. Also in the cast of eight was Ruth Buzzi, who at twenty-seven had already brightened several New York and Provincetown revues.

The January 6, 1964, opening received the first mixed reviews of any of Monk's New York shows. Wrote Milton Esterow in the *New York Times* (January 10, 1964): "[Monk] has served up an entertaining platter that has been well-baked but, unfortunately, needs more dough . . . by putting more seasoning into *Baker's Dozen*, Mr. Monk would have a lot of happy customers." While it was true, as Rex Robbins notes, that "after that first season at the Plaza there was nowhere to go but down," *Baker's Dozen* had more serious problems.

The country was still reeling from the shock of President Kennedy's assassination, a tragedy that destroyed any remnants of the idealized social climate of the '50s. In the face of this rude awakening Monk's shows seemed more frivolous than ever. But nothing would convince him to give them a more incisive analytical tone. "To be polite in the theatre these days is the triumph to achieve," he told the *National Observer* (January 4, 1965).

The show's shining moment came from the pen of Treva Silverman, a brilliant newcomer who later won two Emmy awards as writer of *The Mary Tyler Moore Show.* Entitled "East Side, West Side," it anticipated the cooperative-apartment craze—then in its infancy—by supposing that Mayor Zeckendorf had converted the entire East Side into a giant cooperative complete with artificial gardens, supervised children's play areas, a 9,000-seat barber shop, and a Formica–and–contact paper fortress separating it from the West Side. The havoc it wreaks on the lives of its two and a half million residents is explored wittily and insightfully by Silverman, who could not have known in 1964 that the sketch would become even timelier twenty years later.

Otherwise, *Baker's Dozen* concentrated on James Bond, funeral directors, water pollution, the use of shopping bags as status symbols ("Even you can be a slick chick / With your Barricini"), and similar lightweight topics. The show's two or three ventures onto political ground sounded coy at best ("de Gaulle, de Gaulle / We wish you would get on ze ball"). "White House Comics," a sketch by Robert Elliott and William F. Brown about placing comic strip characters in the White House, ran for page after shallow page without a moment of substance:

FIRST WOMAN: I wonder where we could use Terry and the Pirates.
FIRST MAN: Foreign aid. What Terry gives, the pirates take away.
SECOND WOMAN: How about ambassador to Asia?
FIRST MAN: Punjab? He is an Indian, you know.
SECOND WOMAN: Lovely! A little integration in the foreign service, but we don't go all the way. And the Asp?
FIRST WOMAN: Egypt, of course.
SECOND MAN (TO FIRST WOMAN): Tarnation, Lowizie! Mr. Magoo I could understand, but you take your asp . . . (SHE REACTS, OFFENDED. HE'S EMBARRASSED.) Sorry.

For the moment there was still an audience for this kind of "civilized chic," but the future seemed bleak—a point that Monk's revues were loathe to face.

THE UPSTAIRS appeared to be headed for the same fate. Most of Monk's audience had followed him to the Plaza, leaving 56th Street with a series of shows that won occasional critical praise but were often embarrassingly ill attended. Not even two evenings directed by Ronny Graham, *Graham Crackers* and a book musical entitled *Money*, could arouse much interest.

Probably the most entertaining of the later shows was *Twice Over Nightly*, a major departure from the Monk approach. An improvised revue with only the outline of each sketch planned in advance, *Nightly* was a close relative of Second City, the acclaimed Chicago improvisational group. The cast consisted of Second City veteran Paul Dooley, Richard Libertini, MacIntyre Dixon, Jane Alexander, and Mary Louise Wilson, who had left *Dime a Dozen*. "We wanted to call it *The William Howard Taft Memorial Revue: An All-Protestant, All-Heterosexual Show*," Wilson recalls. "But Irving wouldn't let us."

Neither topical nor intellectual, *Nightly* took an offbeat, slapstick look at some clever premises: the jail privileges, for example, of gangsters who turn state's evidence (such as an unlisted cell number) or the plight of a newly settled suburban couple trying to impress their pretentious neighbors just as a loud, vulgar acquaintance drops by. Leonard Harris in the *New York World-Telegram and Sun* cheered (December 9, 1963): "With *Twice Over Nightly*, the Upstairs at the Downstairs has at last come to realize that Julius Monk is no longer on the premises and there's no use behaving as if he were. The result is a revue which is neither slick, topical nor sophisticated—just funny."

Nevertheless it ran only three months. Haber demanded a return to Monk's style, hoping this would revive the club's SRO status. Starting with 1964's . . . *And in This Corner* the new compere was Rod Warren, a young songwriter who stayed with the Upstairs until 1971. Born into a simple, unsophisticated family in East Orange, New Jersey, Warren had penned several tunes for Monk and directed regional musicals in Baltimore and Rhode Island. He had always loved revues and joined the Upstairs filled with optimism about restoring it to its past glory.

The next seven years, regrettably, were a trial for Warren, redeemed only by his passion for guiding young performers and writers toward an image of Manhattan at its wittiest and most elegant. He had full artistic control, although he fought constantly with Haber to retain it. The accountant demanded that he emulate Monk as closely as possible, but Warren wanted to create a fresher style that would combine the chic of the past with penetrating sociopolitical commentary. Sometimes he succeeded, but overall his shows merely pointed up Monk's strengths. However pallid the material, Monk's revues were always slickly professional and performed with consummate polish. Beside them, Warren's often appeared amateurish, ill paced, ill directed, and ill cast. And whereas Monk's shows were accepted as the apogee of sophistication, Warren's were obviously the product of a group of enthusiastic youngsters who wanted to be chic without quite knowing how.

Nevertheless his work represented the final flowering of the nightclub revue and drew scores of young performers for whom a job at the Upstairs was like a key to the city. Warren chose more colorful casts than Monk and was not afraid to hire actors who might outshine their colleagues. Certainly Monk would never have picked Lily Tomlin or Madeline Kahn, two Warren discoveries.

Warren's writers and players shared a philosophy that lay awkwardly between Monk's generation and their own. They poked fun at the shallowness of '60s youth and its attachment to Bob Dylan and psychedelic drugs, while extolling Fred Astaire, Rodgers and Hart, and the Sunday *Times*. They wanted to awaken viewers to some of the harsh realities of modern life, ranging from Senator Barry Goldwater and Congressman Adam Clayton Powell, Jr., to the torture of a job interview. Even in such an uncommercial setting as the Upstairs, they were sure they would succeed. The '60s were sparked by a belief that the small voice could make a difference, and this idealistic sense had always pervaded the club.

Though the company held a deep affection for New York City they still liked to satirize its daily perils:

For a thriller, ride with me
On the downtown BMT
Pay Miss Liberty a call
See the smut upon the wall

Why, there's P.S. 84
Watch the teacher hit the floor . . .

["New York Is a Festival of Fun"
(Gene Bissell), *Mixed Doubles*]

Optimistically, they were sure that someday the past grandeur would return. As one of Warren's nostalgic valentines to Manhattan asserted: "It was wonderful then . . . and will be again."

From the onset his shows were handicapped by a lack of quality material. Most talented writers were aiming directly for the burgeoning television market, which was now moving to California; few in New York were interested in contributing to Warren's shows for a weekly ten-dollar royalty.

A handful of pieces suggest what heights his revues might have reached. Treva Silverman gave Warren several of his best sketches. In "The Envelope, Please" from . . . *And in This Corner* the cast enacted an Oscar presentation for the best single line of movie dialogue, reciting each nominee in turn:

Forget the contest, Marco. It's suicide to try it without a net!

Unchain the Jewess! She has found favor in the eyes of Marcus Maximus.

The Volcano God is angry. You must leave island. We kissy-kissy no more. But first, I dance for you.

Sure, I'll give you a chance, Tex. The same chance you gave my brother.

As the train sped closer to Budapest, the wheels seemed to be saying, "*Be* a ballerina . . . *be* a ballerina . . . *be* a ballerina . . ."

Warren's 1965 revue *The Game Is Up* included "Eye on New York" by Dee Caruso and Bill Levine, whose work took an irreverent view of the seamier aspects of Manhattan. This sketch, based on a popular local TV interview program, starred singer-comedienne Marian Mercer as a woman discussing the latest of her sixty-two rapes on the subway: "Well, this man just stood up and asked me to come with him into another car, and he seemed so sincere that I followed him."

"What did he look like?" asks the interviewer.

"I don't know, because he was wearing a mask."

Finally she concludes that better lighting would help. "It may not stop the attacks, but at least you could see what you're doing."

Fannie Flagg, a '70s TV game show regular, penned and starred in a sketch for *Just for Openers* about a Southern waitress interviewed by *Newsweek* on integration. Warren should have adopted its biting commentary more often:

REPORTER: Now, Miss Coursey, I wonder if you might give me your opinion on integration here in Tupelo.
COURSEY: Oooooh, we get lots of 'em in here now.
REPORTER: Well, just how do you feel about the Negro situation?
COURSEY: I just hate 'em, that's all, I just hate 'em.
REPORTER: Why is that?
COURSEY: They talk funny.
REPORTER: Yes, and now, how do you feel about equal opportunities for education?
COURSEY: Oh no, sir, you can't educate 'em, I don't care what you say.
REPORTER: Well, how do you feel about Negroes like Ralph Bunche?
COURSEY: Ralph who?
REPORTER: Ralph Bunche.
COURSEY: Oh, he's one of those smarties I don't know.
REPORTER: Miss Coursey, how do you feel about integration in the school system?
COURSEY: Well, Geneva [her daughter] ain't goin' to school with 'em. I'll just keep her outta school before she goes to school with 'em. (PAUSE) You know, we'd 'a won that war if we'd 'a had more guns.

Naturally Warren included many of his own songs and sketches. One of his better numbers, "Daytime Sunday Television," panned that day's home viewing:

Nine to six on Sunday video
Makes you long for Sunday night
Unless you're held in total thrall
By the erudition of Erasmus Hall

His moments of inspiration, alas, were few, but so lackluster was most of the other material that even mediocre efforts stood out. His shows revealed the fine line between pointed topical humor and the epicene variety that fell back on snobbery and insults. The revues contained liberal putdowns of such personalities as Carol Channing ("She does every play / The same old way") and Doris Day ("Doris! Have you saved too little / For too late?") as well as gratuitous name-dropping that rivaled Monk's. They also displayed a tendency toward cheap homosexual innuendo, for no apparent reason except to titillate gay viewers and to shock the rest. And Warren's predilection for effeminate actors rendered ludicrous many numbers about husbands, family men, and even peeping toms ("Come to your window, naked lady / Queen of the Night, ascend into sight and wiggle around"). As one of the waiters recalls, "The shows got gayer and gayer every season, and so did the audiences. Straight people were offended by it. One night Rocky Graziano came as a guest of Irving's. I came over to his table just as he was saying to his lady friend, 'It's a good thing there's no window in here, or a lot of these guys would fly out!' "

One of the best revue writers of the '60s was Michael McWhinney, a homely, round-faced young man who had worked as a schoolteacher before moving to Manhattan and turning into a full-time songwriter. His ex-wife and two children stayed behind in Riverdale. McWhinney's marriage had crumbled largely due to his homosexuality, a quality in himself that he detested. A lifelong alcoholic, he missed many crucial rehearsals only to be found unconscious in his apartment. He turned much of his self-hatred outward and gained a reputation as an acid-tongued, deceitful man who alienated friends and supporters without a thought. "Michael used to make people tremble, he was so evil," says John Paul Hudson. "People would actually call you and say, 'Michael said something nice last night!' "

Nevertheless McWhinney became one of the most sought-after comedy writers in revues, specializing in breezy social satire such as "Suburbia Square Dance," an ensemble hoedown about the newly relaxed marital standards:

Now Jim's gonna sleep in a postwar jeep
On a backroad in Mount Kisco
In the morning Peg will fry an egg
In somebody else's Crisco
And Gert's gonna test that tube of Crest
And Blanche's brush and comb

All join hands and try the brands
In somebody else's home

McWhinney stood at the center of a close-knit group of writers and performers. "We all knew one another, often in the biblical sense," Hudson says. "It was incestuous." Most of them were youngsters trying to create a place for themselves in show business, without a paternal and dictatorial figure such as Monk to guide them. Warren welcomed everyone's suggestions, which gave them a feeling of freedom but obliterated the focus that a stronger ruling hand would have imparted.

In any case, optimism was high. A few Upstairs alumni, notably Nancy Dussault and Jane Connell, had graduated to Broadway and TV. It was obvious, however, that despite the many club and stage revues of the '60s the genre had long overstayed its welcome. That decade begot elaborate failures such as Leonard Sillman's *New Faces of 1962* and *New Faces of 1968*; modest flops such as *Fourth Avenue North*, a 1961 off-Broadway revue of which critic John McClain wrote, "An earnest cast [which included Linda Lavin] fails to avert a disaster"; and charming near-successes such as *4-West*, presented in the back room of Palmer's Restaurant at 4 West 49th Street. Even with the bright material of John Paul Hudson, Treva Silverman, and others, and appealing performances by Hudson, Richard Blair, and comediennes Cari Stevens and Elsie Downey (the wife of film director Bob Downey and mother of screen idol Robert Downey, Jr.), it closed six weeks into its open-end run.

Monk's and Warren's shows seemed prestigious by comparison, for they generally received good notices and gave their casts a full season of work. The Upstairs still had the feeling of a family operation, ruled by Haber and Doris Dreyfus, by now his wife. Although Haber sometimes treated the cast kindly, inviting them to his home in Lake Mahopac, New York, and to parties at his Sutton Place apartment, most considered him the antithesis of the elegance that they hoped to capture—a fat, sloppy, coarse businessman whose rumpled clothes reeked of cigarette smoke. He would walk by the bar and grab fistfuls of peanuts, stuffing them in his mouth as half of them rolled down his tie and bounced off his enormous potbelly.

His cheapness was sometimes tinged with dishonesty. In 1962 Ben Bagley signed Marian Mercer and comic R. G. Brown for *No*

Shoestrings. Shortly after, the producers of the Andy Williams TV show offered them a weekly spot at a handsome salary. Although reluctant to lose them, Bagley agreed that he could not deprive them of a fine opportunity by binding them to a $125-a-week revue. Haber agreed to waive their contracts but secretly told Williams's producers that Bagley had demanded a percentage of the team's salary—a blatant lie. Haber pocketed the money.

His blood pressure rose as he saw all the empty seats. "Where are the customers, Rod?" he grumbled. "We never had this problem with Julius. The critics'd say, 'SRO at the Upstairs.' Big headlines. When's the last time they said that, Rod? I don't know how much longer we can keep this up. Unless business improves . . ."

A frequent subject of gossip was Haber's brother Billy, the bartender. According to Upstairs doorman Mike Milius, "Irving's father told him on his deathbed to take care of Billy, so Irving gave him a job as bartender, but they treated him like shit." The cast loved him, though, and after closing gathered at the bar, chatting until early morning. "Irving left at about nine with Miss D, as he used to call Doris," Milius says. "After that Billy would take over and give free drinks to everybody. It was his way of getting even with Irving." Haber also occasionally used his son Harvey as maître d'. The cast called him "Baby Beef," for he was so fat and clumsy that he had trouble taking three steps without bumping into a table or knocking something over.

In his 1965–1966 revue *Just for Openers* Warren introduced to revue audiences the twenty-three-year-old Madeline Kahn. A recent graduate of Hofstra University, Kahn possessed a singing voice of operatic caliber as well as a natural flair for comedy. In the summer of 1965 she put both to use at Green Mansions, a Westchester summer resort similar to Camp Tamiment. Hired to do a concert program, she sang an occasional classical parody for fun. Two fellow players, actor Virgil Curry and pianist–musical director Michael Cohen, were Warren alumni and urged him to hear her. Warren offered her a job immediately, and for the next two years she gave his shows many sorely needed moments of comic brilliance.

Kahn's flexible voice enabled her to sing the solo part in a Handel-style oratorio that spoofed Lyndon Johnson, to portray an "operator" at the office of a phone-in sex line, even to mimic the singsong delivery of a fashion show announcer introducing a series of informal designs for the modern nun: "And now, ladies, to begin the festivities, this chic number is a knit three-piece double wool habit with the all-new slim skirt and habit cutaway jacket with pompon buttons. *We* love it in salmon, olive green, and the *enchanting* cherry red. It's *almost* forbidden!"

Cast member Richard Blair, an impish, exuberant singer-comic, recalls seeing Kahn for the first time. "Her hair was stringy, she looked a little unkempt, she seemed slightly overweight. Well, when she opened her mouth to sing she had the most glorious voice. She was genuinely funny without trying." Others remember her as friendly but rather vague and preoccupied, as though she sensed levels of the situation that eluded them.

"When I entered that job," says Kahn, "I did not know what a revue was. I had never been to one. I was studying to be a classical singer and hoped to get a job as an actress. I did a good job that first year, but I don't think I judged anything with a great deal of discrimination. I was just so pleased to be in something that important people came to see. I got to be one of only six people, dressed in a glamorous, simple black gown, singing and doing comedy every night. I also thought I deserved it, because I always thought I was very talented. If we're going to combine singing with sophisticated humor, I always knew I was very, very good at that.

"*But*—I really didn't like the revues that much. This chic, sophisticated-as-it-were stuff was, I felt, too arch, it was sarcastic, and I don't like sarcasm unless it's incorporated into a role. But humor simply based on these fresh people putting everything down—I didn't like it. It was very gay, and this is not an antigay statement, but there was a certain effete atmosphere that I found wearing, and it really got to me. After a while I didn't feel very feminine. I started to feel that parts of me were not seen or regarded highly at all. Words like 'fag hag'—a very vulgar term—leap to mind. I wondered, gee, am I becoming that? It was not at all what I was heading for."

One quality that distinguished Kahn from most of her colleagues, and that contributed to her eventual stardom, was her intelligence. She recognized the inferiority of most of her material and knew how much effort it would take to make it sound substantial. "I had to be very smart in picking from the material Rod presented at the beginning of the season. You had to *make* these things work, and it was hard. At first I did whatever he asked me to. But then I got more savvy and realized, be sure you have a very good solo, be sure the other material is stuff you really feel you can make work. Rod gave his opinions, but it was basically up to you.

"And I think it was hard for him to find people. You did two shows a night, six nights a week, and you weren't paid that much. Maybe performers who were very talented didn't want to be tied up in some robotic show like this. During my first year Betty Aberlin left pretty quickly and was replaced, and soon after that Fannie Flagg left to go into TV. Both of them were very unique and talented in this area and, I stress, unique. Betty was replaced by someone who was competent but not uniquely, comically gifted. And Fannie was replaced by someone who was competent but not uniquely, comically gifted but sort of looked like Fannie. I started to get upset and didn't think anyone knew what they were doing.

"One night I went to the Improv with friends and I saw this person doing her material, which I didn't quite understand but thought was very interesting. It was Lily Tomlin. I said to her afterward, 'I'm going to mention you to Rod Warren, so if he comes you'll know who he is. I hope you get to work at the Upstairs.' Rod went to see her, and she did come into the show. Not everyone got what she did at that time, but she sure was interesting. I was anxious to have a group of comic minds to work with."

Usually she did not. Ben Bagley recalls praising her lavishly after a performance. "I began to notice angry stares from the other girls in the dressing room," he says. "Madeline said, 'Come on, Ben, let's go outside.' She closed the door and said, 'Now, Ben, you've got to do me a favor. I want you to go in there and tell everyone else they were wonderful, too.'

" 'Oh, Madeline, I can't!'

" 'Ben, please! I have to work with these people!'

" 'Well, what do you want me to do, tell them they were horrible?'

" 'No, you'd better not do that!' "

"What you hoped for in those shows," says Kahn, "was that David Merrick would come in and say, 'Have I got a part for you!' And that's exactly what happened. In the summer of 1967 he gave me a small part in his new musical *How Now, Dow Jones*."

Subsequently Kahn appeared in *New Faces of 1968* singing "Das Chicago-Song," a Kurt Weill parody by Michael Cohen and Tony Geiss that she had introduced at the Upstairs. By now nightclubs were a none-too-pleasant memory for her. "The time was right to leave. I had gotten in right under the wire. I felt, 'This is gonna end soon.' I didn't miss it. I never got to know anyone in the cast that well, because I couldn't be with them that much. There was just too much static."

None of them seemed to share her feelings about the quality of the revues. "It's almost a thorn in my side, but I am always the one, it seems to me, who is saying, 'The Emperor's New Clothes? Doesn't anyone see that this guy is naked?' Alice at the tea party. And no one sees it, they don't want to see it, and you can't even say to them, 'I've got news for you. This is no good.' They don't want to hear it. You sit there thinking, maybe I'm wrong, maybe I'm crazy. Then later on you find out you weren't."

Passing through the Downstairs in the summer of 1966 was Dixie Carter, acclaimed in the '80s and '90s as Julia Sugarbaker, Southern firebrand of the hit CBS television series *Designing Women.* Then known as Genna Carter, she appeared in *Below the Belt*, a retrospective of highlights that also starred Kahn and Lily Tomlin, whom Warren regarded as his greatest discovery. Her appearances in four of his shows inspired Vincent Canby to write in the *New York Times*, "It's as if Beatrice Lillie and Dracula's daughter had come into some kind of lunar conjunction."

Tomlin's apocryphal biography, reprinted in the program, was certainly Lillie-esque in its wry self-effacement:

> *LILY TOMLIN*: Detroit, Michigan, Wayne State University preceded by Miss Pickett's School for Genteel Young Women, Fort Wayne, Indiana; a superb monologuist, with classical ballet and mime study in Vienna (Austria), she has appeared in concert performing an evening of her own writings; as a model, she has twice been cover girl of the Frederick's catalog—in Autumn 1965 and Winter 1967; with her third husband, the late Robert Paisell, she co-invented a lot . . . She is known for her incessant charity work.

In fact, her early training consisted of stand-up gigs in Detroit coffeehouses before she moved to New York in 1962 with fifteen dollars in her pocket. Born Mary Jean Tomlin in 1939, the comedienne supported herself through office work and as a waitress at Howard Johnson's on 49th Street and Broadway. "That was the lowest-class Howard Johnson's," she told Merv Griffin in an October 1968 appearance on his show. "But I loved that job, and one day they sent me over to a very big, high-class Howard Johnson's on 52nd Street, where they served liquor. I saw a plaque on the wall that said, 'So-and-so is Howard Johnson's Waitress of the Week.' I went back to the other place and said, 'Why don't we have a Waitress of the Week too?' They said, 'We're too small, we don't have the regional supervisor come around and check your hairnets or anything.' So I made up a ballot and had them elect me.

"We had a microphone that you used to call down to the kitchen, but the place was so small that it would echo through the house. Every day when it got real slow I would duck under the counter and say, 'Attention, diners, your Howard Johnson's Waitress of the Week Miss Lily Tomlin is about to make her appearance on the floor, and let's give her a great big hand.' "

True recognition came when Tomlin won a week at Café Au Go-Go, across the street from the Upstairs, and was later hired by Warren. *Below the Belt* was her first experience performing comedy material written by others, and she wondered if she could do it well. ("Do you think I'm funny?" she asked Richard Blair in a coffee shop one night.) She also doubted her singing abilities. The summer of 1967 proved both. In May she headed out to Provincetown, Massachusetts, where revues had thrived since the '50s. The glut of tourists provided a built-in audience, making the town a popular place to try out Manhattan-bound productions. John Paul Hudson planned a two-person revue at the Madeira Club for himself and an actress-singer who became ill and canceled just before rehearsals. Remembering Tomlin from *Below the Belt*, Hudson called her, and within days she joined him.

Most of *Two Much*, as the show was called, consisted of material by Hudson and by Philadelphia writers Don Brockett and Joanne Pasquinelli. Hudson and Tomlin made it shine, especially when they portrayed a scientist and his wife in "The Horrors," a William Dyer–Don Parks satire on '50s science fiction movies:

TOMLIN: Oh, Butch, it's horrible, horrible!
HUDSON: Good God, woman, what happened?
TOMLIN: Mrs. Bassett was just raped by a giant grasshopper!
HUDSON: I was afraid of this. [PHONE RINGS] Hello, yes? Of course. We'll do what we can.
TOMLIN: What is it, Butch?

HUDSON: It's Washington. The country's been alerted. Martial law has been declared. The entire city of North Truro was just swallowed by the blob.

TOMLIN: Little Marjorie! We must get home.

HUDSON: We will, honey.

TOMLIN: I wouldn't want anything to happen to that pink party dress.

Tomlin's two solo spots, however, were the standouts. That summer she presented, for the first time in memory, several of her funniest characters: the "rubber freak" obsessed with everything from erasers to elastic bands to panties, the aging beauty expert Lupe, and a gauche woman mingling at a party:

> What is this, a brownie? Well, goodness no, I just had a cub scout before I came . . . Don't breathe a word of it, but have you heard about Charles? I was speaking with him just before his sister Felicia died. He said he couldn't afford a tombstone, he's planning to bury her with her head out of the ground.

Tomlin also gave her famous dissertation on how her mother raised her to be a lady:

> Like any lady-to-be, Mother thought I should have dancing lessons. I studied the ballet for ten years. Unfortunately my dancing career was cut short one morning when Mother and I were having breakfast. She dropped a six-pack on my instep.
>
> I also went to school in a cab. I took a taxi every morning, and sometimes Mother wouldn't even put the meter on. And, of course, she always insisted I protect my skin against the sun. I was the only one in the first grade recess who wore gloves and a heavy veil.

As director and choreographer Hudson found he had a surprisingly cooperative costar. "She always wanted to learn, she wanted feedback. She even took over as hostess of the afternoon show because it was bombing. That was not in her contract, but she wanted to get down there and work on her bits. She'd come in these outrageous gowns, with her wedgies, and talk to the audience and the people at the bar, welcoming them to *her* nightclub."

The three-month run progressed smoothly, Tomlin's occasional quirks notwithstanding, notably a fear that men were peeking at her as she showered—an odd one given that the Madeira Club was almost exclusively gay. Near the end of the run a legitimate crisis occurred. "Lily's lover had undergone a very serious operation and was in critical shape," recalls Hudson. "Came showtime the next day, and Lily had skipped town. I was frantic. We had about three weeks to run. Joanne Beretta, one of the star acts, said, 'Well, I'll have to learn the show. I've seen it plenty of times.' She started rehearsing. The next day I was sitting on the gallery wondering what the hell would happen next, when Lily returned looking haggard as hell. I understood why she'd left—it was a matter of the heart, you know? Later she wrote me the most beautiful letter, saying, 'When Lily lands on her two feet she will have you to thank.' "

Two Much closed on Labor Day, and in February 1968 Tomlin returned to a severely faltering Upstairs to replace singer Janie Sell in a revue called *Dark Horses*. Warren's weakest show to date, it played to dismal houses night after night. Irving Haber, it was rumored, was about to replace the revues with something more profitable. Instead he decided to close the show, fire most of the cast, and have Warren open a new revue with new players. Richard Blair, knowing that he was about to be dismissed, accepted an understudy job out of town in a play headed for Broadway. He quit the Upstairs about a week before his last night, and Haber was so infuriated he sent the producers a telegram slandering Blair and claiming he had walked out on his contract. No contracts existed, of course, for him or any of the actors. Blair's colleagues loved him, and Haber's deed only harmed morale further.

On March 8 *Photo Finish* opened; only Tomlin remained of the old group. To no one's surprise she was the raison d'être of a show that only marginally surpassed *Dark Horses*. Wrote Vincent Canby in the *New York Times* (March 9, 1968): "It isn't that all the barbs are misdirected; rather, that they have no sting . . . It is Miss Tomlin who dominates the evening and gives it appropriately mad purpose . . . She may well be headed for the big time."

One of her monologues concerned the misfit of a computer dating service. "This is my third date tonight," she announced, as she flicked cigar ash into her rose corsage. Another, "Lupe," spotlighted a glamorous but ancient Helena Rubinstein–type character who demonstrates her personal beauty regimen, a routine based "not so much on compound as technique of application." Tomlin twisted her face into a series of pained contortions as she showed how to apply moisturizer "using only the very soft pads of the fingertips ... round, round, round ... soothing and smoothing away those ugly scowl lines, tea stains, and aluminum pot marks."

After *Photo Finish* Tomlin performed in Warren's summer Downstairs revue *Instant Replay*. By now Irene Pinn, her first important manager, had seen her at the club and decided to represent her. "Irene was an Englishwoman," says Hudson, "heavyset and tough as she could be, but because she spoke British I don't think people realized how tough she was. She saw Lily and said, 'I'm gonna make you a star.' One night Ruth Buzzi asked Lily, 'Is Irene going to come every night?' Lily said, 'Isn't it awful? I just can't keep her away.' Of course, that wasn't it at all. There was always someone to go into a club or anyplace else and fight the battles. Lily's smart that way."

With Pinn's help, Tomlin was signed by NBC to debut on *Laugh-In* on December 29, 1968. As hopeful as she was, Tomlin didn't foresee such an immediate reaction. "Lily and I went to California together just after the premiere episode," Hudson says. "She was wearing baggy slacks and a terrible sweater and no makeup. On the flight she was trying out her 'rubber freak' routines, and I don't think I ever laughed so loud. As we were leaving the plane somebody said, 'Aren't you the new girl on *Laugh-In*?' People started asking her for autographs. She said, 'What shall I do?' I said, 'Well, for one thing you'd better run to the ladies' room and put on some lipstick."

THE DOWNSTAIRS at the Upstairs helped keep Haber's duplex afloat in its later years. In 1963, on the suggestion of Ronny Graham, he hired Mabel Mercer, who sang there off and on for three years. As always, Mercer sat in a straight-backed chair, hands folded peacefully in her lap, making time hover serenely over moments of love and loss that became infinitely explorable when she sang about them. Mercer was adored by the waiters and staff and left a deep impression on all but one listener, Irving Haber. "I'm sure to his last moment he never understood what the attraction was to her legion of fans," says Gary Haber. " 'She can't carry a tune!' he said. I kept saying, 'It's phrasing!' 'Phrasing, schmasing!' he answered. 'She can't carry a tune.' " As always, the money was all that mattered. "One night," recalls an Upstairs doorman, "Mabel became very ill and couldn't go on, and it was packed. Irving somehow got her to do the show when she should have been in the hospital." Ronny Graham, Milt Kamen, and Jackie Vernon also played there, and Lily Tomlin tried out her early solo act between revues. In 1967 Joan Rivers began a series of informal, improvisational evenings that lasted through 1969, bolstered by her guest spots on the *Tonight Show*.

During a four-week hiatus in Rivers's final season she had a surprise replacement. A few weeks before, the twenty-three year-old Bette Midler had auditioned for Haber, singing several songs in a dramatic floor-length black cape. Haber liked her but forgot her quickly. "Before Joan left," says Downstairs maître d' Archie Walker, "Irving asked me whom we should get for the room. I said, 'I think you should bring in Bette Midler.'

"He wasn't crazy about the idea. Bette had, to say the least, a very gay following. Irving had been surrounded by that sort of thing for years—I mean, who could have a gayer following than Mabel Mercer? Every old queen with four days to live came to see her. But Bette's group was of its day, and they were not wearing jackets and ties. I said, 'Irving, for a seven-dollar minimum they may not want to wear ties, but I'm telling you the place will be packed.'

"So he brought her in for one week, with an option for the other three weeks. He paid her two hundred and fifty a week, and out of that she had to pay her three musicians. That left her with nothing, but after all this was mainly a showcase to get people in to hear her. Well, they were lined up on the street. Irving was happy about that, even though in her act she talked about how cheap he was and how terrible the stage and piano were. She decorated the piano herself with velvet and flowers, and that made it look a little better.

"Irving said, 'Bette, we're doin' okay, you got your three weeks.'

"She said, 'That's fine with me, but it's fifteen hundred dollars a week, and *you* pay the musicians.' He groaned, 'Awwwww, Bette, come on . . .' But she got it."

The Downstairs was important for Midler in at least one respect: it introduced her to Barry Manilow, who played cocktail piano upstairs between shows and, downstairs, teamed with a singer named Jeannie Lucas for an act of show and pop tunes of the day such as "Georgy Girl." Manilow made little impression at the time, and he and Midler rejoined in 1971 at the Continental Baths, where she would refer to the Upstairs as the "House of Wax."

Spirits continued to fall Upstairs, as Warren and the cast wondered when Haber would drop the ax. Often only two or three customers showed up, which made the performance of a six-person revue ludicrous. According to AGVA regulations the actors did not have to appear for an audience of fewer than six, but Haber would never have paid them not to work. He instructed the doormen to go into the street and accost passersby. "Hey, you wanna see a nice little show? You won't have to pay for anything, just your drinks, if you have any." Thus he was assured of at least $30 or so in the till.

The waiters were no happier than the cast, for their tips had shrunk drastically. Most of them needed the money to support their acting careers—or so they claimed. "So much of that was bullshit," says Archie Walker. "The actors were the ones who threw their books down at closing and went home, because they had to get up in the morning and make rounds. The others sat at the bar until four in the morning. To me they were ashamed of being waiters, so they pretended they were actors trying to make ends meet."

Morale was further shattered by the death of waiter Mike (Miguel) O'Brian, a young man from the Lower East Side with a black mustache, black hair, and handsome Latin features. O'Brian played two or three minor film roles, but is better remembered as the lover of then-unknown actress Faye Dunaway, with whom he shared a tempestuous affair. "She was in a play at the time called *Hogan's Goat*," says Mike Milius, "and we were waiting for her to come home, because she was gonna cook spaghetti for a bunch of us. She came in and said, 'Otto Preminger was there tonight and offered me a contract.' 'Yeah, yeah,' we said, 'you're full of shit, go cook the spaghetti.' But it was true. She got into *The Happening* with Michael Parks and Anthony Quinn—her first feature." During the filming O'Brian and Dunaway had their last altercation and broke up. According to Milius, O'Brian became terminally depressed and never recovered. "He freaked out and OD'd on sleeping pills. That really broke everybody's heart and destroyed the spirit of the place."

Just as shocking was the death of Michael McWhinney. In October 1969 he invited to his home a young pianist-singer named Ronny Whyte, who had appeared in his Showplace revue *New York Coloring Book* and with whom McWhinney was painfully in love. He told Whyte to look through his record collection and take whatever he wanted. A few months later McWhinney attended a party thrown by some neighbors and became severely drunk. His own house stood on a cliff with a treacherous drop. Instead of going home via the roadway, he announced to a couple of fellow guests, "Look! I can climb the hill to my house!" Amazingly, he made it. After they left, he tried to repeat the stunt.

McWhinney was later discovered in a heap on the ground, his neck broken. The handful of earth and grass that he still clutched did not make his death wish any less obvious to his friends; apparently he was just waiting for fate to intervene.

By 1964 Julius Monk had begun his own decline. That season's revue, *Bits and Pieces XIV*, drew barely enough business to cover costs, and *Pick a Number XV*, a 1965–1966 retrospective of old highlights, was brought up short by Robert Alden in the *New York Times*:

> Regretfully, it must be reported that Julius Monk's *Pick a Number XV*, which opened last night, is a bore. Any topical revue that pokes fun at the mores of our time must be of a substance of diamond-hard quality. It must be able to scratch without being scratched itself.
>
> A revue that depends for laughs on describing the color of the new checkbooks as "terra cotta pink" or "eggplant purple" is vulnerable. A revue that tells the housewife it is safer to let the laundry get brown than to run the risk of being knocked down by the "white tornado" misses the mark.
>
> It is not that this edition of Mr. Monk's hearty perennial, blooming as it has these last three seasons at its home in the Plaza Hotel, is tasteless or that its performers are artless. The show fails because it lacks good material, witty material, original material, lively material.
>
> We all are a little tired of jokes about soup cans constituting pop art. We do not need more jokes about dances called the monkey, the frug and the watusi.
>
> Would this world be any the less if we were spared a serious love song that tells us that "Happiness Is a Bird" (that we don't miss until it flies away)?
>
> It is presumed that the geriatric set was supposed to turn cartwheels when they heard a number harking back to the past called "The Good Old Days." More likely the geriatric set were wishing they were down in Greenwich Village with the Revuers—Betty

> Comden, Judy Holliday, Adolph Green, etc.—when the material was fresh and everyone was 25 years younger.

Although it eked out a full season, by mutual agreement with the management Monk announced that the show would be his last. At first he tried to blame the decline of his series upon a mugging that had taken place in front of the Plaza, but he later made a guarded acknowledgment of changing tastes. "Like Alice in Wonderland," he told Vincent Canby in the *New York Times* (August 5, 1966), "we've overtaken ourselves. We cannot deny the pocketbook. We cannot deny a certain venality . . . I have a whole drawer full of 'sick' sketches that I find killingly funny, but I wouldn't use them."

PLaza 9- brought in Charlotte Rae, Alice Ghostley, and Ronny Graham, whose roller coaster career was headed for its all-time low. Jobs had become so scarce that Graham's income nearly vanished. He fell over a year behind in his $115 weekly alimony payments to Ellen Hanley, who desperately needed money herself. In the summer of 1967 she sued Graham for $6,700 in back alimony and won. Graham was sent to a jail in the bleak neighborhood of 37th Street and Tenth Avenue with little more than the shirt on his back. Hanley's lawsuit left him with only $30 in his bank account and wiped out his ASCAP dividends of $3,000 a year.

A month later she hit him with a second suit for $8,000 in additional unpaid alimony that had accumulated since her first suit, a sum that, as Earl Wilson wrote in the *New York Post* (October 30, 1967), "he stands little chance of paying unless he holds up the other seventeen guys in jail." The latter suit was thrown out of court, but Graham was still incarcerated with no money for bail. All his wealthy and "concerned" showbusiness friends were nowhere to be found. One night Ben Bagley dined with Nancy Walker and David Craig, old pals of Graham's. "Isn't it terrible?" said Walker. "We *must* do something to help Ronny." Bagley reports that she called Carol Burnett, by then a millionaire. Yet within three weeks the supposedly altruistic project was forgotten, with not a penny raised.

In February 1968, after Graham had been in jail for six months, his lawyer worked out a payment schedule with Hanley, and he returned home to rebuild his career from scratch. Twenty years later the health problems caused by his cold, damp cell still plagued him. With typical candor he discussed his hard times on the *Tonight Show* and in several interviews. "I have a multiplicity of talents," he told *Newsweek* (April 30, 1968). "I never handled them right. I just did the things that kept me amused. I would have liked to become something in one of them. I hope it's not too late."

It came as a surprise when PLaza 9- invited Monk back in 1968 to try one more revue. Excited by the opportunity, he played it safe by combining a dozen new numbers with eight favorites and by enlisting two old pros, Rex Robbins and Mary Louise Wilson, to head the cast of five. He called the show *Four in Hand* and subtitled it *The All New Déjà-Vu Revue*, which had overtones that he did not intend. As immersed in the past as he was, Monk had never designed his shows as exercises in nostalgia, but since *Pick a Number* his style had grown increasingly stale. The opening strains carried one back to past seasons, when his revues were the toast of Manhattan and when young and old revered the Plaza:

Day after day we go out of our way to the Plaza
Time after time we regard that sublime nonpareil
Night after night by the beautiful light of the Plaza
We come to the marvelous, fabulous Plaza Hotel . . .

Monk tried to make the show more contemporary, poking fun at the drug generation with such numbers as "Take a Trippie with a Hippie":

Seeds, beads, poetry, and flowers
That is all we've got
We find that since we gave up showers
Flowers help a lot

June Reizner's gospel sing-along, "That New-Time Religion," spoofed the trend to "pray for just a smidgen" and spend the rest of the time manipulating bingo chips, raffle tickets, and Ouija boards. The old numbers were welcome, especially "The Race of the Lexington Avenue Express," and for once Monk had chosen a thoroughly inspired cast, with three fine unknowns named Terry O'Mara, Liz Sheridan, and Alex Wipf. As ever, Mary Louise Wilson was the standout. Vincent Canby in the *New York Times* (November 10, 1967) said that she "manages at various times to look and sound exactly like Lady Bird Johnson and like a matron from some demi-Darien taking her first LSD trip ('Allen, you wouldn't believe it, but I just grabbed a handful of God!')." Overall, however, *Four in Hand* was a charming but quaint anachronism that examined '60s society with far too much politesse for the day. "What we need is a revue with a less chic and perhaps a more lost and disenchanted, that is, an angrier point of view," wrote Canby.

National Educational Television taped the show for its March 15, 1968, edition of *NET Playhouse*. "The sad truth is that the rendezvous was a couple of years too late," wrote George Gent in the next day's *Times*. "A few seasons back, the group's satiric barbs at politicians, liberal intellectuals and religion might have seemed devilishly daring on timid TV; but, in the wake of Rowan and Martin and the Smothers Brothers, it all seemed very genteel and just a little old hat."

Business died for the rest of the run, and once more television was the culprit. Those who had seen the program had no reason to view it again in person, while others were deterred by the poor reviews. *Four in Hand* closed on June 29, and the Plaza did not invite Monk back. Optimistically he told the press that he would present a new revue elsewhere after elections, which would provide fresh grist for his satirical mill.

For the 1968–1969 season PLaza 9- began a series called *PLaza 9- and All That Jazz*, presenting Dizzy Gillespie, Oscar Peterson, Earl Hines, and other jazz stars in an unusually plush setting. Monk was mostly inactive in those months. His modeling career had dwindled—men his age were simply not in demand—and his efforts to interest another club failed. In the summer of 1970 he accepted a job as pianist in the cocktail lounge of the St. Regis Hotel on Fifth Avenue, a lonely and humiliating job that ended quickly. Between sets he discussed his later career with John S. Wilson of the *New York Times* (July 27, 1970):

> My success at PLaza 9- did me a great deal of harm. There's a Dorothy Parker story about a girl who danced with the Prince of Wales. After that, nobody ever asked her to dance again. I had created a superb room. But one is frightened to try again. One would be expected to top oneself after doing fifteen revues in twelve years.
>
> For the past two years I've felt as hollow as an old gourd. Race,

> Vietnam, the Young Lords, the Black Panthers—these subjects are so dangerous with a drinking public. Everything is so iconoclastic now in TV and journalism: Blood must be drawn. I think people are so busy with the mating instinct that they haven't time to be entertained. What can you do that has not been done?
>
> And there's such a propensity to youth now. It's as if a curtain had descended. The experience that once seemed so valuable . . . I really think we've all been drummed away for the time being.

That was Monk's last job. Friends tried to persuade him to mount new revues, but he admitted that his shows would never have succeeded in 1970s and '80s New York. He moved to a small but plush apartment on the West Side and entered a quiet retirement, spending his time dining with friends, browsing in antique stores, and receiving treasured phone calls from Ellen Hanley, Bibi Osterwald, and others from his past.

Some of them worried that he did not have enough money—a surprise to those who remembered the many years he commanded a weekly salary of $1,000 and managed it carefully under the guidance of Thomas Hammond. Says Rex Robbins, "One day I ran into Tommy, who was then managing Bernadette Peters. He said, 'Don't ever worry about Julius. He's well taken care of.' "

By the late '60s the city once famous for having an intimate nightclub on every other block now hardly remembered what the term meant. In the Bon Soir's later years, long after Jimmie Daniels, Mae Barnes, and the Three Flames had gone, the room as well as the bar became predominantly gay. Joanne Beretta, female impersonator Lynne Carter, and the loyal Felicia Sanders gave the club its last touches of distinction; the stage was otherwise dominated by Borscht Belt comics and mediocre singers. Like the entire young generation, gays opted to make their own entertainment in discos and dance bars rather than quietly watching someone else. Near the start of 1967 the Bon Soir closed. It would open again briefly in a couple of later, doomed reincarnations.

After the Showplace folded, Jan Wallman went back to the Duplex, which she managed until 1968. She gave it an impressive last lease on life, capitalizing on the final days when the major TV talk shows originated in New York. They signed two of her acts, Joan Rivers and comedienne Joanne Worley, later a star of *Laugh-In.* "Once Joan appeared on the Carson show and Joanne on Merv Griffin, the people from those shows would come down to see anyone I asked them to see. Performers wanted to work for me, because that was direct entrée to the talent coordinators. And when they mentioned us on the show that brought in customers."

One performer who sought out the Duplex was Rodney Dangerfield, who began his comedy career there and introduced his trademark "I don't get no respect" routines. The former Jacob Cohen from Babylon, Long Island, then forty-three, had decided to resume a show business career after a fifteen-year hiatus, during which he married, raised a family, and worked as a paint salesman. He entertained at the Duplex for free, refusing Wallman's $40-a-week salary. "Kill the forty dollars, I'll have a few drinks instead," he told her. Dangerfield recorded his first album there, and after moving on to the Living Room, the Improv, and other clubs opened his own on First Avenue, Dangerfield's, which thrives to this day.

In 1965 Jack Rollins brought Wallman a young comedy writer named Dick Cavett, whom he wanted to present as a comedian. "They weren't intending to make him a full-time comic," Wallman says. "They wanted him to have the experience because they were grooming him to be the next in the Jack Paar–Johnny Carson line. And within five years he had his own show." Cavett's dry humor made little impact in nightclubs, which he claimed to hate. But through Rollins's promotion he appeared at the Bon Soir, the hungry i, and several others, switching to television in short order.

Also fondly remembered is singer-comedienne Claiborne Cary, a petite blonde with a clear, plaintive voice that touched the heart in such ballads as Stephen Sondheim's "Anyone Can Whistle" and "Where's the Boy I Saved for a Rainy Day?" a superior torch song by Baldwin Bergersen from the Showplace revue *The Prickly Pair.* Cary's madcap, mischievous comic sense was rare in someone so winsome and feminine; it brightened such chestnuts as "The Trolley Song." "He asked my name / I held my breath / I couldn't speak / Well, how do you tell someone your name is Claiborne?" Cary became busy in television commercials and reduced her New York club appearances until 1987, when she made a welcome return.

Wallman's own hiatus was about to start. "Acts had always moved from my clubs to the bigger rooms—the Blue Angel, the Bon Soir.

Once they weren't around anymore those performers didn't have that next step up to take. And when the talk shows moved out to the west coast we really had no more raison d'être. The staff and I would sit around and play a game called 'Movie Star,' because we didn't have any customers. Sometimes we'd keep our coats on, because there wasn't enough heat in the place." The owners tried to cut expenses. Wallman fought with them frequently for "hashing" the booze—pouring cheap liquor into expensive bottles—but they ignored her. Finally Wallman decided it was hopeless to remain at the dying club and resigned in 1968.

Soon afterward the Duplex was closed for liquor violations and other legal infractions. More than two years passed before it was allowed to reopen. "Everybody was in tears but me," says Wallman. "I'd already closed in my mind. And I knew the business was over."

WHY IRVING HABER kept the Upstairs at the Downstairs alive until 1974 is a mystery; it may be the only instance in which a sentimental attachment overrode his business sense. By then columnists were describing Rod Warren's efforts as "valiant." Ernest Leogrande wrote in the *New York Daily News* (June 19, 1969), "You have to commend the Upstairs for its convictions in carrying on." *Free Fall*, *Weigh-In (Way Out)*, and *The Manhattan Arrangement*, Haber's last three revues, all suffered from mostly undistinguished performers and material and met with indifference. Journalists cited *Laugh-In* as his prime opponent, and with a cast that included Lily Tomlin, Ruth Buzzi, Arte Johnson, Goldie Hawn, and Joanne Worley it is not hard to see why. Warren and Haber tried to update the shows, dressing the men in jumpsuits and the women in pantsuits, but it was just too late. The final revue, a compilation of nonpolitical material entitled *Let Yourself Go*, opened on October 28, 1972. Despite some of the best notices that an Upstairs show had commanded in years and the presence of Marcia Lewis, an enormously gifted singing comedienne, it did not have a chance.

Haber presented a series of comedy and musical acts both Upstairs and Downstairs and finally closed on January 22, 1974. Like Julius Monk, he and Doris found it difficult to admit failure. As George Gent reported in the next day's *Times*:

> Mrs. Irving Haber, wife of the owner of the split-level nightclub, said she and her husband were closing the door on three decades of pleasurable memories with yesterday's auction of the club's lighting and sound equipment and other memorabilia.
>
> She said the closing was for personal reasons and was not a result of declining audiences or difficulties in attracting talent, although she admitted that major talents had priced themselves out of the club's market.
>
> "It took us seven months to make the decision," Mrs. Haber said in a telephone interview. "I wanted to pack everything up and move it into our living room. But we did the right thing."

Haber spent his remaining days managing his accounting business and restaurants. Overweight and a heavy smoker all his life, he suffered a decline in health and on April 7, 1975, died in his Sutton Place apartment of a heart attack at age sixty-six. "Head of Downstairs Dies—Staged Julius Monk Revues," read the *Times* obituary. Doris was left to handle his many business concerns. She was also left a very rich woman.

Haber's brother Billy was less fortunate. "After the Upstairs closed," says Archie Walker, "Billy's wife, who had checked coats there on Saturday nights, left him. He ended up in an apartment building for the aged. One day I ran into him in a supermarket and tapped him on the shoulder. When he saw who I was he started to cry. It was so sad. He talked about how much he missed everybody."

The company and staff went on to varying degrees of success. Brandon Maggart eventually became a full-time actor, starring for five seasons on a cable TV sitcom entitled *The Brothers*. Betty Aberlin became Lady Aberlin on *Mister Rogers' Neighborhood*. Judy Graubart, another cast member, performed a slew of TV commercial voiceovers and appeared on *The Electric Company*, another children's series. Marian Mercer kept busy in television, as did Fannie Flagg. Most of the others were scarcely heard from again.

"In those days," says Madeline Kahn, "there were people who were just depressed and not going anywhere, juxtaposed with people who were healthy and focused and very definitely going somewhere—Dixie Carter, Lily Tomlin, Fannie Flagg, myself. We were up against people who, you sensed, were very fragile and were going to self-destruct."

Rod Warren left the Upstairs with a sense of relief. He had struggled to make his company heard above the deafening roar of Vietnam-era protest and to keep alive a certain brand of studied elegance long after the country had decided it no longer mattered. But Julius Monk was right: in a decade characterized by violence, blood had to be drawn in order to gain attention. The topics of importance in the '60s required nothing less. The small voices that remained were snuffed out rather harshly.

By the mid-'70s Warren had established himself as a writer of TV variety specials for such performers as Cher, Bette Midler, Cheryl Ladd, and Lily Tomlin. His songs and sketches proved perfectly tailored for the home audience and eventually won him two Emmys (for a pair of Tomlin shows), five additional nominations, and five Writers Guild nominations. His income rose tremendously, a fitting reward for the years spent working for Irving Haber for $125 a week.

Warren's multitude of assignments left him little time to handle his finances, so he hired a business manager and gave him full power of attorney. Years passed before he became curious about the state of his earnings. He began to investigate and learned that his trusted manager had been using his money to make private and faulty investments. The bulk of his fortune, approximately $500,000, was lost.

The news took a heavy toll on Warren's already precarious physical and emotional health. Like Irving Haber he had always been a chain smoker, and later in life developed a heart condition compounded by his hectic pace and frequent travel. In the fall of 1984 he flew to London to work on the Perry Como Christmas special. One day he did not show up for rehearsal. Members of the staff became concerned, for they knew of his rundown condition. They alerted the security manager at his hotel, who unlocked his door and found him in bed. Warren had died of a heart attack in his sleep. He was fifty-three.

New York City might never have experienced a nightclub renaissance in the '70s were it not for the famous Stonewall riot of 1969 and the advent of gay liberation. The Stonewall Inn was a bar near Sheridan Square in Greenwich Village with a flamboyant gay and lesbian clientele. One evening in June a handful of police and detectives arrived for what seemed like an ordinary raid. That night, however, customers fought back with bottles and cobblestones, set a fire, and gathered outside in a violent show of resistance. An outgrowth of the increasing antigay repression of the mid-'60s, gay lib set out to ensure that even "fairies, nances, swishes, fags and lezzes," as a *New York Daily News* editorial called the Stonewall protesters, could live as openly as a suburban couple.

This did not mean that they would be accepted as part of the mainstream; it meant that they would no longer permit the heterosexual majority and the traditional legal system to dictate their life-styles. Within three years, many old barriers had burst, and New York became "wonderfully free, loose, and trashy," to quote a maître d' of the period. "If you were gay, there was no limit to the trouble you could get into or the fun you could have, and there was nothing to worry about. We're paying for it now, I guess."

As the 1970s began, the night held greater promise for gays than ever before, encouraging them to go out more often and, by necessity, to create new places to go. Among these were dozens of intimate nightclubs. The casual climate of the times allowed little hope for a return to the days of starched white shirts, dark suits, and black dresses with pearls; the club business would have to be re-created in modern terms. Its earliest manifestation, located beneath New York's Ansonia Hotel on 74th Street and Broadway, was the Continental Baths, one of several gay bathhouses created for easy, anonymous sex. Its owner was Stephen Ostrow, an athletic middle-aged man with a mass of conditioned, sprayed, and blow-dried blonde hair. Ostrow had opened the baths with funding from his wealthy wife Joanne, an opera singer whose father had produced the hit TV series *Sky King*. Ostrow created a glitzy fun palace, rife with mirrors and Plexiglas. He converted a sprawling low-ceilinged room into a nightclub of sorts, complete with a large pool, ubiquitous ferns and other hanging plants, pillars in all the worst places, and a towel-clad male audience that wandered in and sat on chairs or on the floor. The room contained a sizable stage with a separate space for the house band, a good sound system, decent lighting, and a lighting designer named Pinky Rawsthorne, who had graduated from being the house sentinel. "My first job was to keep the women out of the area where the rooms were. I had to distinguish the women from the drag queens in the dark. I learned to go for that adam's apple right away."

In the winter of 1971 Ostrow hired a redheaded Jewish singer from Honolulu named Bette Midler to perform on Fridays and Saturdays for fifty dollars a night. Within eighteen months both she and the baths would become nationally famous, helping to set the city's nightlife on its new course. Midler had come to New York in 1965 to pursue acting. She played one of Tevye's daughters on Broadway in *Fiddler on the Roof* and won a bit part in the 1966 film *Hawaii* before drifting into nightclub work. Between brief appearances at the Bitter End and the Improv she worked as a hatcheck girl, a glove saleswoman, a waitress, and a typist.

Given her natural flamboyance, Midler could have found no better place for a full-scale debut than the baths, where listeners came to have a good time, loved the outrageous, and roared their approval. Encore piled upon encore, and sixty-minute shows often stretched to an hour and a half before acts managed to return to their "dressing room"—Ostrow's office, which was cluttered with shelves of hair products as well as a water cooler filled with Lavoris.

Midler sensed the potential of that setting and designed her act appropriately. She billed herself as "Trash with Flash," a tacit assurance that to be trashy—or to be anything once scorned by society—was now chic and could even have a flair all its own. Wearing platform shoes, toreador pants, strapless or backless tops, lamé, sequins, and garish black eye makeup, Midler transformed herself into a gleeful self-parody. She opened and closed with her signature song "Friends" and in between threw in "Boogie Woogie Bugle Boy," the Andrews Sisters hit that would soon become her first gold record; "Superstar," the Carpenters' ballad about a rock groupie whose guitarist love has moved on to the next gig and the next girl; "Marahuana," a Carmen Miranda takeoff; two early rock numbers, "Easier Said Than Done" and "Chapel of Love"; and Bob Dylan's anthem of social liberation "I Shall Be Released" ("This is for all of you . . . and for me"). Thrashing around onstage, leaning over and shaking her breasts at ringsiders, Midler belted with gusto and casually dished the audience, the baths, and even icons of the past. "You know what I remember about the '50s? Rosemary Clooney. That's what I remember. Have you seen her lately? I said to myself, oh, Rose. Rose . . . what happened, honey? She was on TV for that '50s record collection, you know? She looked like she had the whole collection under her dress!" The lamest jokes about her hairdresser or Fire Island's Cherry Grove ("I was supposed to sing there, but they couldn't find room for me in the bushes") drew thunderous laughter. She even poked fun at the distractions in the room. "I know that all of you have very short spans of attention. You tend to wander off. But listen, I have very good eyesight, and I know just who is here and who is not here, and if I happen to see that some of you are not in your respective places . . . I'm going to call your mothers!" One night she said, "I've never played a Sunday here before, but you're really nice. I know, it's the same group from Saturday. It's just too dark for me to see. I thought you had to pay more if you stayed two days. That one's hiding in the hamper with the dirty laundry. This one's hiding under the bed. This one's in room fifty." To a solemn customer at ringside: "Laugh, you muthafucka, you're sittin' in the first row!"

Crass? Of course. Exploitative? Maybe, but Midler certainly knew how to read an audience. For the crowd at the Continental she could do no wrong. The spirit of the '70s shone through her performances: the go-to-hell outspokenness, the party mood in which sadness was just a passing note, the eagerness to try anything at least once, whatever the results. Her indifference to taboos about vulgarity and tastelessness was not original; after-hours comediennes such as Belle Barth and Rusty Warren had long ago exhausted the power of shock value. But Midler's natural authority made it all seem purposeful, funny, even inoffensive.

No popular female performer in memory could match her empathy with gay audiences, including Judy Garland, who basked in their adoration but spoke about it hatefully offstage. But Midler let them know she was as much a "misfit" as they were. By now homosexual behavior in New York may no longer have been illegal, but homophobia had surfaced, as the nation was forced to confront a minority that many had preferred to ignore. The emotional conflicts inherent in homosexuality showed no signs of subsiding either, and Midler mined this to the hilt. "I was playing to people who are always on the outside looking in," she told *Newsweek* (December 17, 1973). "To create the semblance of someone like that can be wonderful. And so I created the character of The Divine Miss M. She's just a fantasy, but she's useful at showing people what that outsider's perspective is."

Midler fed off their enthusiasm. As she said in *Time* (December 31, 1976), "They gave me the courage to be tacky, cheesy, to take risks. They encouraged my spur-of-the-moment improvisations." She even offered herself as a protective mother figure. "When you go out on the street and they hurt you and don't tell you why, remember you have a home with Miss M at the Continental." Some critics dismissed her as another fag hag, a camp figure demeaning to gays, but even they acknowledged her tremendous raw talent. No mere caricature could sing ballads with so much heart or uncover such a unique sense of the ridiculous in everyday life. Years after hearing her at the Downstairs at the Upstairs, Ahmet Ertegun, who produced her first recordings at Atlantic Records, commented in the *New York Daily News* (November 4, 1979), "People of all types—grandmothers, couples, drag queens, everyone was screaming and jumping up and down on tables for this woman. You could discern a great wit there—she was trying to appear raunchy and tasteless *and* exude a certain elegance, and she pulled it off. What she had was *style*."

Midler's early shows benefited from the piano and arrangements of Barry Manilow, Ostrow's house pianist in 1971 and 1972. Manilow had previously worked as a vocal coach and accompanist and as musical director for several Ed Sullivan specials. Midler had already appeared at the baths when he came aboard. As he told Gerrit Henry in *After Dark* (June 1976):

> Usually a singer got two rehearsals at the Baths. Well, Bette called for an extra rehearsal. "Oh, yeah? Who's gonna pay for it?" "Steve will pay." "Okay, come on over."
>
> And she did, and it was death. I thought I was hot shit, just coming back from the Sullivan gig, and she had just come back from killin' 'em as an opening act at Mr. Kelly's, so she thought *she* was hot stuff. Bette did not impress me at my home that afternoon, and I did not impress her. We met again Thursday at the Baths—same thing. Saturday afternoon—we didn't have a good time. Then Saturday night she came on and I had never seen anything like it. I was crying during the ballads, laughing at her jokes, playing my ass off at the piano! I was feeling this energy four feet from me—a comet, a meteor. I went backstage and said, "Whoa, how did you *do* that?" She said, "Oh, really, did you like it?"

Ironically, Manilow's own solo act flopped there, partly because he had not yet developed into an interesting performer and partly because few men were accepted on that stage.

The extraordinary press for Midler enabled Ostrow to book Sarah Vaughan, Cab Calloway, Lillian Roth, Melba Moore, and even the retired Metropolitan Opera star Eleanor Steber. He arranged a series of "black towel nights" in which customers watched the show in a black towel and black bow tie. A few newcomers besides Midler made a strong impression, notably Laura Kenyon, a fearless singer with a rich, robust voice, a superior jazz-oriented repertoire, and a comic sense almost as wild as Midler's.

Nevertheless, the baths were not to be mistaken for a serious listening room. Some performers were amused by the novelty of the setting, but others bristled at the realization that they were there mainly as an adjunct to sex. Joanne Beretta, who normally commanded concert-hall attention, found the experience maddening. "I hated it, I hated everything about it. It was hot as hell in there, people were lying around, they were high, it was all unfocused. At one point I said, 'I'm shocked! I can't believe there are so many boys in the pool without their bathing caps!' And they thought I really meant it."

During later appearances there by Midler and others, regular customers resented having to push their way through fully dressed couples who had come to hear the show and ogle the gays as if at a sideshow. "It began to feel like the lobby of Bloomingdale's," says one patron. They grew disgusted and took their business elsewhere, and the Continental Baths closed and was replaced by Plato's Retreat, a sex club for heterosexuals.

Many of Midler's early friends and supporters complained that she cut them off after reaching the big time. At a New Year's Eve concert at New York's Philharmonic Hall she bid a bold farewell to her gay audience, thanking them for getting her where she was but telling them that she had to move on. "Who could blame her?" says a colleague. "She realized that being Queen of the Faggots wasn't enough."

If Midler gave the nightclub renaissance its biggest single push, she also left in her wake a rash of imitators who tried to copy her raunchiness but possessed none of her charisma. "Self-expression" became an end in itself, whether or not one had anything meaningful to express. Asked by David Tipmore of the *Village Voice* (September 15, 1975) to describe the ideal nightclub act for a newcomer, vocal coach and accompanist James Litt said, "The main thing for the young performer to concern himself with is 'I-Am-Me.' Don't try to be somebody else. If you've got pimples, go on with pimples. If you're fat, go on fat." As a result, most nightclubs were crowded with unskilled poseurs who won praise for their daring and "honesty" at a time when these qualities were often confused with actual talent. Old pros such as Murray Grand were dismayed. "The '70s were a time when you could get up on a stage and fart, and critics would write about what a natural performer you were."

Between 1972 and 1982 at least forty intimate clubs opened and closed, along with a multitude of bars and discos. Recalls Gene Bland, a staff member at Backstage and Onstage, two prominent rooms of the period, "There was no end to the nightlife, beginning when nightlife should begin, at ten or eleven o'clock. You could go class, you could go sleaze, and the worst price you had to pay was a hangover or hepatitis. People would sometimes call you in tears saying they'd found out they had the clap and had given it to you. I'd say, 'I'd rather have the clap than a cold.' I'd go to my doctor and get a couple of shots, and the clap would be gone in thirty-six hours. I might carry around a cold for a week.

"On a Friday night we never wondered, 'My God, what are we gonna do tonight?' It was, 'Which two shows should we see? We can catch the early show here and then run and see the late show there.' I mean good acts in a club where you would be reasonably comfortable and have a fairly good time. I'm not talking about hanging out in a piano bar, which you could do too."

Countless young performers were desperate for exposure—for a stepping-stone to Broadway, television, or movies. More specifically, to stardom. New York had not had such a stepping-stone in several years, but Midler's success suggested that fame could once more be won in a small club. These rooms could also refuel fading café and musical comedy careers. The nostalgia craze was soaring, creating an audience eager to give the old stars the attention that they craved. It is no surprise that so many would-be entrepreneurs smelled a fast buck.

The vogue that followed gained a lot of its momentum from the motion picture *Cabaret*, released in February 1972. It glamorized the decadence and impending tragedy of '30s Berlin, offering as an emblem the mythical Kit Kat Club, whose walls seemed to shut out the "prophet of doom" while enclosing a party that felt as if it would go on forever. "The movie served as an inspirational directive," wrote David Tipmore, "not only for the show-business gypsy but for all those who aspired to being *peripatetic*, *poetic* and *chic*. Meaning: wintergreen nails over the steno pad. 'Come to the Fabergé' in the drugstore window. Hundreds of articles on decadence. ('Divine decadence, darling,' said Liza Minnelli as Sally Bowles.) Hundreds of articles on bisexuality." One club opened after another: Reno Sweeney, the Grand Finale, Brothers and Sisters and the Ballroom (two restaurants turned nightclubs), Upstairs at the Spindletop, Gypsy's, Once Upon a Stove, Seesaw, Tramps, the Bushes, Barbarann, Les Mouches—the list goes on. Arthur Bell of the *Village Voice* dubbed them "the K-Y Circuit," a catchy nickname for a field dominated by gays. Several reasons are given: intimate clubs gave men the freedom to express "feminine" emotions; within the nightclub subculture they were surrounded by other homosexuals with a similar interest; they could bask in the presence of the old leading ladies they loved. Margaret Whiting offers another popular theory. "It was the Rex Reed syndrome," she says, "the young boy who grew up in a Southern town, whose mother would take him shopping with her. He'd say, 'Hey, mama, I wanna go to the movies.' He grew up watching Esther Williams swim, and he fell in love with movies. These were people who dealt in fantasies. Guys from small towns all came to big towns so they could express them."

Expressing fantasies became the keynote of the '70s. Some involved notoriety, others wealth, still others freedom of behavior. Often they were enacted recklessly. Several of the new clubs were opened with Mafia money and run with boundless enthusiasm—but little taste or business sense.

Perhaps the most celebrated of these rooms was Reno Sweeney, named after the character created by Ethel Merman in Cole Porter's *Anything Goes*. Lewis Friedman, a Columbia University graduate, opened it in October 1972 with a vague notion of bygone glamour inspired by Marlene Dietrich movies. He and Eliot Hubbard, who handled the room's publicity, took over an old steak house on West 13th Street and furnished it with objects from their apartments. On the bare brick walls of the outer bar hung a series of posters advertising the acts, stylishly designed by Hubbard. In the rear showroom were eighty-six hard black chairs that looked as if they came from a thrift store. Barely edible food was served on black tables that had initials scratched on them. The wooden floor frequently needed a mop. Above the black-and-white-tiled stage hung a neon sign of a yellow-and-green palm tree, a crescent moon, blue neon waves, and the words "The Paradise Room."

Friedman tried to pretend that he had reinvented chic, and his maître d' characterized Reno's as a "supper club" with "country elegance." But most of their customers had never been exposed to traditional elegance and did not particularly care. ("Who could face the formalized stiffness required of true elegance?" wondered one writer.) Jeans were a conservative uniform there; even Friedman walked around in an enormous pair of sneakers that added an inch or two to his short frame. Everything about the club put its youthful, post-hippie following at ease in a way that the Blue Angel would never have done.

The acts were anyone Friedman thought nostalgic, bizarre, or famous enough to fill the room. They included showbiz veterans (Cab Calloway, Barbara Cook, Blossom Dearie, Maxine Andrews), actresses taking a stab at club performing (Geraldine Fitzgerald, Diane Keaton, Ronee Blakley, Sally Kellerman), pop-rock singers (Janis Ian, Phoebe Snow), a handful of newcomers who won all the renown predicted for them (Peter Allen, Melissa Manchester, the Manhattan Transfer, Meatloaf), and a gallery of curiosities ranging from *Gone with the Wind*'s featured actress Butterfly McQueen to—in the words of Eliot Hubbard in the *Village Voice* (July 23, 1980)—"strippers, jugglers, transvestites, my former college professor of Ancient Greek Tragedy, an all-girl orchestra, an airline stewardess who levitated, [and] a showgirl who had been the Toast of the Great White Way when she headlined Earl Carroll's Vanities of 1928."

At Reno's, distinctions among such groups melted. The pseudo-French pretensions of singer Jane Olivor (née Linda Cohen of Brooklyn) held as much validity as the artistry of Barbara Cook or Anita O'Day. Cab Calloway, belting "Minnie the Moocher" in a performance that glittered with '30s showmanship, seemed as campy to them as transvestite Holly Woodlawn of Andy Warhol fame, who donned an apron and sang the Fanny Brice classic "Cooking Breakfast for the One I Love."

The favorite acts, however, involved the customers. Seldom had an audience so eagerly offered its participation, whether by assisting singer-actress Ellen Greene in the refrain of the risqué "He's My Man of War" or by joining in a question-and-answer session with Butterfly McQueen. One sensed a roomful of egos desperate to share the spotlight, and star customers did just that. Friedman reserved table D-5 for the likes of Liza Minnelli, Mick and Bianca Jagger, Diana Ross, and Bette Midler, illuminating it during the performance with a soft, hidden spotlight.

The eager crowds groomed the styles of several acts, notably Peter Allen, Reno's most illustrious alumnus. When he debuted there in 1973, Allen was known mainly as the husband of Minnelli and as half of Chris and Peter Allen, a singing duo who opened many of Judy Garland's '60s concerts. In 1972 Allen recorded two obscure albums of original songs, and when Ellen Greene sang a few of them to warm response, Friedman offered Allen his own engagement.

In his first act Allen just sat at the piano and sang, with little of his later flamboyance. "The same people kept coming back and back," he says. "I could see the audience wanted to have a good time, so I stopped singing so many sad ballads and switched to a lot of up-tempo things. We didn't have a drummer, so I got the audience to clap and do the beat to keep time. Then I started to get up and dance around to the stomping of their feet. You would look out and see boys holding boys' hands and girls holding girls' hands. When you did a ballad, the most unlikely combinations gravitated toward each other."

Other acts drew on Reno's audience for emotional support. One was Judith Cohen, a winner in the club's Monday night talent showcases, during which unknowns competed for full engagements. A homely, overweight girl with chalky skin and wild red hair, Cohen seemed to thrust her insecurities at her listeners in a desperate attempt at mutual catharsis. "Welcome to the experience of my life," she beckoned, as she tore out the viscera of a tortured adolescence with such songs as Janis Ian's "At Seventeen." "I look at all of you," she moaned, "and we're all so different. But I believe there is a human denominator—that we are all vulnerable." Perhaps so, but Cohen was merely shrill, artless, and undisciplined, a welter of tears and hysteria. Nonetheless, she had an undeniable appeal for certain lonely souls who saw in her the tragic figure that they perceived themselves to be.

Cohen illustrated how secondary simple talent and professionalism had become. The key to popularity now lay in reaching an audience at its own level, in giving them something to identify with—something they could do themselves if they had the chance. If you sang, an untrained "natural" sound fell pleasingly upon their ears. If you wrote songs, write them the way your listeners spoke. Give their egos a chance to shine, just as you did your own. For wasn't it ego that impelled Diane Keaton to sing Rodgers and Hart and Gershwin so badly that it was a relief when she reverted to speaking the lyrics? Didn't ego inspire actress Joan Hackett to explain about herself, "She sings, she dances!" and then, as David Tipmore wrote in the *Village Voice* (August 22, 1974), to "shuffle through a waltz clog, tell a story about a dinner party that she once gave in Los Angeles, and sing a couple of Dory Previn songs in a weak '40s warble"? Most of all, didn't ego give Hubbard's strippers, jugglers, and airline stewardesses the courage to stand before a paying audience, armed with nothing more than chutzpah?

Or was it the fact that this same paying audience applauded them?

THE LONGEST-LIVED of the new clubs was the Grand Finale at West 70th Street. Loudly decorated in red and black, the room seemed ill chosen for its purposes, full of pillars that blocked sight lines. But it accommodated about 250 customers at tables and at a bar opposite the stage, which became popular among chorus boys who could not afford the $5 table minimum.

Harry Endicott, who ran the club, usually booked young performers of local interest, but also managed to attract Bernadette Peters, Sarah Vaughan, Dorothy Collins, Mimi Hines, and dancer-choreographer Peter Gennaro. None of them, however, made a greater impact than Chita Rivera, featured in Broadway's *West Side Story* and *Bye Bye Birdie*; her energetic hour of dancing and singing became the talk of the town. Ultrarehearsed, fashionably tasteless, and as phony as a wooden nickel, Rivera's act gave another example of how to please a theatrically inclined New York audience of the day.

No one could deny its slick packaging, which included special material and direction by John Kander and Fred Ebb, choreography by the late Ron Field, and a pair of chorus boys in skintight pants. Nor could one ignore Rivera's limitless ebullience and musical comedy savvy. A synthesis of Las Vegas and Fire Island, her act commingled all the hype of both places. Writer Fran Lebowitz, no nightclub habituée, was bemused by what she saw. "The Grand Finale is very large and ungainly," she wrote in *Interview* (February 1975). "It is very red and very black and while I have never been to one, the Grand Finale looks like a gay bar in Dayton, Ohio . . . The crowd appeared to be composed entirely of boys who have been on unemployment ever since *West Side Story* closed in 1959."

Rex Reed praised Rivera's performance in the *New York Daily News* (January 10, 1975):

> The bongos throb, two libidinous chorus gypsies in white cling pants chant "Nothin' could be sweeta than to sing and dance with Chita in the evenin'," and we're off to the races. Chita Rivera has a face like an oatmeal cookie with a smile formed by a child's spilled crayola box, her feet have wings, and her show is slick and sassy.

Its centerpiece was "Trash," a showstopper written for her by Kander and Ebb that voiced the battle cry of so many in the '70s: "It's simple as ABC / I like trashy people / Trashy people like me":

Wanna know what trash means?
Trash means being free!

Wanna know what it looks like?
Mida-mida-mida-*ME!*

Midway through the song Rivera gestured toward one of her dancers. "I love buns," she declared. "It has nothing to do with the dance world. I just love pretty buns, and Chris has pretty buns. Chris, would you say something, please? Just say something that is truly, truly trashy."

"Ann-Margret!"

"I love it! Ooooh, I *love* Ann-Margret. She's the epitome of trash. She would be the first one to admit it."*

Her other dancer chimed in. "I've got one, I've got one! Frederick's of Hollywood."

"Hands and holes," cooed Rivera, "just nothing but hands and holes. Have you noticed how the trash just rolls from my tongue? You know why? Because I never, *ever* will be accused of being closet trash."

Rivera approached a table. "Hello. I know *you're* trash. Because you're sitting next to trash. And you came to see trash." One evening she spotted the man who had introduced her to off-Broadway audiences in 1955.

"Oh, there's Ben Bagley. I know you're trash."

Bagley rose to his feet in a rage. "I MOST CERTAINLY AM NOT TRASH! I'll have you know my grandmother was a D.A.R. and . . ."

Rivera froze and her accompanist Peter Howard stopped playing, his hands held motionless above the keyboard. "Somebody hit me in the head with a roll," remembers Bagley, "and those rolls at the Grand Finale were hard as rocks."

Finally Rivera walked over to a boy seated nearby.

"Well, you're trash, aren't you?"

"Oh, *yes*, Chita, I'm trash! I'm trash!"

Other veterans held forth more tastefully at Brothers and Sisters at West 46th Street. Initially a restaurant, the room turned over its back room to entertainment in April 1973 and for several months booked unknown pop and theatre singers. In 1974 it began to present some of

* Ironically, however, whereas Rivera would continue to perform much the same act nearly twenty years after its heyday, Ann-Margret matured into an actress of depth and versatility, as evidenced by *Carnal Knowledge* and the TV version of *A Streetcar Named Desire*.

the great ladies of Broadway and nightclubs past, among them Dolores Gray, Julie Wilson, Vivian Blaine, Hildegarde, Greta Keller, Barbara Cook, Helen Gallagher, and Sylvia Syms. They sang on a small stage at the front of a long, narrow, undecorated room, accompanied by a tinny spinet. "The place looked like an air-raid shelter," says William Roy, a frequent pianist there. "It was a terrible firetrap. There was no back exit, only a narrow front door, and we were always terrified to be there because if there had been a fire we would never have been able to get out. It was an old, rundown building, and David Vangen, who owned it, lived on the third floor in complete disarray with his lover and their pet chimpanzee, who bit me once." On the second floor was a piano bar–restaurant whose bare brick walls and fireplace gave it the feeling of a tenement living room. Broadway gypsies came to perform, and occasionally the evening's star would walk upstairs after the show and sing, then chat with fans. Many unemployed actors will never forget the sense of "belonging" that the club gave them.

It may seem odd that such a dilapidated place could attract so many stars, but most of them had worked little in recent years and appreciated the attention. Past their commercial primes, they were still marvelous entertainers who wore their decades of experience proudly. To sing for a roomful of adoring fans—largely young men who had grown up with their recordings and who greeted even their rarest numbers with orgasmic sighs and cheers—gave their egos a much-needed boost. As singer-actress Karen Morrow, the youngest of this group, told her audience: "I was beginning to feel a little . . . unloved . . . unwanted . . . and more specifically . . . *unknown*." Dolores Gray, who starred on Broadway in the '50s in *Two on the Aisle* and *Destry Rides Again* as well as in a number of Hollywood musicals, appeared at the club after a successful comeback in the London production of *Gypsy*; prior to that she had spent seven years in retirement on a California horse farm. Her opening night at Brothers and Sisters ran almost thirty minutes overtime, as fans cried, "We missed you!" and "Welcome home!" Finally she told them, "Unless I say good night I'm gonna have to start scrambling eggs in the kitchen!"

Barbara Cook began a nightclub and concert career there that brought her wider renown than she had ever known on Broadway. And singer Julie Wilson re-created some of the glamour of a stylish era of New York clubs, her hair sleeked back into a chignon with a white gardenia, and her sylphlike figure poured into some of the same beaded gowns that she had worn during her fifteen years at the Maisonette Room of the St. Regis Hotel. Wilson still relied heavily on her naughty-lady special material of that period, but her renditions of Cole Porter's "I Loved Him" and Rodgers and Hart's "This Funny World" gave evidence of the definitive nightclub artist she would become in the '80s.

Some of these women made light of the seediness. "You think the flowers have gotten a little stale since opening night?" asked Karen Morrow, as she glanced at a bouquet that seemed to have been reclaimed from a trash bin. And on a sweltering July evening Barbara Cook made her entrance in the non–air-conditioned club saying, "How is everybody? Welcome to the equator."

To be sure, some stars sank to the level of their surroundings. Helen Gallagher demonstrated how to lose a Brothers and Sisters audience within thirty seconds when she announced, "Everybody here probably thinks I'll sing all my old showtunes. Well, that's not true, because I don't remember any of them. And that means I'd have to learn them all again, and I find that very boring. So rest assured, there's one person here tonight who's not gonna be bored—it's me." Audiences did not find off-key renditions of "Danny Boy" and "Surabaya Johnny" a worthy substitute.

Such missteps were overshadowed by many other heartwarming evenings. Near the end of her December 1974 appearances Karen Morrow paused for a toast. "Lift your glasses to your neighbor. I want to hear a clink, just a little clink. *Oh*, that's a nice sound!" By the time she finished Noel Coward's "I'll See You Again," the shabbiness of the room had faded, holiday tensions were eased, and time seemed to stand still, uniting a roomful of strangers in a moment that they would not soon forget.

THE BULK OF THE CIRCUIT, as it was called, comprised the "showcase rooms," where unknowns appeared for a night, two nights, or sometimes a week. Their dream, of course, was discovery—perhaps not by David Merrick but by some lesser light who would cast them in a road company of *Auntie Mame* or in the chorus of *Chicago*. These clubs drew so many young hopefuls that even in 1977, when audiences had begun to diminish, new rooms kept opening, competition to perform in them continued, and small publications churned out an ever more ludicrous brand of hype. Cabaret at Cecil published an ad for singer Harriet Leider, an enormously overweight camp figure known as the Divine Diva. It included a lengthy quote from *Michael's Thing*, a gay "going out" guide distributed free in local bars:

> Wonderful, a definite "must-see" . . . She is a dynamite songstress . . . a combination of great singing and incisive dialogue . . . As she said, "If you've found me rude, crude and totally tasteless, wait till my second show, you ain't seen nothin' yet!" . . . You could hear the cheers for blocks.

The ad announced Cabaret at Cecil's "Premier Open Stage" policy. "YOU Present & Promote Performers, YOU Discover and Launch the STARS of 'GALAXY '77 ShowPeople'—COME now and bring a performer who you believe can 'Shine With The Stars.' WHO WILL MAKE IT THIS YEAR?"

No one made it that year at Cabaret at Cecil, nor at Tramps, Gypsy's, the Bushes, Trude Heller's, Spindletop, Reno Sweeney, or any of the other rooms touted as launching pads for "young, fresh" talent. Most of them had acquired such a reputation for mediocrity that no reputable agent or casting director would go near them. Quality of performance seldom mattered in these showcases; the only requirement was to bring in enough friends and family to fill the room. It was a disturbing change from the Blue Angel or the Bon Soir, where faithful audiences came to see a reliable flow of talented, professional performers. The men who booked them were expert judges of club performance and never hesitated to insist that improvements be made. Substantial time and money were spent on clothes, rehearsal, material, musical arrangements, and on the rooms themselves, which were designed to focus attention on the acts. If Julius Monk or Herbert Jacoby sensed hidden potential, he gave the act weeks to develop. As a result, casting scouts came to these clubs every week, and discoveries were made.

John Lombardi of the *Village Voice* noted how little of that atmosphere remained as he took in the ambience at Reno Sweeney. The audience reminded him of "extras in a movie they seemed to be writing themselves," and the waiters made themselves even more prominent:

Pretty soon you see that they're not waiters at all. They're here to stand around and have a good time, to *shoop* along with the music ... [They] look good on the Paradise Room floor, their Torso T-swathed silhouettes slim against the background of candlelight and fresh flowers, below the Pacific Moon Reno Sweeney logo.

I tell Lewis Friedman that I think Reno Sweeney's is the Continental Baths [disguised] as The St. Regis Roof.

Friedman is shocked. "How can you *say* that?" Friedman has on a Torso T, a studded belt, and pants as tight as Oscar Mayer weiners. "I want my waiters to have personality, to talk back if it's called for, and I want them to *blend* with the decor, if you know what I mean. But you're suggesting that they're the show, that I want them to be bitchy ..."

"But aren't they?"

"No!"

Friedman lights another cigarette. His gaze is troubled. He exhales smoke through his nose with the attitude of a man spraying mosquito fogger on a county road in Ship Bottom, New Jersey. "Reno Sweeney exists because of talent," Friedman says very carefully. "We're responsible for bringing back quality live entertainment in this city ... I guess Steve Ostrow at the Tubs is responsible too, but that's all we have in common. Talent is what sells this place, not gayness. I let my boys wear earrings, but not *dangle* earrings."

... I ask what major acts have developed at Reno's, or the Continental Baths, or any of the little clubs that I think of as the Bathhouse Circuit—100-seat nightspots that opened in major cities in the last few years to service audiences with gay sensibilities, and people who want to ogle said audiences.

Friedman looks incredulous. "Why, Bette Midler!" he tells me.

Who else?

Now Friedman is getting pissed off. There are *hundreds* of examples: Novella Nelson. Patti Smith. Manhattan Transfer. Holly Woodlawn.

I tell Friedman that I think all Bathhouse Circuit performers caricature professionalism. The women are so exaggerated *as* women, they're camp. If the men have a common denominator, it's affectation ... It's hard to imagine them in the real nightclubs of the past ...

Friedman just looks at me. "The only thing they lack is exposure," he says icily. Like a cash register closing, Friedman's face rings the conversation up.

It all constituted one of the more hopeless fantasies of the '70s. One was still grateful for the chance to hear Barbara Cook, Margaret Whiting, Anita O'Day, Julie Wilson, and the handful of other pros, young and old. As for the rest, more than one observer likened their acts to "jerking off," a description carried out when Whiting's lover, gay-porn star Jack Wrangler, gave an "act" at the Grand Finale. Wrangler entered fully clothed and made halfhearted attempts to sing and play the piano, admitting after each that "this isn't the real Jack Wrangler." Finally he revealed "the real Jack Wrangler" when he turned around and pretended to take out his penis and masturbate to climax.

DURING THE 1970s another set of rooms made an appeal to a more sophisticated, mature audience. Foremost among them was the Café Carlyle, a dining room and piano lounge within the fashionable Hotel Carlyle on Madison Avenue and 76th Street. The Café had opened in 1955 with Hungarian pianist George Feyer, whose schmaltzy Viennese melodies and showtunes provided a pleasant enough background for the supper and conversation of an older society crowd. Then, as now, the café was the most elegantly appointed room of its kind, highlighted by wall murals by the great French painter Marcel Vertès. It was also one of the most soporific until 1968, when Bobby Short stepped in to replace Feyer during what Short calls his "fatal vacation." Like most of his colleagues Short had suffered a number of lean years courtesy of Beatlemania, and he did not take this opportunity lightly. "I did my best to make those two weeks as successful as anything I'd done," he says. He called upon every wealthy or powerful figure he knew, and so many dropped by that when Feyer's contract ended shortly after, the room became Short's.

It was the setting that Short had always dreamed of, patronized by royalty, high society, presidents, old money, new money. By Jacqueline Onassis, Nancy Reagan, Elizabeth Taylor. Until then Short had enjoyed the sort of cult following known to many café singers: one that could fill a small room for the early show and occasionally the late, make possible some obscure albums, and create little celebrity outside New York. He wanted more, and knew that the Carlyle would give him the opportunity to endear himself to a moneyed white audience. Colleagues had joked for years that Short did not know that he was black; Ben Bagley even wrote in an album biography that Short was born "in the fashionable section of Danville, Illinois." But the fact remained that no singer-pianist deserved this most prestigious of jobs more than he. Decades of experience struggling nightly in clubs to make himself noticed had molded Short into a commanding *performer* and not just a purveyor of background music. The influences of his idols—the vivacity of Fats Waller and Cab Calloway; Duke Ellington's suave, refined manner; the supreme dignity and self-assurance of Ellington's late vocalist Ivie Anderson—combined to give Short a polish that none of his colleagues could equal. And unlike most of them he presented a genuine act, with carefully planned patter and an impeccable, thoughtfully paced repertoire of songs by Porter, Gershwin, Coward, Rodgers and Hart, and other masters.

The Carlyle was just as excited by Short's potential there, and the fortune that they spent on publicity was rewarded: interest in his work had not run out after twenty years. Short's engagement marked a rare union of an intimate café entertainer and a rich society audience—a crowd who had never cared much about that style of performing. They still did not, but they adored the trappings that Short brought to it. Nearly every show became comparable to opening night at the opera: a justification for wealthy patrons to outdress one another, to be seen, maybe to impress an important client. Short's genuine fans could not bear to sit among one of the rudest, most disruptive audiences that a club performer had ever faced. But along with money and social standing apparently came the license to behave any way one wanted. Carlyle habitués assumed that *they* were the raison d'être of the evening, and in this respect the room differed little from Reno Sweeney or the Grand Finale.

Those who knew Short were not surprised at how well he played the game. Others could be forgiven for raising an eyebrow at his offstage chatter, which *New York* magazine reporter Marie Brenner overheard on several evenings (December 19, 1983):

> "See you in Hobe Sound!" "I'll be amused if . . ." "Did you see Gloria's bib?" "*Tellement Mexique.*" "Oh, Mrs. Glazier!" "An hour out of São Paulo . . ." All of this Eurojabber coming from Bobby Short, and only Bobby Short, table-hopping before the actual performance begins because he understands exactly what his audience

> wants. They want *him*. Not just his music or his rasping vibrato—they want his sophistication, gossip, and epicene remarks, which tumble out like vintage Porter. Night after night in the Café Carlyle it is the same phenomenon, the do-nothings and the go-everywheres, the rich and social flocking to see the saloon singer who is their darling and who is raking in $9,000 a week plus a percentage of the house. But it is still impossible to tell who is pandering more to whom. And it really doesn't matter, because Bobby Short has become indistinguishable from the Café and the Carlyle itself. He certainly understands the mores of the neighborhood. "New York is so phony, all you need to make it here is a few good suits and real jewelry," he once confided as he changed shirts between shows.

Whereas Mabel Mercer gave the elegant lyrics and melodies of Porter, Coward, and Rodgers and Hart a warm human quality that illuminated the humblest romance or heartbreak, Short made them seem like caviar for the general—a commodity in whose presence anyone became grander, more sophisticated. The Carlyle experience became "a kind of shorthand for writers, to evoke a mood," Short said. "All they have to say is, 'We went to the Carlyle to hear Bobby Short,' and they've saved pages of description."

By the early '70s Short had become a national symbol of "style," "elegance," and "good taste." To Madison Avenue kingpins he became a symbol of money. They hired him for a series of TV commercials for Charlie perfume and for his friend Gloria Vanderbilt's line of designer jeans. The rewards were unheard of for a "saloon singer," as Short called himself: a huge midtown apartment, a personal secretary, a house in the south of France, and a life-style that cost more and more to maintain. Short's yearly salary demands pushed the Carlyle's cover charge ever upward: $20, $25, $35. It seemed as if those songs, and his highbrow treatment of them, were a luxury that only the rich could afford.

THERE WAS ANOTHER AUDIENCE, comfortable rather than affluent, who had lived in New York during the 1950s nightclub heyday and regretted its passing. Now middle-aged, it had a natural respect for the finer performers of the past, unlike many younger clubgoers who tended to regard them merely as antiques. Fortunately, several veterans tried to re-create that golden age.

One of the first efforts was a 1972 television special produced by South Carolina Educational Television entitled "An Evening with Mabel Mercer, Bobby Short and Friends." Filmed on a studio set designed to look like a sprawling East Side living room, the show was hosted by critic and columnist George Frazier, an unashamed snob who bemoaned "living in a time when the world was awry, when a sense of style was vanishing, when taste was succumbing to tawdriness, when slobs from Seventh Avenue were beginning to punish the parquet at El Morocco, and Le Pavillon was presuming to serve frozen orange juice."

Indeed, the show gave a sense of a stylish era on the verge of slipping through the fingers of the few who still cared. The quietly dominating presence was Mercer, of course, then seventy-two and on the brink of a new flowering. Bobby Short sang enchantingly and spoke pompously. ("De*li*cious!" he exclaimed after Mercer sang "These Foolish Things." "Just *grand*!") Among the friends seated around them were composer Alec Wilder; Cam Walter, widow of the sorely missed Cy Walter, who had died of cancer in 1968; Bart Howard; and William Roy—a group whose maturity and sophistication mirrored the audience that this music had always had.

Also produced in South Carolina was a forty-part radio series called *American Popular Song*, first broadcast from 1976 to 1978 on National Public Radio. Hosted by Wilder and based on his book of the same name, it saluted the great pop songwriters and some of their finest interpreters, including Short, Tony Bennett, Anita Ellis, and Thelma Carpenter. Pianist-arranger Loonis McGlohon provided the accompaniment and acted as co-host. Many of the singers were lesser known but still cherished, among them Teddi King, a Boston-born pop-jazz singer whose rich, honeyed contralto was characterized by a fast vibrato and a throb that lent it a uniquely moving quality. Another was Irene Kral, a onetime big-band vocalist who had matured into a superb, no-nonsense interpreter of ballads. The sister of Roy Kral (of Jackie and Roy), she sang of romance not in the breathless, wistful manner of a swing-era canary but as a woman who entered into it with her head as well as her heart. Tragically both King and Kral died in the late '70s, before either had reached the age of fifty: King of the debilitating and incurable disease lupus, Kral of cancer.

The most highly touted guest was Mabel Mercer, once more a happily accessible treasure of New York nightlife. A 1972 engagement at the newly opened St. Regis Room atop the St. Regis Hotel marked her return; prior to that Mercer had not played a New York club since the Café Carlyle in 1969. More than ever her superb grace and refinement stood out, at a time when such assets were out of fashion. Encountering it in Mercer, critics all but handed her a crown and scepter. "The *grande dame* of the supper clubs," "the reigning monarch of that after-dark world," "the grand duchess of song"—such titles embarrassed her slightly. When her longtime companion Harry Beard called her a living legend, Mercer merely said, "It makes me *veddy ner*vous."

In the mid-'70s she was showered with enough awards and recognition to make up for a lifetime of cult-figure obscurity. In 1975 Boston's Berklee College of Music granted her an honorary doctorate; that year *Stereo Review* featured her on its cover and gave her its first annual award of merit. Five of her old albums were reissued, making available nearly her entire recorded catalog. And at her gala seventy-fifth-birthday party at the St. Regis Roof, a plaque was unveiled renaming the St. Regis Room the Mabel Mercer Room.

While hardly unaware of the impression she had made on so many lives, Mercer brushed over it, changing the subject when anyone paid her a grand compliment. If pressed, she replied self-effacingly. "As long as they're willing to listen, I'm willing to screech at them," she told a Boston interviewer.

Mercer was enormously dedicated to her art, but her heart resided upstate at her country farm, Red Rock. No amount of hyperbole went to her head. She continued to make her own dresses, travel by train ("At my age, what's the hurry?"), and put every cent she could into the farm. In 1974 she told Richard Dyer of the *Boston Globe*, "After I bought my house I never really wanted to leave. Every time an opportunity came up, the house would need a repair, and there the money went. And I would regret spending any money that didn't go into the house, because one day I am going to have to settle down and live there all the time."

Even in her mid-seventies, her health and vitality were astonishing. "She would climb upstairs two steps at a time," says Buddy Barnes. "You wondered where this amazing energy came from, because she never slept. And she *never* talked about mortality. She was too concerned with living." Only her vocal chords betrayed the passing years. Whereas her parched voice could once at least approximate a melody, she now reverted to *parlando*, or pitched speech. But the change mattered little. Her singing had taken on an autumnal serenity that lightened listeners' hearts rather than providing a great emotional catharsis. It assured them that the pain of everyday life left in its place a wisdom that more than justified the heartbreak. "When you're young, you cry a lot," she told William Livingstone of *Stereo Review* (February 1975). "I thought I'd never survive certain things in my life, that if it didn't go the way I wanted it to, life was not worth living. Later you learn to shrug your shoulders, and say, well, it was great fun. The young are very sensitive. They haven't experienced much, and when they're hurt they feel it very deeply. Nothing hurts like young love that's been slapped in the face. I've known a great deal of suffering, and young people sense that in my songs and are comforted by it. This all becomes easier as you grow older."

Amid engagements at London's Playboy Club and at nightspots around the United States, Mercer settled into a new East Side room called Cleo's for much of 1977. Her small but devoted audience knew full well that they should savor her while they could. Wrote Arthur Bell in the *Village Voice* (April 11, 1977):

> At Cleo's, Mabel Mercer is making banal lyrics sound like Robert Frost poetry every night. As I listened to her "Trouble Comes" I realized that she is Mother New York and we are her children, sipping Campari and soda at an hour when the milkman comes in Cleveland.

Elsewhere in town, other veterans returned to the fold. In 1976, at age eighty-one, Bricktop began a long engagement at an East 74th Street club called Soerabaja, appearing with her old friend, singer-pianist Hugh Shannon. Once more the singer-hostess held forth in the grand European manner, and those who did not understand what that meant certainly knew by the time she left. On opening night she wore a Schiaparelli gown and boa, with house slippers that cost $4.75. "When I tell people the shoes aren't custom-made, they think I'm lying. Style, darling. You're born with it. Even if it's a bitch dog, if it's there, there ain't nothing you can do to hide it."

The next year Jimmie Daniels opened a regrettably short-lived club on East 64th Street. Barney Josephson had better luck with the Cookery, an informal Village restaurant that become a jazz club when he hired pianist Mary Lou Williams. Josephson later booked other respected blues and jazz artists, among them Helen Humes, Joe Turner, and the remarkable septuagenarian blues singer Alberta Hunter, then in the midst of a much-publicized comeback.

In 1973 a new Michael's Pub opened at 211 East 55th Street, bearing no relation to a '40s piano lounge of the same name. It achieved something of the "country elegance" that Reno Sweeney tried to affect. There were two performance areas: the "Bird Cage," a small space filled with flowing greenery, where Anita Ellis returned to singing; and a larger room in which such singers as Sylvia Syms, Jackie and Roy, Irene Kral, and David Allyn performed.

Since leaving the Duplex in 1968, Jan Wallman had supported herself through bartending and other jobs. In 1976 she opened a restaurant bearing her own name at Cornelia Street, in Greenwich Village. An undecorated hole in the wall that seated just forty, it became a nightclub when singer Ronnie Welsh asked her if he could break in his new act there. The only person who made any money there was the landlord, but Wallman was happy to be back in the business, and a lot of unknown singers appreciated having a place to perform, however inauspicious.

A new minicircuit of clubs opened in other cities, including the Café Lafitte in Philadelphia, the Mocambo in San Francisco, and the Merry-Go-Round Bar at Boston's Copley Plaza Hotel. (The last got its name from the platform on which customers sat: an enormous, creaky old carousel that revolved around the performers during the show.)

Just like the old days? Not quite. The music that these boîtes championed had held limited commercial interest even in its heyday. Thirty years later only a small core of listeners remained, and few younger ones had joined their company; as a result most of these rooms languished. Jobs for singers, though somewhat easier to come by than in the '60s, were hardly plentiful, and the major record labels had dropped even such stars as Tony Bennett and Peggy Lee from their rosters. Few clubs recalled the '50s style of elegance that they hoped to recapture; things had become too expensive, and the returns were minimal. Michael's Pub is one of the only survivors of this period, having adopted a policy of booking big names whenever possible. Otherwise, the "renaissance" represented a labor of love for all concerned. This art of singing seemed fated to die with its veteran practitioners, a fear that the years since have almost confirmed.

A single new club combined the best of the old and the new with outstanding critical and commercial success. It opened in SoHo, a Manhattan neighborhood south of Houston Street, the southern border of Greenwich Village. Now primarily an artists' colony, SoHo was virtually devoid of nightlife until Greg Dawson, a Yale graduate and press agent, joined with eight partners to open a restaurant called the Ballroom on May 26, 1973. The cost: $1,500 per partner, and a rent of $800 a month. They designed the perfect image of SoHo: a long, narrow room whose high ceiling hung with blue-green mobiles, ball lights, and potted greenery, and whose white walls were lined with paintings by local artists, all for sale. The white Formica tables, generously spaced, seated seventy-five.

Despite raves for the bargain-priced food, the Ballroom got off to a slow start; its first eighteen months left Dawson and his two remaining partners $10,000 in debt. They decided to install entertainment and hired Judith Cohen, whose successful run convinced them to make the Ballroom a nightclub-restaurant.

At first, naysayers dismissed it as another room booking cultish curiosities to make a quick dollar. After Cohen came Jane Olivor, who apparently fancied herself the new Piaf. Olivor applied her pained, tremulous voice to a repertoire ranging from "Some Enchanted Evening" to such pop pabulum as "Come Softly to Me." The emotions she tried to express had all the profundity of a little girl dressing up in her mother's evening gown and high heels; nevertheless her young, mostly gay following grew large enough to take her to Carnegie Hall.

All pretension at the Ballroom was dispelled by singing comedienne Marilyn Sokol, whose credits include a memorable series of TV commercials for York Peppermint Patties, and by Chad Mitchell, formerly of the folk-singing Chad Mitchell Trio, who scored a hit in his solo nightclub debut while appealing a five-year prison sentence for allegedly smuggling 480 pounds of marijuana from Mexico to Texas. Subsequently Dawson inaugurated "Broadway at the Ballroom," in which Sheldon Harnick, Andrew Lloyd Webber, Carolyn Leigh, and other Broadway composers performed evenings of their own songs. The shows were directed by Craig Zadan, future theatrical director and coproducer of the 1983 movie *Footloose.*

An offshoot of the series was soprano Jo Sullivan's tribute to the songs of her late husband Frank Loesser, the composer of *Where's*

Charley? Guys and Dolls, and *The Most Happy Fella*, the last of which starred Sullivan. In this gemlike thirty-five-minute act she returned to performing after years of married retirement. Loesser's death had left her a multimillionairess, but her desire to keep his songs alive, coupled with her wish to sing again, convinced her to accept the Ballroom's offer.

Sullivan's seraphic singing of such Loesser ballads as "Spring Will Be a Little Late This Year" and "My Heart Is So Full of You" revealed the softer side of two of the tougher individuals in show business—a union that began when Loesser divorced his first wife to marry Sullivan. In the act she recalled their mornings: "Up at four A.M., three cups of coffee, then the required reading, the *Oxford English Dictionary*. He always joined me for breakfast at eight A.M. I had one cup of coffee and he was on his second martini. Then, to the office.

" 'Hey Frank, what are you gonna do today?'

" '*Everybody in.*' "

After marrying Loesser in 1959, Sullivan relaxed and toned down an opportunistic instinct that had become quite well known. Broadway insiders had laughed for years at a story told by Mildred Hughes, a stunning six-foot showgirl from the '30s and '40s whom Cole Porter had adored. In 1949 Hughes appeared in *As the Girls Go*, a lavish Mike Todd musical whose chorus included the demure young Sullivan. One Friday the singer phoned in to say she had the flu. She missed that weekend's performances and returned on Tuesday in a full-length mink coat. Hughes said, "My God, Jo, that must have been some bout with the flu!"

To which Sullivan snapped in her childlike voice, "Oh, shut your hole!"

Another memorable engagement came in 1977 with *The Best of New Faces*, a program of highlights from the Broadway revue series hosted by its creator, Leonard Sillman. Hoping to bring the show to Broadway, Sillman spent several years trying to raise the funds, an effort thwarted by his death in 1982. The Ballroom show featured *New Faces* alumni June Carroll, Virginia DeLuce (both '52), and Brandon Maggart ('68) as well as Ann Anello and Jeremy Wind, Sillman's newest discoveries. Their mentor remained as feisty and volatile as ever at sixty-eight, despite a heart ailment that eventually took his life. The show's eighty-minute length was problematic in a nightclub, where at least an hour was needed to seat late-show customers and serve supper. Sillman was asked to shorten it. He stepped onstage for the late show in a rage.

"Well, they asked me to *cut*," he announced. "So I'd like to cut—right out—you know? Anyway, what I'd like you all to know is, you're not gonna see a revue—you're not gonna see a cantata . . . I don't think I will go on." He stormed off.

Brandon Maggart hastily took over: "We'll be doing some of the numbers from Leonard Sillman's *New Faces*—" Back came Sillman. "Now I would like to talk to you people . . . The reviews were terribly good, we had a marvelous audience for the first show—they cheered, they screamed . . . Instead of thanking me, or thanking the cast, he said—CUT IT! . . . Now I will continue the show, because I think I *am* a professional."

"*I* asked him to cut it," says Greg Dawson. "It was too fucking long."

The rest of the run was no less eventful, as Maggart remembers. "Leonard had angina, and one evening he left his pills home. We did the first show, and the pain came on. We said, 'We can't do a second show, you're gonna die!' He said, 'No, we'll do the show!' We went out and dragged Leonard into a cab and sped through traffic to get to his house. He was lying in the backseat screaming, 'I'M DYING! I'M DYING!' We got up to his house, and he discovered he'd left his keys in his coat at the club. We got the cabdriver to take us to Lenox Hill Hospital, and they wouldn't let us in. Leonard started screaming, 'DO YOU KNOW WHO I AM?' He didn't have his prescription, but finally somebody broke a rule and gave him nitroglycerin. We got back into a cab to do the second show, and he was laughing about the whole thing."

Not all the club's presentations were so successful. Joseph Papp, artistic director of the New York Shakespeare Festival, attempted a woeful evening as a song-and-dance man, doing soft shoe and old vaudeville tunes undaunted by his apparent inability to sing, dance, or act. Friends and colleagues cheered him on, then some of them whispered among themselves about how awful the show was.

Estelle Parsons had the potential to do a superb nightclub act but under Zadan's direction wound up performing a confessional "autobiography in song" that epitomized the '70s "tell all" syndrome at its worst. By now famous as the costar of *Bonnie and Clyde* (for which she won an Oscar) and *Rachel, Rachel*, Parsons spent several hours in recorded conversation with Zadan, who fashioned her reminiscences around an ill-chosen set of standards. The show sadly misused her earthiness and wry humor, focusing instead on personal reflections better left unspoken. She recalled her troubled first marriage to a young author: "Like the night that I chased him around the house with a carving knife, and he slammed the door of his office just in time. Or the night we got home from this wonderful party when his first book was published, and I was pregnant, and he kicked me right in the stomach." True to form, critics praised the evening as "shattering," "honest," and "a delight."

More often the Ballroom allowed talented veterans to do what they did best, particularly Austrian folk singer Martha Schlamme, who presented her acclaimed interpretations of Kurt Weill in tandem with actor Alvin Epstein. And the room introduced such promising newcomers as singer Dean Pitchford, later known for his original lyrics for the movies *Fame* and *Footloose*, and Baby Jane Dexter, a hefty young woman whose lusty voice sounded like a combination of Janis Joplin, Bessie Smith, and Kate Smith.

The many piano bars during these years were tailor-made for customers who simply wanted to drink, talk, hear some old tunes, sing along if they pleased, or nurse a wound, without the formality of a show or a cover charge. "At four in the morning," recalls singer-pianist Ronny Whyte, "they'd still be there, stoned out of their minds, almost falling asleep." At the Apartment and many other rooms, Charles DeForest sang his original songs of experience as well as the best and often most neglected numbers from Broadway and Hollywood, with an emphasis on ballads for the heavy of heart. The atmosphere was lighter downtown at the Village Green, where Murray Grand sparked every evening with a bonhomie typical of the better '50s house parties. In the late '70s an East Side restaurant called David K's became a home for Hugh Shannon, who belted out standards in a growling barroom style, to the rhythm of his stomping foot. And the "sophisticated song" lived on at Crawford's, an elegant gay bar whose walls were lined with framed photographs of Joan Crawford. On duty at the piano was Ava Williams, a hearty brunette of late middle age and the queen mother of gay barflies for decades. William's risqué one-liners and reworkings of standards ("I'll be loving *yours*/Always") recalled the days of Nan Blakstone and Charley

Drew, but her dialogues with customers might have shocked even them. "Hey, honey, how's your ass?" she used to ask one regular. "Mine's a little sore tonight. My boyfriend stuck a dildo up it, and it was the kind that has a spine, you know?"

The most popular piano bar of all resided in a corner of Backstage, a restaurant in the midtown theatre district that became a second home for Ethel Merman, Liza Minnelli, Ann Miller, Debbie Reynolds, Rock Hudson, Cher, and countless other celebrities. A modern-day Stork Club without the pomp, Backstage brought showbiz lovers eye to eye with the Technicolor images on their late-night TV screens and with the living legends of Broadway. It was owned by Ted Hook, the room's host and still the quintessential starstruck kid, even though he was in his forties. Hook had danced in the choruses of many film musicals and later worked as secretary for Tallulah Bankhead, Joan Blondell, and other stars. To surround himself every night with the celebrities he worshiped was his ultimate fantasy come to life. "Ted knew all these stars, but he always had this excitement around them," says Richie Ridge, a waiter there. "He was like a little kid."

Unlike so many entrepreneurs, Hook spared no expense in designing and launching his room. The piano bar and vast dining room on the left were partitioned by flowers, with a lengthy social bar on the right. The walls were lined with photographs of Bankhead, Merman, Angela Lansbury, and other stars Hook had known. It was uncommonly elegant yet intimate enough to feel like a living room.

He opened on December 17, 1975, by offering the entire Broadway community and their friends a free three-day bar and buffet that cost thousands of dollars. Within a year demand for tables was so great that reservations had to be made days in advance, especially for Star Alley, as Hook called the front portion of the dining room. No one came for the mediocre food; they came for the atmosphere that Hook created. He was his own press agent and generated endless publicity, as staff member Gene Bland remembers. "Earl Wilson of the *New York Post* used to call every night and say, 'What have you got?' Ted would feed him items for the column. Liz Smith and Rex Reed were there all the time, and Ted was in their columns. You could hardly pick up a newspaper without finding some mention of Ted Hook's Backstage."

Every night at the peak of business Hook took over the microphone and introduced celebrities, listing their credits with the help of reference books kept on hand. "At this time it gives me great pleasure to introduce to you a woman who played the part of Bianca in the motion picture *Kiss Me, Kate*, and if it weren't for her there would never have been Technicolor or MGM, because she personifies everything that was, is, glamour. She's here tonight—Ann Miller!" He offered Backstage T-shirts, tank tops, sweatshirts, umbrellas, and canvas bags; named drinks after his regulars ("Chita Beata," after Chita Rivera, and "The Merm"); and even held "Teddy Awards" ceremonies to honor Tony Award losers and unnominated actors. The awards were custom-made battery-operated lamps designed after the spiral staircases in the old Ziegfeld Theatre. These lamps lit the restaurant's tables and became so popular that many customers tried to steal them, including a tipsy Estelle Parsons during rehearsals for her one-woman Broadway play *Miss Margarida's Way*. In the coatroom were over 500 lampshades stenciled with the names of star regulars. "People would have their secretaries call ahead to make sure their lamp would be on their table," says Bland. "Celebrities who came in unexpectedly would send the waiter to get the lampshade and take it back to the table. Ethel Merman would take Liza Minnelli's lampshade off and put hers on."

One evening Hook announced, "I don't know how to introduce these two celebrities, but they *are* MGM. Ladies and gentlemen, Miss Ann Miller and Miss Debbie Reynolds!"

"They came out from the bar and danced their way together down the aisle," says Ridge. "Fans were screaming and cheering. I thought, my God, this is like *The Wizard of Oz* come to life."

Hook's presence contributed to the room's amazing electricity. "You would walk in the door and know in a minute whether Ted was there," says maître d' Bruce Laffey. He spent much of his time darting around, introducing showbusiness guests who had arrived alone to others who shared their interests. One night he flew through the room on roller skates, zooming out the door onto 45th Street. "Somebody better go get him!" said Laffey. "He might not know how to stop!" Such antics inspired Elizabeth Taylor to call the room a circus, but most customers hated to go home. Says Steve Oxendine, another Backstage maître d': "I would literally have to turn up the lights at four A.M. and say, 'Folks, it's been real, but we're leaving here now.' "

The piano bar became just as crowded as the restaurant when Hook hired Steve Ross, a Washington-born singer-pianist with an enormous repertoire of showtunes. "There was a wonderful unspoken competition between Steve and Bobby Short," says Oxendine, "when Steve was named 'Crown Prince of the Piano Bars' by the *New York Times*. His repertoire was twice what Bobby's was. You could sit and listen to Steve and be very comfortable and relaxed and charmed without having to wade through Bobby's pretension. Bobby's pretension worked in a room like the Carlyle, but at Backstage you didn't have to deal with that." Ross's boyish vivacity and skill as an accompanist encouraged many stars to rise and perform. One night Ginger Rogers sang "But Not for Me," the George and Ira Gershwin ballad that she had introduced over forty years before on Broadway in *Girl Crazy*. The reclusive Kay Thompson literally climbed over the piano bar and made her way over to the keyboard to sing in public for one of the last times. Liza Minnelli sang Kander and Ebb's then-unknown "New York, New York" prior to the release of the film. Some stars even gave complete shows. Ventriloquist Wayland Flowers of *Hollywood Squares* fame once called to say he would be dropping by with Madame, his trashy sexagenarian puppet. In his cups, Flowers sat on the piano bar for an hour and let loose with all his best routines, such as Madame's recollection of a Hollywood party. "I finally got tired and went out to hail a cab. One pulled up. I said, 'Can you take a case of Scotch and a tray of hors d'oeuvres?' He said yes. So I threw up in the back."

A party thrown in 1983 for Debbie Reynolds on her closing night in the Broadway musical *Woman of the Year* lasted until eleven the next morning. Around midnight Reynolds got up and performed for about ninety minutes, re-creating her great MGM moments, imitating Lauren Bacall and Raquel Welch (her predecessors in the show), even ruminating on how Elizabeth Taylor had stolen her former husband, Eddie Fisher. The party dwindled until only Reynolds, producer Harry Rigby, and two friends remained. As daylight flooded in, the waiters went into the kitchen to make bacon and eggs for everyone, then went home to sleep the day away.

"It was fun, but it was all bullshit," says Gene Bland. "It was interesting to see who the assholes were and who the nice people were. I generally found that the bigger the name and the bigger the talent, the nicer the person. The assholes were the second leads, and the biggest assholes were the hangers-on. You'd never want to deal with anyone's secretary. You'd never want to deal with the faggot who takes Liza Minnelli out every chance he gets. But one of the reasons the stars came off as well as they did was that they had these people to do the dirty work for them. Somebody else bitches about the lampshade. Somebody else bitches about the table, the food. *They* never bitch about anything—except for the really awful ones with no class at all, who couldn't even maintain hangers-on."

There were glimpses of stars at their most vulnerable, particularly Richard Burton. "He used to sit at a table in the rear corner of the back room, because he loved his privacy," Bland says. "Very few people even knew he was there. He had supposedly quit drinking. There was a great deal of press about it: Burton hasn't had a drink in two weeks, three weeks, four weeks. He came in with his wife Susan Hunt and a friend. He called over his favorite waiter and said, 'Excuse me, where is the men's room?' The waiter thought this was odd because Burton had been there many times, and he knew that from his table he could go through the kitchen to the end of the bar, where the men's room was, and he didn't have to pass anyone. But the waiter told him again. Over the next two hours Burton had to go to the men's room five times. Well, we found out from the bartender that he never went near the men's room. He went through the kitchen to the end of the bar, ordered a double vodka neat, downed it in a gulp, and went right back to the table, where he didn't drink at all."

As THE PARTY that was the 1970s continued, the nightclub craze, like any other, soon began to wear thin. Female impersonator Gypsy (Jim Haake), the flamboyant and frequently hilarious host of the East Side club Gypsy's, summed it up more humorously than most. "How, you may ask, does it feel to be a star in cabaret? How would I know? But I think it would be like being a social director on the *Titanic*. You know you're going down, but you don't know when."

For others, the old carefree mood was sinking under a burden of rising costs and declining attendance. In 1975 Lewis Friedman put Reno Sweeney up for sale, tired of working eighteen hours a day at an unprofitable pursuit. He sold out in April 1976 to New Orleans restaurateur James Maxcy, real estate agent Sally Strickland, and publisher Robert Hobbs. Maxcy would book the acts, even though he knew nothing about nightclubs. "I'll tell you one thing," he informed John S. Wilson of the *New York Times* (June 11, 1976). "Even if we don't make a cent, Helen Gallagher is one person who is going to play here." Yet despite such beacons as Annie Ross and Blossom Dearie, the fare sank even below Friedman's standard, and except for showcase nights audiences were sparse. Maxcy foolishly ignored one problem until it was too late: Friedman had never obtained a cabaret license. Anyone close to Reno's could see the handwriting on the wall.

Brothers and Sisters closed in 1977. For some time David Vangen had had trouble paying bills; performers often sang by candlelight or hurricane lights. Worse still, some of his employees seemed to be robbing him blind. There were bartenders who doled out free drinks to friends and to male customers they hoped to pick up; one chef had a habit of closing the kitchen at 10:30 or 11:00 and leaving to go dancing. But Vangen blamed his financial problems on poor attendance downstairs. He cited the example of singer-comedienne Marcia Lewis, whose act received rave reviews and TV exposure. "And still we have empty seats," he told the *New York Daily News* (January 30, 1977). "If it were a Broadway show with two thousand seats, we would have been sold out. It seems to me there is resistance to cabarets. Everybody thinks we're rich and successful, but we haven't really built an audience."

Building an audience involved more than booking acts that might fill a room with family and friends or lovers of nostalgia, but it was too late for such considerations. There were still swarms of ambitious amateurs, but by now few musical comedy veterans cared to mount an act that would probably cost them more than they earned.

Other nightclubs ended more abruptly. Much excited word of mouth had greeted the opening of a new Blue Angel at a charmed address, 123 East 54th Street, the former site of the old 1-2-3 club and La Vie en Rose and a block south of the old Angel. The press release stated, "The Blue Angel has been designed to recapture the total nightclub environment combining glamour, excitement and frenetic ambience so identified with that time in history when New York City was the nightclub entertainment capital of the world."

But this Blue Angel was different from the old one. The featured show was *Zou*, an elaborate French drag production with thirty singers and comedians. Some were actually women, and the audience was invited to guess which. The opening night party on December 4,

1973, was planned as the social event of the season, with a guest list that included Dyan Cannon, Paul Newman and Joanne Woodward, Anthony Perkins and Berry Berenson, Bill Blass, Oscar de la Renta, and Andy Warhol. As ever with such evenings, reviews focused on the guests' clothing (sequins predominated). The lavishly costumed and designed spectacle inspired only ennui among a group accustomed to feeling little else. "It's like seeing our kids in a school play," complained Saks Fifth Avenue's Ellin Saltzman to her decorator husband Renny, but the show delighted less jaded viewers. At its conclusion waiters covered drinks with coasters, as confetti and balloons fell everywhere.

Two years and two weeks later, on December 18, 1975, *Zou* played its final performance. At about 1:45 A.M. about fifty people remained in the club. The haze of cigarette smoke was so heavy, and the customers so drunk, that no one noticed a faint smell of burning electrical wiring. At 2:16 the curtains and stage decorations burst into flames. The whole club was plunged into darkness, soon illuminated by the spreading orange glow at the stage. Instead of fleeing, customers rushed to claim expensive topcoats and furs at the checkroom; Sherri, the attendant, tried to leave but was trapped. As the club filled with dense smoke a mad scramble took place toward the single exit.

The next morning, firemen nursed the still smoldering heap of wood, glass, and twisted metal. Six people had been injured, and seven died. Among them was Sherri, whose body was found at the bottom of the lower staircase. According to a report, the fire began in an electrical distribution box above the stairs, then spread to the stage decorations. A source close to the investigation reported that a key exit had been blocked by furniture; Paul Sapounakis, the handsome young Greek owner, denied this. "I'm miserable, it's on my conscience, all those people who died in my place," he said that day. "Something happened electrically, something in the air conditioning," he told the *New York Post* (December 19, 1975). "I ran into the kitchen. They were screaming for milk. They said milk puts out fire quicker than water."

The next nightclub to go, surprisingly, was the Ballroom. Its six-year lease expired in 1979, and the landlord hiked the rent from $1,300 to $3,500 a month. Two years later Dawson reopened on West 28th Street.

In 1980 Reno Sweeney closed its doors forever. The "creative bookkeeping" that press agent Jonathan Craig admitted to the *SoHo News* (May 21, 1980) may have begun much earlier; many customers had long complained about seemingly padded checks. But there were other problems. The club had operated illegally as a cabaret since its opening, ignoring a local zoning ordinance that allowed only three people onstage at one time, including musicians, and no use of percussion instruments. Many neighborhood residents complained about the noise, and as a result Jim Maxcy's belated request for a cabaret license was refused. But soon it no longer mattered. On May 12, 1980, the club was evicted for nonpayment of rent. Singer Whitney Houston was scheduled to open there.

Backstage had remained so profitable that Ted Hook decided to invest in another of his dreams, to create "the world's biggest piano bar" as a showcase for Steve Ross. He found a location on West 46th Street and again spared no expense. The result, called Onstage, featured a spacious center stage surrounded by three tiers of tables and by gray, white, and black banquettes. The walls were painted with an image of the New York skyline. One waiter described it as "Catskills chic": it looked expensive but lacked the warmth and elegance of Backstage. Hook spent a fortune on a high-tech lighting and sound system, complete with one of the first cordless microphones in use. He outfitted the waiters in Philip Morris bellhop's uniforms, with pillbox hats and trousers specially tailored to show off their behinds; the maître d's wore white tie and tails. A '30s-style cigarette girl walked from table to table.

Nevertheless, the room—which Hook called his "gift to New York"—seemed doomed from the start. Construction costs soared over budget, leaving little money for further capitalization; employees wondered how Onstage could possibly meet its costly rent and overhead. To Steve Ross's dismay, Hook abandoned his notion of a piano bar, choosing instead to book star acts. He opened in December 1979 with a show by Rosemary Clooney and a lavish party.

Subsequently Rip Taylor, Hildegarde, John Raitt, Margaret Whiting, and female impersonator Charles Pierce appeared, but most of the big names that Hook wanted preferred to work in Atlantic City or Las Vegas, where they could earn $15,000 or more a week. By now there seemed to be little reason to play for a lower fee in a city of fading prestige.

And so Onstage become another "showcase" room, usually booking two unknowns a night, seven nights a week, in an effort to draw family and friends. Gene Bland, whom Hook had placed in charge of booking, says, "There were seven or eight rooms competing for maybe a dozen acts that you could guarantee would fill a house for two nights, and by filling a house we're talking a hundred people. My first question to them was, what was the last room you played, and when? An act who had just played five nights at the Duplex was not going to draw at Onstage two weeks hence."

Perhaps because it was obviously faltering, Onstage rarely captured the exuberance of Backstage. Lee Gray recalls the night that Tennessee Williams came in to see *Jerry's Girls*, a revue of Jerry Herman songs. "He was just a mess. He was with his male secretary, and they ordered a bottle of wine. He had six or seven yellow capsules in his hand, and he was playing with them on the table while I filled the glasses. He swallowed them all with his wine. The show started, and he began making rude comments about the performers. 'Oh, come on, get her off the stage and let's get on with something else!' 'God, she's so fat, why doesn't she go on a diet?' There was nothing we could do. Finally a guy nearby said, 'If you don't shut up I'm gonna come over and punch you in the mouth!' He calmed down a little, but then something else would set him off again. At the end of every show Ted would introduce the stars in the audience, and of course he introduced Tennessee Williams. After the applause died down Tennessee looked over at the guy and shouted, 'Now that you know who I am, do you still wanna punch me in the mouth?' "

Hook continued to spend most of his evenings at Backstage, and Onstage suffered from his absence. He usually barred photographers from the former room, which stars appreciated. But one evening Richard Burton came into Onstage after a performance of *Camelot* to catch the act of his costar Christine Ebersole. "There were lights everywhere from the moment he came in," says Gray, "and as soon as the show ended all the photographers started snapping his picture. I said, 'Now I can see why he always asks to sit in the back room of Backstage.' "

When present, Hook did his best to add a spark to the atmosphere. During Rosemary Clooney's engagement he persuaded her ex-husband José Ferrer to come to the club and see her for the first time in years. Hook himself also supplied a few lighter moments. Occasionally he sat at the controls with a live microphone, making wisecracks and rude comments during the shows. "A microphone in Ted's hands was like a weapon," says one employee. But he didn't stop at that. "Ted was known for mooning people," says Gray. "Onstage had a long hallway stretching from the entrance to a small flight of steps that led up to the showroom. Ted would stand at the top of the stairs and drop his drawers, so whoever had just walked in would see him bare-assed down the hallway. You'd hear roars of laughter, and then you'd see Ted at the top of the stairs with his pants up, looking around and smiling."

Overall, however, Onstage was a great disappointment to him, and now Backstage had started to fade as well. Some blamed the decrease in new hit Broadway musicals, which limited the local trade of avid theatregoers while attracting more and more bus and tour groups. "Ted used to teach us to watch the showbills," says Steve Oxendine, "so we would know who was in the restaurant. When you saw a lot of old showbills you knew you were dealing with tourists as opposed to New Yorkers. In the last year we were seeing a lot of *Chorus Line* showbills."

The main problem, however, was Hook's laissez-faire attitude as a businessman. While concentrating on his role as host and resident bon vivant, he appointed a number of managers and accountants whose follies he never seemed to notice. Says Lee Gray, "Ted's attorneys used to warn him all the time, 'Be careful, watch the books. You don't know how many restaurants have closed that had lines around the block.' " In 1979 Hook hired a married couple as manager and bookkeeper for both his rooms. Staff members thought this unwise—and with good reason. After a year or so maintenance had deteriorated, and supplies were not arriving as they should. Employees grew suspicious of the couple's secrecy over money matters and of their frequent and expensive "business trips." Finally they realized that a vast flow of money was leaving both rooms. "Ted was very trusting of people he hired and, in that case, too trusting," says Gray. "Finally the staff got up in arms. While the manager was in Las Vegas on vacation, Gene, the waiters, and bartenders called a house meeting with Ted and told him what was happening." By the time Hook fired them it was estimated that thousands upon thousands of dollars had vanished.

Onstage expired in the winter of 1982. Lola del Rivero, the sister of Chita Rivera, took over management of Backstage. In the coming months several attempts were made to raise funds for Hook, including a $100-a-plate benefit dinner advertised as an "anniversary," but the restaurant had lost too much money to be salvaged.

Hook ended it several months later in an unfortunate way. "We all got to work one night," recalls Gray, "and during the evening a lot of Ted's old friends were showing up. The lamps had disappeared the week before from all the tables. Gradually we suspected that this was it, but none of us had been told. I said, 'I'm gonna clean out my locker, because I don't think we'll be able to get back in here tomorrow.' I left near closing, and Ted was still there, but nothing was said. When the restaurant closed, padlocks were put on the door."

Several employees would later report a series of events that were a mystery that night. Unknown to most of his staff, Hook had declared total bankruptcy. The court had claimed Backstage and scheduled it for auction to the highest bidder. Hook planned somehow to gather the money and place the winning bid himself or to get backers to do so who would then allow him to continue fronting the restaurant. Allegedly Hook had hidden this from his staff in order to prevent word about the auction from leaking out and possibly attracting other bidders, but the waiters wondered why he had so freely informed his friends.

According to one source, bidding was scheduled for a Friday, but the judge became ill and rescheduled the auction for Monday. Over the weekend another bidder learned that Backstage was up for auction, and Hook was outbid. Later he told a friend how much he wished he could get back the fortune he had spent on free champagne and dinners for celebrity guests, whose checks were always "on Mr. Hook." "He'd have Ethel Merman there," says one associate, "and he'd say it was a comp for her and her guest. The next night Ethel would come with four boys, and it was another comp. The night after that she'd come with eight people, and he'd comp that too. I said, 'Ted, my goodness, she's using you, can't you see?' He'd say, 'Oh, it's wonderful publicity to have her here.' "

The closing devastated him and left his employees with a lot of ill feelings. "It was a combination of disappointment and bitterness over not having been told," says Oxendine. "The people there on that last night were the most faithful; they felt they deserved to know."

By then, padlocks had also been placed on the door of the Grand Finale. The "backers" had decided it was time to say good night.

Marty's, an elegant and expensive East Side jazz club, closed around that time. Despite acts that included Vic Damone, Mel Torme, Joe Williams, Anita O'Day, and Kenny Rankin, the room could not meet expenses.

In 1984 Hook made a halfhearted attempt to re-create the past. With the financial help of several showbusiness pals, among them Dorothy Loudon and James Kirkwood, he opened Ted Hook, a miniature replica of Backstage down to the original Ziegfeld table lamps. It lasted only a few months. Hook swore he would never open another restaurant—the moment had simply passed.

Some say that Backstage might still exist today had it been managed all along by the capable Lola del Rivero. Others, like Oxendine, feel that it had overstayed its welcome. "It had been there since 1975, and like everything in New York it was cyclical. Nothing really lasts. It was a place to see and be seen, like Studio 54. After a while everybody had been introduced, everybody had been met, the great evenings had been used by Broadway people for what they were worth. And because the place was so high-charged, it was difficult to maintain that energy the way a laid-back restaurant could.

"We were coming out of very heady days of activity in the city. Broadway had been at a remarkable high throughout the '70s, and that brought an influx of people into the city. The Village was absolutely alive, and there were discos like 54, and there was this amazing tempo in the gay community, with places like 12 West and the Flamingo and the Saint. It was also a time when you had different cultures meeting and crossing, and that was another unique thing about Backstage. Ted could put Harvey Fierstein and a couple from Iowa in the same room, and they would have a wonderful time. Then we were smacked in 1983 and 1984 with the full realization of what the AIDS crisis was, and you saw clubs closing left and right after that. So many people who contributed to the energy of the city at that time are no longer here—a great deal of that talent bank and spirit is simply dead. The Perry Ellises and the Michael Bennetts and the Steve Rubells—all of them are gone, and there was an incredible artistic energy at the center of all that craziness."

Many of the Backstage and Onstage waiters are gone as well. At a reunion in May 1989 at the Red Blazer Too, a restaurant on the site of Onstage, the warm sense of reacquaintance was tinged with a sadness about those who were missing.

Many voids in those postdisco, postnightclub, and postpromiscuity days have never been filled. After Reno Sweeney and so many other clubs closed, the late Arthur Bell—himself a victim of AIDS—commented in the *SoHo News* (May 21, 1980), "Sociologically, it's a very funny thing. In the mid-seventies gays thought they were better than everyone else, or worse than everyone else. Today they think they're just the same and they don't aspire to that kind of entertainment."

Just as likely, the combination of rising costs, diminished chances for exposure, and sinking performance standards made the future of intimate clubs seem less encouraging than ever.

Chapter ELEVEN

During the 1980s, going out for its own sake extended mainly to movies, bars, restaurants, or the homes of friends. Most people undertook an evening at the theatre or a nightclub only when they wanted to see a show badly enough to bear the high cost. Some places warranted the trouble, however, especially the Hotel Algonquin, famous for decades as a home of Manhattan literati and showbiz elite. In 1981 the management hired Steve Ross to play and sing in its Oak Room, an oblong, oak-paneled dining room where Greta Keller, Cy Walter, and others had entertained in the '30s. Ross liked to say he was "dragged reluctantly" from those days; and with his tuxedo, slicked-back hair, and marked resemblance to Cole Porter he recreated that era so timelessly that fifty years seemed to melt away. For four seasons Ross provided the sort of nights that an older generation of New Yorkers had grown to miss and that a substantial young audience had yet to discover.

For now the genre survived mostly in the hands of its veterans, many of whom were near the end of their careers. By 1980 Mabel Mercer had ceased to work, except on rare occasions. The octogenarian singer had suffered for some time from arthritis, vertigo, and other ailments and seldom ventured from her farm. But her friends and colleagues would not forget her. On January 5, 1981, they planned a lavish tribute at New York's Whitney Museum, attempting to recapture the elegance of Tony's and other old Mercer haunts. With the fourth floor draped in black silk moiré and illuminated by candlelight, her signature songs were sung by Carolyn Leigh, Bart Howard, Sylvia Syms, Dolores Gray, Sammy Cahn, and the queen of geriatric café society, the Incomparable Hildegarde, who seemed to have wandered into the wrong tribute. "I want to thank you, Mabel, for singing all those wonderful songs that I introduced," she said, then followed with a corny medley of war tunes that Mercer never touched. "Let me see, which war was it?" In all, though, it was a heartwarming display of gratitude for a woman who had affected them all. Mercer remained as humble as ever. "I just did my work through the years," she said afterward. "I never realized I was an influence to anybody."

In the coming months she grew noticeably feebler and let her hair turn gray for the first time. "It was a sign that the spirit was failing," says Buddy Barnes. Occasionally music could still "reendow" her, as she put it. On June 27, 1982, she sang two songs at a Carnegie Hall memorial for her beloved friend Alec Wilder. Escorted onstage, she lowered herself tentatively into a chair and began to huskily speak the words to Wilder's "Did You Ever Cross Over to Sneeden's?" After a few bars some intangible force took hold of her, and suddenly Mercer was singing again. Other performers listened backstage with tears in their eyes, as did many in the audience. For the finale she joined the cast in "While We're Young":

Though it may be just for today
Share our love we must, while we may . . .

When it ended, she pranced away almost as buoyantly as if she were dodging off between vaudeville turns in 1926.

The next afternoon Mercer teamed with soprano Eileen Farrell for a concert at Lincoln Center's Alice Tully Hall. Farrell, a hearty ex-opera star with a deep fondness for popular music, helped give her the confidence to get through a performance that she would never have attempted alone. Mercer made one final appearance at a benefit at New York's Grand Hyatt Hotel before she died at age 84 on April 20, 1984.

Those whose hearts belonged to the golden age of Manhattan boîtes called it the end of an era. On June 10 publicist Donald Smith, Mercer's longtime manager and the man responsible for reactivating her career in the '60s, gathered about thirty singers and composers—

among them Thelma Carpenter, Cy Coleman, Jimmie Daniels, Anita Ellis, Bart Howard, Bobby Short, and Sylvia Syms—for a Town Hall concert of songs and remembrances. Many in the cast hadn't seen one another in years, so things became quite emotional. "We were all crazy backstage," says Ellis.

The show was billed as a celebration and, as such, contained a few jolly moments. Syndicated columnist Liz Smith joked about "the petty, ordinary and sometimes even sordid love affairs of my own that Mabel raised to grandeur . . . One has to bless her for giving us romantic memories that one can bear to live with." But an elegiac feeling underscored the afternoon, so full of timeless performances that had arbitrarily received nostalgia status. Strains of the passing years recurred, some mournful, as in "The Days of the Kerry Dancing" ("gone, alas, like our youth, too soon"); others philosophical, such as Bart Howard's "It Was Worth It":

Oh, why should I browse through my wrinkles regretting them?
After all, I sure had a ball while getting them!

A FEW NIGHTCLUB SINGERS in town were still capable of providing some restorative insight into your feelings. Sylvia Syms continued to perform impeccably at Michael's Pub, Marty's, and elsewhere, although these bookings were growing fewer, most owners pronouncing her too difficult to work with and not popular enough to fill their rooms except on opening and closing nights.

In 1985 Julie Wilson returned to the business after eight years in Omaha raising her teenaged sons. Just before New Year's she reluctantly accepted a last-minute offer to open at Michael's Pub with an evening of Cole Porter. With only six hours of rehearsal, Wilson won perhaps the biggest raves of her career. Then sixty, she looked amazingly similar to the reedlike figure in a skintight red beaded gown, gardenia tucked in her hair, that appeared on the cover of the 1957 album "Julie Wilson at the St. Regis."

As Bobby Short recalled in a Boston interview, "Julie opened during the so-called dull period right after the holidays. You're worn out, your pockets are empty, your kids have bored you to death, and you just want to go away someplace. But her engagement was like the return of Cleopatra. I know how blasé New Yorkers can be, but every performance was packed with the very best people in New York—by that I mean people who cared about Cole Porter, who cared about Julie."

William Roy, her steady accompanist thereafter, compiled programs of Sondheim, Rodgers and Hart, Berlin, Gershwin, Arlen, and others. At Michael's Pub and at the Algonquin, where they appeared for three seasons, couples held hands and exchanged glances as if on their first dates. Wilson sang as if those mature sentiments had been fighting to burst from her for years, as indeed they had. She had long outgrown the naughty ditties that had quickened the heartbeats of tired businessmen at the St. Regis Hotel's Maisonette Room in the '50s and '60s—"Every Baby Needs a Da-Da-Daddy," "I Refuse to Rock and Roll," and other tunes about big-city girls who put out and were rewarded with Tiffany bracelets and real estate. But friends tried to discourage her from singing anything better. "Julie," asked one, "why are you trying to compete with Peggy Lee and Ella Fitzgerald and all these other great singers? Why don't you do your material? Nobody does *material* like you do."

"But I want to broaden, I want to really sing. I'm working on my voice. I know I'm not a great singer, but I want to try."

Now the years had given her dry, intense voice the power to express nearly every emotion, and her sweeping hand and body movements spoke with heartbreaking eloquence. In Irving Berlin's "Supper Time," the Ethel Waters classic about a woman's struggle to tell her children that their father has just been lynched, Wilson's fists clutched at the air as if trying to seize him back. In the face of reviews proclaiming her the greatest nightclub singer of the day, Wilson retained an earthiness that surpassed even Mabel Mercer's. "I'm not a great singer—I never was," she often said. "But I love songs." When complimented on her looks, she would blurt out, "It's all paint! It took me *two hours* to put all this together!"

But glamour was mainly a vehicle through which she communicated a lyric. After her second show had ended and she had greeted her last fan, Wilson would retire to her dressing room, remove her gardenia and tie her hair into a long braid, doff her gown for an old blouse, ratty slacks, and tennis sneakers, and lug her enormous suitcase (Roy called it a "mobile home") over to the PATH train, which took her back home to Jersey City.

In more jazz-oriented rooms, the spirit of Billie Holiday lives on in

Carmen McRae, a revered vocalist who, since her emergence in the late '40s, has used her improvisational skills as a direct means of drawing out the guts of popular lyrics. A native of Brooklyn, McRae has matured into a matronly woman with a short-cropped, graying Afro; big, dark eyes that can light up or wither a room in one glance; and a toughness born of forty years on the road. Not for her the penchant of other café singers to wallow in the romantic; her deep, reedy voice examines phrases with a hard-edged wisdom that leaves no room for hollow sentiment.

Since the mid-'80s she has made her New York base the Blue Note, a deep blue Art Deco jazz club in the Village whose attractions have included Sarah Vaughan, Ray Charles, Miles Davis, and Dizzy Gillespie. For McRae its greatest asset is its simpatico audience, which creates an atmosphere that she feeds on. A moody, uncompromising artist, she has always required the right performing conditions as well as an appreciative crowd in order to give her all. Without them she is likely to freeze up and cut her set short. Such was the case at Marty's, the elegant East Side jazz room whose wealthy clientele often sat as if waiting for her to prove that she was not wasting their time. Peter Reilly of *Stereo Review* magazine visited her there one night in 1980:

> Time: Elevenish on a warm fall night. Place: Marty's, a glossy Upper East Side spot with a window-wall facing an illuminated fountain and an entertainment policy that's bringing some of the greatest names in jazz to the New York public. Not your usual jazz lair; there's scarcely a scoobey-doo turtleneck, a pair of onyx-glass shades or Wilson running shoes in sight. Instead, a lot of men in Swiss banker suits with the requisite display of cuffs, and women who look as if they can tell the difference between Gucci, Pucci and Hermès at a hundred paces even in this dimmer-manufactured twilight.
>
> A narrow door to the left of the stage opens and McRae makes her way to the platform. First impression is of an elegant, healthy-looking, tennis-playing matron. But once the lights hit the face, particularly those magnificent eyes, you know that you are In a Presence. She slips into the show with a casual calmness that borders on preoccupation. The voice, however—that throaty, reedy, unforgettable voice—is a lot more involved. It stings and lashes, wheedles and cajoles as if it were an entity separate from the body it inhabits. The set ambles along. McRae fumbles a lyric, introduces her trio,

even sneaks a glance at her watch. She acknowledges her applause with a set smile that indicates she's not too wild about you either. Then she glides into Gershwin's "But Not for Me." The verse—"Dear Abby, don't you dare / Ever tell me he will care . . ."—is sung with a playful, admonitory lightness. End of verse, and then a long two-beat silence. With a sudden twist, a thrust of her head and shoulders, she signals that Playtime is over. Throttling down to a slower beat, she sizzles that great song into a heap of glowing embers. At the finish the feeling is rather like that one associates with watching sparks fly into a dark-blue night from a guttering bonfire. Oh, so *that's* Carmen McRae! Took a while, but worth the wait.

McRae recalled that club at the Blue Note in 1988. "I used to get the damnedest people you ever saw, and it cost a *fortune.* There was one table of six people sitting right underneath my nose, and they could not have gotten out of there without spending five hundred dollars, just to eat and drink. And this broad is sittin' there talking out loud. 'I don't know what's wrong with Alvin's teeth! I have taken him to the orthodontist, and they can't figure it out!" And I'm singing, like, 'Lover Man.' Which goes to show your how impressed *she* was!"

All these singers share Mercer's ability to strip songs to their essence, filling the silence between phrases with their presence. As the '90s began, so few successors had come along that one wondered if that priceless art might vanish when McRae and her peers were gone.

THE NEW BALLROOM opened in 1981 at 253 West 28th Street with a large restaurant and a performance room set up in theatrical fashion, its three ascending levels of tables facing an off-Broadway—size stage. It began with a popular double bill of Margaret Whiting and Rosemary Clooney, but nosedived with the overexposed Chita Rivera, who failed to draw sufficiently to justify Greg Dawson's oversalaried monthlong December booking. Undercapitalized in general, the room was forced to close until 1983, when it reopened and gradually regained its momentum. In addition to its 9:00 and 11:00 P.M. shows it inaugurated 6:30 performances by Blossom Dearie and by the team of singer-comic Bertram Ross—Martha Graham's former choreographer and lead dancer—and composer-pianist-singer John Wallowitch, whose songs had long been championed by Dearie, Joanne Beretta, and other singers. An owlish, bald, and bespectacled man whose deadpan expression was often betrayed by mischievously sparkling eyes, Wallowitch uncrated a library of songs that either sliced to ribbons the sillier behavior of the deliriously-in-love, or stripped away every bit of jest to reveal a vulnerability born of the late hour, a few martinis, and an overwhelming need to share the deepest part of himself:

It takes a life to realize what life is all about
And life is all about . . . this moment
I'm here with you,
Before we're through
What secrets will we tell?
I'll learn to know you well
This moment
How soon, too soon the hours fly
I feel my life go rushing by
I only hope that time will be your friend
We live a life to give a life with love, oh don't you see?
And so if you'll agree
Then come along with me
I only guarantee . . .
This moment . . .

Although Dawson gave many lesser-known performers a chance, his room is best known for such veteran pop stars as Peggy Lee. Lee's last New York engagement had taken place at the Waldorf-Astoria in 1976, at which time she slipped on a heavily waxed elevator floor and brought a $15 million lawsuit against the Hilton Hotel chain and Johnson's wax. Chronic ill health and accidents have threatened to snuff out her career ever since, but amazingly she has never stopped singing, her vitality diminished but not her determination.

Lee's 1985 Ballroom debut was one of the most exciting bookings of the decade. One had to overlook her ghoulish appearance: she wore a white Cleopatra wig and huge dark jeweled glasses (to help conceal a partially paralyzed face) and dressed in white satin with maribou feathers and other costumes ill suited to her amorphous figure. Barely ambulatory, she hobbled onstage in 1986 with a jeweled cane; in 1988 her pianist Mike Renzi escorted her to a velvet-covered swivel chair. Minutes after a Saturday night late show, fans watched uncomfortably as the mink-clad star left her dressing room at the front of the club and ceremoniously worked her way toward the exit, dragging herself down the center of the packed house with a walker.

On her best nights Lee was still capable of giving an object lesson in jazz-inspired pop singing, binding phrases with a subtle rhythmic pulse and coloring lyrics from a palette that had grown almost infinite with the years. A continued perfectionist, she employed the complex lighting that was her trademark, as well as a superb quintet led by the extraordinary Renzi. Her own gift for bringing songs vividly and theatrically to life with no apparent effort remained quite magical. Such artistry did not come cheap. Tickets cost $45 and $25 plus a $12.50 minimum—a price necessary to meet Lee's enormous salary demands. The singer needled Dawson about how she had "started the place," a slight to Blossom Dearie and the other artists who preceded her.

Naturally, Lee never expected to be upstaged by a monkey. One night interior designer Mario Buatta, a friend of Lee's, brought in a chimpanzee as a publicity stunt. The animal wore a red jacket emblazoned with his name, Zip, and charmed much of the audience. Lee apparently realized that the monkey was stealing her show, and stormed off without completing the first half. When she returned, the chimp was gone.

In 1987 Dawson hired another living legend, Eartha Kitt, who had not hissed and slithered across a New York club stage in about seven years. Still remarkably slender and lithe in her sixties, doing full justice to low-cut and high-slitted gowns most women half her age would not have touched, Kitt stalked the stage like a force of nature and held forth with alternately chilling and coquettish authority. As always, however, she provoked a few diva headaches of her own. One evening she failed to show up for her sold-out performance, and Dawson and his assistant Scott Gleason could find her nowhere. Later, after all the customers had gone, the phone rang.

"Scottie, will you protect me?"

"PROTECT YOU?"

The next night she showed up, but her consciousness had drifted skyward. She gave a slurred, giggling explanation of the night before:

> I got lost yesterday, can you believe it? Ah, where's my glass? Come, baby, because if you give me one, two, three, four guys up here we

need a glass of champagne, don't we? Oh, you know? Yesterday I wound up in jail! I wound up in jail because I could not find my way here! I'm telling you my secret situation at the moment, because lots of times I don't even think my daughter understands me. I had to go to jail to find out whom [sic] I am. It's very true . . . and when I got here, I thought I had already done the show! And I turned around and went home! I got to a point where I touched my face, and I started to realize . . . Eartha, you don't have any makeup on! When I touched my face, Eartha Kitt wasn't there!

Martha Raye played a smash engagement in 1985, her sweet voice and high spirits intact but marred by an excess of corny shtick. In 1987 came the return of Yma Sumac, the "Legendary Sun Virgin" of Capitol Records fame and an icon of '50s pop culture. Allegedly born in the High Andes, Sumac won international stardom by treating a repertoire of Peruvian-style vocalises to the pyrotechnics of her supposed five-octave vocal range, with which she clucked and swooped like some rare Incan mountain bird. A camp favorite who took herself with the utmost seriousness, Sumac had been semiretired from the early '60s until 1984, when she was coaxed back into activity. She created such a sensation at the Ballroom that the club held her over for several weeks and added special late shows. "These young boys screaming," Sumac marveled to *New York Newsday*'s Blake Green (February 21, 1989). "I was shocked. But they explained to me that it was because they *adore* Yma Sumac. All the big stars came to see Yma Sumac. What is the name of that one, I think Madonna?"

The sixtyish Sumac stood onstage between a pair of Styrofoam Incan statues, her bare-midriff gown—and her once high-flying voice—exposing the curses of gravity. Her command of English was still limited but not enough to restrict her from writing "over five thousand songs," two or three of which she growled indecipherably. Nor did she have any problem milking applause in the best old-time hoofer's tradition. "I'm very tired right now, you know? But I *love* to sing, especially for you, my dear people. And I *hope* you enjoy it. I hope so!" Her expert jazz accompanists, however, did not enjoy being scolded during the show ("Get the beat!"), and the loving and trustworthy publicist responsible for her comeback did not enjoy being accused of stealing from her. Sumac's renaissance did not last long.

A shadowy, mirrored East 49th Street supper club called Freddy's ended its eight-year existence in 1987, not long after AIDS-stricken owner Freddy Martini sold it to businessman Frank Nolan. It left memories of a roster that alternated such established acts as Tammy Grimes, Margaret Whiting, Jane Harvey, female impersonator Charles Pierce, and jazz singer Chris Connor with just about every second-string canary who had ever appeared in a road company of *A Chorus Line*. The more durable Michael's Pub has concentrated on such pop-jazz veterans as George Shearing, Mel Torme, Anita O'Day, Mark Murphy, and the remarkable composer-pianist-singer-arranger Bobby Scott. Best known for his hit compositions "A Taste of Honey" and "He Ain't Heavy, He's My Brother," Scott made his strongest impression at Michael's Pub and similar rooms with his powerful, reflective piano and a moving voice that ranged from a raspy, Ray Charles-inflected blues quality to a full-throated baritone.

But the personality most associated with the room is its owner Gil Wiest. Anyone who has ever worked there has his own stories of Wiest's behavior, as do many customers. After a Kaye Ballard appearance Ben Bagley, whose 1965 revue *The Decline and Fall of the Entire World as Seen Through the Eyes of Cole Porter* had starred Ballard, stood in the outer bar waiting to greet her. A middle-aged woman approached him. "Excuse me, but I wonder if you wouldn't mind taking me back and introducing me to Kaye Ballard. Everybody says I look just like her."

"I'd be delighted."

Up marched Wiest. With the woman two feet away, he shouted, "DON'T YOU TAKE HER BACK THERE! She doesn't look anything like Kaye Ballard! This woman is at least ten years older, and she has a bald spot!"

The next night a couple walked up to him at the reservation desk. "Hello, we're here to see the show. We don't have a reservation, but we're friends of Kaye Ballard's."

"Oh, you're friends of Kaye's."

"Yes, we are."

"BIG DEAL!"

THE MODERATE SUCCESS of Michael's Pub and the Ballroom belied the faltering state of other rooms throughout the country. Except for piano bar players and a handful of older café stars, it had become nearly impossible to make a living in clubs. During the health-conscious '80s most people smoked and drank less and went to bed earlier. It seemed much safer—and cheaper—to rent a movie for $3.00 than to visit an oftentimes cramped, uncomfortable club and spend anywhere from $20 to $60 for a show that probably would not be worth it. This was a particular consideration in Manhattan, where the cost of living had skyrocketed and where a cityful of rent-poor residents planned their evenings out very carefully.

People were especially reluctant to gamble on performers they didn't know. The '70s tradition of vanity showcases lived on in such clubs as Don't Tell Mama, the Duplex, and Eighty-Eights, where countless neophytes appeared for one night, two Tuesdays, a month of Fridays. These rooms still offered the dim prospect of "discovery," although they usually did little more than give amateurs a chance to perform for friends in a quasi-professional setting. Quality sank so low that most of these clubs were hardly taken seriously or even noticed by the general public.

It was a sorry system for the rare acts who deserved greater attention. One of them was singer Karen Mason, whose appearances at Don't Tell Mama, Eighty-Eights, and other clubs built her a devoted cult following. Among Mason's assets are a big belting voice capable of considerable delicacy and nuance, a fearless versatility that recalls the young Barbra Streisand, and an ability to communicate the theatrical center of material that includes Beatles songs, showtunes such as "Something's Coming" and "Mr. Snow," and deftly crafted ballads and comedy tunes by her accompanist Brian Lasser.

Mason left a successful club and concert career in her hometown of Chicago to enter the showbiz crucible that New York still represented to out-of-town youngsters. When she moved there in 1980, however, nightclub and musical comedy opportunities had reached a discouraging low. She and Lasser were hired for a series of Saturday nights at the Duplex, where they learned the frustrating realities of trying to showcase oneself in such a room.

"The Duplex seated forty people. I think we started out with a six-dollar cover, so our gross potential was two hundred and forty dollars. Every week we ran an ad in the *Village Voice* that cost about two hundred and fifty dollars, and we footed the entire bill, plus doing fliers and posters. It cost us a fortune. We operated at a severe loss for many years. I don't know any other career where, as you're learning, you're also going broke. In a company like Motorola or IBM you work yourself up and still make money. In this business the overhead is outrageous, and it's all on the performer to pay for the musical director, the advertising, the mailing list—everything. We would go back to Chicago and do a concert to make money just so we could come back here and spend it. How did we get by? Support from family, borrowing money from wherever we could. Borrowing from Peter to pay Paul. I've been very fortunate to have a partner who is willing to make no money with me.

"When we arrived in New York we saw that nightclubs were not given a great deal of credibility, and I found that very frustrating. In Chicago there was a value seen in what we did. You knew that talent and thought had gone into it. But in New York the smaller clubs were seen as bastard children. They were something you did between shows. A lot of the acts we saw were by people who put together all their favorite songs and sang for forty-five minutes. I was very offended by that. There was more to it. We were kids, we were still making mistakes, but we had a grasp of what we were doing."

Performers who shared that grasp had little chance to flower through experience. The polish displayed by most veteran singers owed much to the era of nightly band singing, local live radio, and vast nightclub and recording opportunities, but today's youngsters are denied these advantages. "As with any craft you learn by doing it over and over," says Mason, "and the sooner you can get back up on the horse and ride, the better off you are."

Intimate clubs were now a sheer labor of love, requiring entrepreneurs willing to settle for minuscule profits—if any—in return for their headaches. Naturally, these dedicated few had little money for publicity and could count on minimal support from television or major record labels, both of which devoted their budgets to promoting attractions that ensured top financial return. The days when a tiny New York revue such as *4-West* or Jerry Herman's *Nightcap* wound up on Ed Sullivan or Jack Paar had long passed. Says Mason, "You know what the *Today Show* and *Regis and Kathie Lee* told me when we were at the Algonquin, which is considered a prestigious room? 'When you have something national, let us know.' I sang at Carnegie Hall with the New York Pops. Then I did *Jerome Robbins' Broadway*. How much else has to happen before you get discovered? If you're not national they don't want to know about you. It just doesn't make sense to me. Where does the sense of discovery in this city start? We've lost it."

In today's nightclubs, discovery usually starts and ends with stand-up comics, whose broader, timeless craft appeals to a wide audience that club singers can seldom reach. Rooms such as the Improv, Catch a Rising Star, Dangerfield's, and Caroline's thrive, and their performers appear regularly on cable and commercial TV. As talk-show hosts know, comics have not only reached a peak of popularity but also present fewer of the financial worries attendant on buying musical sound equipment, hiring musicians, and paying song royalties. Just as important, today's promising comic talents far outnumber their gifted musical counterparts, a fact that the amateur boîte circuit refuses to acknowledge.

Owners who persevere face other hurdles, such as exorbitant real estate costs. Jan Wallman's tiny Village room ended with a jolt in 1985, when the landlord doubled her rent. Luckily she returned two years later with a jewel of a new club on West 44th Street, elegantly mirrored and upholstered in red velvet. As before she could usually afford only unknowns; Sylvia Syms, appearing for two weeks at a high guaranteed salary, failed to attract enough business to recoup costs. But even though Wallman maintained an admirable standard under the circumstances, she was back to the day-to-day struggle that she had known all her life. "Cabaret is my world, so I think it's beautiful," she told critic Jacques le Sourd of the *Gannett Westchester Newspapers* (April 9, 1989), "but it's not what it was, and I don't think anyone can say it's back or coming back."

Even pessimists agree that attendance would improve if more people knew about these rooms. Stars such as Kitt and Lee would always draw through reputation, but unknowns need the kind of exposure only television can provide. National and local newspapers cover major engagements, but the short bookings in many clubs preclude reviews, for acts are usually gone before publication. And since the smaller rooms book almost anyone who can bring in his own audience, coverage is hardly worth the newsprint. Old-timers look around despairingly at the apparent dearth of new talent, but younger observers have a different perspective. "I think it's just harder for talent to grow, to get that chance," says Mason. "A lot of it is financial. Doing something for the sake of art, you can only go so far. Then you have a thousand-dollar rent and all the other expenses of living, and a lot of very talented people don't stick with what they should be doing."

Amid such negative conditions are a few encouraging signs. A handful of pros such as Tony Bennett, Carmen McRae, and Joe Williams signed with major record labels for the first time in years, and pop-rock singer Linda Ronstadt recorded three platinum-selling albums of standards, arranged and conducted by the late Nelson Riddle. Although Ronstadt's fame was such that anything she recorded would become a hit, the venture suggested that perhaps she had tapped a longing for the great romantic ballads of the '30s and '40s. Willie Nelson, Carly Simon, and Dionne Warwick were among the stars who followed suit.

An ironic note was sounded by Marlene VerPlanck, a top studio and jingle singer who later took her clear, supple voice into many nightclubs around the country. One morning she heard Ronstadt's recording of "Skylark" on the radio. "It sounds just like my record!" she said. A comparison between Ronstadt's rendition and VerPlanck's, recorded years earlier for Georgia-based Audiophile Records, revealed that they were indeed phrased almost identically. VerPlanck later reported that producer-arranger Quincy Jones, a mutual friend of hers and Ronstadt's, had given Ronstadt copies of VerPlanck's albums to study.

Occasionally a newer act illustrates the heights that today's club performers so seldom reach. Singers Jeff Harnar, Sandra King, Nancy LaMott, Susannah McCorkle, and Mary Cleere Haran have displayed admirable taste in songs and a professionalism that places them far above most of their contemporaries. At Steve McGraw's, a relaxed, unpretentious room on West 72nd Street, the style of such '50s vocal quartets as the Four Lads, the Four Aces, and the Ames Brothers came back to life in *Forever Plaid.* Stan Chandler, David Engel, Jason Graae, and Guy Stroman enacted a tale of a promising vocal group who died in 1964 when their car collided with a busload of schoolgirls on their way to see the Beatles on the *Ed Sullivan Show.* Now, through a time warp and a gap in the ozone layer, they return to give the concert they never lived to perform. A silly premise, it still suited this loving sendup of an era of apple-cheeked, wholesome innocence. More important, it allowed the group to re-create with breathtaking purity and accuracy such '50s pop standards as "Three Coins in the Fountain," "Moments to Remember," and "Undecided," spoofing the synchronized hand movements and grins of '50s quartets as vividly as if they had grown up watching Ed Sullivan every Sunday night. Opening in November 1989 on a weekend schedule, *Forever Plaid* graduated to off-Broadway status in May 1990 and was recorded by RCA.

Starting in the spring of 1989, a warm Southern breeze blew new life into the Café Carlyle in the person of Tennessee-born Dixie Carter, by now a star of CBS-TV's hit series *Designing Women.* For fifteen years or so after her 1966 appearances at the Downstairs at the Upstairs, Carter's career had reached no higher peak than a long-running role on the ABC soap opera *Edge of Night*; much of her time was spent raising her two daughters. In November 1983 she opened at Freddy's with a hodgepodge of Cole Porter, Bob Dylan, Bruce Springsteen, country, and light rock. With an overwhelmingly sexy-vulnerable-madcap personality that no other medium had unleashed, Carter transformed this material into a sixty-minute marvel of deeply felt emotional revelations and high comedy. Few who heard her would forget her cavorting on the piano in a tight black dress, her mop of brunette hair tumbling over a come-hither glance, as she drawled Porter's "Let's Do It." And it was difficult to remain untouched by her spare and poignant "Bill" or by "Hold Out for the Real Thing," a declaration of romantic hope by her accompanist Michele Brourman.

At the Carlyle, Carter further polished that act into a tour de force of the kind rarely seen in nightclubs. For Porter's "Come on In," the beckonings of a 42nd Street burlesque show barker, her high kicks revealed a pair of legs to rival any Rockette's. "We have spared no time or effort," she purred, "in our determination to bring you simply the most *refined* material . . . presented in simply the most *refined* fashion . . . Don't tell it to Bobby Short!"

She spotlighted her early coach John Wallowitch's songs, among them "Cosmetic Surgery," about a rich old crone's obsession with the surgeon's scalpel, and "Come a Little Closer," a ballad about an early morning moment of Manhattan intimacy. In that song Wallowitch and Carter tenderly captured the feelings of a group of strangers huddled together at an hour when most people were fast asleep:

Four o'clock, Sunday morning
New York town is quiet once again

We're alone, Sunday morning
All alone
Don't go to bed, my sleepy-headed friend . . .

Other café performers achieved far more mileage with far less. A showbusiness phenomenon of the '80s was the rise to stardom of Michael Feinstein, a fresh-faced young singer-pianist who has brought American standards to a wider national audience than almost any performer in the last thirty years. Born in Columbus, Ohio, in 1957, Feinstein moved to Los Angeles and was hired by Ira Gershwin to catalog his brother George's collection of music and memorabilia. Feinstein longed to perform the rare Gershwin songs that he had uncovered, and even though he had little experience he was blessed with a degree of chutzpah that made this secondary. At parties he was known to take over the piano whenever the hired pianist stepped away for a break. Before long he won several party gigs of his own, and at one of them, in the home of screen actor Robert Stack, he made an immediate fan of Liza Minnelli. Minnelli threw a Hollywood party for him whose guests included Elizabeth Taylor, and the publicity officially launched Feinstein's career. On the opening night of his first engagement at the Algonquin, Minnelli fêted him again; not surprisingly, he sold out his sixteen-week run.

Thereafter Feinstein toured Europe with Minnelli, appeared frequently on network television, completed three Broadway concert engagements, entertained at the White House, played selected parties for a reported $20,000 fee, signed with Elektra Records, and won write-ups in nearly every major American publication. All this hype placed before millions a performer whose bland piano style, follow-the-bouncing-ball phrasing, and unvarying emotional temperature do little to illuminate the songs he loves. For some, his success proves the durability of the great standards and gives hope for aspiring pop singers. Others consider it a testament to the power of hype and evidence that anything can be sold to a national audience when celebrities such as Minnelli and Taylor endorse it. But many listeners wonder what all the fuss is about. According to one theatrical director, "Kids hear him and think that all showtunes sound this way, and they never want to hear them again. I took a young musician to Michael's first Broadway show, and during intermission he said, 'If this is what theatre music is about then I don't want any part of it.' I give Michael credit for hiring top arrangers and musicians, who help take the curse off his singing, but every song still sounds like every other song."

It is unfortunate that so much money and celebrity clout were not invested in a greater talent. Ann Hampton Callaway, a Chicago-born singer-pianist, has molded that undervalued art into an entertainment as funny, affecting, and theatrical as the best full-scale club act. A six-foot-tall brunette with a model's face and figure and a lustrous three-octave voice, Callaway has a stylistic range that extends from comic imitations of Sarah Vaughan and Bob Dylan to ballads sung with an emotional urgency that few singers twice her age can equal. Her desire to "bring back romance" becomes obvious from the first measures of "I'm Glad There Is You" or "Too Late Now," as she sinks into long, langorous phrases as seductively as if she were stretching out in front of a fireplace. In an "instrumental" version of "I Can't Get Started" she mimicks a trombone, muted trumpet, guitar, and bass in the style of the Mills Brothers. Her own "At the Same Time" is an eloquent plea for peace published by Mikhail Gorbachev in his book *Americans Write Gorbachev*. Callaway stamps every performance with her sassy sense of humor and with a passionate lyricism. By the end of her shows a roomful of listeners stare up at her with an apparent desire to sweep her into their arms and take her away from it all—if only they were strong enough to carry her.

Callaway began performing in New York piano bars in 1979 at age twenty. Her primary training ground was Les Tuileries, a bar-restaurant on Central Park South. She worked in a corner formed by the central revolving door and a mural window that exposed a strolling panorama of city life, complete with clip-clopping horse-drawn carriages. Sometimes a senior citizen tour group pressed their noses against the glass, looking in at a bar in which every third customer seemed to be of ill repute. "It was the theatre of the absurd in a way," she says. "I'm very spontaneous, and I thought there were so many ingredients that made it a theatrical setting: the park, the revolving door behind me, the bar, the prostitutes, the drug pushers, the celebrities, the horse smells. I thought, if I'm going to compete with all that, I'd better use it. I remember nights thinking, 'Nobody's listening to me. I'm gonna try something.' "

At those moments she might gasp in mock amazement and pretend that 1940s film star Kathryn Grayson had just walked in and agreed to sing a chorus of "Make Believe," which Callaway mimicked with deadpan accuracy. At the final high note the bartender smashed a glass behind the bar. When the outdoor parade became too distracting, she announced, "I'd like to tell those of you who are looking at the people passing by that they are not actually real people. The New York Tourist Association has hired all the unemployed actors in New York to pretend to be drug dealers, pimps, prostitutes—they are very accurately portraying some of the types of people you will encounter in New York. And I think that whenever they walk by you should acknowledge them with some applause." Drunks were introduced as her ex-husbands ("By the way, honey, the mail was a little slow this month!"); song request notes were read into the microphone as bogus mash letters ("Dear Ann, I'm with this woman, but you're the one I really want"). Through such devices Callaway drew listeners in one by one, until even the softest late-night rendition of Irving Berlin's "How Deep Is the Ocean?" could often be sung in a hush.

Since then her biggest frustrations have been at the hands of management, whose insensitivity can surpass any drunk's. A glaring example was at the Oak Room of the Plaza Hotel, managed by owner Donald Trump's wife Ivana for a dollar a year and all the dresses she could buy. "I put a lot of money into press," says Callaway, "and tried to build it into a serious place for people to come after the theatre. I told them, 'In order to make this special you have to present me. You have to have lighting, you need a small stage, I should be introduced, the smoking section should not be in the front where I'm going to choke to death.' We finally got most of that done, and the Trump people came in and took it all away and turned down my volume. I said, 'If you want background music, don't hire me. I didn't work ten years to become a background.' So I left."

Callaway has made a living through performing since she came to New York and has worked in top clubs and made a few minor TV appearances. But as the '90s began she had still not found a satisfactory record contract, which hindered her chances for further television or prime concert work. "The basic comment is, 'She's great, but she's not national,' " she says. "They don't want to take any chances on some newcomer."

In 1989 two expensive new rooms reached, quite literally, for the stars. One of them, the ninety-seat Rainbow and Stars, opened on the sixty-fifth floor of 30 Rockefeller Plaza, adjacent to the famous

Rainbow Room. A thirty-five-dollar cover brought customers acts not seen in a New York club in years, in some cases decades: Tony Bennett, Phyllis Diller, the McGuire Sisters, Gloria DeHaven, Lisa Kirk, Rosemary Clooney, and many others. They performed against a backdrop of windows that gave a stratospheric view of the Manhattan skyline. The rest of the room resembled an Art Deco ocean liner, with licorice-red wall siding, a fiber-optic lighting effect that flashed a multicolored rainbow on the glass, and two levels of tables.

Although the high cost made the room unaffordable for many fans, those with the money were nearly always assured of an act that bespoke talent, preparation, and expense, giving a much-needed reminder of how pros perform. And the room had a warmth and comfort that were just as rare, with comfortably arranged seating and a respectful staff. Moreover, it was the only such club in New York—perhaps in the country—that enforced a jacket-and-tie dress code. For those who cared about such things, the pleasure of sitting in a roomful of elegantly dressed, well-mannered people brought back distant memories of the days when New Yorkers aspired to a sophisticated atmosphere.

Rainbow and Stars provided a lot of uniquely memorable evenings. Singer-actress Gloria DeHaven, as glamorous and affecting of voice as in her MGM heyday, offered a nostalgic trip through those years that made one long to turn back the clock. The McGuire Sisters, whose harmonies had grown richer with the years, continued to demonstrate the easy, unpretentious charm that endeared them to a nation of TV viewers in the '50s. Carol Lawrence and Larry Kert, original stars of Broadway's *West Side Story*, reunited for the first time in over thirty years for a graceful, seamless evening of showtunes and standards that relied little on nostalgia for its appeal. Tony Bennett, Julie Wilson, Rosemary Clooney, and Julius LaRosa held forth with an authority born of forty years of showbiz experience, as did Patti Page, who united past and present with a skill that few could equal. Near the end of her act Page entered the audience, shaking hands and greeting every customer as she sang a long medley of her hits. What may sound like a corny gimmick became nostalgia at its most heartwarming. Older guests felt renewed as they touched the hand of a part of their youth—someone who looked and sounded nearly identical after four decades. Listeners who could rouse themselves from her spell might have wondered how the singer managed to time her songs and hellos so as to shake the last hand on the last phrase.

Two or three acts seemed caught in a time warp, particularly Lisa Kirk, costar of Broadway's *Allegro* (1947) and *Kiss Me, Kate* (1948). Looking as if she had been preserved on ice for thirty years, Kirk revived her Persian Room act not as an essay in nostalgia but as an eerie exercise in déjà vu, as if she truly believed it were still 1958. Only her frayed voice betrayed the passing years. Her opening number, "Manhattan's Merry-Go-Round," celebrated '50s New York as if it still existed:

Of all the places I've been to
New York's the best that I've found
Where else can you see the Yankees
Or travel under the ground?

Holy terror Lainie Kazan griped onstage nightly that the room was too hot, even as snow dusted the window behind her. One evening patrons waited for the late show to begin as the disgruntled maitre d' walked around covering the overhead vents with black electrical tape. Finally Kazan emerged in a tie-dyed muumuu and proceeded with her show, pausing occasionally to comment on the temperature. "Oh my GODDDDDDD, it's so HOT in here! *JEE*-sus *CHRIST!*"

One attempt to book a commercial act made regulars wince. Lanky six-foot California actress Susan Anton made her New York club debut in September 1990 after several all-too-evident years in Las Vegas and Atlantic City. After her opener, the Aretha Franklin hit "It's My Turn," Anton ran her hand through her long sun-bleached hair and greeted the crowd. "Ah, good evenin', ever'body, welcome to Rainbow 'n' Stahs. How y'all FEELIN'?" A few murmurs of "fine." "Oh, you had to *think* about it! Now, I'm goin' to ask you again. How ya feelin'?"

"Great, great," said a few people.

"Good, good, good, I'm glad. Well, you must be feelin' good, all the way sixty-five floors up, checkin' out this incredible view, sittin' there all comfortable. Great food on your plate! Whatcha got, pasta? Oh, you can eat while I'm singing! *Mangia*, absolutely!" ("That's called 'working the room,' " explained a *chanteur* at ringside to his companion.) Like Kazan, Anton commented on the heat. "WOOOOO, 's hot in here, right? Look out! Mmmm-hmmm . . . I think I might have to . . . get rid of somethin' . . . Are you ready?" At the close of her program of vapidly sung rock tunes and standards, Anton introduced "the terrifically talented young man playin' the piano and the synthesizer and conducting and arranging and . . . jus' doin' 'bout every single thing I can think of . . . I haven't asked you to do my laundry yet! Heh-heh-heh . . ."

Outside in the lobby afterward the "talented young man" passed her and said, "Well, Susan, if you give me your panties I promise I'll do the rest of your laundry."

Another touch of Las Vegas came to 45th Street and Broadway with the September 1989 opening of the Criterion Cabaret, part of the $7.5 million Criterion Center theatre-cinema complex. A massive, underheated gray room with seating for 370 and more levels and staircases than the nearby Times Square subway station, the Criterion made no pretentious claims toward anything except giving a series of big-scale acts such as Nell Carter, Leslie Uggams, David Brenner, and Chita Rivera a club space that New York had not offered them in years. Sixties rock star Little Anthony closed the room that New Year's Eve. As with Ted Hook's Onstage, one of the suggested factors in the room's failure was Atlantic City, which had inflated so many stars' salaries. Numerous customers said they wished they had sprung for a Broadway show instead of the Criterion, which charged a thirty-dollar cover plus food and drink costs. "We really wanted this to work," said Charlie Moss, the courageous owner of the complex. "We wanted to bring something special back to New York that isn't here anymore, and we tried hard. There's really no room in New York that has the size to take a major league star and present him in the right way and yet isn't so overwhelming that the star has to fill two thousand seats."

Can anything be done to create a solid audience? Donald Smith believes the key lies in promotion. Shortly after Mabel Mercer's death he established the Mabel Mercer Foundation to "perpetuate the memory and the spirit of Mabel Mercer by the stimulation and promotion of public interest in cabaret and supper club performance." "Many club owners don't realize that you can't just book an act, even a well-known one, and expect to fill a room without advertising and promotion," Smith told Jacques le Sourd. "A cabaret needs a machine working all the time and pushing." While the question remains as to how these troubled rooms would finance that machine, Smith has fought tirelessly and resourcefully to bring café performance to a wider public. He has produced a successful series of one-night acts at a lovely sixty-seat room upstairs at the Russian Tea Room; an annual program of concerts at New York's Weill Recital Hall by Julie Wilson, Ann Hampton Callaway, Kaye Ballard, and others; and a "cabaret convention" series at Town Hall that began in October 1989. It consisted of four marathon concerts featuring dozens of singers and three afternoon panel discussions by journalists, singers, and club owners on how to bolster business. The last of them pinpointed the greatest problem: when a panelist asked which of the 200 or so audience members was a performer, about half of them raised their hands.

Another organization, the Manhattan Association of Cabarets (MAC) announced its goal "to promote cabaret as a viable art form and as an alternative to a night at the theatre," but so far has merely furthered the business's reputation as a self-contained, incestuous subculture. Most of MAC's membership came from the local amateur circuit, who gathered for meetings and seminars on such topics as "How to Choose a Musical Director," "How to Do Your Own Publicity," and "Videotaping Your Show." MAC's annual award ceremonies exposed every reason why the business *should* expire. Between the presentation of a group of ludicrously chosen awards were performances by a parade of transvestites, epicene male singers, and female self-parodies, who received thunderous applause from their assembled claques. During a midsong ovation given to a tortured Colombian female vocalist, one veteran singer-pianist whispered to another, "I think we're a little too old for this."

IT SEEMS LIKELY that piano bars will always exist, as well as lounges and restaurants where singer-pianists can work. And singers willing to perform at their own expense for a night or two will probably never lack a place to do so. How much else of the business will survive remains to be seen.

Amid hopes that small clubs will regain some of their former eminence, one must remember that popular music and comedy have always mirrored the social climate of the day. Intimate spaces and quiet, modest sentiments had a special place in a society not obsessed with big concerns, be they skyscraper office buildings or life-threatening national issues. The sly gesture, the wink, the double-entendre—in short, much of the mystique of romance—went hand in hand with a naïveté that this tell-all, know-all age has shattered. Understandably, many take a dim view of what has contributed to this.

"Change occurs, and you can't stop it," says Portia Nelson. "A lot of it had to do with the drug generation. People began to care less about excellence than about doing as they pleased. The kind of thing we did took a certain discipline and work and cooperative artistry to bring about. And we had an audience who cared about that. In the '50s and '60s many performers were not of the caliber we knew earlier on. They played the guitar and sang a song that somebody liked and were put on records and built into something, but they were not genuine artistic talents. When an unskilled singer can make a million dollars—that's what everybody's after. It's competition, it's who's making the most money, who's the most famous. I think mediocrity has become the norm, rather than a striving for excellence. We have let the barriers down to include more, rather than making people climb to be their best. In some ways maybe that's good, but it has eroded the level of quality. And when that changes, the level of expectation changes along with it. I rebelled so against rock and roll in those days, although it was fun once I opened my head to it. But I thought that if people could only hear what was good, if rock wasn't all that was available, they might develop a taste for it. It's like education. If you don't *have* to study certain things and be good at them to get a passing grade, you aren't going to do it. All of us are lazy by nature. We have to learn not to be lazy. I think the biggest problem is that the easy way out has taken over."

And yet our growth away from a period of dewy-eyed romanticism, and daily concerns that ventured no farther than the secure terrain of house and community, has not been without advantage, as Pat Carroll points out. "The fact that comics like Robin Williams, Whoopi Goldberg, and Billy Crystal can do a comedy show on television and interest people all across the country in the homeless—wow! That's fantastic! Except for Mort Sahl's sociological and political humor, the modus operandi of performers in the '50s was entertainment. People weren't into the big issues yet. We were happy where we were. The only stress we had was worrying about our acts, whether they got applause or not.

"But looking back, I don't think I knew anything politically. I don't even think I decided what political party I'd vote for until I had two children. Then I realized that all the laws that were passed had an effect on what my kids ate, on their education, on the amount of taxes we paid for our home. I was very naive. The entire country was naive."

Which is why remembering that era is like remembering childhood. Today's youngsters are born into an atmosphere that makes that innocence seem archaic.

Where does this leave an endangered art form that asks us to strip away our urban defenses for an hour and admit a little vulnerability? "I think people inherently hunger for music and what it does for the soul," says Ann Hampton Callaway. "In order to merit people's undivided attention you have to live and feel to a degree that may be beyond the average person. One of the things I love about intimate performing is the magic of sharing with a roomful of people. It's a sense of family that happens in few things: around a table, with special friends, at a game where fans are rooting for the same team. Otherwise, we're either alone or shoved in with busy people in streets or subways with whom we feel little if not hostile connection. The power of music and laughter and whimsy is that there you are in a dark room with others like yourself, and you can laugh, cry, yearn, and imagine all you like. When the show is over, I think you feel a little closer to yourself, your partner, and the people around you. And in this day and age, to be part of that experience is worth the humbleness of being a nightclub performer, worth the frequently small wages, the smoke, the noise, the late hours. It's a love affair as special as any two people can share."

DISCOGRAPHY

The following is a selective discography of long-playing recordings, including year of original release. Every effort has been made to list current domestic compact disc reissues, where available. This listing is not comprehensive; recordings are chosen that best illustrate the café style or the work of a particular performer, with emphasis placed on live sessions. Releases that, in the author's judgment, endure as outstanding achievements in the genre and provide lasting pleasure are marked with an asterisk. Broadcasts, private audio tapes, 78s, and 45s are not listed. Inquiries or information about other existing recordings, films, and video are welcome and may be directed to the author in care of Limelight Editions

PETER ALLEN

Peter Allen — Metromedia KMD 1042, 1971
Tenterfield Saddler — A&M SP-69826, 1972
Continental American — A&M SP 3643, 1974

WOODY ALLEN

*Woody Allen [recorded live at Mister Kelly's, Chicago]
Colpix SCP 518, 1964

Woody Allen, Volume 2 [recorded live at the Shadows, Washington, D.C.]
Colpix 488, 1965

The Third Woody Allen Album [recorded live at Eugene's, San Francisco]
Capitol ST 2986, 1968

DANNY APOLINAR

Come By Sunday — Stereoddities C-1904, ca. 1964
A Spot in the Sun Presents . . . — Entertainment Assocs. 101, ca. 1968

(Singer-songwriter-pianist Danny Apolinar has been a fixture in Manhattan piano bars since the 1960s. These two rarities are the only commercial recordings of his sometimes riotous, sometimes heartrending style.)

BEN BAGLEY'S "REVISITED" SERIES

*Rodgers & Hart Revisited, Volume I — Painted Smiles PSCD-116, 1961
*Cole Porter Revisited, Volume I — Painted Smiles PSCD-121, 1964
*Jerome Kern Revisited, Volume I — Painted Smiles PSCD-113, 1966
*Irving Berlin Revisited — Painted Smiles PSCD-118, 1970
*Harold Arlen/Vernon Duke Revisited, Volume II — Painted Smiles PSCD-127, 1975
*Cole Porter Revisited, Volume V — Painted Smiles PSCD-122, 1992

[Many of Ben Bagley's "Revisited" CDs of obscure showtunes feature top cafe veterans—among them Bobby Short, Blossom Dearie, Dorothy Loudon, Kaye Ballard, Charlotte Rae, Barbara Cook, Nancy Andrews, Tammy Grimes, and Julie Wilson—along with dozens of new tracks recorded by Ann Hampton Callaway.]

KAYE BALLARD

Live? [recorded live at the Bon Soir, New York] — U.A. UAS 6155, 1959

BUDDY BARNES

*The Magic Time — Audiophile AP-139, 1980

MAE BARNES

*Fun with Mae Barnes [with Garland Wilson and the Three Flames] — Atlantic ALS 404, 1954
*Mae Barnes — DRG CD 8434, 1959

ORSON BEAN

At the hungry i — Fantasy 7009, 1959

RICHARD RODNEY BENNETT

*Harold Arlen's Songs — Audiophile AP-168, 1983

Take Love Easy: The Lyrics of John Latouche — Audiophile AP-206, 1985

*Lush Life — Ode CD 1292, 1988

*I Never Went Away — Delos CD DE5001, 1990

(British classical and film composer Richard Rodney Bennett's prolific scoring has enhanced *Murder on the Orient Express, Far from the Madding Crowd, Equus, Nicholas and Alexandria,* and many other movies and television dramas. In Manhattan jazz clubs and piano bars, he stylishly indulges his passion for singing and playing popular songs in an insinuating, jazz-tinged style.)

JOANNE BERETTA

Sings at the Madeira Club [Provincetown, Massachusetts] — A La Mod 101, 1967

SHELLEY BERMAN

*Inside Shelley Berman [recorded live; location unknown] — Verve MGVS-6106, 1958

*Outside Shelley Berman [recorded live; location unknown] — Verve MGVS-6107, 1959

*The Edge of Shelley Berman [recorded live; location unknown] — Verve MGV-15013, 1960

NAN BLAKSTONE

An Evening with Nan Blakstone [1930s anthology] — Gala 1000

RAE BOURBON

An Evening in Copenhagen [1950s anthology] — UTC 1

Around the World in 80 Ways [1950s anthology] — UTC 8

Let Me Tell You About My Operation [1950s anthology] — UTC 101

JANET BRACE

Special Delivery — ABC-Paramount ABC-116, 1956

(This sprightly, diminutive singer performed at Le Ruban Bleu in the early '50s.)

STELLA BROOKS/GRETA KELLER

Songs of the 1940s — Folkways FJ 2830

MICHAEL BROWN

Sings His Own Songs [with the Norman Paris Trio] — Jubilee LP-2010, 1954

Alarums and Excursions — Impulse AS-24, 1962

LENNY BRUCE

*The Lenny Bruce Originals, Volume I — Fantasy FCD-60-023 (F-7001/7003), 1959

*The Lenny Bruce Originals, Volume II — Fantasy FCD-60-024 (F-7007/7011), 1959

GEORGE BYRON

*Jerome Kern Songs — Desto D501, 1953

*Rediscovered Gershwin — Desto D502, 1953

(Baritone George Byron enjoyed the friendship and respect of such songwriters as Ira Gershwin and Jerome Kern, whose songs he featured on radio and in nightclubs, notably the Café Gala in Hollywood.)

ANN HAMPTON CALLAWAY

*Ann Hampton Callaway — DRG CD 91411, 1992

THELMA CARPENTER

Thinking of You Tonight — Coral CRL 757433, 1960

DIXIE CARTER

Come a Little Closer — Vining HH85001, 1985

*Sings John Wallowitch—Live at the Carlyle — Vining CD LL-9001, 1991

JUNE CHRISTY

*Something Cool	Capitol CDP 796329 2, 1955
*Duet [with Stan Kenton, piano]	Capitol T 656, 1955
*The Misty Miss Christy	Capitol CDP 798452 2
Fair and Warmer	Capitol T 833, 1957
*Gone for the Day	Capitol T 902, 1957
*June's Got Rhythm	Capitol ST 1076, 1958
*The Song Is June	Capitol ST 1114, 1959
*Ballads for Night People	Capitol ST 1308, 1960
*Something Cool	Capitol ST 516, 1960

[A stereo re-recording of the 1955 mono release.]

*Off Beat	Capitol ST 1498, 1961
*Impromptu	Discovery DSCD-836, 1978

(The late pop-jazz singer June Christy remains closely associated with the café genre, although her club appearances were limited mostly to dates with Stan Kenton and other big-band leaders. Christy's signature song, Billy Barnes's "Something Cool," depicts a boozy middle-aged woman reminiscing to a silent stranger at a bar about her better days, perhaps imagined. Herself an alcoholic, who died of kidney failure in 1990, Christy could communicate a sense of defeat as heartbreakingly as any singer discussed in the text. The feeling of melancholy that her husky voice imparted even to love ballads makes the above albums required listening for the postmidnight glad-to-be-unhappy.)

ROBERT CLARY

Meet Robert Clary	Epic LN 3171, 1955
Lives It Up at the Playboy Club [Chicago]	Atlantic 8053, 1961

CHARLIE COCHRAN

I Sing, I Play	Dorian LP-1011, 1961
*Haunted Heart	Audiophile AP-177, 1983

(A warm-voiced, no-nonsense singer-pianist, Charlie Cochran has enjoyed the admiration and friendship of Lee Wiley, Judy Garland, Anita O'Day, and Jeri Southern, who called his 1983 album "some of the most exquisite singing I've ever heard . . . Every time I hear him sing I feel that it's just for me.")

BETTY COMDEN & ADOLPH GREEN

The Revuers/Bonanza Bound [original late-'30s recordings by the Revuers, plus songs from a 1947 musical]
Box Office JJA-19764

BARBARA COOK

*From the Heart: The Best of Rodgers & Hart
MMG MMCD 900, 1959
*Barbara Cook at Carnegie Hall — Columbia M 33438, 1975
*It's Better with a Band — MMG MCD 10010, 1981

IRWIN COREY

*The World's Foremost Authority [recorded live at Le Ruban Bleu, New York]
Jubilee LP-2018, 1954
Win with Irwin [recorded live at the Playboy Club, Chicago]
Atlantic 1326, 1961

JILL COREY

Sometimes I'm Happy, Sometimes I'm Blue
Columbia CL 1095, 1958

LESTER CROSLEY

*In the Heart of the Dark — Jubilee JLP-1082, 1956

(One of the most respected café pianists of the 1940s, Lester Crosley is best remembered as Mabel Mercer's accompanist at Tony's in the mid-'40s.)

DARDANELLE

Echoes Singing Ladies — Audiophile AP-145, 1980
*The Colors of My Life — Stash ST-CD-541, 1979–82

(This Mississippi-born singer-pianist has used her soft, supple voice and swinging piano style to enrich a fine repertoire of Broadway, film, and jazz songs that range from the well worn to the unjustly obscure.)

MARTHA DAVIS & SPOUSE

*Martha Davis & Spouse — ABC-Paramount ABC-160, 1957
*A Tribute to Fats Waller — ABC-Paramount ABC-213, 1958

BLOSSOM DEARIE

Blossom Dearie Verve CD 837 934-2, 1956
*Give Him the Ooh-La-La Verve MGV-2081, 1957
*Once Upon a Summertime Verve 827 757-1, 1959
Sings Comden & Green Verve MGVS-6050, 1959
*My Gentleman Friend Verve MGVS-6112, 1960
*May I Come In? Daffodil CD BMD-114, 1964
*Blossom Time [recorded live at Ronnie Scott's, London]
Fontana SRF 67562, 1967
*Sweet Blossom Dearie [recorded live at Ronnie Scott's, London]
Fontana STL 5399, 1967
*Winchester in Apple Blossom Time
Daffodil BMD 104, 1977
*Needlepoint Magic [recorded live at Reno Sweeney, New York]
Mastermix CDCHE3, 1979

CHARLES DEFOREST

Daydreams and Nightdreams Version VLP-102, 1954
Arbiter of Elegance Purist 1, ca. 1962

MATT DENNIS

Plays and Sings Matt Dennis [recorded live at Tally-Ho, Hollywood]
Trend TL-1500, 1955
*She Dances Overhead: The Songs of Rodgers & Hart
RCA LPM-1065, 1955
Dennis, Anyone? [recorded live; location unknown]
RCA LPM-1134, 1956
Play Melancholy Baby RCA LPM-1322, 1957

(The composer of such oft-recorded songs as "Angel Eyes," "The Night We Called It a Day," "Will You Still Be Mine?" and "Everything Happens to Me," Matt Dennis sang both originals and standards in a clean, flexible, expressive voice, accompanying himself with a jazz musician's verve and sense of swing.)

JOE DERISE

*Sings Bethlehem BCP 1039, 1955
*Joe Derise Bethlehem BCP 51, 1957
*Vintage '64 Palm Tree AKPT-10001, 1964

(Like Dennis, singer-pianist Derise gave cuddly, jazz-inflected readings of an impeccable repertoire of well-known and unknown tunes, especially from lesser-known film musicals.)

FAY DEWITT

Through Sick and Sin — Epic BN 596, 1961

(This rich-voiced comedienne-singer, familiar at the Bon Soir, Le Ruban Bleu, and other clubs, got her one solo recording opportunity with this barely existent collection of pseudo-risqué special material by Charles Strouse and Lee Adams, Fred Ebb and his early collaborator Paul Klein, Harold Rome, and others. The highlight is Ebb and Klein's "London Town," about a maiden who becomes progressively debauched as she attempts a long journey to visit her love.)

PHYLLIS DILLER

Wet Toe in a Hot Socket [recorded live at the Bon Soir, New York] — Mirrosonic SP 6002, 1959

*Laughs [recorded live at the Bon Soir, New York] — Verve V6-15026, 1961

*Are You Ready for Phyllis Diller? [recorded live at the hungry i, San Francisco] — Verve V6-15031, 1962

RITA DIMITRI

An Evening with Rita Dimitri at La Chansonette — Private Pressing

(This justly obscure release is included as an example of the depths to which nightclub performance so often sinks. Chantoosie Dimitri—"I ahm hahf F*lll*ench and hahf G*lll*ick"—was the featured singer at an East Side restaurant financed by her wealthy businessman husband Stanley Brilliant, who makes a sorry appearance on this disc as singer-guitarist. *Caveat emptor*—even at the twenty-five cents this issue usually fetches in a thrift shop.)

JACK DOUGLAS

With the Original Cast [recorded live at the Bon Soir, New York] — Columbia CS 8357, 1962

CHARLEY DREW

Sings Witty Ditties, Album 1 — Gala GBR-1, ca. 1955

Sings Witty Ditties, Album 2 — Gala GBR-2, ca. 1955
Sings Witty Ditties, Album 3 — Gala GBR-3, ca. 1955

FRANK D'RONE

*Sings — Mercury SR 60064, 1958
In Person [recorded live at the hungry i, San Francisco] — Mercury SR 60721, 1960

(Pop-jazz vocalist Frank D'Rone performed at the Bon Soir and other clubs starting in the late '50s, singing standards in a lean, swinging voice and often accompanying himself on guitar.)

EADIE & RACK

Piano Moods — Columbia CL 6176, 1950
*Play Songs from *Fanny* — Liberty Music Shop 1009, 1954

JONATHAN & DARLENE EDWARDS

*The Piano Artistry of Jonathan Edwards — Corinthian 104, 1957
*In Paris — Corinthian 103, 1958
*Sing Along with Jonathan & Darlene Edwards — Corinthian 120, ca. 1963
*Greatest Hits [anthology] — Corinthian COR 101 CD

(These classic parody albums by singer Jo Stafford and arranger Paul Weston present an imaginary couple encountered in any number of lounges and restaurants: a leaden, tone-deaf, but well-intentioned vocalist accompanied by her dizzy-fingered, metrically and harmonically hopeless pianist. The brilliant satire on these sides could have been achieved only by two such consummate musicians.)

ANITA ELLIS

*I Wonder What Became of Me — Epic LN 3260, 1956
Hims — Epic LN 3419, 1957
*The World in My Arms — Elektra EKS-7179, 1960
*A Legend Sings [with Ellis Larkins, piano] — Orion ORS 79358, 1979

MICHAEL FEINSTEIN

Live at the Algonquin — Elektra-Asylum CD 9 60743-2, 1987

Remember: Michael Feinstein Sings Irving Berlin
Elektra CD 9 60744-2, 1987

Isn't It Romantic — Elektra-Asylum CD 9 60792-2, 1988

The Burton Lane Songbook, Volume I
Elektra-Nonesuch CD 79243-2, 1990

GEORGE FEYER

Plays *My Fair Lady* [side two recorded live at the Café Carlyle, New York]
Vox VX25-340, 1957

A Nightcap with George Feyer [recorded live at the Café Carlyle, New York]
Decca DL 74625, 1965

DWIGHT FISKE

Sophisticated Songs and Patter, Album 1 [1940s anthology]
Gala GLP-100

Sophisticated Songs and Patter, Album 2 [1940s anthology]
Gala GLP-101

Sophisticated Songs and Patter, Album 3 [1940s anthology]
Gala GLP-102

Musical Satires [1940s anthology] — Monarch 206

Songs His Mother Never Taught Him
Jubilee LP-17, 1954

DWIGHT FISKE/NAN BLAKSTONE

Tongue with Cheek [1930s/'40s anthology]
Jubilee JGM-2026

PHIL FOSTER

Alive? [recorded live at the Bon Soir, New York]
Keynote LP 1103, 1963

STAN FREEMAN

*Piano Moods — Columbia CL 6158, 1950

At the Blue Angel — Epic LN 3224, 1956

*Not a Care in the World — Audiophile AP-202, 1986

(In the '50s and '60s Stan Freeman was considered second only to Cy Walter as a café pianist, although his extraordinary technique surpassed even Walter's. Freeman's additional skills as singer and raconteur have contributed to a career of greater longevity than that of any of his early colleagues.)

DAVE FRISHBERG

*Classics [1982–1983 collection] — Concord Jazz CCD-4462

Live at Vine Street [Hollywood jazz club] — Fantasy F-9638, 1985

Can't Take You Nowhere [recorded live at the Great American Music Hall, San Francisco] — Fantasy FCD-9651-2, 1987

(West Coast composer-singer-pianist Dave Frishberg views such subjects as baseball, Marilyn Monroe, one-night stands, and nostalgia for a forsaken Manhattan through a cynical, diamond-hard lens, and sings about them in a voice whose rural Hoagy Carmichaelish rasp cannot mask his worldly wisdom. "I'm Hip" and "Peel Me a Grape" have long been highlights of Blossom Dearie's repertoire, but no one sings his wry, witty, complicated, and often heartfelt songs as effectively as Frishberg himself.)

DODY GOODMAN

*Sings? — Coral CRL 57196, 1957

DICK GREGORY

*East and West [recorded live at the Blue Angel, New York, and at the hungry i, San Francisco] — Colpix CP 420, 1962

TAMMY GRIMES

Julius Monk Presents Tammy Grimes, Debut—Downstairs at the Upstairs — Offbeat OB-401, 1959

DICK & KIZ HARP

*At the 90th Floor — 90th Floor SLL-901, 1960

*Again! At the 90th Floor — 90th Floor SLL-902, 1961

(These discs are highly prized by the handful who own them. Pianist-singer Dick Harp and his singing wife, Kiz, were a charming young couple who converted an old warehouse behind a Dallas grocery store into a nightclub visited by Marlene Dietrich, Tony Bennett, Phyllis Diller, and many others who admired the couple's unpretentious way with a tasty, "in" New York repertoire. Kiz died of a cerebral hemorrhage in 1960 at age twenty-eight, making these two live albums all the more treasurable.)

PAT HARRINGTON, JR.

Some Like It Hip! [recorded live at the Blue Angel, New York]
U.A. UAS 4088, 1960

JANE HARVEY

*I've Been There — Audio-Fidelity AFSD-2149, 1965

*You Fats, Me Jane [Fats Waller songs]
Classic Jazz CJ 15, 1975

GOLDIE HAWKINS

Goldie Plays by the Sea — Atlantic ALR 125, 1953

An Evening at Goldie's [with Wayne Sanders, piano]
Mercury SR 60218, 1959

Goldie's New York Revisited [with Sam Hamilton, piano]
U.A. UAS 6320, 1963

Goldie's Two Pianos [with Wayne Sanders, piano]
Ruby FRS-1736, 1967

HILDEGARDE

I'm in the Mood for Love [1940s anthology]
Stanyan SR 10056

Hildegarde [side two recorded live at the Cotillion Room, New York]
Seeco CELP-400, 1957

CLAIRE HOGAN

*Boozers and Losers — MGM SE-4501, 1967

(Ex-band vocalist Claire Hogan appeared only once in a New York solo club engagement but is still identified with the genre thanks to this cult favorite, elaborately produced by Cy Coleman, for whom she worked as girl Friday. "I'll Pay the Check," "I'm Always Drunk in San Francisco," "Sometime When You're Lonely," and especially the title track conjure up a world of 2 A.M. piano bars, booze-and-cigarette-voiced female singers, and stoned customers. Camp tragedy and urban alcoholic despair are chillingly united in Hogan's ravaged baritone.)

WILL HOLT

The Exciting Artistry of Will Holt
Elektra EKS-7181, 1960

WILL HOLT & DOLLY JONAH

On the Brink [recorded live at the hungry i, San Francisco]
Atlantic 8051, 1961

ELSIE HOUSTON

*Sings Brazilian Songs [recorded 1941]
RCA LCT 1143

BART HOWARD

Bart! The Songs of Bart Howard [with Julie Wilson, William Roy, and K. T. Sullivan] Painted Smiles PSCD-114, 1990

JACKIE & ROY

*Jackie & Roy Storyville STLP 904, 1954
*Sing, Baby, Sing! Storyville STLP 915, 1955
*The Glory of Love ABC-Paramount ABC-120, 1956
*In the Spotlight ABC-Paramount ABCS-267, 1959
*Double Take Columbia CS 8504, 1961
*Like Sing! The Songs of Dory & Andre Previn
Columbia CS 8504, 1963
*Lovesick Verve-Polygram CD839 291-2, 1967
Concerts by the Sea [recorded live at Concerts by the Sea, Redondo Beach, California] Studio 7 ST7-402, 1977
*A Stephen Sondheim Collection [recorded live at Michael's Pub, New York]
DRG CDS 25102, 1983
*One More Rose: A Tribute to Alan Jay Lerner
Audiophile ACD-230, 1987
*An Alec Wilder Collection Audiophile ACD-257, 1990

T. C. JONES

Himself! [recorded live at the Crescendo, Hollywood]
GNP 602, 1961

JUST FOR OPENERS (Upstairs at the Downstairs, 1965)

With Betty Aberlin, Richard Blair, Stockton Brigel, R. G. Brown, Fannie Flagg, and Madeline Kahn

UD 37W56

GRETA KELLER

Greta Keller and Other Chanteuses [anthology of Liberty Music Shop 78s from the late '30s; also features society singers Eve Symington, Adelaide Moffat, and Frances Maddux; pianist-singer Joan Edwards; and musical comedy singer Teddy Lynch]

	Box Office NLM1989
XII O'Clock	Dolphin 5, 1955
Remember Me	London LL 1305, 1961
In the Waldorf Keller	ABC-Paramount ABCS-429, 1962

JOHN KELLEY, JR.

Café Society Piano	MI 101, 1986

(Another ubiquitous Manhattan café pianist of the '50s, Kelley plays in the charming but unobtrusive manner that once underscored late-night conversation so appealingly.)

SANDRA KING

*In a Concert of Vernon Duke	Audiophile AP-197, 1985

(British pop-jazz vocalist Sandra King's deep, seductive voice is familiar to BBC and Dutch radio listeners, who often have the treat of hearing it against sumptuously arranged orchestral backgrounds. In 1982 King made her American debut at the Corcoran Gallery of Art in Washington, D.C., where this elegant album was recorded with a piano-bass duo.)

TEDDI KING

Round Midnight [1953–1954 recordings]

	Japanese Storyville PA-3116
*Now in Vogue	Storyville STLP 903, 1954
Bidin' My Time	RCA LPM-1147, 1956
To You from Teddi King	RCA LPM-1313, 1956
*A Girl and Her Songs	RCA LPM-1454, 1957
All the King's Songs	Coral 757278, 1959

Marian Remembers Teddi [with Marian McPartland, piano; recorded live at the New York Public Library, Lincoln Center]
Halcyon HAL 118, 1974

*This Is New — Inner City IC 1044, 1978

LISA KIRK

*Sings at the Plaza — MGM SE 3737, 1959

EARTHA KITT

Sings at the Plaza — GNPD CD2008, 1962
*Love for Sale — Columbia (U.K.) SCX 3563, 1965
*Live in London — Ariola CD353852, 1990

JIMMIE KOMACK

Inside Me . . . — RCA LPM-1501, 1957
At the Waldorf . . . Delicatessen — Ember ELP 800, ca. 1960

IRENE KRAL

*The Band & I — U.A. UAS 5016, 1959
*Better Than Anything — Ava AS-33, 1963
Wonderful Life — Mainstream S/6058, 1966
*Where Is Love? — Choice CRS 1012, 1975
*Kral Space — Catalyst CAT 7625, 1977
*Gentle Rain — Choice CRS 1020, 1978
Angel Eyes—Live in Tokyo — AllArt K18P 9419, 1978

ELLIS LARKINS

*Blues in the Night: The Melodies of Harold Arlen
Decca DL 5391, 1952
*Perfume and Rain — Storyville LP 316, 1954
*Do Nothin' Till You Hear from Me: In an Ellington Mood
Storyville STLP 913, 1955
*The Soft Touch — Decca DL 9205, 1957
*Blue and Sentimental — Decca DL 9211, 1958

(A master accompanist for Ella Fitzgerald, Anita Ellis, Chris Connor, Jane Harvey, and many other singers—as well as leader of the Blue Angel house trio for several years—Ellis Larkins has a light, airy, instantly recognizable touch that lends itself just as well to the solos on these superb albums.)

JOHN LA SALLE QUARTET

Jumpin' at the Left Bank — Capitol ST 1176, 1960

BARBARA LEA

A Woman in Love — Audiophile AP-86, 1955/1978

With the Johnny Windhurst Quintets — Prestige OJCCD-1713-2, 1957

Lea in Love — Prestige OJCCD-1742-2, 1957

JULIE LONDON

Julie Is Her Name — Liberty LRP 3006, 1955

Lonely Girl — Liberty LRP 3012, 1956

Calendar Girl — Liberty SL 9002, 1956

*About the Blues — Liberty LRP 3043, 1957

Make Love to Me — Liberty LRP 3060, 1957

*Julie — Liberty LRP 3096, 1957

*London by Night — Liberty LRP 3105, 1957

Julie Is Her Name, Volume Two — Liberty LST 7100, 1958

*Your Number Please — Liberty LST 7130, 1959

*Julie at Home — Liberty LST 7152, 1960

Around Midnight — Liberty LST 7164, 1960

Sophisticated Lady — Liberty LST 7203, 1962

Love on the Rocks — Liberty LST 7249, 1962

In Person—Live at the Americana — Liberty LST 7275, 1964

*All Through the Night—Julie London Sings the Choicest of Cole Porter — EMI CDP-7-93455-2, 1965

DOROTHY LOUDON

*At the Blue Angel — Coral CRL 757265, 1960

PAUL LYNDE

*Recently Released — Columbia CL 1534, 1960

JIMMY LYON

*Plays Cole Porter's Steinway and His Music [recorded live at Peacock Alley, Waldorf-Astoria, New York]
Finnadar SR 9034, 1982

CARMEN MCRAE

*By Special Request — Decca DL 8173, 1955
*After Glow — Decca DL 8583, 1957
*Carmen for Cool Ones — Decca DL 8738, 1958
*In London—at the Flamingo Club
Ember 5000, 1961
*Bittersweet — Focus 334, 1964
*Second to None — Mainstream S/6028, 1965
*Haven't We Met? — Mainstream S/6044, 1965
*Woman Talk—Live at the Village Gate
Mainstream CD MDCD 706, 1966
*Live at the Century-Plaza, Japan — Japanese Atlantic, 1968
*The Great American Songbook [recorded live at the Great American Music Hall, San Francisco]
Atlantic CD 2 904-2, 1972
*Live at the Dug—Carmen McRae Alone [recorded live in Tokyo]
Victor CD VD5-1570, 1973
Ronnie Scott's Presents Carmen McRae "Live"
Pye NSPL 18543, 1977

PENNY MALONE

Sings? An Album of Sophisticated Songs
Jubilee LP 16, 1954

JOHNNY MATHIS

A New Sound in Popular Song — Columbia CL 887, 1956

MABEL MERCER

The Art of Mabel Mercer [anthology of three Atlantic 10″ LPs from the early '50s] — Atlantic 2-602
Mabel Mercer Sings Cole Porter — Atlantic 1213, 1955
*Midnight at Mabel Mercer's — Atlantic 1244, 1956
*Once in a Blue Moon — Atlantic SD-1301, 1959

Merely Marvelous	Atlantic SD-1322, 1960
Sings	Decca DL 74472, 1964

MABEL MERCER & BOBBY SHORT

*At Town Hall	Atlantic SD2-604, 1968
Second Town Hall Concert	Atlantic SD2-605, 1969

MIXED DOUBLES/BELOW THE BELT (Upstairs at the Downstairs/ Downstairs at the Upstairs, 1966)

With Judy Graubart, Madeline Kahn, Larry Moss, Robert Rovin, Janie Sell, Gary Sneed, Richard Blair, Dixie Carter, and Lily Tomlin
UD37W56 Vol. 2

JULIUS MONK

Simply Plays (and/or Vice Versa)	Offbeat OB-400, 1959

REVUES:

Take Five	Offbeat O-4013, 1957
Demi-Dozen	Offbeat O-4015, 1958
Pieces of Eight	Offbeat O-4016, 1960
Four Below Strikes Back	Offbeat O-4017, 1960
Dressed to the Nines	MGM SE 39144OC, 1960
Seven Come Eleven	Columbia 55478, 1962
Dime a Dozen	Cadence CLP 25063, 1963

HELEN MORGAN/FANNY BRICE

*Torch Songs by Helen Morgan and Fanny Brice [anthology, 1928–1934]
"X" LVA-1006

*Fanny Brice—Helen Morgan [anthology, 1921–1934]
RCA LPV-561

MARK MURPHY

*Rah!	Riverside 395, 1962
*That's How I Love the Blues	Riverside OJCCD-367-2, 1963
*Midnight Mood	Pausa PR 7023, 1968
*Stolen Moments	Muse MCD 5102, 1978
*Bop for Kerouac	Muse MCD 5253, 1981

*Brazil Songs — Muse MR 5297, 1984
Sings Nat's Choice, Volumes 1 & 2
Muse MCD-6001, 1986
*Night Mood — Milestone MCD-9145-2, 1986
*September Ballads — Milestone MCD-9154-2, 1988
*Kerouac, Then and Now — Muse MCD 5359, 1989

(Since the mid-'50s, singer Mark Murphy has proven himself one of the most daring, restless, and eccentric spirits in jazz. In clubs from Europe to New York City, Murphy reconstructs American standards, Brazilian music, bop vocalese, and contemporary ballads in a grainy but fluent baritone, his off-the-wall sense of humor never quite concealing a palpable ache. To spend an hour with Murphy is to enter a world where time dangles, stops short, or races frantically; where tensions build and never fully subside, even at the end; and where no moment is predictable. Somehow the message of the lyrics comes through in ways the listener never imagined. All this is most evident on his 1981 album "Bop for Kerouac," a tribute to the ballads and jazz of Jack Kerouac's era. It is capped by a gut-wrenching version of Tommy Wolf and Fran Landesman's "Ballad of the Sad Young Men," a song supposedly inspired by the customers at the bar of the Crystal Palace in St. Louis, which was managed by Landesman's brother-in-law Fred. Few singers have delved as deeply into the recesses of disillusionment and uncertainty as Murphy does here and in many other recordings.)

PORTIA NELSON

*Love Songs for a Late Evening — Columbia LM 4722, 1953
Autumn Leaves — Dolphin 4, 1955
*Let Me Love You: The Songs of Bart Howard
New Sound NS 3002, 1956

PARADE [based on Jerry Herman's *Nightcap*]

With Dody Goodman, Charles Nelson Reilly, Richard Tone, Lester James, and Fia Karin — Kapp KS-7005, 1960

NORMAN PARIS TRIO

*An Evening with Paris — Columbia CL 6179, 1951

CHARLES PIERCE

Live at Bimbo's, San Francisco — Blue Thumb BTS 30, ca. 1972

HUBBELL PIERCE

*Cole Porter: Sung by Hubbell Pierce, Played by William Roy
Private pressing, 1973

(Singer-pianist Hubbell Pierce performed regularly at Upstairs at the Downstairs, the Left Bank, the Drake Room, and other clubs. Near his fiftieth birthday in 1973 Pierce's mother died, and he and his sister discovered [and gleefully cashed in] some old Coca-Cola stocks they found under her bed. The windfall allowed him to record, privately press, and distribute to friends this delightful album of Porter obscurities, sung in his highbrow yet swinging manner.)

LOVELADY POWELL

Lovelady — Transition TRLP M-1, 1956

CHARLOTTE RAE

Songs I Taught My Mother — Vanguard VRS-9004, 1955

SUE RANEY

*Quietly There: The Songs of Johnny Mandel
Discovery DSCD-939, 1988

(Liquid-voiced Sue Raney, whose blonde beauty is one of the modeling profession's greatest losses, shares these assets with clubgoers all too seldom. This collection of songs by arranger-composer Johnny Mandel is a gem of warm, sexy pop-jazz singing, tasteful and deeply felt.)

SUSAN REED

Sings Old Airs — Elektra EKL-26, 1955
Susan Reed — Elektra EKL-116, 1957

JORIE REMUS

*The Unpredictable Jorie Remus — Everest LPBR5102, 1960

JOAN RIVERS

The Next to Last Joan Rivers Album [recorded live at Upstairs at the Downstairs, New York]
Buddah BDS 5048, 1969

ANNIE ROSS

*A Gasser — Blue Note CD JB2-46854, 1957

*Sings a Song with Mulligan	Blue Note CD JB2-46852, 1958
*Annie by Candlelight	Pye GGL 0316, ca. 1965

STEVE ROSS

Steve Ross	Stolen Moments 1938, 1979
*Live at the Algonquin	Stolen Moments 1939, 1982
*At the Don Burrows Supper Club [Australia]	ABC L38638, 1986
*Most of Ev'ry Day	Audiophile AP-217, 1988

WILLIAM ROY

When I Sing Alone	Audiophile DAP-213, 1986

MORT SAHL

The Future Lies Ahead [recorded live; location unknown]	Verve MGV-15002, 1959
Mort Sahl at the hungry i	Verve MGV-15012, 1960

FELICIA SANDERS

At the Blue Angel	Columbia CL 654, 1955
That Certain Feeling	Decca DL 78762, 1959
*I Wish You Love	Time S/70002, 1960
*Songs of Kurt Weill	Time S/2007, 1960
*Live [recorded at the Bon Soir, New York]	Special Editions 801, 1965

BOBBY SCOTT

*Sings the Best of Lerner & Loewe	Atlantic MGVS-2106, 1958
*For Sentimental Reasons	Music Masters CIJD6 0229 Y, 1990

HUGH SHANNON

Sings and Plays	Atlantic ALS 406, 1954
*Disgustingly Rich [with Blossom Dearie]	Harlequin HQ-703, 1958
As Time Goes By	SRL 201, 1967

BOBBY SHORT

*Songs by Bobby Short	Atlantic 1214, 1956
*Bobby Short	Atlantic 1230, 1956
*Speaking of Love	Atlantic 1262, 1957
*Sing Me a Swing Song	Atlantic 1285, 1957
*On the East Side	Atlantic SD 1321, 1959
*My Personal Property [Cy Coleman songs]	Atlantic SD 1689, 1963
*Nobody Else But Me	Atlantic SD 1574, 1970 [recorded 1957]
*At the Cafe Carlyle	Atlantic SD2-609, 1974
*Late Night at the Cafe Carlyle	Telarc CD 83311, 1992

JERI SOUTHERN

*The Southern Style	Decca DL 8055, 1954
*You Better Go Now	Decca DL 8214, 1955
Prelude to a Kiss	Decca DL 8245, 1955
*When Your Heart's on Fire	Decca DL 8394, 1956
*Jeri Gently Jumps	Decca DL 8472, 1956
*Southern Hospitality	Decca DL 8761, 1957
*Coffee, Cigarettes and Memories	Roulette 25039, 1957
Southern Breeze	Roulette 52010, 1958
Sings with Johnny Smith	Roulette 52016, 1958
Sings Cole Porter	Capitol ST 1173, 1959
At the Crescendo	Capitol ST 1278, 1959

LARRY STORCH

At the Bon Soir	Jubilee JGM 2033, ca. 1962

RALPH STRAIN

Only These People Are Permitted to Buy This Album	Riverside 847, 1958

(This album by debonair pianist and sometime singer Ralph Strain is so titled because the jacket is covered with the names of nightclub and café society personalities as well as familiar club-hoppers—a veritable who's who of the '50s "intimary" scene.)

BARBRA STREISAND

*Live—1963 [recorded live at the hungry i, San Francisco]
Bel Canto 5001

*Just for the Record [anthology] Columbia C4K 44111

[This 4-CD retrospective includes eight previously unissued tracks recorded live at the Bon Soir.]

MAXINE SULLIVAN

*St. Louis Blues [1938–1939 collection]	Japanese RCA RJL-2586
*Maxine Sullivan, 1944–1948	Tono TJ-6001
*Maxine Sullivan, 1956	Period RL 1909, 1956
*Maxine Sullivan, Volume Two	Period SPL 1207, 1957
Close as Pages in a Book	Monmouth-Evergreen MES 6919, 1969
*With the Ike Isaacs Quartet	Audiophile AP-154, 1981
*The Queen, Volume One	Kenneth KS-2052, 1982
*The Queen, Volume Two	Kenneth KS-2053, 1983
*The Queen, Volume Three	Kenneth KS-2054, 1984
*The Queen, Volume Four	Kenneth KS-2055, 1985
*I Love to Be in Love	Tono TDJ-101, 1986

SYLVIA SYMS

*After Dark	Version VLP 103, 1954
*Sings	Atlantic 1243, 1956
*Sings	Decca DL 8188, 1956
*That Man: A Love Letter to Frank Sinatra	Kapp KS-3236, 1960
*Torch Songs	Columbia CS 8243, 1961
*Sylvia Is . . .	Prestige 7439, 1966
*Lovingly	Atlantic SD 18177, 1976

KAY THOMPSON

*Kay Thompson 1935–1957	Box Office JJA 1975510

THE THREE FLAMES

*The Three Flames at the Bon Soir
Mercury MG 20239, 1955

MEL TORME

Live at Marty's — Finesse W2X 37484, 1981
Encore at Marty's, New York — Flair PG 8200, 1982

JOHN WALLOWITCH

*My Manhattan — GP JW 5023, 1982
*Back on the Town — DRG CD 91406, 1984

CY WALTER

*Piano Styles of Cy Walter [early '40s anthology]
Liberty Music Shop LMS-1007
*At the Drake Room Piano — Apollo 14, 1948
*Piano Playhouse [with Stan Freeman]
MGM E-514, 1950
*Piano Moods — Columbia CL 6161, 1951
*Holiday for Keys — Columbia CL 6202, 1952
*Manhattan [with Stan Freeman] — Epic LN 3114, 1955
*Rodgers Revisited — Atlantic 1236, 1956
*Gershwin Classics — Atlantic 8016, 1957
*Hits from the Great Astaire-Rogers Films
Camden CAS-533, 1959
At the Drake — MGM SE-4393, 1966

ANNETTE WARREN

*There's a Man in My Life — ABC-Paramount ABC-183, 1956

(A striking brunette with a creamy, impeccably schooled voice, Annette Warren graced the Blue Angel and other clubs throughout the '50s.)

KEN AND MITZIE WELCH

A Piano, Ice Box and Bed — Kapp KS-3039, 1959

RONNY WHYTE

The Songs and Piano of Ronny Whyte
Bandbox 1015, 1968

We Like a Gershwin Tune [with Travis Hudson]
Monmouth-Evergreen MES-7061, 1973

It's Smooth, It's Smart, It's Rodgers, It's Hart! [with Travis Hudson]
Monmouth-Evergreen MES-7069, 1974

Ronny Whyte at the Conservatory
Audiophile AP-151, 1980

ALEC WILDER

The Songs of Alec Wilder [anthology drawn from Wilder's National Public Radio series *American Popular Song,* 1976–1978; features Hugh Shannon, Anita Ellis, Mark Murphy, Mary Mayo, Johnny Hartman, Barbara Lea, Bobby Short, David Allyn, Marlene VerPlanck, Ed Monteiro, Woody Herman, and Tony Bennett]
Box Office JJA 19795

LEE WILEY

*The Songs of George & Ira Gershwin and Cole Porter [1939–1940 Liberty Music Shop recordings]
Audiophile ACD-1

*The Songs of Richard Rodgers & Lorenz Hart and Harold Arlen [1940 Liberty Music Shop/1943 Schirmer recordings]
Audiophile ACD-10

*Night in Manhattan [1950 Columbia recordings]
CBS Special Products CD A 656

*Sings Vincent Youmans [with Cy Walter and Stan Freeman, pianos]
Columbia CL 6215, 1952

*Sings Irving Berlin [with Cy Walter and Stan Freeman, pianos]
Columbia CL 6216, 1952

*Sings Rodgers & Hart — Bethlehem LP 312, 1954

*West of the Moon — RCA LPM-1408, 1957

*A Touch of the Blues — RCA LST-1566, 1958

*The Legendary Lee Wiley [anthology, 1939–1956]
Tono TJ 6004

AVA WILLIAMS

A Night with Ava [recorded live; location unknown]
Borderline BL 23, ca. 1962

JULIE WILSON

Love — Dolphin 6, 1956

*At the St. Regis — Vik LX-1118, 1958

At Brothers & Sisters, Volume One
Arden B&S 1, 1976

At Brothers & Sisters, Volume Two
Arden B&S 2, 1976

JONATHAN WINTERS

*Down to Earth — Verve MGVS-615011, 1960

*Here's Jonathan [recorded live at the hungry i, San Francisco]
Verve V-15025, 1961

*The Wonderful World of Jonathan Winters
Verve MGVS-6099, 1961

*Another Day, Another World [recorded live; location unknown]
Verve V-15032, 1962

*Whistle-Stopping with Jonathan Winters [recorded live at the National Press Club, Washington, D.C.]
Verve V-15037, 1964

TOMMY WOLF

Wolf at Your Door — Fraternity F-1002, 1956

Spring Can Really Hang You Up the Most
Fraternity F-1010, 1958

(Songwriter Tommy Wolf, best known for his collaborations with lyricist Fran Landesman—among them the hippest of '50s torch songs, "Spring Can Really Hang You Up the Most"—played and sang in a breezy, conversational style at such clubs as Gatsby's in New York and the Crystal Palace in St. Louis.)

ANTHOLOGY

The Erteguns' New York: New York Cabaret Music [recordings from the Atlantic vaults; features Mae Barnes, Joe Bushkin, Barbara Carroll, Eddie Condon, Chris Connor, Jimmie Daniels, Goldie Hawkins, Greta Keller, Jimmy Lyon, Carmen McRae, Mabel Mercer, Joe Mooney, Hugh Shannon, Bobby Short, Ted Straeter, Sylvia Syms, Billy Taylor, Mel Torme, and Cy Walter]
Atlantic 3-CD 7 81817-2

Permission to quote from specific sources, published and unpublished, is hereby acknowledged with thanks:

SHELLY BERMAN: Monologue used by permission of Shelley Berman; LOUIS BOTTO: "After Burton, Who?" used by permission of Louis Botto; MICHAEL BROWN: "New York Has A New Hotel," Copyright © 1962 Alley Music Corp and Trio Music Company. Copyright renewed by Hudson Bay Music. Reprinted by permission of Hudson Bay Music; GENE DEPAUL and DON RAYE: "I'm In Love With You," Copyright © 1950, 1977 by MCA MUSIC PUBLISHING, A division of MCA Inc., 1755 Broadway, New York, NY 10019 and BIG FOUR MUSIC CORPORATION. International Copyright Secured. All Rights Reserved. MCA MUSIC PUBLISHING; PHYLLIS DILLER: Monologues used by permission of Phyllis Diller; GEORGE AND IRA GERSHWIN and DUBOSE HEYWARD: "I Loves You Porgy," Copyright © 1950, 1977 by MCA MUSIC PUBLISHING, A Division of MCA Inc., 1755 Broadway, New York, NY 10019 and BIG FOUR MUSIC CORPORATION. International Copyright Secured. All Rights Reserved. MCA MUSIC PUBLISHING; HERBERT HARTIG: Monologues used by permission of Herbert Hartig; JACK HOLMES: "Names," Copyright © 1959 by Jack Holmes; "Thor," Copyright © 1960 by Jack Holmes; "Festivals," Copyright © 1959 by Jack Holmes. All used by permission of Jack Holmes; BART HOWARD: "Fly Me to the Moon, (In Other Words)," Words and Music by Bart Howard, TRO Copyright © 1954 (renewed) Hampshire House Publishing Corp., New York, NY. Used by permission. "Year After Year," Words and Music by Bart Howard, TRO Copyright © 1955 (renewed) and 1957 (renewed) Almanac Music, Inc., New York, NY. Used by permission; TOM JONES and HARVEY SCHMIDT: "The Race of the Lexington Avenue Express" and "The Holy Man and the New Yorker" from *Demi-Dozen* used by permission of Tom Jones and Harvey Schmidt; BUD MCCREERY: "Lollipop Lane" and "Guess Who Was There" used by permission of Gall and Wormwood Publishing Company; TREVA SILVERMAN: Excerpts from "The Envelope Please" and "And In This Corner" used by permission of Treva Silverman; CHARLES STROUSE and LEE ADAMS: Excerpts from "The Last of the Red Hot Mamas" used by permission of Charles Strouse; LILY TOMLIN: Excerpts from the monologues "Gauche Lady at a Party," "Being a Lady," and "Lupe, The World's Oldest Beauty Expert, on Applying Moisturizer" used by permission of Lily Tomlin; JOHN WALLOWITCH: "Come a Little Closer," Copyright © 1973, Fisher Music, Inc. "This Moment," Copyright © 1975, Sky Witch Music, 411 East 51st Street, New York, NY 10022. (Renewed) All rights reserved. Used by permission. KURT WEILL: "We'll Go Away Together" used by permission of Warner Chappell Music, Inc; KURT WEILL and LANGSTON HUGHES: "We'll Go Away Together," Copyright © 1947 Tro-Hampshire House Publ. Corp & Chappell & Co. (Renewed) All rights Reserved. Used by Permission; KEN WELCH: "I Made a Fool of Myself Over John Foster Dulles," Copyright © renewed 1985 by Kenneth H. Welch, published by Little Jug Music, Inc.; G. WOOD: Excerpts from "Daisy" and "Mona Lisa" used by permission of G. Wood.

INDEX

Unless otherwise indicated, all clubs listed are or were located in New York.

Index

Index